Museum Worthy

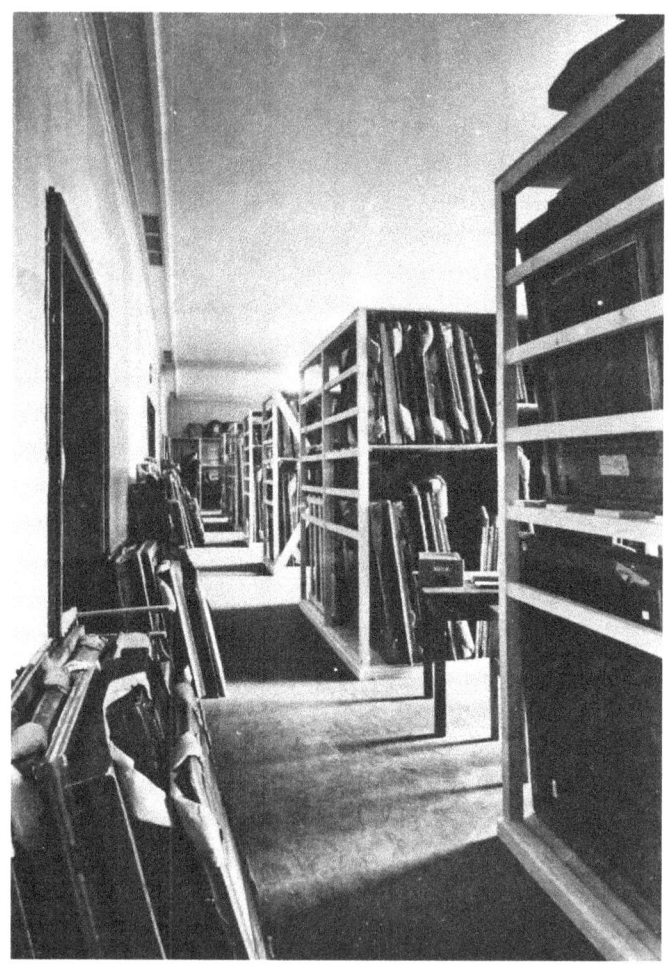

The Central Collecting Point in Munich. Pictures on the left have been taken from the racks for examination in various national storage rooms. Courtesy United States National Archives and Records Administration (RG 260-MCCP-1-27)

Museum Worthy

Nazi Art Plunder in Postwar Western Europe

ELIZABETH CAMPBELL

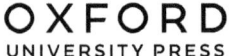

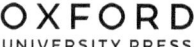

Oxford University Press is a department of the University of Oxford. It furthers
the University's objective of excellence in research, scholarship, and education
by publishing worldwide. Oxford is a registered trade mark of Oxford University
Press in the UK and certain other countries.

Published in the United States of America by Oxford University Press
198 Madison Avenue, New York, NY 10016, United States of America.

© Oxford University Press 2024

All rights reserved. No part of this publication may be reproduced, stored in
a retrieval system, or transmitted, in any form or by any means, without the
prior permission in writing of Oxford University Press, or as expressly permitted
by law, by license, or under terms agreed with the appropriate reproduction
rights organization. Inquiries concerning reproduction outside the scope of the
above should be sent to the Rights Department, Oxford University Press, at the
address above.

You must not circulate this work in any other form
and you must impose this same condition on any acquirer.

CIP data is on file at the Library of Congress

ISBN 978-0-19-005198-3

DOI: 10.1093/oso/9780190051983.001.0001

The manufacturer's authorised representative in the EU for product safety is
Oxford University Press España S.A. of El Parque Empresarial San Fernando de Henares,
Avenida de Castilla, 2 – 28830 Madrid (www.oup.es/en or product.safety@oup.com).
OUP España S.A. also acts as importer into Spain of products made by the manufacturer.

For
Mary Ann Courtney,
Bob Campbell,
and
James Marsh

We'll always have Paris. And New York.

Contents

List of Illustrations	ix
Acknowledgments	xiii
Abbreviations	xvii
Introduction: Plunder and Patrimony	1
1. Nazi Art Plunder in Western Europe	11
2. Allied Victory and Art Recovery	47
3. Negotiating Cultural Restitution	87
4. Recovered Art as French Patrimony	116
5. National Heritage in the Netherlands	146
6. Restoring Belgian Artistic Heritage	177
7. Contested Patrimony	204
Conclusion: A New Age of Museum Ethics	242
Notes	251
Selected Bibliography	307
Index	321

List of Illustrations

Figures

Frontispiece:	The Central Collecting Point in Munich. Pictures on the left have been taken from the racks for examination in various national storage rooms. Courtesy United States National Archives and Records Administration (RG 260-MCCP-1-27).	ii
Figure 0.1:	Salon of the Gutmann home in 1928, with Jacob de Wit grisaille above the door. Courtesy of Simon Goodman.	2
Figure 0.2:	A slightly faded but moving image: Lili Gutmann with Chinese vases. Courtesy of Simon Goodman.	3
Figure 1.1:	*Adele Bloch-Bauer I* (1903–1907), restituted to Maria Altmann, now at the Neue Galerie in New York. Courtesy of Neue Galerie New York / Art Resource, NY.	12
Figure 1.2:	"Degenerate" paintings, as defined by the Nazis, at the Jeu de Paume museum. Valland referred to the space as the "Room of Martyrs." Alamy Stock Photo.	36
Figure 1.3:	Works by Picasso, Braque, and Laurencin in the Paul Rosenberg gallery stairway, ca. 1935–1936. Digital Image © The Museum of Modern Art/Licensed by SCALA / Art Resource, NY.	39
Figure 1.4:	Paul Rosenberg in his office, rue la Boétie, Paris. Digital Image © The Museum of Modern Art/Licensed by SCALA / Art Resource, NY.	43
Figure 2.1:	Notice to Allied soldiers at Mont Saint Michel. Courtesy of National Gallery of Art, Washington, D.C., Gallery Archives.	58
Figure 2.2:	Cache of books in a German repository, Paris. Courtesy of National Gallery of Art, Washington, D.C., Gallery Archives.	65
Figure 2.3:	Recovered household effects at the Foire de Paris. Courtesy of National Gallery of Art, Washington, D.C., Gallery Archives.	66
Figure 2.4:	American soldier with cultural stash at a church turned German repository in Ellingen. Courtesy United States National Archives and Records Administration (RG 111-SC-204899).	70

X LIST OF ILLUSTRATIONS

Figures 2.5 & 2.6: Photograph of Neuschwanstein Castle in Bavaria, given by Rose Valland to James Rorimer in the spring of 1945. It appears she wrote on the back of the photograph twice, the second time, in August 1945, in friendship and gratitude. Archives of American Art, Smithsonian Institution. 73

Figure 2.7: James Rorimer, at top, with American soldiers and recovered art, Neuschwanstein Castle, 1945. Photo by Universal History Archive / Universal Images Group via Getty Images. 76

Figure 2.8: Generals Bradley, Patton and Eisenhower examine paintings at the Merkers mine, April 1945. Courtesy United States National Archives and Records Administration (RG 111-SC-204516). 77

Figure 2.9: American soldiers with Edouard Manet's *Wintergarden* from the National-Galerie in Berlin, evacuated by the Germans to the Merkers mine for safekeeping. Courtesy United States National Archives and Records Administration (RG-111-SC-203453-5). 81

Figure 2.10: In the Alt Aussee mine, George Stout (center) oversees protection and removal of Michelangelo's Madonna sculpture, stolen by the Germans from the Church of Our Lady in Bruges. Courtesy United States National Archives and Records Administration (RG 239-PA-1-7). 86

Figure 3.1: Main entrance to the Munich Central Collecting Point, formerly the Nazi Party headquarters. Courtesy United States National Archives and Records Administration (RG 260-MCCP-1-36). 94

Figure 3.2: German paintings on display at the National Gallery in Washington, D.C. Courtesy of National Gallery of Art, Washington, D.C., Gallery Archives. 100

Figure 3.3: Chaplain Samuel Blinder examines a Torah scroll, one of hundreds stolen from across Europe. Courtesy United States National Archives and Records Administration (RG 111-SC-209154). 103

Figure 3.4: Rose Valland and Edith Standen examine sculptures at the Wiesbaden Collecting Point. Archives of American Art, Smithsonian Institution. 106

Figure 4.1: Giovanni Battista Tiepolo, *Alexander the Great and Campaspe in the Studio of Apelles* (c. 1740), selected by the French committee. Restituted to heirs of Federico Gentili di Giuseppe in 1999. Courtesy of the J. Paul Getty Museum, which purchased the painting in 2000. 131

LIST OF ILLUSTRATIONS xi

Figure 4.2: Fernand Léger, *Woman in Red and Green* (1914). Confiscated by the Nazis from the Paris gallery of Paul Rosenberg in 1941. © 2022 Artists Rights Society (ARS), New York / ADAGP, Paris. Bridgeman-Giraudon / Art Resource, NY. 133

Figure 4.3: Jean-Baptiste-Camille Corot, *Genzano* (1843). Oil on canvas, 14 ½ x 22 ½ in. The Phillips Collection, Washington, DC. Sold by the French state and acquired in 1955. 144

Figure 5.1: Floris Gerritsz van Schooten, *Still Life* (1625). Courtesy of Frans Hals Museum, Haarlem, purchased with the support of the Rembrandt Society and Fonds J-P de Man. Photograph by Arend Velsink. 147

Figure 5.2: Johannes Lencker, *Ewer in the shape of a triton and a nereid* (c. 1620), selected by the Dutch state. Restituted to heirs of Fritz Gutmann. Courtesy of the Rijksmuseum, which purchased the item in 2003. 161

Figure 5.3: Jean Siméon Chardin, *Soap Bubbles*, ca. 1733–1734, restituted by the Dutch state to the widow of Fritz Mannheimer. Sold to Wildenstein, New York. Courtesy of the Metropolitan Museum of Art, which purchased the painting in 1949. 163

Figure 6.1: Jan Denens, *Vanitas* (seventeenth century), selected by the Belgian state. Courtesy of the Royal Museum of Fine Arts, Antwerp. 190

Figure 6.2: Jacob Jordaens I, *The Fruit Seller* (seventeenth century), selected by the Belgian state and today at the Royal Museum of Fine Arts, Antwerp, inv. No. 5049. Photograph by Hugo Maertens, courtesy of Collection KMSKA — Flemish Community. 193

Figure 7.1: Hans Petoltz, *Double-Cup* (1596), selected by the Dutch state. Restituted to heirs of Fritz Gutmann in 2002. Courtesy of the Detroit Institute of Arts, which purchased the items. 230

Figure 7.2: Hans Ludwig Kienle, *Horse and Rider* (1630), selected by the Dutch state and restituted to heirs of Fritz Gutmann in 2002. Courtesy of the Art Institute of Chicago / Art Resource, NY. 231

Figure 7.3: Salomon van Ruysdael, *River Landscape with Ferry* (1649), selected by the Dutch state. Restituted to heirs of Jacques Goudstikker in 2006. Courtesy of the National Gallery of Art in Washington, D.C., which purchased the painting. 234

Maps

Map 1: Occupied Western Europe, 1940 15
Map 2: The Partition of France, 1940–1944 32

Tables

Table 4.1:	Location of works repatriated to France by 1950	121
Table 4.2:	Restitution to owners of repatriated works	122
Table 4.3:	Items liquidated by French government	122
Table 6.1:	Public sales of ownerless cultural assets at Palais des Beaux-Arts (PBA), Brussels, in BFr	194

Acknowledgments

It is late afternoon in early January—conference season for many scholars. Dozens of professors, students, and history enthusiasts mill around the book fair in a hotel ballroom, as dim light from the setting sun beams through tall windows. The book fair provides a respite from intense scholarly panels, roundtables, and a few too many audience queries that are more a comment than a question. One historian, an expert in the social history of Vichy France, finds the paper edition of this book, glances at the cover, and starts flipping through the pages. The aftermath of Nazi art looting in western Europe. A fascinating topic, and a book she would like to own. Her personal library includes the digital version of many books but still appreciates the tactile pleasure of reading a paper book, feeling the weight of it in her hands. She buys it (yes!), slips it into her shoulder bag, and heads off to the Aspen Room for a roundtable on teaching and the digital humanities. For her, the newly purchased book has personal meaning and value beyond the price point.

In our digital age, humans continue to value tangible objects—watches, phones, books, works of art. These items can be lost or stolen and, with some luck, returned. Our ascribed valuation can be monetary and sentimental, and, in the case of books, cultural and intellectual. Any historian hopes that a paper book resulting from a decade of labor will be valued by many readers over time, pulled from shelves, not just sitting on them. For me, this book is far more than a mere object—paper or digital. It represents countless hours of work, passion, and determination, shaped through conversations, peer review, and guidance from many individuals across the United States and Europe.

This book, apparently about artworks, ultimately is about people. For the heirs of Holocaust victims and claimants of Nazi-era art, the return of a family's cultural patrimony goes far beyond material or aesthetic value. It provides tangible connections to the past and ancestors, persecuted, exploited, and in some cases killed by the Nazis and their collaborators. The claimants I have had the honor to meet are the first in a long list of individuals I wish to thank for making this book possible. Their stories and insight fundamentally shaped my sense of purpose for the book. From Simon Goodman, I learned how one can turn the Golden Years of retirement into a quest to restore the family patrimony. Marianne Rosenberg similarly helped me understand family history and explain cases analyzed here. Marei Von Saher offered welcome encouragement to continue the search for knowledge and rightful restitution. And locally in Denver, I have been delighted to know Nina McGehee, descendant of Siegfried Laemmle, and learn about the meaning of restitution of cultural items that may not have great monetary value but provide treasured connections to lost family members.

Scholars, like artists, require patrons to support our research and writing. I am grateful for support from the United States National Endowment for the Humanities and the volunteer peer reviewers who saw intellectual value in the project. From the University of Denver, I received support from Professional Research Opportunities for Faculty, the Faculty Research Fund, and an Internationalization Travel Grant.

As I tell my student researchers, archivists know our sources best and are indispensable guides. In France, Anne Liskenne provided clear and careful guidance at the archives of the Ministry of European and Foreign Affairs in La Courneuve, at a time when French archives in this area were going through a crucial process of declassification and digitization. At the Archives des Musées Nationaux, formerly located at the Louvre and now absorbed into the Archives Nationales, Alain Prévet provided exceptional assistance as I was transitioning my research from my last project to this book. I will always cherish memories of accessing the reading room, far away from throngs of tourists in the public galleries, squeezing into a slim elevator or opting to climb a narrow winding stairway. The salle de lecture, only large enough to accommodate several researchers, was packed to the brim with books, manuscripts, and archive boxes, and felt like the perfect place to absorb details about French museum policy.

At the Ministry of Culture, I received further expert guidance from Thierry Bajou and David Zivie and am grateful for their willingness to discuss with me complexities in French restitution policy. Attorney Corinne Hershkovitz also generously provided a much-needed legal perspective and helped me understand dynamics in French historiography of the Shoah and art restitution debates.

At the National Archives of Belgium, I was fortunate to work with Filip Strubbe on multiple occasions. At the beginning of my research, he was in the process of cataloguing asset recovery and restitution archives, and fortuitously was able to guide me to exactly the sources I needed. I returned two years later and benefited from his exceptional finding aid and additional conversations to examine a wider range of documents.

I again benefited from remarkably astute assistance at the Nationaal Archief in The Hague. Perry Schrier has provided guidance consistently over the past several years, and very generously identified relevant files for my research. Eelke Muller was similarly gracious in answering questions by email once I was back home and drawing conclusions from the documents. Staff at the Institute for War, Holocaust, and Genocide also guided me to helpful secondary sources that were unavailable in the United States.

During a research trip to Britain, staff at the National Archives in Kew were exceedingly helpful, as were those at the Imperial War Museum in London, where I read the diaries of Monuments Woman Anne Olivier Popham Bell. I then had the great privilege of meeting the delightful Ms. Bell at her cozy cottage in Sussex, on a cold December day. At the age of ninety-eight, she told fascinating and humorous stories about her postwar adventures, the living room brightened by soft rays from the setting sun. I am grateful to have shared a resulting article manuscript with Ms. Bell before her passing in 2018.

Closer to home, Greg Bradsher, now retired from the US National Archives and Records Administration, generously spent time discussing available resources, some of which early in my research were newly digitized and made available at fold3.com. At the archives of the National Gallery of Art, Jean Henry helped me navigate resources produced by the officers of the Monuments, Fine Arts, and Archives division. At the Archives of American Art, Erin Kinhart and Marisa Bourgoin also provided astute assistance. My editor at Oxford University Press, Nancy Toff, saw the book's promise from the initial prospectus. I thank her and her colleagues for greatly improving the manuscript. Any errors or omissions, of course, are my own.

Any scholarly work also results from fruitful exchange of ideas in community of scholars. I continue to appreciate strong ties to the Institute of French Studies at New York University, my graduate alma mater, and am grateful for continued exchanges with Edward Berenson, Herrick Chapman, Stéphane Gerson, Frédéric Viguier, and Isabelle Genest. An international network of scholars and writers has shaped this book, through their own research and many conference presentations, telephone conversations, and discussions enjoyed over meals, coffee, or cocktails. I am especially indebted to Evelien Campfens, Jean-Marc Dreyfus, Sarah Fishman, Shannon Fogg, Patrick Fridenson, Bianca Gaudenzi, Sarah Gensburger, Ophélie Jouan, Lisa Leff, Mary Lewis, Marc Masurovsky, Lynn Nicholas, Lisa Nieman, Pascal Ory, Robert Paxton, Jonathan Petropoulos, Inès Rotermund-Reynard, Daniel Sherman, and Wouters Veraart. David Stephenson helped to ensure the correct translation of Dutch Sources. At the University of Denver, I am grateful for remarkable camaraderie among many colleagues, and especially for support from Chairs in the History Department, Carol Helstosky, Susan Schulten, and Jonathan Sciarcon, and Deans of the College of Arts, Humanities and Social Sciences, Danny McIntosh, and Rhonda Gonzales.

I am also fortunate to have wide support from friends and family on both sides of the Atlantic. In France, Stéphanie and Erwan Papin, Catherine Tamburini-Bonnefoy and Fabrice Faure Dauphin, and Peggy Robinson and Daniel Berrous offered hospitality, convivial conversation, and loyal friendship. Here in the United States, special thanks to Julia Bartlett, Kristen Beatty, Leslie Beck, Pamela A. Bonnie, Janelle Donovan, Jim Hogan, Vandna Jerath, the Karlsgodt/Schaeffer family, Jennifer Kremer Matt Lantz, Patti Perrin, Arlyne Reichert, Kay Sheridan, and Betsy Wilcox. Aradhna Malik bolstered my morale from India, and my brother T. J. Campbell offered just the right mix of encouragement and probing questions. I am delighted that my sons, Ryan and Grant, also are drawn to art and history and enjoy discussing complex ideas around the dinner table.

As I complete this decade-long project, I also feel bittersweet gratitude for the support of three beloved elders who passed before the book finally came to fruition. My mother, Mary Ann Courtney, had loved learning French and encouraged me to do the same. That wise advice would set the course for my entire intellectual and professional journey. A decade later, we spent two magical weeks in France, finally speaking French together as we explored Paris, Normandy and Brittany. Thanks to my father, Bob Campbell, I joined a six-week educational program in France as a sixteen-year-old and came home a Francophile. His encouragement never wavered, through every phase of my academic journey. We, too, shared unforgettable moments in the City of Light. My uncle, James Marsh, an accomplished Marxist philosopher who finished his scholarly career at Fordham University, taught me what it meant to pursue "a life of the mind" while I was a graduate student at New York University. In bars, restaurants, and coffee shops across Manhattan, he repeatedly told me: don't get a job; find a vocation. The message stuck. As we explored the City together, he taught me to love art and museums, to carry out research rigorously, and, when warranted, to argue courageously. In many ways, he remains my role model as a scholar, teacher, and citizen.

All three elders shaped my life and vocation beyond measure, and I dedicate this book to them.

Abbreviations

AAA	Archives of American Art, Washington, D.C.
ACC	Allied Control Council
ACLS	American Council of Learned Societies
ALIU	Art Looting Investigation Unit, US Office of Strategic Services
AMGOT	Allied Military Government
AMN	Archives des Musées Nationaux (National Museums Archives), France
AN	Archives nationales (National Archives), France
BHG	Bureau Herkomst Gezocht (Origins Unknown Agency), Netherlands
BRüG	Bundesrückerstattunggesetz (Federal Restitution Law), West Germany
BTG	Brüsseler Treuhandgesellschaft (Brussels Trust Company)
CCP	Central Collecting Point, Munich
CFLN	Comité Français de Libération Nationale (French Committee of National Liberation)
CGR	Commissariaat-Generaal voor de Nederlandse Economische Belangen in Duitsland (Office of the Commissioner General for Dutch Economic Interests in Germany)
CIVS	Commission for the compensation of victims of spoliation resulting from the anti-Semitic legislation in force during the Occupation (France)
CORC	Coordinating Committee of the Allied Control Council
CRA	Commission de récupération artistique (Art Recovery Commission), France
DER/ORE	Dienst Economische Recuperatie/Office de récupération économique (Office for Economic Restitution), Belgium
DGER	Direction générale des études et recherches (General Directorate for Studies and Research), France
EAC	European Advisory Commission
ERR	Einsatzstab Reichsleiter Rosenberg, Nazi Germany
FRG	Federal Republic of Germany
FRUS	Foreign Relations of the United States
HERGO	Bureau Herstelbetalings en Recuperatiegoederen (Office for Reparations Payments and Restitution of Property), Netherlands
IARA	Inter-Allied Restitution Agency
ICN	Institute for Cultural Heritage (Netherlands)
ICOM	International Council of Museums
IS	Islamic State

IWM	Imperial War Museum, London
JCR	Jewish Cultural Reconstruction
JRSO	Jewish Restitution Successor Organization
JTC	Jewish Trust Corporation
MEAE	Ministère de l'Europe et des Affaires Etrangères, La Courneuve, France
MFAA	Monuments, Fine Arts and Archives division (western Allies)
MNAM	Musée national d'art modern (National Museum of Modern Art), Paris
MNR	Musées nationaux récupération (National Museums Recovery), France
NAN	Nationaal Archief, The Hague, Netherlands
NARA	United States National Archives and Records Administration, College Park
NGA	National Gallery of Art, Washington, D.C.
NIOD	Nederlands Instituut voor Oorlogsdocumentatie (Dutch Institute for War Documentation: Institute for War, Holocaust and Genocide Studies), Amsterdam
NK	Nederlands Kunstbezit (Dutch Art Property)
OBIP	Office des biens et intérêts privés (Office for Personal Property and Interests), France
OMGUS	Office of Military Government, United States
OSS	Office of Strategic Services, United States
RAF	British Royal Air Force
RB	Rijksarchief in België (Royal Archives of Belgium), Brussels
RDR	Directorate of Reparations, Deliveries and Restitutions in the Allied Control Council
SCAP	Office of temporary administrators, France (Service du contrôle des administrateurs provisoires)
SHAEF	Supreme Headquarters Allied Expeditionary Force
SiPO-SD	Sicherheitspolizei-Sicherheitsdienst (Third Reich Security Police)
SNCF	Société National des Chemins de Fer (French national railway company)
SNK	Stichting Nederlands Kunstbezit (Dutch Art Property Foundation)
SS	Schutzstaffel (Third Reich Protection Squads)
TVK	Treuhandverwaltung von Kulturgut (Fiduciary Administration for Cultural Assets), West Germany
UKNA	The National Archives, Kew, United Kingdom

Introduction

Plunder and Patrimony

On the afternoon of May 26, 1943, a black Mercedes pulled into the long circular driveway of the Bosbeek estate, near the Dutch city of Haarlem. The car stopped in front of an elegant brick mansion, an imposing seventeenth-century structure with symmetrical rows of shuttered windows framing stately front steps. The historic building boasted an impressive exterior, but the Nazis had reduced it to a mere pretty shell, having stripped the home of nearly all furniture and personal belongings. On the walls inside, shadowy rectangles were the only traces of recently plundered artwork. The estate owners, Fritz and Louise Gutmann, were home when the car arrived, enduring a kind of house arrest. A young SS lieutenant got out of the Mercedes, climbed the front steps, and urgently knocked at the door. Once inside, the officer locked the door behind him, briskly inspected the common rooms, and told Fritz and Louise they had a few hours to pack up the rest of their things. The Nazis were putting them on a train, headed east.[1]

It was a scene unimaginable to the Gutmanns a few years prior, even as Europe had descended into chaos and the Wehrmacht overran the Netherlands. Millions of people around them had appeared far more vulnerable to the circumstances of war and occupation. The Gutmanns were Protestants, Dutch citizens, and enormously wealthy. They were both born into the German upper class of the late nineteenth century and had known privilege all of their lives. Building on a foundation of inherited wealth, Fritz had become a successful banker in his own right, and carried on his father's passion for art collecting. Having settled in the Netherlands, he and Louise were known in cultural circles throughout Europe. They travelled extensively, and during a trip to Paris in 1926 sat for portraits by Man Ray in his Montparnasse studio.[2]

Before the war, the opulent Gutmann mansion housed an art collection worthy of a fine museum, with paintings by Boucher, Guardi, Hubert Robert, and Vigée-Lebrun. Aubusson tapestries graced the walls, cabinets displayed an array of Meissen porcelain, Renaissance gold and silver-gilt pieces, and Ming and Qing vases. Louis XV and Louis XVI furniture rested on sumptuous Chinese carpets.[3] These items were mere things but precious, magnificent things, some inherited from Fritz's father and others collected by the couple themselves, at a time when property ownership seemed immutable, a right guaranteed by the laws of modern civilized society.

But the Gutmanns had a central and tragic vulnerability: they were ethnic Jews living under the Nazis. They quickly learned that laws are, in fact, perilously malleable, and even fragile in extreme circumstances. The Nazis had demonstrated that a handful of individuals can refashion notions of legality, strip away individuals' rights and belongings, separate loved ones, and end lives with remarkable ease. Since the Dutch surrender in May 1940, art dealers in the Nazis' employ had pressured Fritz into selling pieces at prices far below market value, dangling a promise that he and Louise might be granted safe passage out of the Netherlands as a reward for their cooperation. These forced sales gave way to more extreme "safekeeping" measures, a favorite euphemism for Nazi theft. Operatives repeatedly barged into the home and assessed the Gutmann belongings, as if the home were a commercial art

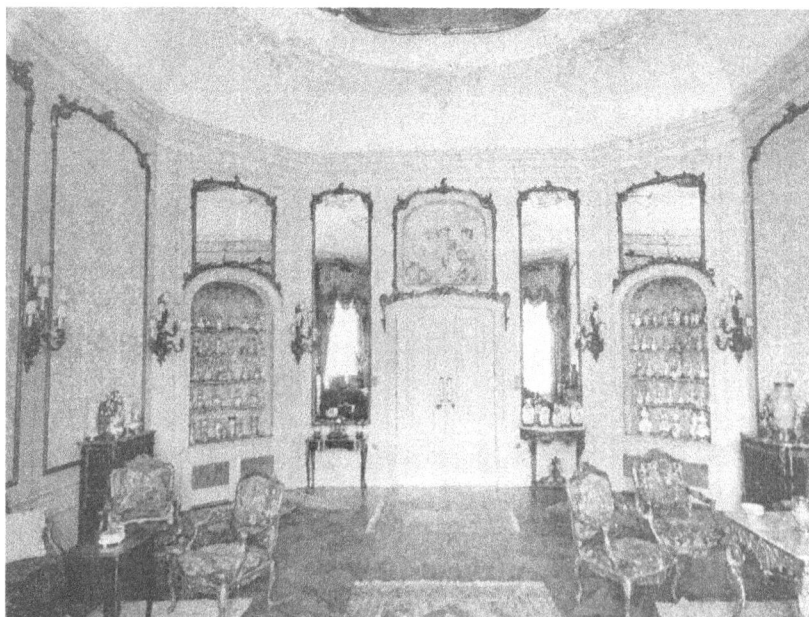

Salon of the Gutmann home in 1928, with Jacob de Wit grisaille above the door. Courtesy of Simon Goodman.

INTRODUCTION 3

gallery, while the owners could only look on helplessly. The dealers' minions then successively seized all the valuable artworks, leaving only some fine china and silverware.[4]

On that May afternoon, the SS lieutenant told Fritz and Louise that a car would pick them up shortly and escort them to The Hague, where they would board a train for Berlin. They would be safe, he reassured them, and would continue to Prague and Vienna, ultimately reaching Italy, where family members had been trying to negotiate their safe passage. The Nazis even gave the couple first-class train tickets and a private sleeping car. As the Gutmanns

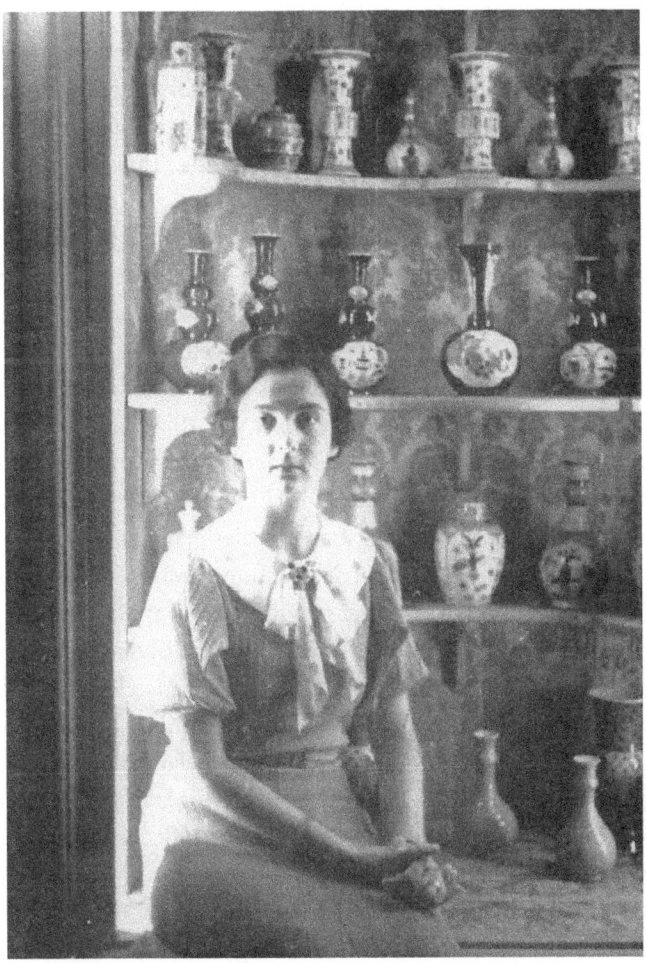

A slightly faded but moving image: Lili Gutmann with Chinese vases. Courtesy of Simon Goodman.

packed clothes, linens, toiletries, and some food items, Fritz hoped his gamble had paid off. He had relinquished treasured items from the family art collection, but he and Louise at least would survive and reunite with their grown daughter, Lili, in Florence.[5]

He was wrong. Near Dresden, the Germans joined their private car to another train, this one headed for the Theresienstadt concentration camp in Bohemia. Ultimately, Fritz was beaten to death at a nearby prison in April 1944, and several weeks later Louise perished at Auschwitz. Back at Bosbeek, the Germans confiscated all the remaining Gutmann assets, including the china and silverware.[6]

The magnificent Gutmann art collection was only a small portion of Nazi plunder amassed across the European continent, which totaled several hundred thousand works of art and millions of rare books, manuscripts, archive collections, and other cultural objects. But the fate of this single collection illustrates the full range of Nazi looting methods. They stole items from homes, bank vaults, and museum storage facilities, and dominated the art market, using threats and intimidation to coerce owners to sell items below market value. Jews were not the only victims of Nazi art plunder, but they were the central victims. The seizure of Jewish assets writ large—bank accounts, real estate, insurance policies, gold, jewelry—was part of the Nazi mission to destroy European Jewry and thus must be understood within the broader framework of the Final Solution. It was "thefticide," as defined by Canadian legal scholar Irwin Cotler, a former justice minister and founding chair of the Raoul Wallenberg Centre for Human Rights: "the greatest mass theft on the occasion of the greatest mass murder in history."[7]

Yet in the context of postwar reconstruction, western European officials assessed the impact of Nazi looting across the entire population, without distinguishing Jewish losses due to antisemitic persecution and expropriation. According to a 1947 French government report, German looting had "aimed to diminish the historic, artistic, and literary patrimony of occupied countries," while expanding that of the Third Reich.[8] Belgian and Dutch officials similarly viewed the losses in national terms.[9] This framing of looting and destruction on a national scale elides the very specific loss of life and property by Jews in the context of the Final Solution.

The phenomenon of Nazi looting is now well known through the commercial success of films such as *The Monuments Men* (2014) and *Woman in Gold* (2015), and books by best-selling author Robert Edsel.[10] Stories about the Monuments Men and Women, the cultural officers of western Allied forces, tend to focus on the dramatic rescue of Europe's art treasures from castles and salt mines used as repositories by the Nazis. And with good reason. These officers saved many of the great art masterpieces in Europe, and they returned thousands of items to rightful owners.

Less known is the story of items that were not returned to private owners and instead were held by governments in western Europe to enrich museum collections and adorn government ministries, embassies, and other public buildings—more than two thousand pieces in France, some four thousand in the Netherlands, and more than six hundred in Belgium. These were so-called heirless or orphaned works that had not been successfully claimed within a few years of their repatriation to the country of origin. Some items were worthy of the Louvre, the Rijksmusem, and Belgian royal museums, providing an unusual opportunity to enhance state collections at little cost to public treasuries. Among the orphaned artworks, French curators selected paintings by old and modern masters: Frans Hals, Tiepolo, Veronese, Boucher, Monet, Manet, Degas, Cézanne, Matisse, Picasso. The Dutch chose paintings by Cranach the Elder, Rembrandt, and Jacob van Ruisdael, plus Meissen porcelain, Renaissance gold and silver pieces, Chinese vases. The Belgian custodianship included works by Van der Weyden, Jacob Jordaens, and Frans Snyders. Many were highly coveted items.

There were several reasons why the artworks had not been returned to rightful owners. In some cases, the owners had perished, and their heirs lacked the ownership documentation required in postwar claims processes. Through the twentieth century, the governments of France, the Netherlands, and Belgium placed the burden of proof on claimants, without proactively carrying out provenance research to find rightful owners. The burden imposed on victims and their descendants became increasingly onerous as time went on. In addition, objects that had been purchased by the enemy in under-duress sales reverted to state control in the countries of origin and were especially difficult to recover. All three governments viewed the repatriated artworks as a form of cultural reparations that would mitigate the wartime looting and destruction inflicted by the Nazis. However, this compensation extended the injustice of Nazi plunder, as it was paid not by Germany, but the victims themselves, especially Jews.

Not all objects in the custodianships were owned by ethnic Jews at the time of the German invasion. Such works included dozens of pieces from the collections of Otto Lanz and Franz Koenigs, who had lived in the Netherlands, and at least forty-six items in the French custodianship. In Belgium, about half of the selected objects most likely had been owned by Jews.[11] However, the misappropriation of Jewish assets is more significant than these numbers might suggest, given that Jews made up a small minority of the population in each country at the beginning of the war—around 1.5 percent in the Netherlands, and less than 1 percent in France and Belgium.[12] Jewish assets thus constituted a vastly disproportionate segment of the items held by the postwar governments.

The extent of state ownership varied among the three countries. In France, the selected artworks, most commonly known as the Musées Nationaux Récupération or MNRs, retained special status in trusteeship and were not legally acquired by the state. The chosen works in the Netherlands also were recorded in a special inventory, the *Nederlands Kunstbezit-collectie* (NK), or Dutch Art Property collection, but were officially owned by the state. Belgium absorbed the selected items into state collections without grouping the items into a separate inventory. In the Dutch and Belgian cases, state control thus eventually extended the state's role beyond trusteeship to outright acquisition.

This book situates government use of recovered art in the broader context of the Final Solution and argues, above all, that postwar cultural policies extended the dispossession of Jewish assets wrought initially by the Nazis and their collaborators. While the governments of western Europe restituted tens of thousands of artworks to rightful owners, an amalgamation of civil law, legal norms, and national cultural interests deterred more extensive restitution. This approach to art recovered from the Third Reich is an example of patrimania, defined here as state appropriation in the name of cultural patrimony.[13] It is a concept derived from the French term *patrimoine national*, meaning cultural assets conserved by the state for the good of the nation, and passed from one generation to the next. In the 1940s, officials in all three countries invoked the term in reference to their nations' cultural patrimony.

Despite this core similarity in the three countries' approaches to the art custodianships, there are some important national differences in notions of cultural heritage. The French cultural meaning of "patrimony" dates to the Revolution, when the state became the custodian of artworks formerly owned by the monarchy, church, and nobility. Royal art and library collections became national, in part to protect them from iconoclasm of radical revolutionaries. The preservation of art and heritage in France became more centralized over the course of the nineteenth century, with the creation of a historic monuments commission under the July Monarchy in 1837, and extension of state preservation and intervention during the Third Republic (1870–1940).[14]

Centralized institutions devoted to the pursuit and preservation of a national cultural heritage developed later in Belgium and the Netherlands. Competing regional and religious identities—Catholic and Protestant—persisted in Belgium well after independence from the Netherlands in 1830. Notions of a Belgian cultural identity largely developed in the last two decades of the nineteenth century under King Leopold II. In the context of imperial expansion in the Congo, this narrative of Belgian cultural greatness was deliberately constructed by writers, art experts, and other elites, locating a common artistic heritage in Flemish masters such as Rubens and Pieter Brueghel the Elder.[15] In the Netherlands, King William I established important public art museums in the wake of the Napoleonic wars—the Rijksmuseum in Amsterdam (1815) and Mauritshuis in The Hague (1816). Yet through the mid-nineteenth century, art collecting largely remained a private and royal pursuit. Liberals who dominated the government believed in limited state intervention in artistic affairs, lest the monarchy assert excessive control over Dutch culture. A shift toward greater centralization occurred in 1875, when a division of arts and sciences was created in the Ministry of Home Affairs, an administrative reform that separated the arts from education and recognized the importance of a national cultural heritage that needed centralized protection. A truly national Dutch cultural policy developed only in the 1940s, in the aftermath of the plunder and destruction during the Second World War.[16]

The French term *patrimoine national* has been popularized since the 1980s, and today it refers to an ever-expanding range of objects, structures, folklore items, music, and oral traditions. The United Nations Educational, Scientific and Cultural Organization (UNESCO) similarly recognizes a wide definition of cultural heritage, from historic and archeological sites to underwater and intangible heritage.[17] But in the 1940s, the cultural meaning of *patrimoine* referred to a more narrow realm of artistic heritage—fine and applied art objects, antiquities, and historic sites, such as cathedrals and chateaux.[18]

In all three countries, the cultural nationalism evident in postwar art appropriation illustrates a reassertion of sovereignty in the wake of the German occupation. Having emerged from a period of brutal German exploitation, all three remained exploitative imperial powers themselves and in the early postwar years defended their right to extract resources, including cultural objects, from their colonies in Africa and Asia.[19] While membership in international institutions such as the United Nations and UNESCO (1945), NATO (1949), and the European Steel and Coal Community (1951) promised greater security and prosperity, state-sponsored heritage conservation remained a cultural defense of the national ideal.[20] In this context, the cache of ownerless art recovered from the Third Reich provided a means to fortify public museum collections and the national heritage.

This book builds on a rich and ever-growing literature produced by scholars, journalists, and art experts. The first contributors were those involved in the art recovery and restitution process themselves—the Monuments Men and Women who served in the Monuments, Fine Arts, and Archives (MFAA) division of western Allied forces. Many went on to become leaders in the mid-twentieth-century American art world—James Rorimer as director of the Metropolitan Museum of Art, Thomas Carr Howe as director of the California Palace of the Legion of Honor, Lincoln Kirstein as cofounder of the New York City Ballet—and several wrote riveting memoirs.[21] In the early postwar years, Janet Flanner, Paris correspondent for *The New Yorker*, wrote essays about Nazi art looting and the MFAA, some of which appear in the collection *Men and Monuments* (1957).[22] But after this initial rush of interest, the art world and journalists moved on. Cold War realpolitik toward Germany contributed to acceptance of the restitution status quo by 1955, and the history of Nazi looting largely receded in public memory for forty years.

With the fall of the Berlin Wall came a flood of new inquiries into the Nazi seizure of assets, and ways that states, corporations, museums, and other entities continued to benefit from the plunder. In eastern Europe, the collapse of communism spurred investigations into property seized by the Nazis or communist regimes or both. In the United States, Cold War pragmatism gave way to moral concerns about the incomplete compensation of Holocaust victims and heirs. With the fiftieth anniversary of the war's end, European governments declassified wartime archives, allowing journalists and historians to document human and material losses.[23] This combined scrutiny by writers, historians, heirs, and activists prompted governments in the United States and western Europe to investigate the continued impact of Nazi-era looting and spoliation. Important scholarship resulted from these extensive and in some cases multi-volume reports issued at the turn to this century by the United States Presidential Advisory Commission on

Holocaust Assets, and study commissions in France, the Netherlands, and Belgium.[24]

The scholarly literature on Nazi plunder and limited postwar restitution is now voluminous, investigating the impact on fine art, financial assets, real estate, household effects, books, and archives. In the context of headline-grabbing multi-million dollar lawsuits, researchers and legal experts have explored alternatives to litigation in Nazi-era art disputes.[25] Scholars also are situating the history of Nazi art looting and restitution in transnational and global perspective, offering insight from research in migration and postcolonial studies. Bianca Gaudenzi and Ingrid Swenson, for instance, place Nazi looting in a wider geographic and chronological context, identifying common trends in imperial plunder and postcolonial restitution from the nineteenth century to present times.[26]

While the literature on Nazi plunder and postwar restitution has expanded in important ways, the dominant emphasis on national studies has created an overly fragmented field. Comparative history can tease out similarities and differences across national cases to shed light on the phenomena of art looting, restitution, and state appropriation of "ownerless" assets. Up to now, scholars have used comparative analysis to reveal occupation mechanisms in western Europe that enabled the Holocaust, interrogating differences, for instance, in deportation rates of the Jewish population in France (25 percent), Belgium (46 percent), and the Netherlands (76 percent).[27] Comparisons on the seizure of Jewish property are more scarce.[28]

Using a comparative approach, this book argues that the dispossession of Jewish Holocaust victims is an injustice that has yet to be fully rectified. It underscores striking similarities in the three governments' approaches to "orphaned" art, despite differences in the extent and nature of Nazi plunder, postwar institutions and personnel, and national laws and norms. Extending the comparison to current times, it also examines recent disputes over works that were still held by the governments in the early twenty-first century, proposing a more ethical path in museum collection stewardship.

Several factors justify the comparative analysis of art looting, restitution, and state appropriation in France, the Netherlands, and Belgium. All three countries experienced significant cultural plunder during at least four years of German occupation. The case of Luxembourg is excluded, as only a small number of items, some forty paintings, were lost there by Jewish owners and were never recovered.[29] The other western European countries all participated in the MFAA, and civil servants in all three postwar governments managed important caches of ownerless works of art. Their successors in the 1990s, in turn, were all forced to come to terms with this history, and created similar study commissions to offer restorative solutions. While plundering and restitution agencies differed in the three cases, as we will see, there is substantial overlap in institutions and actors. National postwar policies shaped and were shaped by one another.

Nazi art plunder and restitution in eastern Europe and the Soviet Union remains a crucial area of under-explored research, but one beyond the scope of this book. Soviet art trophy brigades seized objects as a form of reparations for looting, destruction, and atrocities committed by the Germans on the eastern front. Though soldiers in every Allied army succumbed to the temptation of looting and vandalism, and there were comparable temptations among some western Allied leaders to confiscate art from Germany as reparations, the overriding restitution logic and mission of the MFAA was diametrically opposed to Soviet interests. While access to Soviet and Russian archives remains a dilemma, research by Konstantin Akinsha, Grigorii Kozlov, Patricia Kennedy Grimsted, and Sophie Coeuré reveals the vast potential for additional study of plunder of art and archives.[30]

Soviet my own comparative approach will, I hope, provide a better understanding of origins of the postwar art custodianships, and clarify the legal and ethical responsibility of museums, galleries, auctions houses, individual collectors, and other actors in the art market to carry out provenance research on items that might have changed hands in Europe during the Nazi era. May this ethics-driven research and transparency, echoing Michael Marrus, eventually lead to some measure of justice.[31]

1
Nazi Art Plunder in Western Europe

The mechanisms of Nazi art plunder first developed not in Paris, Brussels, or Amsterdam, but in Vienna. Far from the smash-and-grab tactics commonly associated with art heists, this form of theft often maintained the appearance of civility. On January 28, 1939, for instance, a group of distinguished Austrian museum directors and curators gathered at an elegant private home in a posh district near the Ringstrasse. After greeting one another at the front door, they entered an opulent salon, brimming with museum-quality artworks. An array of shiny *objets* tastefully decorated antique furniture pieces, arranged atop luxurious rugs. Glass cases displayed a four hundred-piece collection of eighteenth- and early nineteenth-century porcelain, and fine paintings graced the walls, featuring works by Austrian artists such as Rudolf Alt, Jakob Schindler, and Ferdinand Georg Waldmüller.[1]

The host for this gathering was not the homeowner, Jewish sugar magnate Ferdinand Bloch-Bauer, but Erich Führer, an attorney, zealous Nazi party member, and temporary administrator of Bloch-Bauer's property. After the curators strolled through the home's common rooms, they worked their way to the private bedroom and salon of Ferdinand's late wife, Adele. This personal space at the time displayed five paintings by Austrian modernist Gustav Klimt, including two portraits of Adele. The assemblage had served as a memorial first to the artist, who died from a stroke in 1918, and then to Adele after her premature death in 1925 from meningitis, at age forty-three. In the first portrait, painted in 1907, glittering gold shapes swirl around a bejeweled and fair Adele. A golden gown drapes her slim figure as she clasps her hands next to her bare right shoulder and returns the viewer's gaze with a slight, sensual smile—the now world-famous "woman in gold" painting, commonly known as the Austrian Mona Lisa.[2]

The Third Reich had given curators access to these sumptuous private spaces to help determine how the government would allocate the homes' contents. Ferdinand, who had supported an anti-Nazi workers' movement, fled Vienna in March 1938 after the German invasion and relocated repeatedly to stay a step ahead of the Germans. He landed first in Czechoslovakia,

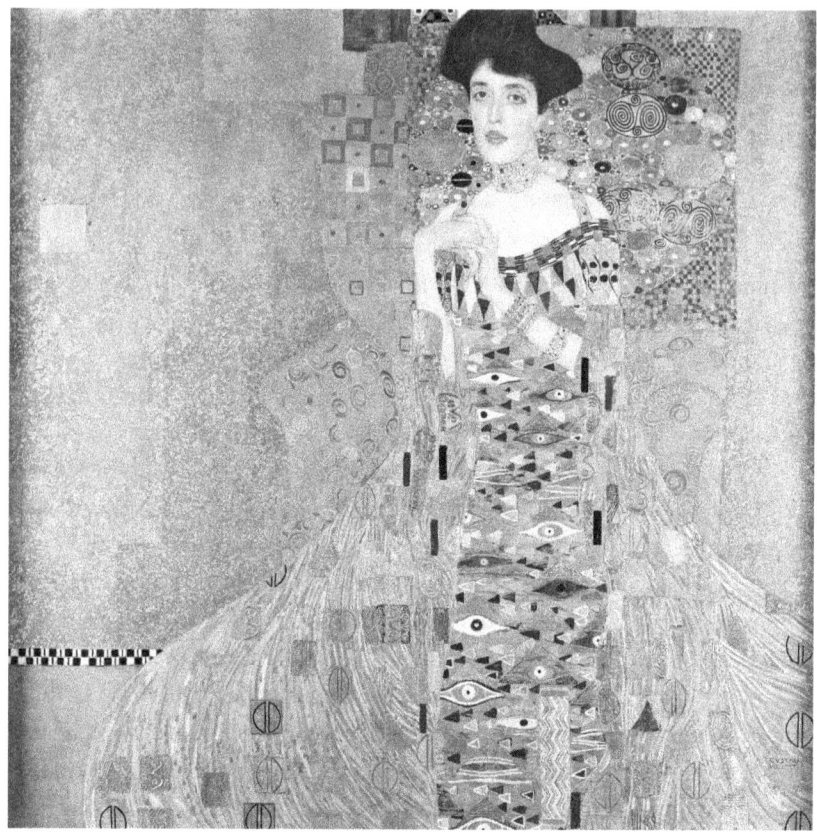

Adele Bloch-Bauer I (1903–1907), restituted to Maria Altmann, now at the Neue Galerie in New York. Courtesy of Neue Galerie New York / Art Resource, NY.

where he owned a castle near Prague, then traveled to the city of Vichy in France, and finally to Switzerland by September 1939. Reich authorities initiated a tax evasion investigation as a pretext for seizing his property in Austria—his factories and the home in Vienna, with all the valuable contents. The museum officials who gathered at the Bloch-Bauer home on that winter's day were charged with selecting pieces for distribution to Austrian museums, as a way of protecting the national cultural heritage and preventing the sale of valuable pieces to Germany or foreign buyers.[3]

But the Austrian curators did not have first choice among the spoils, which was always Hitler's prerogative. Agents collecting on his behalf declined the Klimt portraits of an elite Jewish woman, as did other top Nazi officials. Erich

Führer, who had hoped to maximize proceeds for the Reich treasury, was able to negotiate only an exchange with the Österreichische Galerie in Vienna. The golden portrait remained there until 2006, when Bloch-Bauer's niece, US citizen Maria Altmann, successfully won restitution of the "Woman in Gold" and four other Klimt paintings in a landmark case.[4]

The Nazi seizure of Jewish assets in Austria, including art collections, provided a model for subsequent plundering operations within Germany and throughout occupied Europe.[5] Hitler aimed to dominate the continent militarily, economically, and culturally. He mobilized top German art experts to help him build a world-class art collection for a new museum—the finest in the world, one that would far outshine the Louvre and the Rijksmuseum. This planned *Führermuseum* would be the crown jewel in a cultural complex envisioned for his childhood hometown of Linz, Austria that would also house a library, theater, and symphony hall.[6] The plans never came to fruition, but during the war top Nazi leaders pursued Hitler's vision, competing for influence in this area of great personal importance to the Führer. They also built their own private collections, employing an array of nefarious methods to acquire artworks, from outright theft to purchases carried out through varying degrees of threat and coercion, especially from Jewish collectors and art dealers. Nazi "plunder" thus includes works either stolen from owners or sold by them under duress.

Following the seizure of Jewish art collections within the Third Reich, the invasion of western Europe and occupation, secured by mid-June 1940, gave the Nazis access to a vast wealth of cultural property. A handful of men controlled the fate of thousands of items in private collections.

Agents of Plunder

In this as in other areas of the Third Reich, Hitler deliberately fostered rivalries among the Nazi leadership to limit the control of any single official. Among those vying for authority was propaganda minister Joseph Goebbels, who already had played an important role in Nazi art policy. Before the *Blitzkrieg* invasions, the Third Reich had scrutinized its own art collections and developed an aesthetic doctrine that denounced "degenerate" modernist trends, targeting surrealist, cubist, and expressionist works. Goebbels oversaw a commission that purged over sixteen thousand modernist pieces from German state museums. In July 1937 a Degenerate Art Exhibition opened in Munich with the intent of educating the public about the harmful influence of modernism, which according to the Nazis had been orchestrated by Jewish artists and critics. Prominently displayed below the "degenerate" artworks was provenance information that detailed the previous museum location, with the acquisition date and price, aiming to scandalize the public. In a convergence of anti-modernism and antisemitism, the Reich also purged works by Jewish artists or with Jewish subjects from German museums.[7]

With the fall of France, Goebbels extended his influence into the occupied territories and received authorization from Hitler to secure "German" works of art held in western Europe. He enlisted the expertise of top German art historians to create a list of works previously owned by Germans since the sixteenth century, but which over time had scattered to other countries. Pieces looted by French forces in the Napoleonic wars held cultural and political value and were a top priority. Leading this team of experts was Otto Kümmel, director of the Berlin State Museums, who became special commissar for securing foreign museums. The resulting Kümmel reports also identified works that were stylistically "Germanic," an elastic notion that included Dutch and Flemish masters.[8]

Hitler mobilized other German art experts to acquire artworks for the Linz collection and in June 1939 appointed Hans Posse, director of the Dresden Gemäldegalerie, to head the effort. According to Petropoulos, Posse's collaboration with the Nazis illustrates a Faustian bargain struck between the Third Reich and numerous art experts, historians, and dealers. Posse had enjoyed an illustrious career as a museum director and had been temporarily dismissed in 1938 for acquiring modernist works by Dix, Klee, and Kandinsky. At that point, his career could have remained on a principled trajectory. Yet at the recommendation of Berlin-based dealer Karl Haberstock, Hitler ensured that Posse regained his position in Dresden, and about a year later offered him the chance to build the Linz collection. Haberstock also had a stake in the appointment, knowing he could reap tremendous benefits from the connection. Posse likewise could not resist the opportunity to direct the project, with vast sums of the Reich treasury at his disposal.[9]

During the war, Posse traveled extensively in the German-occupied territories of western Europe and capitalized on favorable exchange rates to purchase works of art for Linz. He was well aware that some of the acquired pieces had been plundered from Jewish owners.[10] However, a fatal cancer ended Posse's quest in December 1942, and he was succeeded by Hermann Voss, director of the Wiesbaden Landesmuseum and former head of the

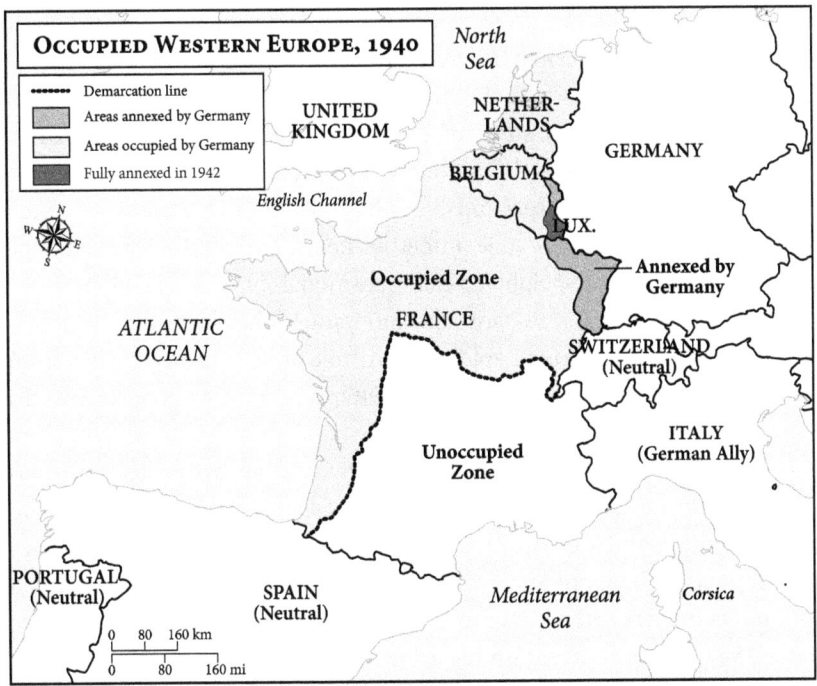

Occupied Western Europe, 1940

Kaiser Friedrich Museum in Berlin. Voss was an esteemed expert on Old Master paintings, and by some accounts Posse had recommended him as his own successor as his health declined.[11] By the end of the war, Posse and Voss had spent over RM 100 million on acquisitions for the Linz project, and acquired thousands of paintings—estimates range from five to eight thousand—plus sculpture, tapestries, furniture, and assorted art objects.[12] The accumulation of high-quality artworks was stunningly rapid. For comparison, the US National Gallery of Art, established in 1941, acquired three thousand paintings over the course of fifty years.[13]

Some looting was carried out by German soldiers, but there is an important distinction between more isolated acts of theft and vandalism, carried out in Europe by soldiers in Allied and Axis armies alike, and systematized Nazi plunder against civilian enemies of the Third Reich.[14] Shortly after entering Paris in June 1940, for instance, German soldiers stole some two thousand objects from the Army Museum at Les Invalides, including trophies, armor, and historical maps. They seized military flags that had been stolen before by their Prussian predecessors during the occupation of 1870–71 and were restored to France through the Treaty of Versailles.[15] In 1942, the German military authorized the dispersal of two hundred paintings from the art museum in Lille, some of which were used to decorate German billets and military offices.[16] On the night of September 24, 1943, after the Musée Maritime des Salorges in Nantes had sustained damage from Allied bombing, German soldiers stole numerous items. The curator estimated the museum had lost around eighteen elaborate model ships, several eighteenth-century solar watches, a sextant, and numerous other historical objects.[17] In the Netherlands, German soldiers also stole at least two paintings from the state-run Hooge Veluwe museum in Otterloo—a Cranach portrait and a *Venus* by Baldung Grien.[18]

Within the German military the *Kunstschutz*, an art-protection division created during the First World War, showed some genuine efforts to prevent looting and vandalism. Reactivated and employed in the military governments in Belgium and France in 1940, the Kunstschutz was charged with protecting art and heritage and, in theory, ensuring German adherence to the 1907 Hague Convention regarding the treatment of private property. The head of the Kunstschutz in France, Franz Graf Wolff Metternich, had served as a curator in Rhineland-Westphalia before the war, and was well known and respected by French experts. A descendant of the nineteenth-century Austrian diplomat Klemens von Metternich, he oversaw legitimate conservation efforts by the German army. The division posted instructions for German soldiers to respect historic buildings and monuments and to demonstrate that they were carriers of a high culture.[19] A member of the traditional German elite, Wolff Metternich was not a party member and issued numerous protests in response to Nazi looting. Göring removed him from the Kunstschutz in June 1942 on the pretext that his expertise was needed back in the Rhineland. His successor and former assistant Bernhard von Tieschowitz similarly was a trusted liaison for the French national museum office.[20]

In contrast to isolated examples of looting by the German military, the plunder carried out on behalf of the Nazi leadership was far more systematic and relied on a network of willing collaborators within the Third Reich and the occupied territories—civil servants, museum directors, curators, dealers, and art historians.[21] Among the cultural riches in western Europe, the Nazis targeted privately owned collections, especially Jewish-owned items, and left the prestigious national museum collections largely intact. In the Nazi vision of postwar Europe, museums in the Netherlands and Flanders would be part of an expanded Thousand Year Reich, obviating the need to displace the collections. As for France, Hitler planned to demand the most prestigious masterpieces after the German victory. "This restraint," Albert Speer later observed, "was not so unselfish as it seemed." Hitler awaited the final peace treaty, when "the best pieces from the Louvre would have to be delivered to Germany as part of war reparations."[22] In the meantime, the German occupation required stability and a docile population, which might become unnecessarily roiled with the loss of such national cultural treasures as the *Mona Lisa*. Instead, the Nazis swiftly targeted privately held cultural assets owned by their official enemies—Jews, Freemasons, and communists. And among those groups, it was Jews who owned the most extensive art collections.[23]

In addition to supplying works for Hitler's Linz museum project, Nazi art looting nourished the avarice of other top officials, including Joseph Goebbels, Joachim von Ribbentrop, Heinrich Himmler, and *Reichsmarschall* Hermann Göring, whose collection burgeoned to nearly two thousand objects, second only to Hitler's.[24] Göring received Hitler's authorization to assemble a sizeable collection that he intended to donate to the Third Reich, and he enlisted the expertise of Berlin-based dealers Walter Andreas Hofer and Bruno Lohse.[25] Through these advisors, Göring was a particularly ruthless negotiator, manipulating his purchases well below market value and inflating prices in his own sales to dealers, including objects funneled to him by theft—transactions all thoroughly documented in official invoices and receipts. After the war, witnesses reported to members of the US Art Looting Investigation Unit (ALIU) that, despite unlimited resources at his disposal, Göring always bargained, "no matter how small the amount involved." He wanted to maintain the appearance of "correct" dealings and said that he intended to pay for any works he received through Nazi looting. Ultimately, however, Göring's simultaneous use of threats and coercion made him a "consummate hypocrite."[26]

A key partner for Göring in the confiscation of cultural assets was party ideologue Alfred Rosenberg, who had developed plans for the advanced study of National Socialism in a network of institutions. In July 1940, Hitler authorized Rosenberg to seize libraries and archives from Jews, Freemasons, and communists to secure materials for the initiative. By September, the Führer extended Rosenberg's charge to securing all "ownerless" (*herrenlos*) cultural property of the Nazis' enemies. These assets included works of art "abandoned" by individuals who had fled abroad, or objects entrusted to national governments for safekeeping. Rosenberg's staff grew with these increased responsibilities, and developed into an agency that bore his name, the *Einsatzstab Reichsleiter Rosenberg* (ERR).[27] A western Office (*Dienststelle Westen*) established in Paris under Kurt bon Behr dominated the plunder in France, where it eventually oversaw a burgeoning cache of seized books, archives, and works of art. Facing a need for funding, personnel, and transportation to ship the plunder to the Reich in the summer of 1940, Rosenberg courted the support of Göring. The two men struck an agreement that gave the ERR needed financial support, while the Reichsmarschall gained privileged access to the spoils for his personal collection.[28] The ERR also played a key role in art looting in Belgium, but was less influential in the Netherlands.[29]

In all three countries, Jews became increasingly vulnerable through a combination of German and national antisemitic decrees. The result was incremental exclusion and dispossession. The first step was defining a Jew, far from a simple process. In occupied France, a German ordinance of September 27, 1940, defined Jews as anyone who practiced the Jewish religion or had at least three Jewish grandparents. It also required Jews in the occupied zone to register with French authorities, at the *sous-préfecture* of their primary residence, and forbade the return of those who had fled the zone.[30] A week later the Vichy regime, intent to assert its sovereignty in this area, issued the Jewish statute of October 3, 1940, which defined Jewishness on the basis of race—a person with three ethnically Jewish grandparents, or two if married to a Jew. This core definition applied in the Netherlands and Belgium through German decrees issued the same month, while including individuals with two Jewish grandparents who practiced the Jewish religion.[31] The French statute also barred Jews from the highest ranks of government and the military, and positions of public influence—education, publishing, radio, theater, and cinema.[32]

Within a year, the Vichy regime promulgated twenty-six laws and twenty-four decrees further eliminating Jewish influence. A second Jewish statute in June 1941 expanded the list of professions closed to Jews and subsequent decrees established quotas in the liberal professions, affecting Jewish doctors, lawyers, pharmacists, and architects, with the support of non-Jewish members of those professions. A law of November 17 further specified the exclusion of Jews from the commerce of paintings and antiquities. Moreover, the revised statute replaced exclusion by profession with exclusion by entire economic sectors, affecting not "bankers" but "banking." As a result, a given organization could not rehire an affected individual in any capacity.[33]

As the occupation wore on, German plundering agencies proliferated. In all three countries, the Nazis mobilized the *Devisenschutzkommando* (Currency Control Commando) to scour bank vaults and safes, another operation under Göring's authority through the office of the Four-Year Plan.[34] They targeted furniture and household items through the *Möbel-Aktion* (Furniture Operation). In December 1941, Rosenberg, who after the German invasion of the USSR also served as Reich minister for the occupied eastern territories, sought Hitler's approval to seize goods from residences no longer occupied by Jews; some had fled, others had been arrested. With Hitler's assent, the furniture and household items left behind were amassed for the benefit of Germans displaced by Allied bombings and those settling in the eastern occupied territories. And the supply of these assets spiked by mid-1942, with the systematic deportation of Jews in the Final Solution. The Möbel-Aktion stripped Jewish residences of all belongings, including any documents that might later be used in property ownership claims. In all, the operation seized goods from more than seventy thousand homes in the three countries, including forty-five hundred in Belgium, twenty-nine thousand in the Netherlands, and thirty-eight thousand in the city of Paris. The operation mostly amassed household effects, but it also swept up some lower-quality works of art.[35]

In France, an estimated seventy thousand Jews lost assets at internment and transit camps located across the country, where prisoners were detained and transferred prior to deportation to Nazi camps. Some were German and Austrian Jews detained as enemies of the state in September 1939 and May 1940. Others were refugees who had fled invading German forces in the Netherlands and Belgium. In October 1940, the Third Reich deported 6,500 German Jews to the Gurs camp in the foothills of the Pyrenées Mountains, near the Spanish border. In May 1941, more than 3,500 Jews were interned in the northern zone at Beaune-la-Rolande and Pithiviers. Upon entering camps, prisoners were forced to relinquish cash, jewelry, watches—any small items they had been able to carry on their person or pack in a suitcase. In the summer of 1942, the camp of Drancy in a northeastern suburb of Paris became the primary transit camp for deportations to Auschwitz, and prisoners from the region or transferred from camps in the provinces were stripped of all items of value.[36]

A booming wartime art market across western Europe further exacerbated the displacement of cultural property. Beyond Posse and Voss's purchases for the Linz project, a host of buyers took advantage of the circumstances of war and occupation to purchase works, whether the sellers were eager and free actors, reluctant dealmakers, or victims of coercion. Art dealers from the Reich representing museums and private collections fanned out in the occupied countries in search of bargains. Elite buyers from the western countries flocked to auctions in Paris, Amsterdam, and Brussels, in search of safe investments, as a hedge against inflation. Exclusionary measures banned state enemies from all aspects of art commerce, with a devastating impact on Jewish dealers and gallery owners, while other dealers took advantage of their absence.[37]

War profiteers purchased art and resold it abroad to obfuscate all manner of illicit dealings. Prices skyrocketed. A price index for sales at the Drouot auction house in Paris between 1940 and 1943 shows a fivefold increase. By March 1944, coveted modern paintings were selling for 50 percent more than the price paid for similar works in 1942, while the price index of variable-income securities remained flat.[38] In Amsterdam, even more dramatically, an index of sales at the Mak an Waay auction house from 1940 to 1943 reveals a 2,300 percent price increase. In Belgium, newspapers during the occupation reported "intense activity" in the art market.[39] As writer Jean-François Elslander later recalled, "people were buying a tremendous amount of ugly daubs, just because they hoped that one day, maybe, these daubs would reach really high prices."[40] According to Belgian journalist Geert Sels, much of the purchased art flowed to France, the Netherlands, and other countries beyond the Reich, thus escaping postwar investigations.[41]

Amid these trends, with individual actors, and agencies common to Nazi art plunder in the three countries, differences in each national case were shaped by several factors, notably demographics, the supply of Jewish collections before the war, the administrative apparatus of each occupation government, national institutions, the applicability of national laws, and the degree of centralization of Jewish assets.

Purchased Plunder in the Netherlands

The German invasion of the neutral Netherlands marked the first battle on Dutch territory since the Napoleonic wars, and meager Dutch forces were no match for the German Blitzkrieg. On May 13, 1940, the Luftwaffe flattened the city center of Rotterdam, the country's most important port city, killing 980 civilians. Queen Wilhelmina and the royal family fled to England along with the Dutch cabinet, which would remain in exile for five years. Facing the threat of continued air raids, the head of Dutch forces, General H. G. Winkelman, capitulated the following day.[42]

The brief but concentrated battle also took a heavy toll on Dutch art and heritage. The extensive bombing of Rotterdam spared valuable collections in the Boijmans Museum but claimed numerous private homes and their contents, as an estimated 13 percent of residents became homeless. The historic city center of Middelburg was destroyed, including the municipal antiquities collection, local archives, and nineteen paintings from the Mauritshuis on loan at the local art museum. Bombs and fires damaged an estimated forty paintings loaned from the Rijksmuseum to Dutch museums across the country.[43]

Following the Dutch surrender, the Germans quickly implemented a civilian occupation administration under Reichskommissar Arthur Seyss-Inquart, an SS high official who reported directly to Hitler. Seyss-Inquart oversaw the most immediate and extensive SS presence in western Europe, headquartered in the former American embassy in The Hague. He had the power to issue executive decrees (*Verordnungen*) while four German commissioners oversaw the Dutch cabinet, including Hans Fischböck, head of economy and finance, and Austrian-born SS officer Hanns Albin Rauter, general commissioner for security and police.[44]

A German ordinance issued on June 24, 1940, swiftly proclaimed control over enemy assets in the Netherlands.[45] The royal family owned the largest private collection in the country, and on September 10, 1941, Seyss-Inquart proclaimed the forfeiture of all assets owned by living Dutch royals. Thanks to negotiations conducted by a Dutch commission, most of the royal art collection remained in the Netherlands, though the Nazis shipped to the Reich some furniture items, archives, and an assemblage of paintings with hunting scenes.[46]

Far more vulnerable were the assets of Freemasons, socialists, and Jews, held by institutions and individuals. In Amsterdam, the ERR seized Masonic archives, rare books, and incunabula from the Biblioteca Klossiana, which had been donated to the order by Prince Hendrik, the late husband of Queen Wilhelmina. The ERR also shuttered the International Institute of Social History, used the building for its Amsterdam headquarters, and confiscated the library's newspapers and some 160,000 volumes. In February 1943, it confiscated the collection of the Jewish Historical Museum in Amsterdam, which had been transferred to the municipal museum for safekeeping in 1940.

The Germans seized 153 crates of valuable Jewish books and manuscripts from the Biblioteca Rosenthaliana, owned by the city of Amsterdam, and shipped them to the Reich in June 1944. Targeting the Portuguese-Jewish community, they seized a seminary's archives and a twenty-thousand-volume library.[47]

Among the assets targeted in Nazi looting operations, the plunder of Jewish property was the most systematic.[48] Having defined Jews in October 1940, the Nazis then required them to register with authorities and provide their name, address, and profession. Most Dutch Jews did so within a matter of months. According to Gerard Aalders, they largely complied due to an overriding respect for authority and a widely held belief that their assimilation in Dutch society had prevented widespread antisemitism; they had seen no violent episodes akin to *Kristallnacht* in Germany.[49] But a flurry of subsequent Verordnungen made the Jewish community in the Netherlands increasingly isolated and vulnerable. All Jewish civil servants were dismissed on November 4, 1940, and a series of measures ordered Jews in various professions to provide services only for Jewish clients.[50]

The process of expropriation accelerated with the German establishment of a phony branch of the Lippmann, Rosenthal & Co. bank (Liro), a Jewish-owned institution located at the Nieuwe Spiegelstraat in Amsterdam and widely respected among Jews before the war. The Germans deliberately used this trusted name to set up a separate branch in Sarphatistraat, commonly known as Liro. It was not a bank, but a repository for a wide range of Jewish assets that were liquidated by the Nazis. Two decrees issued in August 1941 and May 1942 required Jews to deposit assets at the Sarphatistraat branch. Liro accumulated stock shares, bank notes, liquid assets, works of art, antique furniture, precious metals, and jewels.[51] More than thirty-five hundred cultural objects were deposited at Sarphatistraat. Hitler's curators for the Linz project, as always, had first choice among the spoils, while lower-quality objects were sold on the Dutch art market, and the proceeds were used to purchase more coveted items.[52]

Beyond Liro, an agency headed by Austrian Kajetan Mühlmann, a personal friend of Seyss-Inquart, eventually dominated the plunder of Dutch art collections. Mühlmann had experience seizing cultural assets in Poland and capitalized on his connections to the Reichskommissar. He assumed responsibility for works of art seized through a German law on enemy assets, promulgated on June 21, 1940, and established his office, the *Dienststelle Mühlmann*, in The Hague.[53] With the title *Sammelverwalter*, or collection manager, he hunted down works of art owned by Jews and entrusted to Dutch museums for safekeeping. Among them was a collection of paintings owned by Alphons Jaffé, a Jewish doctor and British citizen who had entrusted some ninety pictures by nineteenth-century masters to the municipal museum of Leiden. Mühlmann seized part of the collection and saved the best pieces for Hitler and Göring.[54]

Above all, the Dienststelle functioned as an art dealership for the Nazi elite. Mühlmann created bank accounts that funneled art payments on behalf of Hitler and Göring and accumulated funds from sales of enemy assets. His preferred acquisition method was negotiating purchases far below market value, including seventy-five pieces deposited by Jews at Liro. Mühlmann also worked closely with the Devisenschutzkommando and Gestapo to confiscate Jewish assets. But he did not limit himself to Jewish-owned art. He was willing to manipulate any owner with coveted objects, dropping thinly veiled threats that he had the power to destroy any art business or its owner.[55]

Joining Mühlmann in the occupation art trade were numerous German buyers who seized the opportunity to benefit from a favorable exchange rate and a rich supply of works, due to the circumstances of war and antisemitic persecution. As later described by American MFAA officer Bancel LaFarge, "After June 1940 a horde of buyers descended upon Holland—agents for Hitler, Göring or other notables—museum directors, art dealers and private individuals."[56] Art historian Erhard Göpel served the Linz project in the Netherlands after 1942, assisted by several Jewish art historians who received protection from antisemitic measures as long as they continued to facilitate acquisitions.[57] In April 1941, German purchasing power increased dramatically when the Reich abolished the currency border between the two countries, a move that forced the Dutch central bank to convert all cash guilders to Reichsmarks at a rate favoring the Germans. With no restriction on the number of marks exchanged, German currency flooded the Dutch economy, with lasting repercussions. After investments flowed to Germany, the Dutch central bank was left at the end of the war with about six billion acutely devalued marks.[58]

Göring managed to score the most spectacular art purchase in the Netherlands, securing several hundred Old Master paintings from the stock of Jewish dealer Jacques Goudstikker. Leading up to the war, Goudstikker was an internationally renowned expert on Dutch paintings, and arguably the most successful dealer in the country. After the German invasion of Poland, Goudstikker and his wife Désirée (Dési), a well-known Viennese opera singer, vacillated about whether to flee the Netherlands and leave behind their extensive assets—two castles, the head branch of the Herengracht dealership in Amsterdam, and the gallery's stock of some fourteen hundred paintings. Goudstikker secured visas to the United States in December 1939, but could not bring himself to leave behind the world he had created in the Netherlands. The visas expired on May 9, 1940, the day before the German invasion. Five days later, while flames from Luftwaffe air raids engulfed Rotterdam, they decided to escape with their infant son, Eduard. They boarded the SS *Bodegraven* destined for South America, one of the last ships to depart as the Dutch high command prepared to surrender. They reached Dover but were barred from disembarking amid British concerns that German spies also had boarded the vessel. The night of May 16, Jacques grew restless sitting with his family and other passengers in the ship's stuffy hold, and went up to the deck to smoke. The ship lights had been turned off to prevent an enemy attack and in the darkness, he slipped through an open hatch and fell to his death. Dési grew increasingly worried when Jacques did not return to the hold, and a group of sailors searched for him. One of them fell through the same open hatch and landed on the art dealer's body. The sailor survived but was injured, and the captain reversed course to allow the serviceman to receive medical treatment on land. The ship stopped at the English port of Falmouth, and Dési, without disembarking, quickly arranged Jacques's burial. She and Eduard continued on to Liverpool, where she eventually secured a visa to the United States with the help of influential friends and the American embassy in London. Without access to the Goudstikker assets, Dési earned a living as a singer in New York. It was a far less opulent lifestyle, compared to their past in the Netherlands, but Dési and Eduard were among privileged Jews who escaped Nazi domination and survived the war.[59]

On the night of Jacques's tragic death, he had been carrying a little black notebook, recovered by Dési, with carefully typed pages detailing his firm's inventory. He had noted the title of each painting, the author, and dimensions—crucial evidence of the dealer's art stock. But to Dutch and German authorities, Dési was a Jewish émigré who had abandoned the assets. Compounding her misfortune, the Goudstikkers' attorney and trustee, D. A. Sternheim, had died of a heart attack during the German invasion, leaving the business under the control of Goudstikker's staff. Dési instructed them by telegram not to sell the collection, but she had lost control of the estate. In July 1940, the employees sold Goudstikker's assets to Göring and

Alois Miedl, a German dealer and longtime resident in the Netherlands, for a total of NLG 2,550,000.[60] The sale included the gallery premises at Herengracht 458, country estates in Breukelen and Ouderkerk aan de Amstel (Oostermeer mansion), the trade name, and stock of at least 1,113 artworks. Miedl paid NLG 550,000 for the real estate and trade name, while Göring paid NLG 2 million for some six hundred paintings, including exquisite Dutch works—a still life by Floris van Schooten, a landscape of America by Jan Mostaert, *View of Delft* by Daniel Vosmaer, a river landscape by Salomon van Ruysdael.[61] Miedl purchased some of the works from Göring and continued to operate the gallery during the occupation under the firm's new name, Kunsthandel Voorheen J. Goudstikker NV. Aiming to maintain the appearance of propriety, Miedl deposited a portion of sales proceeds into an account held for Dési, totaling NLG 1,363,752.33 by the end of the war, an amount far below the works' market value.[62]

The Germans also pursued a collection in the estate of Fritz Mannheimer, former director of the Mendelssohn Bank in Amsterdam. A German Jew, he became a naturalized Dutch citizen and maintained homes in Amsterdam and outside Paris. He financed a luxurious lifestyle through the Mendelssohn Bank, eventually running up significant debts in the 1930s. He died in France on August 9, 1939, and a few days later, the bank collapsed, leaving his estate in bankruptcy. Yet his assets included a stunning art collection of around three thousand objects, divided between the two countries. The collection contained paintings, jewelry, and fine furniture, but was best known for its Meissen porcelain, precious silver, medieval gold pieces, and other decorative objects of Germanic origin. The ever-industrious Posse was determined to secure the objects from both countries for the Linz museum, and in 1943 Seyss-Inquart negotiated a deal on his behalf with the non-Jewish trusteees of Mannheimer's estate for NLG 5.5 million.[63]

Non-Jewish art collectors and their trustees also negotiated with the Germans. Posse established an office in The Hague on June 26, 1940, and within days initiated a deal involving several hundred Old Master drawings collected by Franz Koenigs, a German banker and naturalized Dutch citizen who had lived in the Netherlands since the early 1920s. Koenigs had amassed a sizeable collection, the core of which was some 2,600 drawings. He fell on hard times with the economic crisis of the early 1930s and used the collection as collateral for a loan from the Jewish-owned Lisser and Rosencrantz Bank of Amsterdam. He did so, however, on condition the drawings would be on display to the public at the Museum Boijmans in Rotterdam. Several years later, when the German invasion appeared imminent, the bank directors began calling in their loans and wished to sell the Koenigs pieces. The head of the museum, Dirk Hannema, convinced Dutch industrialist Daniël George van Beuningen to purchase the collection of drawings and twelve paintings for NLG 2 million, aiming to keep them in the Netherlands.[64]

A few weeks into the occupation, Posse visited Van Beuningen and offered to purchase the drawings. Van Beuningen needed the cash and was keen to maintain good relations with the Germans, as his company transported German coal to the Netherlands. In December 1940, he reached a deal with Posse and sold 527 of the best Old Master and Italian drawings for NLG 1.4 million. The Germans shipped them to Dresden, where in 1945 they fell under the control of the Red Army. Most of the drawings remain in St. Petersburg today, in an ongoing dispute between Russia and the Netherlands.[65]

Posse also secured a collection of Italian Renaissance paintings, sculpture, and furniture assembled by Otto Lanz, a non-Jewish and Swiss-born surgeon, and longtime resident of the Netherlands. Lanz became a professor of surgery at the University of Amsterdam in 1902 and amassed a valuable collection of around 430 objects, some of which were held at the Rijksmuseum. After Lanz's death in 1935, his widow relocated to Basel but allowed the museum to continue holding much of the collection. During the occupation, Mrs. Lanz was willing to sell the collection for SFr 2 million, but would negotiate only through the Dutch and Jewish dealer Nathan Katz. Such a high price in foreign currency was out of reach for nearly all German buyers, including Göring. But not for Posse. As part of the deal, Mrs. Lanz required a visa to Switzerland for Katz, which Posse dutifully arranged through Nazi party leader Martin Bormann. Posse purchased the collection in April 1941 and Katz relocated to Basel. In another deal with the Nazis, Katz used a Rembrandt painting, *Portrait of a Man of the Raman Family*, to secure visas for twenty-five relatives to escape via Spain. He also secured his mother's release from the Westerbork concentration camp in exchange for another picture that became an SS officer's gift to Hitler.[66]

Mühlmann confiscated works from another non-Jewish owner, art historian Frits Lugt of The Hague. Lugt had fled the Netherlands for Switzerland in 1939, then relocated to Oberlin, Ohio from 1940 to 1945. Mühlmann seized the collection in early 1941 based on reports that the art historian had displayed anti-German sentiment. Mühlmann selected twenty-five paintings for Linz and in July 1941 shipped them to Germany. The alleged legality of the confiscation was called into question when Mühlmann learned that the denunciation of Lugt had been fabricated by the administrator of the estate, appointed by Lugt himself. Conveniently for the Reich, the US entry in the war in December 1941 made Lugt a residential enemy, restoring a "legal" justification for the confiscation of his assets.[67]

While it is impossible to know the exact number of artworks lost from the Netherlands, after the war claimants registered some twenty thousand objects, for a total value of NLG 150 million, based on prewar prices.[68] In neighboring Belgium, the Nazis reaped fewer cultural assets of significant value, but still plundered the assets of Jews and non-Jews alike, and liquidated the household effects of thousands of lower-income Jewish victims.

Plundered Homes in Belgium

During the chaos of the German invasion, Belgian King Leopold III, in contrast to Dutch Queen Wilhelmina, chose not to flee. In a grandiose gesture, he took command of the nation's armed forces, as had his father, Albert I, in August 1914. But much of the government did leave. Most ministers and many members of parliament escaped to southern France, and eventually formed a government in England. Within less than three weeks, three German panzer corps commanded by Field Marshal Gerd von Rundstedt had advanced through Luxembourg and the Belgian Ardennes, and they outflanked French and British forces along the French border. With the collapse of Allied defenses, Leopold surrendered on May 28. Yet he was hardly a martyr, as the victors placed him under rather comfortable house arrest in the royal palace at Laeken.[69]

In contrast to the civilian occupation government established in the Netherlands, the Germans created a military government for Belgium, which included the northern departments of France. General von Falkenhausen headed this *Militärverwaltung Belgien und Nord Frankreich* until June 1944, when the Nazis implemented a final-hour civilian government under SS leadership. Whereas the Germans envisioned the Netherlands within an expanded Third Reich, Belgium would constitute an immediate foreland. Hitler's further intentions for the future of Belgium were unclear, though he instructed the military administration to favor the more Germanic Flemish population over the francophone Walloons.[70]

The German theft of several national treasures held in churches and state museums was a retaliatory measure against the cultural provisions of the Treaty of Versailles, which had forced Germany to relinquish panels from the famed Ghent Altarpiece and *The Last Supper* by Dieric Bouts. In the summer of 1942, German art historian and director of Bavarian State Painting Collections Ernst Buchner oversaw the seizure of the Bouts panels from Louvain and the Ghent Altarpiece panels from a repository in Pau, France, the latter allowed by the French head of government Pierre Laval in Vichy.[71] The Germans also seized at least nine paintings from the Belgian Royal Museum in Antwerp, including *Flute Player* by Emile Godding, *Sheeps and Hens* by Eugène Joseph Verboeckhoven, a landscape by Auguste de Lathouwer, and a seascape by Pieter Jan Schotel.[72] Just a few days before the liberation of Belgium in August 1944, the retreating Germans seized Michelangelo's magnificent sculpture *Madonna and Child* and paintings from the Church of Our Lady in Bruges. They promptly shipped them to the Alt Aussee salt mine in Austria, where the Nazis stored much of the art destined for Linz.[73]

Compared to the Netherlands and France, Belgium had the fewest number of significant Jewish art collections at the beginning of the occupation. Out of around sixty-five thousand Jews in Belgium, more than 90 percent were foreign immigrants who had arrived since the 1920s, mostly refugees escaping persecution in central and eastern Europe. In contrast, roughly 55 percent of Jews in France were citizens, as were 80 percent in the Netherlands.[74] The concentration of exploitable cultural assets found in France and the Netherlands, whether looted or purchased, was not available to the Germans in Belgium. Here, the Möbel-Aktion targeted a higher proportion of libraries and lower-quality furniture.[75]

Over the course of the occupation, the Third Reich secured from Belgium a wide range of goods—raw materials, laborers, gold reserves, and cultural objects—and quickly implemented measures to facilitate the expropriation of Jewish assets. On October 12, 1940, the Germans drew upon Belgian law in creating the Brussels Trustee Corporation (*Brüsseler Treuhandgesellschaft*, BTG) to locate and manage enemy property, including Jewish assets. This reliance on Belgian law created an anomaly in the Nazi seizure of Jewish property, as the trust company could inspect and oversee private property but not liquidate it, in contrast to the German plundering branch of Liro in Amsterdam. Jewish bank accounts are a significant case in point, as the BTG never transferred ownership to the Germans.[76]

In other asset areas, the expropriation was far more systematic and extensive. On October 28, 1940, German occupation authorities required registration of Jewish businesses and real estate. Economic Aryanization advanced further on May 31, 1941, when a German decree allowed provisional administrators to take control of Jewish property. Eventually, the liquidation of Jewish businesses in Belgium generated RM 12 million, which the Germans credited toward occupation expenses.[77] By the end of the occupation, the BTG continued to oversee 637 Jewish enterprises worth an estimated RM 100 million.[78] It also seized works of art from the homes of Jews who had fled or were deported, and transferred objects—quality furniture, silverworks, porcelain, Persian rugs, paintings, and engravings—to the ERR in Paris.[79]

Among entities involved in the plunder, the German Security Police (*Sicherheitspolizei-Sicherheitsdienst*, SiPO-SD) joined the occupation government in Brussels in June 1940 and collected archives and libraries of political enemies, coordinating efforts with the ERR. They targeted Masonic lodges in Brussels, Antwerp, Liège, and Verviers. German agents seized the archives of the leftist newspapers *Le peuple* and *Vooruit*, and shut down socialist libraries of the Houses of the People in Brussels, shipping some of the materials to Germany. The ERR scoured the homes of politicians and professors who had fled Belgium and sought refuge in the United States, Britain, or France. They confiscated the papers of Professor Niko Gunzburg, head of the law department of the University of Ghent, who was also a known Freemason and prominent member of the Jewish community. The Germans also seized documents and libraries of professors at the Free University of Brussels (Université Libre de Bruxelles), including Max Gottschalk, Jacques Errera, and Herbert Speyer, who according to the Nazis had propagated insidious Jewish-Masonic-socialist ideas. Among Jewish institutions, the Germans seized materials from the Federation of Zionists and the Alliance Israélite.[80] All told, the ERR plundered an estimated 56,250 books from Jewish collections in Belgium.[81]

The Möbel-Aktion also had a significant impact in Belgium. As Jews were arrested, deported, or fled from authorities, their homes were ransacked and any objects of artistic value were given to the ERR. By the summer of 1943, one year after systematic deportations began, the Germans had confiscated the contents of nearly four thousand homes in Belgium, totaling an estimated fifty-four thousand cubic meters of household items.[82] The total number of plundered homes grew to forty-five hundred by the end of the occupation, creating a greater proportional loss of household furniture and everyday effects compared to the plunder of higher-value art in France and the

Netherlands.[83] In 1944, representatives of the ERR in Paris selected thirty-two miniature antiques from the stash, and an estimated thirty-five quality paintings.[84]

While the yield of "enemy assets" art was relatively modest in Belgium, the Germans nonetheless seized art collections of value; of fourteen collections confiscated by the ERR, twelve were Jewish-owned. These collections contained 258 objects, of which 249 items, or 96 percent, were stolen from Jews.[85] One such collection was owned by Hugo Andriesse, a financier and industrialist who in December 1939 had entrusted to the Musées Royaux des Beaux-Arts in Brussels a collection of five tapestries, seventeen oriental rugs, and twenty-eight lead-sealed crates of some forty paintings mostly by Flemish and Dutch and masters. They included a canvas each by Ter Borcht, Van Goyen, Jan Steen, and Frans Snyder and three by Salomon van Ruysdael. According to head curator Jean Capart, an eminent Egyptologist, Andriesse had made an oral promise several years prior to donate the pieces to the museum. Due to this potential contribution to "the heritage of the Belgian state," Capart received permission from the education ministry, which oversaw the fine arts office, to safeguard the collection. In December 1939, Andriesse's Belgian chauffeur transported the works to the museum, where they were placed in an air raid shelter. Andriesse paid the same driver to take him to Lisbon in October 1940 and from there fled to the United States, believing his art collection was in safe hands.[86]

The trusted chauffeur, it turns out, was not so trustworthy, and in his own pursuit of personal gain revealed the collection's location to the ERR. When questioned by German authorities, Capart confirmed that the collection was in the care of the Musées Royaux. On March 9, 1942, the Devisenschutzkommando seized the works as enemy assets and shipped them to ERR headquarters at the Jeu de Paume museum in Paris. Capart immediately protested to the Belgian Secretary General of Education, emphasizing that Andriesse had "stated formally on a number of occasions" that upon his death the works were "to have entered into the possession of the Belgian state." A month later, the secretary general in turn tepidly reported the incident to the Kunstschutz in Belgium, which itself was in no position to contest the confiscation.[87] Göring's staff at the Jeu de Paume selected some of the pieces for the Reichsmarschall, and the ERR shipped the remaining objects to a repository in Buxheim.[88]

The Germans also seized at least forty-one eighteenth-century English paintings and drawings owned by Jewish collector Eric-Emil Lyndhurst, stolen from his home in Brussels and a vault in the Belgian national bank. The Lyndhurst works joined other ERR loot at the Jeu de Paume, where Göring's experts selected a few of the pieces for the Reichsmarschall. The Germans sent the rest to a repository at the Castle of Nikolsburg (today Mikulov, Czechia). When the Red Army advanced into the region in April 1945, the castle caught fire in the ensuing battle and an unknown number of objects were destroyed. Lyndhurst recovered only two paintings after the war: a portrait of Lady Spencer by James Northcote and a portrait of a young woman by John Hoppner.[89]

In all, the enemy confiscated an estimated 885 works of art from Belgium.[90] One should not infer that the relatively small yield of museum-quality artworks compared to France and the Netherlands reflects a lower degree of persecution or exploitation of Jews; on the contrary, these statistics underscore the vulnerability of a lower-income, mostly foreign population. As stated by Lucien Buysse, head of the Belgian Study Commission, while the Nazis were not able to carry out the planned full spoliation of Jewish assets in Belgium, "it does remain a fact that the Jewish population was effectively and quasi completely ripped from participation in economic life and that those who survived the holocaust [sic] after the war found only devastation: the devastation of their families and the ruin of their possessions."[91]

Massive Art Plunder in France

The real treasure trove for the Nazis was in France. With a population several times larger than Belgium and the Netherlands, France also had the greatest number of large Jewish-owned art collections and dealerships among the three countries.[92] The German invasion of May and early June 1940 panicked civilians from all segments of society in Belgium and northern France, and several million fled south for safer ground.[93] On June 10, as the Germans approached Paris, the French government joined the civilian exodus. The cabinet first regrouped on June 14 in Bordeaux. In accordance with the 1875 constitution of the Third Republic, Premier Paul Reynaud nominated eighty-four-year-old Marshal Philippe Pétain to form a new government and negotiate armistice terms, and President Albert Lebrun accepted the nomination. Pétain's rise to political power was no military *putsch*. The grandfatherly Pétain was a national hero from the First World War, best known for defending Verdun against the Germans in 1916 and ending army mutinies in

1917. On June 21, French General Charles Huntzinger received the German armistice terms. He did so in the same railway car near Compiègne where the French had delivered peace terms to the Germans in 1918, highly charged symbolism in equal measure irresistible to the Germans and devastating to the French. Both sides signed the armistice the following day.⁹⁴

As in Belgium, the Germans established a military occupation government, the *Militärbefehlshaber in Frankreich*, but the armistice divided the territory into several zones. The Third Reich annexed outright two French

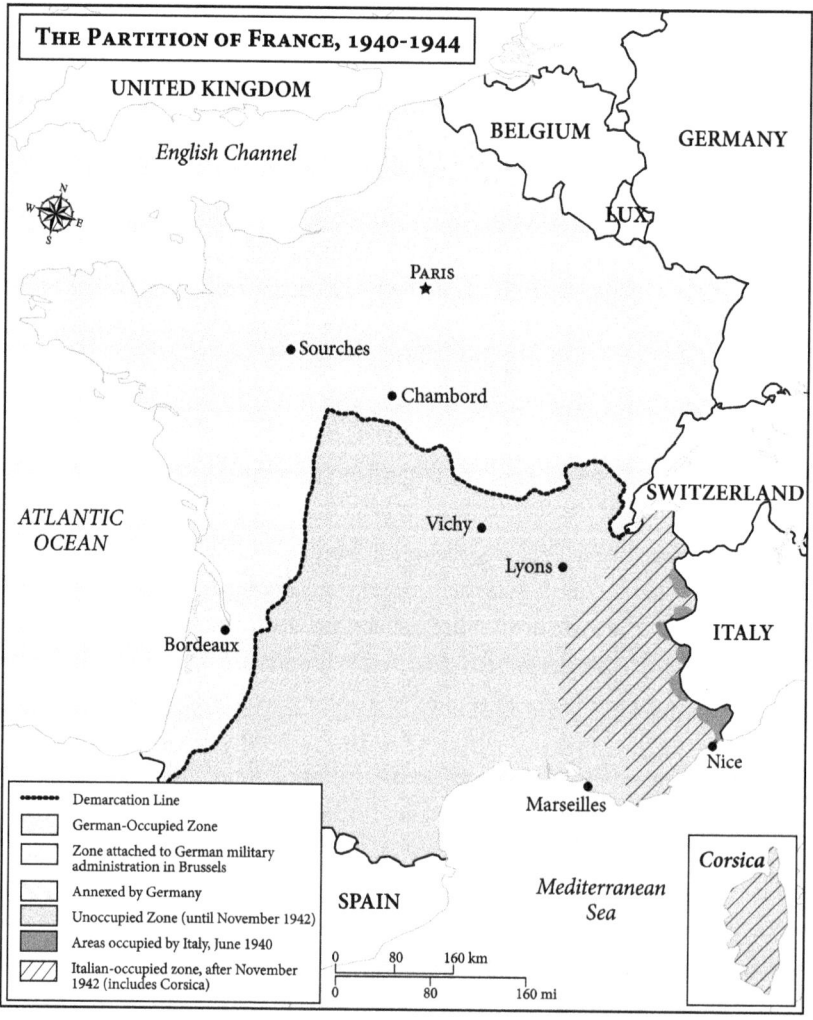

The Partition of France, 1940–1944

departments on the German border, Alsace and la Moselle, and in the northernmost region, the Nord and Pas-de-Calais were absorbed into the military command in Brussels. Just south of the Belgian command zone was a "forbidden" zone, extending north of the Somme and Aisne rivers, and to the west of the annexed territory was a "reserved" zone across eight French departments, both portending possible annexation of what the Third Reich considered the more "Germanic" regions of France. The primary German-occupied zone extended from the English Channel to the Loire River and cut southwest to the Spanish border, incorporating all of the Atlantic coast. The remaining unoccupied territory or so-called "free" zone constituted two-fifths of continental France, in the relatively resource-deprived central and southeastern regions. With the Allied landings in North Africa in November 1942, German forces occupied this southern zone as well, though movement across the demarcation line was still restricted.[95]

With Bordeaux sitting in the German-occupied zone, the French government relocated again, first to Clermont-Ferrand in the Auvergne, south of the demarcation line in the "free" zone of central France. Unable to find enough lodging, the ministers next landed in the spa city of Vichy, known for its natural hot springs. It was an appealing temporary seat of government, situated near the demarcation line with an existing railway line to Paris, and with numerous hotels available for lodging and office space. The armistice allowed the possibility of the government's return to Paris, but negotiations stalled in the summer of 1940, and Vichy remained the seat of government throughout the occupation, while much of the civil service continued to operate in Paris.[96]

Pétain quickly and legally consolidated power in Vichy, while maintaining the Third Republic's dual executive system. On June 23, the cabinet named veteran politician Pierre Laval as deputy premier. Laval later would orchestrate the most egregious acts of French collaboration with the Nazis, including the deportation of seventy-six thousand Jews, and was executed by the French provisional government in October 1945.[97] Yet in the early weeks of the Vichy regime, he believed in the promise of Franco-German collaboration, and he convinced the cabinet to grant Pétain full emergency powers to create a new constitution. A rump parliament—without communists, who were now ineligible to serve, and twenty-seven deputies who had sailed to Casablanca on the ship *Massilia* in opposition to the armistice—assembled in Vichy and on July 10 approved the measure by a vote of 569 to eighty, with seventeen abstentions. The parliament thus voted itself out of existence.⁹⁸ The measure was legal nonetheless, and in contrast to Belgium and the Netherlands, the French government remained on its national territory.

In the important area of French cultural assets, rivalries among high-ranking Nazi officials emerged, preventing any one of them from controlling the seizure of artworks. At the end of June 1940, the head of German armed forces, Wilhelm Keitel, notified the German commandant in Paris that Hitler had authorized German ambassador Otto Abetz to secure historical documents and art objects belonging to individuals, notably Jews. This action would be taken not as a form of expropriation, according to Keitel, but a guarantee for peace negotiations. Abetz took the instruction to mean he had the authority to seize works from state and private collections, and on July 1 sought the assistance of army command in Paris to assist with the transfer the most valuable pieces to the German embassy. Army command, however, was not willing to give up control over artworks so easily and, on July 15, issued an ordinance forbidding the transfer of objects without the express consent of the military administration. The measure further required individuals to declare works valued at over Ff 100,000 to the relevant field commander by August 15. Attempting to clarify who really was in charge of "safeguarding" works of art, Ribbentrop then informed Keitel on August 3 that Abetz indeed had Hitler's authority to secure private and state-owned works of art, especially Jewish assets.⁹⁹

His authority thus confirmed, Abetz proceeded with seizing objects and archives of interest to the Third Reich, enlisting the help of field police agent Eberhard Freiherr von Künsberg, who had overseen art seizures in The Hague and Brussels. Under the authority of Künsberg's special commado unit (*Sonderkommando*), on August 11 German agents seized original copies of the treaties of Versailles and Saint-Germain from an archival repository in Tours. The next day, they stole numerous items from the library of the French Ministry of Foreign Affairs, including a two-volume history of the Council of Pisa, two feather pens that had belonged to Bismarck, and a bust of Frederick the Great.¹⁰⁰

Soon these German "protective" measures extended to private Jewish-owned art collections, including works held in repositories for safekeeping by the national museum office. The Director of National Museums, Jacques Jaujard, had foreseen the particular vulnerability of Jewish assets. In some cases, he drew up phony contracts recording donations to the French state, using old paper, the proper stamps, and official seals. The attention to detail did not deter the

Germans, however, and they invalidated any donation made after the declaration of war, without bothering to verify dates.[101] On August 8, 1940, a German police officer accompanied by two French police agents appeared at the Moire chateau, demanded access to the stashed Wildenstein collection, and walked away with thirty-eight paintings.[102] By the end of the month, Künsberg's unit had seized some fifteen hundred objects from various locations and stored them on the rue de Lille, in a building adjacent to the German embassy.[103]

The plunder elicited protests from Wolff Metternich in the Kunstschutz. He had learned in early August 1940 that Künsberg intended to transfer works in the French national collections from Chambord to Paris, under the pretext of better safeguarding them, and alerted the head of the Militärbefehlshaber in France, General Streccius. The matter reached the highest ranks of the German army and Field Marshal Walther von Brauchitsch ordered the foreign office to cease all transfers of art from French repositories. Wolff Metternich later reported with great personal satisfaction that the French national collections had been saved.[104]

The Jewish-owned art in the repositories did not enjoy such protection. On September 17, Hitler authorized the ERR to confiscate ownerless works of art, including those held in safekeeping by the French Direction des musées.[105] The ERR quickly eclipsed the German embassy as the central plundering agency in France, taking control over all works seized by the embassy and the Devisenschutzkommando, and beginning in January 1942, any objects of value confiscated from victims' homes through the Möbel-Aktion. The high concentration of wealth and cultural assets among a handful of prominent Jewish collectors and dealers led to the Nazi confiscation of more than ten thousand works from four families—Rothschild, David-Weill, Kann, and Seligmann. From members of the Rothschild dynasty alone they stripped nearly four thousand pieces, including Vermeer's *Astronomer*, Chardin's *Portrait of Young Girl*, and Boucher's *Portrait of Madame Pompadour*.[106]

As the stash of plundered art grew, the building used for storage next to the German embassy quickly became inadequate. The ERR transferred 450 cases of art to the Louvre, and in early November, Jaujard authorized German use of the small Jeu de Paume museum in the Tuileries garden, which normally exhibited foreign contemporary art. Jaujard and Wolff Metternich reached an agreement by which a double inventory would be made of all objects entering the museum, with one copy given to French authorities. But Wolff Metternich was in no position to enforce the agreement, and Jaujard never received the inventory. The museum soon became a beehive of activity and became the triage center for art looted by the ERR in western Europe. Under the Paris head of the ERR, Kurt von Behr, a staff of German art experts made lists of incoming works, studied them, and routed them to repositories in the Third Reich. In all, the ERR processed some 30,000 works of art through the Jeu de Paume.[107]

Wolff Metternich continued to oppose Nazi looting and even alerted French authorities in April 1941 to an imminent ERR raid on the Sourches repository. The ERR had set its sights on the collection of David David-Weill, an important patron of French museums who prior to the war had served as president of the national museum advisory council. Armed only with the tip-off from Wolff Metternich, the supervising curator of the repository, Germain Bazin, helplessly watched the ERR cart away 130 cases of art from the collection. A month later, the Germans seized works from the Wildenstein collection at Sourches. By the end of the occupation, twelve additional private collections had been confiscated from repositories, six from Chambord and six from Brissac.[108]

Although Jaujard did not receive the agreed-upon inventory of plundered art, the Germans did allow him to appoint a national museum attaché to the

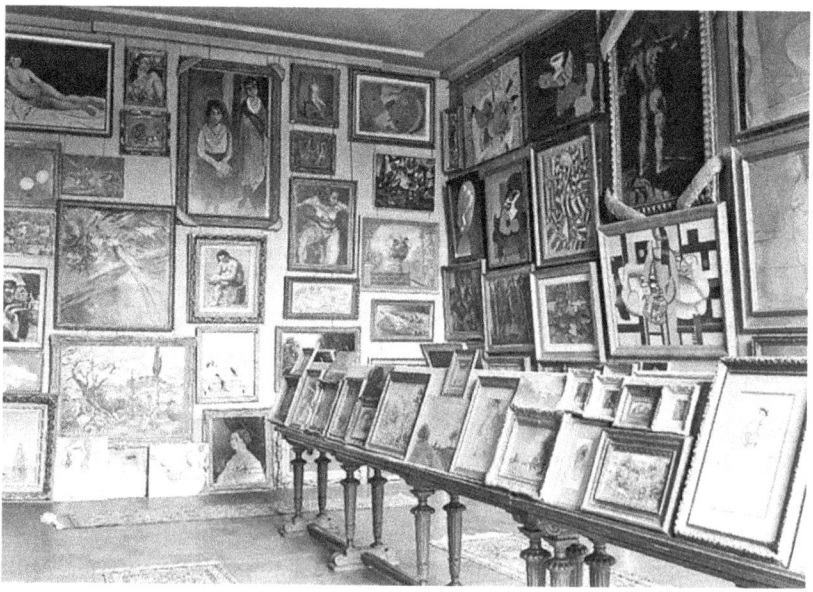

"Degenerate" paintings, as defined by the Nazis, at the Jeu de Paume museum. Valland referred to the space as the "Room of Martyrs." Alamy Stock Photo.

Jeu de Paume. This French representative, Rose Valland, would go on to become a celebrated, if complicated, member of the Resistance and the MFAA. Born in 1898 to working class parents in the Rhône-Alpes region of southwestern France, Valland had excelled in school and earned scholarships to prestigious schools of fine arts in Lyon and Paris. She earned a master's degree in art history at the Ecole du Louvre, a remarkable achievement for a woman at the time, especially from her modest background outside the Parisian social and cultural elite. Securing a paid position in the museum establishment remained an even more challenging task. In 1932 she became a volunteer at the Jeu de Paume to help plan exhibitions of foreign art, an experience that would serve her well during the occupation.[109]

Even after Jaujard asked her to serve as his eyes and ears at the Jeu de Paume, "cost what it may," she was not paid for this work until July 1941.[110] But her work was crucial. A serious and unassuming woman, she attracted little attention from the German men who processed the artworks streaming into the museum. American MFAA officer Thomas Howe later observed that she was "a robust woman with grey hair and the most penetrating brown eyes I have ever seen."[111] To the Germans, she was a lower-level staff member—not even a curator—who appeared merely to communicate with French security guards and workers who maintained the heat and electricity. Yet she also spoke German, a skill she hid from them, and listened to their conversations. She soon engaged in true espionage, working secretly at night in the museum after Von Behr's staff had cleared out. She copied the lists of works registered by the Germans, including the owners and where convoys were being shipped. Documenting the success of their operations, the ERR took photographs of their staff with choice works of art, and she made copies of the film negatives. She knew she was carrying out dangerous work. One day while noting information on a seized collection, she was startled by Bruno Lohse, Göring's key advisor in Paris. He reminded her that the staff were working on a secret operation and anyone who leaked information would risk grave punishment. She reported to Jaujard, "He looked at me and said I could be shot." She replied baldly that of course, everyone working it the museum was aware of the risks.[112] She continued her secret work nonetheless and wrote regular reports to Jaujard, but carefully kept her notes to herself.

In the midst of Nazi art looting in 1940 and 1941, the Vichy regime scrambled to control the liquidation of Jewish assets in France. In June 1941, education minister Jérôme Carcopino and deputy premier François Darlan, who held the position from February 1941 to April 1942, implored the French representative to the German high command, Fernand de Brinon, to negotiate an end to Nazi looting.[113] In August 1941, Xavier Vallat, then commissioner of Jewish Affairs, issued a vehement protest against Nazi looting to Werner Best in the German military administration.[114] These protests were not aimed at the seizure of Jewish assets in principle, but German violations of French sovereignty; the French aimed to seize Jewish cultural assets themselves.

A power struggle then developed over the assets left in France by Jewish émigrés. To the Vichy regime, Jews who had fled France were traitors, and it sought to liquidate their holdings categorized as "enemy assets." There were precedents for this kind of liquidation. During the First World War, the Third Republic seized the assets of German nationals living in France, including some fifteen hundred works owned by Wilhelm Uhde and Daniel-Henri Kahnweiler, mostly modernist paintings and drawings, which were sold at auction between 1921 and 1923.[115] Under Vichy, a French law of July 23, 1940, stripped French citizenship from individuals—Jews and non-Jews alike—who had fled abroad between May 10 and June 30, 1940. The law also allowed the French state to sequester the assets of émigrés and liquidate them within six months to fund a charity agency, National Aid (Secours National).[116] The French government had thus proclaimed "ownerless" the property left behind by individuals who had fled—real estate, businesses, bank accounts, and art collections. Another French law of October 5, 1940 enabled the state property agency (Domaines) to manage and liquidate sequestered assets for "general security" reasons.[117]

While the Germans controlled nearly all of the seized art collections, in 1941 French authorities held works from eleven significant art collections "abandoned" by enemies of the Vichy regime. Ten belonged to Jewish owners (Elie-Joseph Bois, Paul-Louis Weiller, Edouard Jonas, the Bonn family, Jacques-Ernest May, and five members of the Rothschild family—Edouard, Eugène, Henri, Maurice, and Robert), and one to the Bonne-Foy Masonic lodge of Saint-Germain-en-Laye.[118] According to French law, Domaines would normally proceed with the public sale of sequestered assets. However, some of the works in these collections, particularly the Rothschild family holdings, were high-quality objects worthy of French museums.

Under the leadership of Jacques Jaujard, the Direction des Musées asserted a right of first refusal, which it had held in public art auctions since 1921. The purchase of sequestered art was not merely, as asserted in the Mattéoli

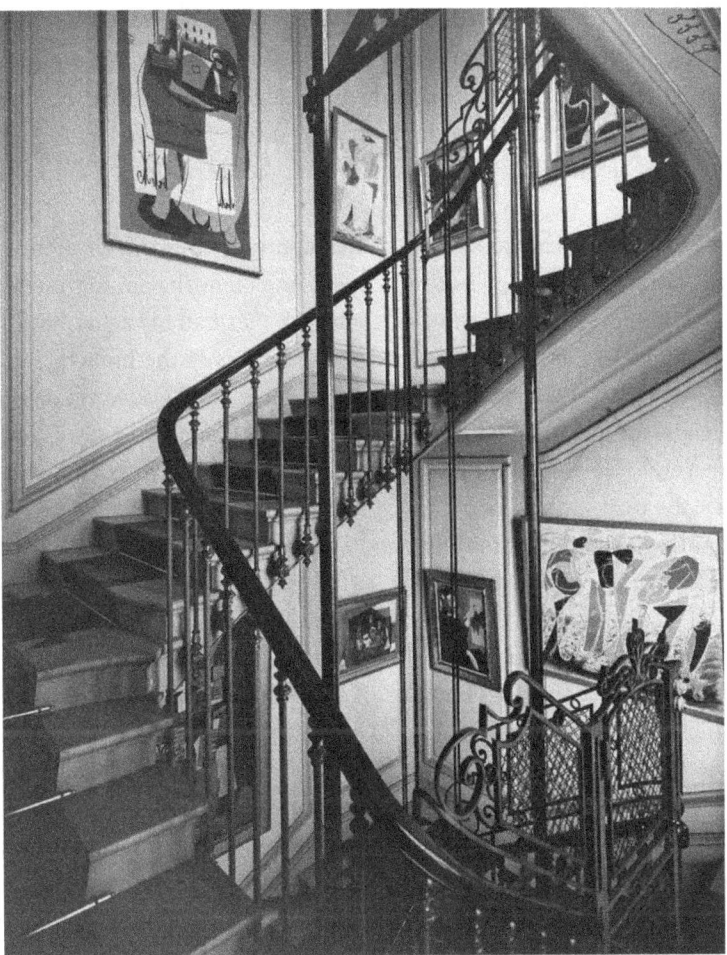

Works by Picasso, Braque, and Laurencin in the Paul Rosenberg gallery stairway, ca. 1935–1936. Digital Image © The Museum of Modern Art/ Licensed by SCALA / Art Resource, NY.

Commission report, a strategy devised by French museums to protect "key elements of the national patrimony, especially those in the Rothschild collections" from "Nazi appetites."[119] At the time, French officials in the finance and education ministries believed the state was truly acquiring works for French museums. Context is crucial. The education ministry first raised the issue of valuable sequestered collections with Domaines in November 1940,[120] leading to lengthy bureaucratic negotiations through 1941—well before the tide of war turned against the Germans. As a result, the acquisition budget for French museums in 1941 and 1942 spiked from 14 to 66 million francs, to accommodate the purchase of works from sequestered Jewish collections and to provide six million francs for works up for sale on the booming art market.[121] The justification: "conservation of the national patrimony."[122]

The Direction des Musées took a similar approach to works from the magnificent Adolphe Schloss collection of Dutch and Flemish paintings, stolen on April 16, 1943, from the chateau of Chambon. German SD agent Emil Hess led the operation, assisted by four armed members of the French Gestapo. When news of the theft reached Vichy, even Pierre Laval was scandalized. He and Pétain both demanded the works' return to French custody. From the German side, Göring initially oversaw the operation and ordered SD agents to place the works in a Bank of France vault in Limoges. The French were able to negotiate a right of first refusal, and Louvre curators Germain Bazin and René Huyghe selected forty-nine pieces for French museums.[123]

In all of these cases, French officials would later claim that they had exercised the right of first refusal as a way to protect the works from the Germans and keep them on French soil. Though they did indeed accomplish this noble goal, the resistance narrative omits the fact that Jaujard and his colleagues believed they were purchasing the works for French collections *à titre définitif*—permanently. Huyghe, director of paintings at the Louvre, ardently pursued the goal of "filling gaps" in the Louvre's permanent collection through these purchases. In justifying the purchase of sequestered pieces to Jaujard, he underscored the importance of two Rembrandt portraits (a "poorly represented" area of Rembrandt's work at the Louvre) and a Renoir still life ("we do not have any still-life paintings by Renoir") from the Robert de Rothschild collection.[124]

Huyghe was especially eager to acquire works from the Schloss collection. He actively cultivated relationships with potential benefactors to the financially strapped public system, and in the late 1930s, had met with Lucie Schloss, Adolphe's widow. According to Huyghe, Mme. Schloss agreed in these conversations to donate several paintings from the world-class collection to the Louvre. However, she passed away in November 1938 before making the donation, and left the collection to five adult heirs who felt no obligation to honor their mother's oral promise. It was a disappointing missed opportunity for Huyghe.[125] Once the collection had been seized in 1943, with the very real possibility it could all fall in Nazi hands, Huyghe's previous agreement with Mme. Schloss led him to believe the Louvre had "legal rights" as well as "special moral rights" to at least some of the paintings.[126] Justifying the acquisition to Jaujard, Huyghe argued that a Rembrandt landscape would enable the Louvre "to fill a notable gap that we have not hoped to be able to address, as there are only about a dozen known landscapes by this master." With the acquisition of this and other masterworks from the collection, "the Louvre's gallery of Dutch painting . . . would become the top Dutch gallery in the world, just after the Rijksmuseum in Amsterdam and the Mauritshuis at The Hague." The acquisition would thus "greatly enhance our museum's prestige."[127]

Correspondence between Jaujard and the museum curators regarding the distribution of works from sequestered collections extended into late July 1944—several weeks after the Allied landings in Normandy. On July 22, Jaujard sent to the head curator of the palace of Versailles museum, Charles Mauricheau-Beaupré, lists of some two dozen items held for the museum. Though some descriptions provide little detail, the lists convey the objects' high quality, fit for the palace of Versailles: from the Robert de Rothschild collection, a small portrait of the Marquise of Pompadour and a Louis XVI desk with inscribed initials "M.A.," understood as having belonged to Marie Antoinette; from Henri de Rothschild, Louis XV and Louis XVI chairs and desks, a watercolor of Louis XVI and Marie Antoinette, and two drawings of the Queen; from the Paul-Louis Weiller collection, two sets of Louis XVI painted silk curtains and four tapestry-covered chairs.[128] On August 5, 1944, the museum confirmed receipt of most of the items and included the objects' descriptions on its official inventory. In addition, the museum received five chairs from the Bonne-Foy Freemason Lodge in Saint Germain-en-Laye.[129] Unlike the other sequestered objects, the museum office did not pay for those from the May collection,[130] perhaps due to the timing of the acquisition just a few weeks before the Liberation of Paris. Yet the intent to acquire all of the sequestered collections is key to National Museum officials' opportunism, during and after the war.

Meanwhile, the art market in Paris was booming, as Germans with deep pockets and an artificially favorable exchange rate snatched up bargains at auction houses and galleries, and the French elite searched for safe investments. In the 1941 and 1942 season, more than a million objects came under the hammer at the Hôtel Drouot in record-breaking sales. Particularly in demand were small, decorative pieces, landscapes, and still-life paintings. Works by Dutch masters drew the highest sales, but modern paintings by

Degas, Renoir, Cézanne, and Seurat skyrocketed in value. A sale of 120 Impressionist works from the estate of Georges Viau in December 1942 fetched more than forty-six million francs—a record sale at the Drouot in a single session. One Cézanne Mont Sainte-Victoire landscape sold for more than Ff 5 million, an amount one could expect to pay for a sizeable property in France with a chateau.[131] By March 1944, coveted modern paintings were selling for 50 percent more than the price paid for similar works in 1942. Art was a hot investment. In contrast, during the same period the price index of variable-income securities remained flat.[132]

The Germans took a key step in Aryanizing art galleries and dealerships through an ordinance of October 18, 1940, that imposed trusteeships on all Jewish enterprises in the occupied zone. The Vichy regime, aiming to maintain control over Jewish property, created an agency of French temporary administrators (*Service de Contrôle des administrateurs provisoires* SCAP) who would serve as trustees, and oversee the management and liquidation of Jewish assets. French control over exclusionary measures in the entire country expanded in March 1941 with the Vichy regime's establishment of the Commissariat-General for Jewish Affairs; in July, Aryanization of Jewish businesses extended to the unoccupied zone.[133] In the art world, especially in Paris, German and French exclusionary measures affected some of the country's most influential dealers and gallery owners, concentrated on the Right Bank in the Faubourg Saint Honoré and on the rue la Boétie. Paul Rosenberg fled to New York and the Aryanized Bernheim Jeune gallery became the Galerie Saint-Honoré Matignon. Other dealers found creative ways to transfer management. Daniel-Henry Kahnweiler, a German Jew, sold his gallery to Louise Leiris, his non-Jewish sister-in-law. André Weil lived in hiding in the French countryside and allowed Louis Carré to manage his gallery featuring modern works on the rue Matignon in Paris.[134]

The most controversial of these arrangements, to this day, is that of Georges Wildenstein, owing to the Jewish dealer's negotiations with Karl Haberstock. In the early months of the occupation, Wildenstein took refuge in Aix-en-Provence while waiting for safe passage to the United States. A loyal employee, Roger Dequoy, managed business operations at the gallery in Paris. Haberstock visited the gallery in October 1940, offering enticements that prompted Dequoy to accompany him to visit Wildenstein in southern France for a few days the following month. Haberstock and Wildenstein both were highly motivated to negotiate.[135] The Berlin dealer later told Allied investigators that Wildenstein was willing to acquire Impressionist works

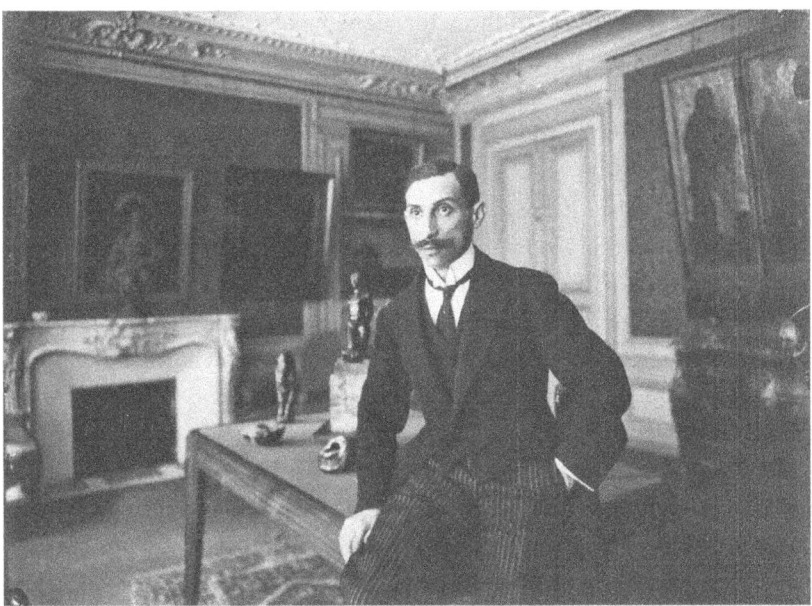

Paul Rosenberg in his office, rue la Boétie, Paris. Digital Image © The Museum of Modern Art/Licensed by SCALA / Art Resource, NY.

from Germany in exchange for more traditional pieces from his own stock, including "a large Tiepolo," which the French dealer considered "unsaleable in the U.S. whereas the Impressionists would bring a high price." Wildenstein then allegedly proposed that Haberstock, with Dequoy's assistance, could have first choice of pieces held for safekeeping at the National Museum repository at Sourches.[136] Meanwhile, the French dealer left for the United States in January 1941 and successfully carried on his business in New York.[137]

Back on rue La Boétie, amid Aryanization, a Monsieur Gras became provisional administrator of the gallery, while Dequoy continued to manage daily operations. Conveniently for Haberstock, Aryanization meant that eighty-seven works from the Wildenstein stock held at Sourches were no longer enemy assets and thus could not be seized by the ERR. The US Office of Strategic Services (OSS) later determined that Dequoy and Haberstock together orchestrated the seizure of Wildenstein pieces from the repository in May 1941. Haberstock, disappointed by the "poor quality" of works, purchased seven, including a Courbet, for FRF 930,000, while Dequoy used the rest of the stock to boost business in Paris.[138] The broader trans-Atlantic scheme imagined by Wildenstein and Haberstock did not come to fruition, and questions remain about the actual agreements struck by these dealers, who all were making the most lucrative opportunities. At the very least, the available evidence suggests the emergence of an important transnational network of dealers in Europe and the United States that would continue after the war.[139]

For other Jewish gallery owners, there were no agreements struck with trusted managers, and their enterprises were simply taken over and liquidated. Léonce Rosenberg, brother of Paul and also a dealer in modern art, reported to French authorities in February 1945 that the Commissariat for Jewish Affairs had first sought cooperation from a syndicate of modern art dealers headed by André Schoeller. To his credit, Schoeller declined the offer and convinced all of his colleagues in the syndicate to do the same. The Commissariat then turned to Paris-based dealer Paul Cailleux, president of a syndicate of antiquarians, whose members were quite willing to profit from the liquidation—all "scavengers," in Rosenberg's frank assessment. His own dealership was taken over by a former partner of Jewish antiquarian Edouard Jonas, and he remained convinced that some provisional administrators "did not finish their task empty handed."[140]

For dealers unaffected by exclusionary laws, the occupation art market boom created tremendous opportunity, and dozens were willing to sell to German buyers. Papers of the Schenker transport company, which shipped works of art from France to Germany, indicate that forty-seven dealers in Paris sold objects to German museums. Investigations by the MFAA in the spring of 1945 found that curators from the Rhineland were especially eager to benefit from the favorable exchange rate, and purchased identifiable paintings as well as "a vast quantity" of miscellaneous objects with "immense value" at a "very reasonable" price, from the German perspective. Museums from several Rhineland cities had spent considerable sums in France: Krefeld FRF 11,253,000, Essen FRF 6,895,550, Bonn FRF 5,450,000, Wuppertal-Elberfeld 992,000, Düsseldorf FRF 3,466,575, and DM 160,000.[141]

An even greater number of dealers in France—144 in the MFAA's estimation—sold works to dealers who bought on behalf of private German collectors as well as museums across the Rhine.[142] One such German dealer was Walter Bornheim of the Galerie der Alte Kunst in Munich, who negotiated purchases for Hitler, Göring, German museums, and private collectors. Bornheim always paid in cash to willing French dealers, and at times kept hundreds of thousands of francs on hand in his briefcase. His cash expenditures during the occupation reached an estimated FRF 100 million.[143]

Another top German dealer operating in France was Maria Almas Dietrich. Though considered by some to be a mere amateur, no other dealer sold more paintings to Hitler.[144] Frau Dietrich had special access to the Führer through Eva Braun, and bought around 320 paintings in Paris during the occupation, including eighty for the Linz project.[145]

Artworks of every genre sold to anyone who could pay, whether the buyers were French, German, collaborationist, or Nazi. German dealer Hildebrand Gurlitt negotiated a Pissarro for Göring while "degenerate" Picassos continued to sell.[146] Even Picasso himself purchased a painting during the occupation by Henri Rousseau via one of the Germans' preferred dealers—Martin Fabiani. The painting had belonged to Jewish businessman Pierre Wertheimer, known for his family's majority stake in Parfums Chanel among other pursuits, and had fled to New York in 1940. When questioned by French intelligence agents in March 1945, Picasso claimed to have documentation proving the sale was legal, though he did not readily provide it.[147]

Corrupt dealers in Paris exacerbated high prices by orchestrating bidding wars among clients and divvying up the proceeds. American Monuments Man James Rorimer investigated this practice in November 1944 and accurately foresaw the legal difficulties stemming from these sales: "If such dealings complicated the sale of works of art during the Nazi occupation, and they no doubt did, it will be impossible to determine the validity of the transactions by which the Germans bought at public auction many works of art."[148] Added to the mix were exchanges on the black market and deals arranged in the back rooms of galleries, without a paper trail. As Laurence Bertrand Dorléac puts it, these were transactions "without an invoice, without a trace, without proof and ultimately without a pedigree."[149] In this environment, dealers and sellers cared little about how works of art ended up on the market. Culling modernist works from its plunder, the ERR traded and sold pieces stolen from Jewish collectors to dealers in France and Switzerland. Lopsided trades illustrate the German agents' disdain for modernism. In some cases they exchanged modern for traditional works at a twenty-five-to-one ratio.[150]

Plunder and Genocide

As art looting operations proceeded in western Europe, a far greater human tragedy was unfolding, one that was directly linked to the seizure of Jewish assets. As a result of antisemitic measures implemented in all three countries, discrimination and expropriation preceded deportation. The highest rate of deportation was in the Netherlands, at 76 percent, where the SS had the strongest presence in the civilian administration. Of an estimated 140,000 Jews living in the Netherlands in 1940, some 107,000 or 76 percent were deported to Nazi camps, and most were Dutch citizens. In contrast, the French Vichy regime assisted with the deportation of roughly 76,000 of 350,000 Jews, or 22 percent, of whom one-third were citizens. Among Jews in Belgium, roughly 25,000 of 65,000, or 40 percent, were deported and killed, of whom 5 percent were citizens. The survival rate of the deported is similarly tragic in all three cases, at around 5 percent.[151] These statistics help us understand postwar art restitution and appropriation rates in the three countries.

The greatest tragedy in this history is the loss of human life, but the loss of Jewish property also had significant long-term repercussions for survivors and descendants, which continue to this day. As historian Tony Judt observed, "The Nazis' attitude to life and limb is justifiably notorious; but their treatment of *property* may actually have been their most important practical legacy to shape the post-war world."[152] Through theft and sales, the Germans drained at least 100,000 art objects and assemblages from France, twenty thousand from the Netherlands, and more than three thousand from Belgium.[153] The Germans and their collaborators, while orchestrating the genocide of the Jewish people on a previously unimaginable scale, had also carried out the greatest cultural heist in human history. As the Allied powers increasingly controlled European territory in 1944 and 1945, their vast challenges—human and material—included recovering immense quantities of cultural property, and launching the protracted and complicated process of restitution to rightful owners.

2
Allied Victory and Art Recovery

Across the Atlantic, American art experts regularly received news of Nazi plunder from their contacts in Europe. International treaties from the previous four decades, signed by all of the major belligerents, had aimed to prevent precisely this kind of theft and displacement. The Hague Conventions of 1899 and 1907 on the laws of war had prohibited the plunder of private property and state-owned cultural property, and forbade its seizure, damage, or willful destruction.[1] In the 1919 Treaty of Versailles, the western Allies had punished Germany for the destruction of cultural heritage during World War I, notably the shelling of Reims cathedral in France and the University of Louvain library in Belgium.[2] But the systematic Nazi plunder in occupied territories across Europe far surpassed prior German cultural transgressions.

With US entry into the war in late 1941, American experts also grew increasingly concerned about the impact of imminent combat operations on European art, monuments, and heritage sites. A group of conservators, curators, and museum directors concentrated in elite institutions on the east coast tapped into political connections to promote the protection of cultural heritage within broader strategic objectives. In 1943, their efforts led to the creation of a US army unit of cultural officers, the Monuments, Fine Arts and Archives (MFAA) division, which would grow to include nearly 350 men and women from fourteen nations, popularly known as "the Monuments Men and Women."[3] These cultural officers would oversee the recovery and restitution of several hundred thousand works of art, plus millions of books, archives, and other cultural items.

Mobilizing Cultural Experts

The US-led campaign to preserve European heritage developed in cooperation with western Allies, including officials from occupied countries who had fled to Britain and formed governments in exile. The Europeans were already discussing these cultural issues well before the United States created the MFAA. Beginning in November 1942, European ministers of education met regularly in London to discuss responses to the cultural challenges in occupied countries—the destruction of heritage, the depletion of national patrimonies through the art market, and the Nazi displacement of art, libraries, and archives.[4]

Among the American experts alarmed by these threats to European heritage was George Leslie Stout, head conservator at Harvard's Fogg Museum. In December 1942, he and Harvard colleagues Paul Sachs, associate director of the Fogg, and George Chase, art historian and dean of the Graduate School of Arts and Sciences, drafted a petition urging the US government to include cultural conservation in its war plans. Preserving historic sites and works of art would "bear witness that these things belong not only to a particular people but also to the heritage of mankind." Safeguarding them, moreover, was a responsibility of the Allied powers, as "these monuments are not merely pretty things," but "expressions of faith" that reflect "man's struggle to relate himself to his past and to his God."[5] Stout and Sachs secured support for their ideas from top leaders of the art world: Francis Henry Taylor, director of the Metropolitan Museum of Art in New York; W. G. Constable, chief curator of the Museum of Fine Arts, Boston; William Dinsmoor, president of the Archaeological Institute of America; and David Finley, director of the National Gallery. The board of the National Gallery also included potential allies with significant political influence, including Chief Justice Harlan Stone, Secretary of State Cordell Hull, and Secretary of the Treasury Henry Morgenthau.[6]

Meanwhile, civilian agencies mobilized more quickly than the government. One was the American Defense Harvard Group, established by faculty and concerned citizens to share academic expertise in a variety of war-related areas. With the guidance of Paul Sachs in the cultural realm, the group drew up lists of monuments in areas of Europe and Asia likely to fall in the path of military operations. Another organization, the American Council of Learned Societies (ACLS), received Rockefeller Foundation funding to create maps of culturally sensitive areas, based on guidebooks and resources provided by military intelligence, the OSS, and the Library of Congress. By October 1943, the ACLS had provided 168 maps for a civil affairs handbook for Italy, and was producing maps of France, Greece, Bulgaria, Albania, Belgium, the Netherlands, and Central Europe.[7]

While discussions with the military continued, the US government created a civilian agency to coordinate conservation efforts. On June 23,

1943, Roosevelt approved the American Commission for the Protection and Salvage of Artistic and Historic Monuments in Europe, commonly known as the Roberts Commission after its chairman, Supreme Court Justice Owen Roberts. Other members included Finley and Huntington Cairns of the National Gallery, Sachs of the Fogg Museum, Dinsmoor of the Archeological Institute, Taylor of the Metropolitan Museum, and Librarian of Congress Archibald MacLeish.[8] The commission was charged with recommending art experts who would advise the military on protecting art and heritage sites in Allied-occupied territories, reflecting "the concern felt by the United States Government and by artistic and learned circles in this country for the safety of artistic treasures in Europe, placed in jeopardy by the War."[9] It compiled a list of fifty potential art advisors and seven architectural engineers in October 1943, and by the end of the year convinced the War Department's Civil Affairs Division to create the MFAA as a branch within the US army.[10] Stout joined the MFAA in early 1944 and quickly emerged as the cultural officers' unofficial leader.

The Roberts Commission also aimed to "aid in salvaging and restoring to lawful owners such objects as have been appropriated by the Axis powers or individuals acting under their authority or consent."[11] These art restitution responsibilities reflected an increasingly determined Allied response to Nazi plunder. In early January 1943 the British government had spearheaded a declaration to notify the enemy and neutral powers that the Allies would not recognize transfers of property carried out in Axis-occupied territories. On January 5, seventeen governments and the French National Committee signed an Inter-Allied Declaration, vowing "to do their utmost to defeat the methods of dispossession practiced by the governments with which they are at war against the countries and peoples who have been so wantonly assaulted and despoiled." The warning applied "whether such transfers or dealings have taken the form of open looting or plunder, or of transactions apparently legal in form, even when they purport to be voluntarily effected."[12] On January 20, the French National Committee issued a complementary declaration, emphasizing that the measure applied in both the northern zone of occupied France and the formerly unoccupied zone, encompassing acts of dispossession carried out by the Germans and the collaborationist Vichy regime.[13]

The British army, for its part, had launched cultural preservation efforts in North Africa well before the Americans had entered the war. In January 1941, British forces under General Archibald Wavell had advanced from

Egypt into Cyrenaica along the coast of Libya, a prized Italian colony. The fascist government had invested significant resources to restore ancient sites at Leptis Magna, Cyrene, and other historic landmarks along the Mediterranean coast in an attempt to revive the glory of the Roman Empire. The British archaeologist Sir Leonard Woolley, known for discovering tombs of Sumerian kings at Ur in present-day Iraq, remarked that scientific accuracy in these fascist projects "was altogether abandoned in favor of theatrical display." But the effort had the intended impact, as "no visitor could fail to be struck by the imposing effect of the excavations, and to the Italian Fascist they did indeed symbolize the glories of his traditional ancestry." Woolley, a lieutenant colonel in the War Office during these operations in Libya, later recalled knowing that the "treatment of the Roman monuments would be jealously watched and any shortcomings used to our discredit."[14]

The Italians regained Cyrenaica in mid-April 1941 with the help of Rommel's forces and promptly launched a propaganda campaign against the British. In a pamphlet, *What the English Did in Cyrenaica*, Italian authorities published photographs of statues allegedly destroyed by British soldiers and heritage sites defaced by graffiti. The photos may have been staged by the Italians themselves, as Woolley later claimed, but the propaganda succeeded in stoking Libyan animosity toward British occupation forces.[15] The incident in Cyrenaica also forced British political and military leadership to recognize the strategic value of heritage preservation. After regaining the region in November 1942, the British developed strategies to protect archaeological sites and museums. The War Office formalized Woolley's cultural role in October 1943, naming him archaeological advisor to the Directorate of Civil Affairs. The most important sites were better protected during this second British occupation, but vandalism continued in outlying areas, as soldiers removed bas-relief fragments and drove military vehicles over historic mosaics. With sites threatened at Leptis and Sabratha, a more concerted preservation effort developed under the leadership of Colonel Mortimer Wheeler, an archaeologist and longtime director of the London Museum (The institution merged with other entities in 1975 to form the Museum of London). Joining Wheeler in the effort was Major J. B. Ward Perkins, a former London Museum curator. Soldiers attended lectures by cultural experts and received pamphlets and guidebooks. The army posted on-site notices in culturally sensitive areas and hired experienced Italian and Libyan personnel to help manage the sites.[16] But Woolley ran a lean operation. He later proudly reported that his staff "consisted of the Adviser himself, Lady Woolley and a clerk," embracing a motto inspired by Pericles's funeral oration: "We protect the arts at the lowest possible cost."[17]

Other experts had broader cultural ambitions and coordinated international efforts to preserve art and heritage. In April 1944, an American delegation to the conference of Allied ministers of education proposed a new commission charged with centralizing information on threatened cultural assets and Nazi plunder. The proposal led to the Inter-Allied Commission for the Protection and Restitution of Cultural Materials, headquartered in London. Commonly known as the Vaucher Commission after its president, French scholar Paul Vaucher, the representatives met regularly to discuss conservation and restitution issues, mindful of the anticipated Allied invasion of western Europe. Among the Big Three powers, the United States and Britain sent representatives as observers, but the Soviet Union ignored several invitations.[18] The Vaucher Commission compiled information from the ACLS committee in New York and the Roberts Commission, and became the first international body to gather data on Nazi looting and cultural destruction.[19]

In May 1944 the British created their own civilian Committee on the Preservation and Restitution of Works of Art, Archives, and other Material in Enemy Hands, charged with advising the government on questions of restitution of cultural property. Like the other civilian agencies, it was known by the surname of its chairman, Hugh Patton Macmillan, and included high-profile members of the cultural and political establishment. Yet it differed from its American counterpart in that it did not address the protection of heritage sites in combat zones, a duty that remained under Woolley in the War Office.[20]

By the eve of D-Day, American, British, and international entities were in place to protect and recover cultural property in territories occupied by Germany. In Italy, however, a handful of American cultural officers had been toiling in the field for several months with little in the way of personnel, supplies, or transportation—shortages that would plague the MFAA through its entire existence.

Making the "Monuments Men"

The first Allied cultural officers in the field were deployed on Sicily in the summer of 1943, before the MFAA was even a formal entity. US

General Dwight Eisenhower, then commander-in-chief of Allied forces in North Africa, had granted the US Civil Affairs Division one British and one American fine arts advisor. The latter was filled by Captain Mason Hammond, a classics professor from Harvard who had been drafted into Air Force intelligence. While the Sicily operation, code-named Husky, remained secret, Hammond departed for Algiers in June, and was told he would be preserving monuments in North Africa. He absorbed the news of his actual assignment on Sicily with some trepidation. Because of the secrecy of the operation, he did not have access to the maps and lists of cultural monuments prepared so diligently by American Defense Harvard Group and the ACLS. Hammond joined other officers in a training center south of Algiers who were elaborating plans for the Allied Military Government (AMGOT), and created a list of the most important Sicilian heritage sites, based in part on information gleaned from a tourist guidebook. Once military operations were underway, he remained in Algeria for three weeks, receiving little additional information and without the assistance of the British colleague who was supposed to join him. He was finally sent to Sicily on July 29, where he found significant damage to the port city of Palermo. Allied bombing had spared some Norman monuments and a twelfth-century cathedral and cloister at Monreale, but sixty other churches and the National Library had sustained significant damage. When AMGOT set up offices in Palermo, Hammond had a desk and chair but little else—no transportation, no assistant, and an utter lack of conservation materials to administer "first aid" to damaged structures. With historic sites exposed to the elements and at risk of collapsing, Hammond needed scaffolding to repair holes in roofs and wooden planks to replace blown-out windows.[21] After five weeks Hammond's British counterpart, Captain F. H. J. Maxse, finally arrived along with an Italian-American sergeant who helped procure a beat-up car. As Hammond inspected sites around the island, he found some graffiti, vandalism, and evidence of souvenir hunting carried out by German and Allied soldiers. But the damage was minor compared to the destruction wrought by Allied air raids.[22]

Anticipating the Allied invasion of the Italian mainland, the Roberts Commission recruited additional cultural officers who were deployed in September 1943. Woolley inspected cultural operations in Italy a few months later and found a wide-ranging lack of discipline—displacement of works of art and furniture, damage to Pompeii, and the theft of books, coins, and decorative objects. If left unabated, he warned, this damage to Italian heritage would surely tarnish the reputation of Allied armies.[23] His admonishments led Eisenhower, who had assumed command of Allied operations in Italy, to issue a directive: the country's heritage sites had shaped "the civilization which is ours," and Allied forces were "bound to respect those monuments so far as war allows."[24] The final phrase was a significant caveat, as revealed in subsequent operations.

Strategic objectives continued to override cultural concerns in early 1944, as Allied and German armies faced off along the Germans' Gustav Line of fortifications stretching across the Italian peninsula, less than a hundred miles south of Rome. Under German Field Marshal Albert Kesselring, a key strategic point along the line was the fortress abbey of Monte Cassino, known as the site where the Benedict of Nursia wrote the founding principles of western monasticism in the sixth century. The abbey was indisputably a valued heritage site, precisely the kind of monument Eisenhower had invoked in his directive. Yet for the Allied soldiers mired in the surrounding hills, in freezing temperatures and with German shells raining down on them, the abbey had become a symbol of the enemy's resilience. Reports of Allied casualties at Monte Cassino in the British and American press prompted heated debates, notably in the British House of Lords, about whether soldiers' lives should be sacrificed to save historic buildings. A growing chorus of British, New Zealander, and Indian commanders, whose troops were poised to take the mountain, advocated bombing the abbey. On February 13, 1944, on the orders of British General Harold Alexander, Allied air forces dropped leaflets instructing monks and civilians sheltering inside the abbey to evacuate, and the bombing began two days later. Waves of bombers repeatedly shelled the abbey, destroying most of the structure. Compounding the cultural disaster, the operation failed tactically, as German troops promptly found shelter among the ruins and in the surrounding mountains. Polish forces finally took control of the site in May, after the Germans retreated.[25] The deliberate bombing of Monte Cassino appeared to contravene all Allied rhetoric extolling the value of European heritage, and was a prime example of futile destruction that art experts and organizations had been working to prevent.

Meanwhile, as Allied plans for a massive invasion of France were underway, a coalition of American and British MFAA personnel slowly expanded. At the end of 1943, Woolley appointed Colonel Geoffrey Webb, Slade Professor of Fine Arts at Cambridge, as British MFAA adviser at Supreme Headquarters Allied Expeditionary Force (SHAEF) in London.

Webb became the overall head MFAA adviser at SHAEF early the next year. An architectural historian, he had a positive reputation among US officers as a competent and energetic administrator.[26] American Monuments Man Thomas Carr Howe later described him in more colorful terms—a "tall, rangy colonel who reminded me of a humorous and grizzled giraffe."[27]

The handful of cultural officers attached to the MFAA at this early stage all were accomplished men in the arts and humanities. Most had been nominated through old boys' networks of the American and British cultural elite. Assisting Webb in a general administrative section were Cambridge historian Captain Ronald Balfour, American Captain Marvin Ross (a Harvard graduate and expert on Byzantine art), and Lieutenant George Stout. A section focusing on France included two Americans, sculptor Captain Walker Hancock and architect Captain Bancel LaFarge. In the German unit were Americans Major Theodore Sizer, director of the Yale University Art Gallery, and Lieutenant Calvin Hathaway, decorative arts curator at the Cooper Union Museum in New York.[28] The officers' first task was writing instructions for Civil Affairs staff on the protection of monuments, fine arts, and archives, while incorporating information gathered by the American Defense Harvard Group and photographic maps compiled by the Frick library. They developed handbooks for each country of planned occupation and produced lists of heritage sites to be spared from air raids.[29] A great number of these vulnerable sites were located in France.

On the Ground in France

With Operation Overlord, launched on June 6, 1944, the noble goal of cultural conservation once again butted up against the reality of military tactics. Leading up to the invasion, Hancock, Ross, and Webb had drafted SHAEF directives from London, which eventually carried the signature of Eisenhower, now supreme commander, and gave the MFAA sorely needed authority in the field.[30] Eleven days before the invasion, Eisenhower issued a secret directive to all commanders under his authority: "Shortly we will be fighting our way across the Continent of Europe in battles designed to preserve our civilization. Inevitably, in the path of our advance will be found historical monuments and cultural centers which symbolize to the world all we are fighting to preserve. It is the responsibility of every commander to protect and respect these symbols whenever possible."[31]

Eisenhower recognized that military necessity might require the destruction of revered sites, as "the lives of our men are paramount." He invoked the bombing of Monte Cassino, not as a regrettable error but an example when "the enemy relied on our emotional attachments to shield his defense." In the interest of military necessity, "commanders may order the required action even though it involves the destruction of an honored site." Yet he demanded restraint: "commanders will preserve centers and objects of historical and cultural significance." Information on the location of historic sites would be communicated to forces at all ranks.[32]

Civil Affairs officers were given an MFAA handbook on French geography, recent history, and politics. "France is a great country," the pamphlet explained, "justly proud of her past achievements and of her enormous contribution to the political, scientific and intellectual progress of humanity."[33] A separate memorandum for naval civil affairs officers conveyed French attitudes: "It will not always be easy for an American to understand how a good Frenchman feels today. As a nation, we have never been beaten. We have not known what it means to be the underdog." The French people "may sometimes seem surly and ungrateful even to their friends because of what they have suffered." They might resent Americans, as they were "known to be blunt. We have not always been tactful in our dealings with other peoples." American soldiers would need to be sensitive to the trauma experienced by the French people during the occupation.[34]

Many of those French civilians would soon witness vast destruction in Operation Overlord, the largest amphibious assault in history, with six hundred warships, four thousand transports and landing craft, and twelve thousand aircraft.[35] As in Italy several months prior, despite the proclaimed best intentions, military objectives often overrode preservation concerns. For SHAEF planners, tactical latitude was paramount, and they forced the MFAA to shorten lists of sites to be spared from bombing and exempted from military use.[36] Even with the MFAA lists, the destruction was massive in strategically crucial areas: 82 percent of Le Havre was flattened, as was 77 percent of Saint-Lô, 73 percent of Caen, and more than 80 percent of port cities Lorient, Saint-Nazaire, Brest, and Bologne.[37]

In early August 1944, James Rorimer painstakingly documented this destruction in France. He had missed a ship from England to Normandy with other American soldiers, so he ended up landing with a group of French soldiers that had been serving in North Africa—a fortuitous result, in his mind. He was assigned to the Advance Section Communications Zone, at the rear of the US First Army.[38] Within two hours of landing at Utah Beach, he began inspecting damaged buildings near the shore. His notes contain the high level of detail one would expect from an accomplished curator:

> 14:00 A8/T40 Chapel called Ste Madeleine. Fr. McAvoy has posted a sign calling for daily services at 1700. Good 16c Ren. Architecture in Maison Carrée style. Fragments which can be used for restoration are in and about the immediate area which is off the highway. Main portal was damaged by fragmentation in the South, or West. 1 lierne rib damaged. Wooden roof with stones is in good condition except for minor damage. Major Kellogg, Beach operations, provided me with transportation to Catz.[39]

The entries, written dutifully every day, reveal his powers of observation but also the impuissance of one lone officer; he could do little on his own to save these structures.

At this point in operations, one officer was attached to the staff of each commander in the British and American armies—a total of ten Monuments Men. Soon after Rorimer's arrival, several MFAA officers, including George Stout and Bancel LaFarge, were able to gather for a rare meeting near Saint-Lô. These men were never part of an organized platoon; they would carry out much of their work in Europe alone or with one partner and greatly valued these infrequent gatherings. But they had to figure out their own transportation. Stout managed to procure a decrepit German Volkswagen, Rorimer hitched a ride with army colleagues, and LaFarge arrived in a small British car.[40]

After this first brief meeting, Rorimer was on his own; he was a commissioned lieutenant assigned to oversee a large sector of Normandy, with no assistant or vehicle. Most immediately, he felt a great urgency to inspect the world-renowned medieval abbey of Mont Saint Michel, built on a small mountain surrounded by swiftly moving waters, becoming an island at high tide. Topography had protected the abbey for centuries, a natural defense overcome by modern air power. "Even a single plane might wreak irreparable havoc," Rorimer observed, "if it were thought that the ramparts with their commanding view of land and sea harbored a look-out post," or if the medieval buildings were used for billeting troops. As Rorimer's assigned army section had advanced a hundred miles away from the abbey, he sought permission to inspect it from his commanding officer. "You idiot," the colonel glowered, "This is twentieth-century war. Who gives a damn about medieval walls and boiling pitch?" He ended up authorizing Rorimer's inspection but did not provide a vehicle. The colonel's deputy, having heard rumors about food and wine available at the town, advised Rorimer, "Get there any way you can." So he did. He first caught rides with Allied trucks, then with French civilians, and he finally ended up "a reluctant foot soldier."[41]

Once he reached the abbey, he was relieved to find it unscathed. Far more troubling, however, was the carousing of American soldiers in the village at the foot of the mountain: "The scene was one of almost indescribable bedlam." Around a thousand soldiers inhabited the village daily and "drank as hard and as fast as they could, and, feeling the effects, became boisterous beyond the power of local control," even looting village shops. Rorimer met with the mayor and the deputy prefect and established new regulations for the village. Troops could visit the site, but military vehicles and alcohol consumption were banned.[42]

The next morning, just when Rorimer was starting to feel there was some dignity in monuments work, he was apprehended by an Air Corps military police captain, incredulous that an American lieutenant would be travelling around Normandy alone, without an assistant or vehicle. Concluding that Rorimer must be a German spy, the captain copied his identification papers and took him to a military office in a nearby town. He was released only when another civil affairs officer confirmed that he was in the MFAA.[43]

Other cultural officers faced similar affronts and frustrations. US Lieutenant John Skilton, for example, had managed artworks evacuated from the US National Gallery at Biltmore House in North Carolina. He later recalled that when he requested a position in the MFAA, "no one in authority had the slightest notion that Arts and Monuments was to become a recognized branch of the service and that the entire subject was regarded as somewhat of a joke."[44] While Skilton was going through basic training, he told fellow soldiers about his cultural aspirations, and they asked him "in typical Army vernacular what the hell art was all about anyway and why it should be considered of any importance of the American Army in the midst of the greatest war in history."[45] American sculptor Walker Hancock similarly recounted that each cultural officer was forced to obtain transportation, clerical assistance, or authority to bring about action "by means of any entreaties, cajolings, or other tricks at the command of the individual officer."[46]

As Allied forces pressed eastward toward Paris in the summer of 1944, Stout could only administer temporary repairs to damaged historic sites. Amid this work he was deeply impressed by the spirit of the common French

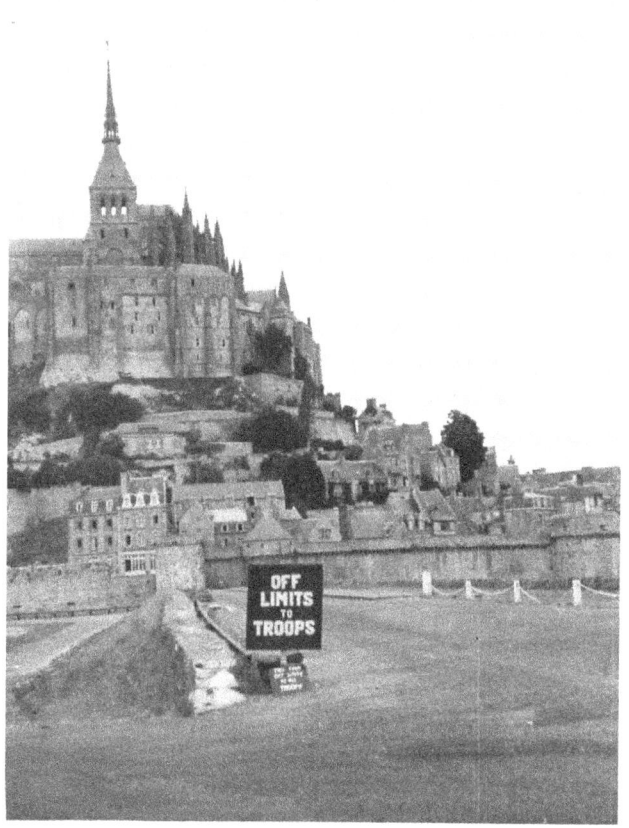

Notice to Allied soldiers at Mont Saint Michel. Courtesy of National Gallery of Art, Washington, D.C., Gallery Archives.

people. "Put me down as saying that I take my hat off to the people of France," he wrote to his wife. "I don't mean the important political people. . . . The valor of the simple country people is touching. . . . Crippled and battered and seemingly unchanged, they keep about their jobs. They are kind to us—more kind than we deserve—and are most friendly." On Bastille Day, July 14, he saw villages festooned with French and American flags: "Their own tricolor is hung out at hundreds of cottage doors and a staggering number of stars and stripes. Where they got them is beyond imagination." Some villagers without their own flags made them by hand with whatever materials they could find: "The stripes sewn out of white and something approaching red, the stars stitched on." Everywhere they went, the French people waved to them, many standing in front of their demolished homes. "No victory parade could match this for meaning."[47]

Meanwhile, the collaborationist Vichy regime was in its final days. On August 9, the French Committee of National Liberation proclaimed a new French Republic, and the battle for Paris began ten days later.[48] Rorimer witnessed the liberation of the French capital, arriving just a few hours after the surrender of the German garrison: "We slept in beds in a hotel where the Germans had been less than twenty-four hours previously." And he observed one of the most consequential moments in modern French history: the arrival of De Gaulle. "The most striking day," he reported, "was Saturday, the 26th, when Paris went mad with enthusiasm, then received De Gaulle—I was on the Champs Elysées as I had been on many an earlier occasion after the last war when Joffre and the other great French heroes came down the Champs—and finally, shots were fired wildly from every house-top."[49]

In the final days of the occupation, Kurt von Behr of the ERR made a last-ditch effort to send works of art from French collections on a train bound for Germany. At the beginning of August, he had ordered the shipment of forty-eight cases of paintings, including works by the most important Impressionist artists and modern masters—Cézanne, Monet, Dufy, Degas, Renoir, Gauguin, twenty-nine by Braque, and sixty-four works by Picasso alone. The ever-vigilant Rose Valland watched as the Germans loaded the crates onto trucks and headed for the Aubervilliers train station just north of Paris. She knew the enemy was racing against the encroaching Allied forces. The Germans had filled five train cars at Aubervilliers but were adding forty-seven other cars with everyday furniture and household goods seized by the Möbel-Aktion. If she could delay the shipment, the artworks might be saved. With Jaujard's approval, Valland convinced French railway workers to intervene and provided the train car numbers she had noted from German records. The workers ensured that mechanical "problems" stalled the heavily packed train, and it remained stuck at Le Bourget for forty-eight hours. It was redirected to Aulnay while a new locomotive was arranged, but by this point, on August 27, Leclerc's army was already in the Paris region. A detachment of French soldiers took control of the waiting train cars, and in a remarkable twist of fate, one was the son of art dealer Paul Rosenberg, whose plundered works were among those on the train.[50]

The Germans also nearly retreated with the famed Bayeux tapestry, a seventy-meter-long eleventh-century embroidered masterpiece that recounts William the Conqueror's victory at the Battle of Hastings. Nazi agents in the Ahnenerbe, an SS division responsible for researching Aryan history and culture, had studied the tapestry at Bayeux during the first year of the occupation. For the SS, the tapestry was evidence of superior racial lineage from the Normans to modern Germans, laden with additional political symbolism of the English defeat. Uneasy with Nazi interest in the tapestry and Ahnenerbe "preservation" tactics, French cultural authorities transferred it in August 1941 to a repository in Sourches. It remained there until late June 1944, when the Nazis ordered its transfer to Paris, again under the pretext of conservation, and it was still at the Louvre during the Liberation. As the city descended into chaos, two SS officers visited the office of the German military governor of Paris, General Dietrich von Choltitz, at the Hotel Meurice and relayed the order. By his own account, the general took the officers to his window, showed them the Louvre rooftops where French snipers were shooting at Germans below, and told them they could go ahead and fetch it there. It remained in the Louvre.[51]

Following the liberation of Paris, Allied forces moved quickly into Belgium and pressed east toward Germany. On September 4, the British Second Army took control of the city of Antwerp, raising hopes that the Allies would soon have access to its port, badly needed by the Allies to distribute fuel and other supplies to the rapidly advancing front. But the Germans maintained control over the sixty-mile estuary between the city and the port until November 1944. Combat continued on Belgian territory with Hitler's bold Ardennes offensive launched in December, the infamous Battle of the Bulge that pushed back the Allies westward in a C curve. In the Netherlands, the Allied advance stalled in September, with the failure to cross the Rhine River in Operation Market Garden. Western portions of the Netherlands remained occupied by the Germans and were subjected to a German blockade of food and supplies. The measure contributed to famine in the devastating Hunger Winter of 1944 and 1945, which claimed some eighteen thousand Dutch lives. The country was not fully liberated until May 5, 1945, just a few days prior to the general German surrender on May 8, known in the west as Victory in Europe (VE) Day.[52]

An American in Paris

As one occupation of Paris gave way to another, SHAEF established a headquarters in Versailles and Webb set up the MFAA office in repurposed stables facing the main palace. His deputy chief was Charles Kuhn, a US naval reserve officer who was better known among cultural experts as an eminent scholar of modern German art and director of the Busch-Reisinger museum at Harvard.[53] Rorimer remained in Paris through the winter. Initially he was put in charge of the civil affairs information desk at the Louvre, tackling a wide variety of tasks. In the first few days, he arrested seventeen German spies in civilian clothes and, he recorded in his diary, "helped with electricity, bomb disposal, police and fire services, locksmiths, hotels, taxis, food supplies, etc."[54] Stout passed through the city at the end of August, and the two officers agreed that no Allied billeting would be allowed in the Versailles gardens. Together, they learned the full extent of Nazi looting from Jaujard.[55]

Rorimer's surroundings soon became far more comfortable and refined than they had been on the back roads of Normandy. He was appointed head of the MFAA Seine section, which meant he was responsible for ensuring adequate protection of every historic building and art collection in the Ile-de-France region. Between September 1944 and February 1945, Rorimer inspected 125 chateaux.[56] His French language skills also enabled him to play an important diplomatic role with top French cultural officials. He had known Jaujard before the war and was able to deepen those connections to earn the trust of French administrators. Through the end of 1944, his primary concern was surveying chateaux, churches, and other historic sites. He spent much of his time visiting buildings in and around Paris and wrote detailed reports about numerous complaints by cash-strapped aristocrats whose property had been damaged by German or Allied troops. He was a frequent dinner guest with current and erstwhile French officials and spent one such evening with Jaujard and Jérôme Carcopino, the former Pétainist education minister. These occasions were more than mere social events for Rorimer; he was gathering intelligence. Time and again, the French elite were willing to "share their 'rainy day' savings to enjoy with their old American friends the great day of our arrival. The Palais Royal offices and private chambers of the scholars," he wrote to friends, "open almost magically."[57]

Rorimer quickly proved an important ally to French cultural officials and took important steps to defend the nation's heritage against damage carried out by Allied soldiers. In September 1944, American troops were using the

Tuileries garden as a parking lot for jeeps and heavy army vehicles and had damaged several historic statues. Jaujard and other French officials opposed military use of the gardens and wanted to open them to the public as a sign that Paris was returning to normalcy. Rorimer suggested the army could park the vehicles on the expansive, paved Esplanade des Invalides instead, a proposal subjected to lengthy discussion before the Americans finally accepted it.[58]

Rorimer also intervened when American officers requested objects from the Versailles museum to decorate Eisenhower's office, located in the former home of Paul-Louis Weiller, a Jewish industrialist who had fled to Canada during war. The Germans had stripped furnishings from the home and Jaujard had approved the request for Versailles pieces, believing it had come from the supreme commander himself. Rorimer happened to learn about the American decorating plan while having breakfast with colleagues in Paris, and he promptly went to Versailles to investigate the matter. He found a very eager Captain Todd, who was quite pleased with the works he had been able to procure for Eisenhower: eleven paintings—including Van Dyck's portrait of Thomas of Savoy, Vernet's *Duck Hunt*, seven engravings, and one terra cotta statue—all of which were in the official catalog of the Versailles museum. The French head curator at Versailles, who "wanted to be helpful," also had been willing to provide an impressive eighteenth-century desk, Persian rug, and additional furnishings. Eisenhower's headquarters commandant, Colonel Brown, bristled at Rorimer's intervention and unsuccessfully tried to contact the commanding general to confirm the planned office decor. In the meantime, Rorimer came up with an effective argument: ". . . Wouldn't the German propaganda office have a holiday if it could report that General Eisenhower had appropriated art objects from Versailles for furnishing his own office?" The colonel finally relented and the pieces returned to the museum the next morning.[59]

Even more disturbing to Rorimer was the American army's improper use and treatment of private historic chateaux in France and elsewhere, following what he called the Germans' "characteristic brutality" toward residences owned by Jews and non-Jews alike.[60] American soldiers in France had burned valuable furniture for fuel and looted personal property, while in Belgium, the education minister demanded MFAA action against the "indiscriminate ravages of billeting" by Allied troops.[61] No single army was to blame; rather, the problem was widespread. In March 1945 Webb reported "wanton damage" carried out by the First Canadian, Second British, and Ninth US Army in the Netherlands and Germany. Soldiers desecrated churches in the Maas Valley of Holland, slashed pictures, and tore open cases of books from the Stadt Bibliotek of Aachen that were stored at Julich. Webb cited Eisenhower's directive to prevent "looting, wanton damage and sacrilege of buildings by troops" and urged SHAEF internal affairs branch to "take strong action," as soldiers increasingly were likely to discover cultural repositories in Germany. "The danger to the whole policy of restitution of enemy looted works of art," he warned, "is a very real one."[62]

Many MFAA reports do not specify the loss of Jewish property, including Stout's summary of his discussions with Jaujard.[63] Rorimer's perspective is all the more notable, as his reports, diary, and memoir say nothing about his own Jewish heritage. His paternal grandparents, Jacob and Minnie Iglauer Rohrheimer, had emigrated to Cleveland from Bavaria in 1849 and were among the first of the city's Jewish settlers. Jacob established a tobacco company and from 1874 to 1884 served as president of the Tefereth Israel, the city's first Reform Jewish congregation. Their son Louis, James's father, founded Rorimer-Brooks Studios, a leading interior design firm in the Arts and Crafts movement, with clients stretching from the Midwest to New York. Unlike his father, Louis did not play a leadership role in the Jewish community. In 1917, amid rising anti-German sentiment and antisemitism during World War I, he changed the surname spelling to Rorimer.[64] James's silence on his own Jewish heritage may reflect an awareness of latent antisemitism in the highest echelons of the museum world in the United States, including among museum board members.[65]

Rorimer went so far as to underscore the non-Jewish ownership of numerous historic residences damaged by Germans. While "the property of Jews was taken more methodically," he explained, it "suffered less on this account since it was usually handled by either experts or self-styled experts." He recorded looting in castles that were "among the hundred finest in the Ile de France, and here none of the Nazi race theories could be applied."[66] Similarly, his reports from fall 1944 and winter 1945 contain few references to Nazi-looted artworks. On September 9, he noted briefly that he planned to see a French official at the Carnavalet museum "about stolen works of art from private people."[67] There is no follow-up information, and even this brief mention of "private" collections does not specify whether the items had been looted from Jewish owners. Perhaps most surprising, Rorimer excluded from his official reports the return to Paris of the art train that had been kept in France thanks to Valland and the SNCF. Reversing the path the works had taken in August, the French museum office unloaded 148 crates of paintings at the Jeu de Paume by October 19, 1944.[68] The omission is explained in part by Rorimer's primary responsibility at the time, which was historic buildings, not looted works of art.

Toward the end of 1944, however, his journal entries reflect a growing preoccupation with mobile cultural assets plundered from private individuals, especially Jews. At Albert Henraux's suggestion, Rorimer contacted Valland to learn more about the fate of artworks during the occupation. He knew she had dropped hints to French colleagues about her secret information on Nazi plundering operations, including Göring's visits to the Jeu de Paume. With battle lines in the Ardennes still fluid, she had shared it with no one. Rorimer, along with her compatriots, began to wonder how much she actually knew.[69]

Little by little, Valland sparingly doled out some of this knowledge by taking Rorimer on a tour of key sites used by the Germans in Paris. On December 18, they visited the temporary residence of Bruno Lohse at 3 avenue Matignon. They learned from the concierge's wife that the Germans had left the building a few days before the liberation with "a truck or trucks containing works of art." They inspected a building at 17, place des Etats-Unis, where the Germans had photographed the art plunder. There was not much to see, as the equipment had been taken to the Louvre and any remaining works of art had been collected by Domaines, the French state property agency. Far more significant was the information Rorimer was absorbing from Valland. She took him to 45, rue de la Bruyère, headquarters for the confiscation of valuable books, and Rorimer photographed mounds of volumes abandoned by the Germans. The enemy had shipped thousands of books to the Third Reich, including fifty thousand volumes and documents from the Alliance Israelite Universelle.[70]

On December 22, Rorimer and Valland inspected some of the contents of the infamous art train that had been stashed at the exhibition center of the Foire de Paris, an enormous annual retail fair that was suspended during the war. The valuable art already had been transferred the Jeu de Paume; what remained was an enormous hoard of furniture, pots and pans, and hundreds of boxes filled with dishes and vases. Rorimer noted in his journal there was no important art in this cache—only "a few insignificant paintings." Valland

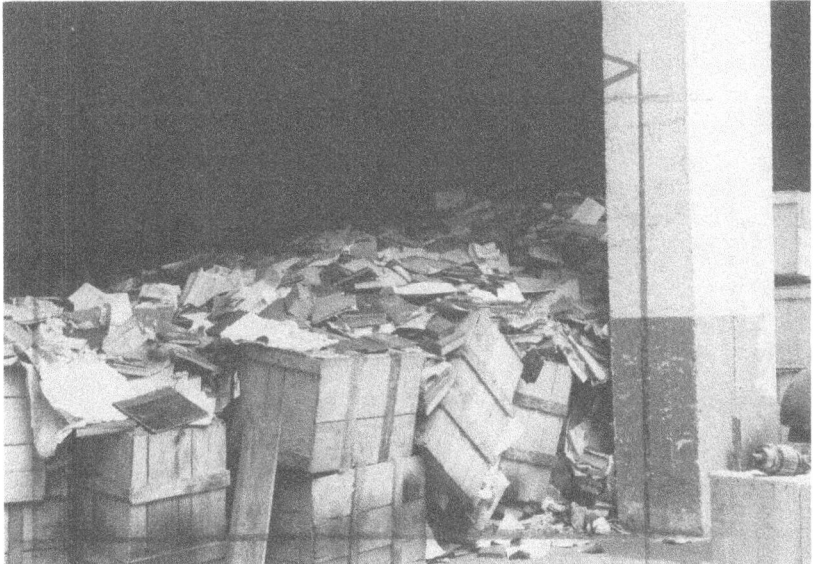

Cache of books in a German repository, Paris. Courtesy of National Gallery of Art, Washington, D.C., Gallery Archives.

took him to two additional warehouses, again, without finding important works of art. Yet he learned something crucial: Valland knew precisely which train cars had held the most valuable objects, indicating, he guessed, that she likely knew far more about Nazi art plunder.[71]

Valland, meanwhile, had been assessing Rorimer's commitment to the French cultural patrimony since he had arrived in Paris. Gradually, he earned her trust.[72] Just before Christmas, she sent him a bottle of champagne, raising his hopes that she might be willing to share more information. He invited her to his apartment to toast their successes thus far, "in the best cloak and dagger tradition." Rorimer found her to be a woman "of shifting moods; at one moment difficult, scheming, making good use of all the feminine wiles and subterfuges—but at all times her absolute integrity and her devotion to France were only too obvious." The champagne softened her demeanor and she became more chatty. She described her espionage activities at the Jeu de Paume, copying the Germans' lists of looted art and the shipments' destinations, and processing the photographic negatives they had created to document the plunder. But even the best French champagne would not

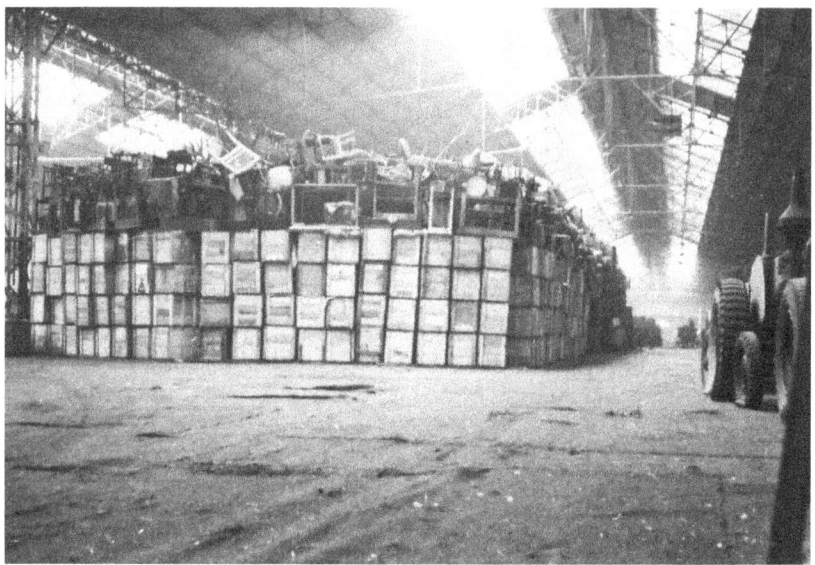

Recovered household effects at the Foire de Paris. Courtesy of National Gallery of Art, Washington, D.C., Gallery Archives.

prompt her to release her notes prematurely. Timing was crucial. She could give the information only to the most trustworthy of officers—those with the authority to secure repositories in Germany.[73]

Valland would keep Rorimer waiting for several more weeks, until he learned of his possible transfer to the US Seventh Army, then battling its way across the Rhine and into Germany. One evening, she invited him to have a drink at her small apartment in the Latin Quarter. They shared cognac, cigarettes, and gossip, discussing rivalries among American and British officials. She told him he must go to Germany himself to secure the repositories. His next assignment still uncertain, Rorimer encouraged Valland to share her information with SHAEF headquarters, through the French mission. She scoffed at the idea: "One fellow is thick-headed and smug, and poof . . . nothing happens."[74] She went into her bedroom and returned with a stack of papers and photographs, along with lists of art shipments to Germany, detailing the contents and destinations. Rorimer finally received his transfer orders in April, just as Valland volunteered to serve as a cultural officer in the French First Army. Her information was crucial to them both in the next phase of the MFAA mission, in which the recovery of Nazi loot superseded the preservation of historic buildings.[75]

Losing the Battle for Preservation

As the Allies moved into territory of the Third Reich, MFAA officers administered first aid to damaged churches and other historic sites as best they could. Often, the destruction exceeded their capabilities. In October 1944, Walker Hancock's unit moved into Aachen, the former capital of Charlemagne's empire. The closer they moved to the city, the more destruction they saw. First, they noticed only some broken windows, then further toward town, collapsed roofs and walls. As they reached the city center, Hancock learned the city had been abandoned and the fronts of brick buildings were mere shells: "I realized at once what I later so often found to be true—that a skeleton city is more terrible than one that the bombs have completely flattened. Aachen was a skeleton."[76]

Hancock walked alone to the cathedral as shells fell nearby. As many had before him since the early Middle Ages, he found sanctuary in the heart of the cathedral: "For more than eleven centuries these massive walls had stood intact. That *I* should have arrived just in time to be the sole witness of their destruction was reassuringly inconceivable."[77] He saw an improvised altar along the west wall and evidence of recently evacuated civilians who had sought shelter—books, toys, dishes, half-eaten meals, and coffee-filled cups. As Hancock observed these items, the vicar, Erich Stephany, appeared and took Hancock to his den and makeshift shelter. Stephany was visibly shaken and his voice stammered as he told Hancock his primary concern: several teenage boys had served as a fireguard at the cathedral, putting out fires created by incendiary bombs. The Allies had caused this destruction, but now German shells were falling and the vicar wanted the fireguard back. The vicar advised Hancock he could find them in a nearby town with other evacuated civilians. Hancock was happy to help, but since the boys had served in the Hitler Youth, he needed approval from the SHAEF Counter-Intelligence Corps.[78] Once Hancock secured the required permissions and passes, the boys were thrilled to return to the cathedral and continue their mission: "Their faces were all alight with a radiant joy. It was as if no further cares existed for them." The group leader, Helmut, accepted the counter-intelligence passes from Hancock and told him ironically, "*Ich bin der Führer*" (I am the leader).[79]

Serving the MFAA in combat zones meant that the art experts were very much in harm's way, and two were killed in the spring of 1945. One of the fallen officers was British Major Ronald Balfour, who had been serving with the First Canadian Army in Kleve, Germany. He relished the work, reporting to Webb on March 3, "It was a splendid week for my job—certainly the best since I came over. On the one hand there is the tragedy of real destruction, much of it completely unnecessary; on the other the comforting feeling of having done something solid myself."[80] A week later, Balfour was moving panels from an altarpiece in a church in Kleve with four other men when an exploding shell killed him. In a tribute to the officer, Woolley observed that Balfour had died while saving works of art, "which he loved so much." His death would leave an irremeable gap in the MFAA, and on a broader level, the entire field of art history had "suffered a tragic loss."[81]

The following month, US Captain Walter Huchthausen, an architect and faculty member at the University of Minnesota, was responding to reports of an important cache of art found near Aachen when he was caught in German machine gun fire. He died from a shot to the head. In a condolence letter to Huchthausen's family, David Finley of the Roberts Commission wrote that Huchthausen was "one of the outstanding Monuments Officers in the field," and his work in the Loire Valley and at Aachen would remain "a signal contribution to the cultural preservation of Europe."[82] With the loss of Balfour and Huchthausen, there were only eight monuments officers in the field with British and American armies, as the western Allies pressed deeper into Germany.[83]

Finding Hidden Treasure

As Allied forces gained control over German territory, they discovered Nazi art repositories in churches, castles, and salt mines, often by accident. At the end of March 1945, two American Monuments Men with Patton's Third Army, Robert Posey and Lincoln Kirstein, had a chance encounter with Hermann Bunjes, one of the most important cultural advisers to the Nazis. This art scholar, an expert on French medieval architecture, had served as one of Göring's experts at the Jeu de Paume, and was now hiding out in a country home near the city of Trier. Posey and Kirstein met Bunjes's father-in-law, a dentist, when Posey came down with a toothache. During the consultation, the dentist mentioned that his son-in-law was an art expert who had recently returned from Paris. The officers casually expressed interest in learning more, and the dentist guided them to his daughter's home, where they found a cottage decorated with pictures of French monuments, and Bunjes. The startled art historian quickly discerned that these Americans might be able to shield him from prosecution. He assumed they already knew about ERR looting operations and Hitler's plans for the Führermuseum. In fact, his eager cooperation provided some of the first key intelligence acquired by the MFAA. He divulged that the great Rothschild collections of France were at Neuschwanstein castle in Bavaria and that numerous masterpieces, including the Ghent Altarpiece, were stored in salt mines at Alt Aussee, Austria.[84] As Kirstein put it, ". . . information tumbled out, incredible information, lavish answers to questions we had been sweating over for nine months, all told in ten minutes."[85] At the time, the American officers did not have enough incriminating evidence to arrest Bunjes, nor could they offer him immunity. They left without him and reported to superiors what they had learned. After another interrogation by other officers, in which Bunjes requested a nice, quiet home in Paris, he realized the Americans would not, in fact, protect him. Bunjes chose suicide over dishonor—as did Hitler, Göring, Himmler, and Goebbels—and shot his wife, their child, and himself.[86]

By mid-April, Rorimer reported to the Seventh Army in Germany, armed with Valland's notes and photographs. Allied forces had already discovered 175 German repositories in a band of territory stretching roughly from Frankfurt to Salzburg, with an average width of eighty miles, and Rorimer knew they would find more. As additional caches were discovered, commanders took greater interest in the artworks, attracted by the prospect of finding "hidden treasures" with the attendant publicity. The cultural officers, having been criticized up to that point for impeding military operations, suddenly were deluged with requests for assistance and had to prioritize the most urgent cases.[87]

Assisted by John Skilton, Rorimer aimed to secure the largest repositories holding foreign-owned works.[88] Valland had told Rorimer that the town of Füssen in southern Bavaria was the center of ERR activity in Germany and gave him a photograph of Neuschwanstein and Hohenschwangau castles, nestled in the Bavarian Mountains near the Austrian border. On May 1, he learned that the castles had been secured by Allied forces, but his command post was in Schwäbisch Gmünd, about 120 miles away, and he was stranded without a vehicle. He vented his frustrations to a Red Cross worker, who offered Rorimer a spare jeep if he could drive himself. He seized the opportunity and set off with Skilton to inspect the castles. The red crosses on the

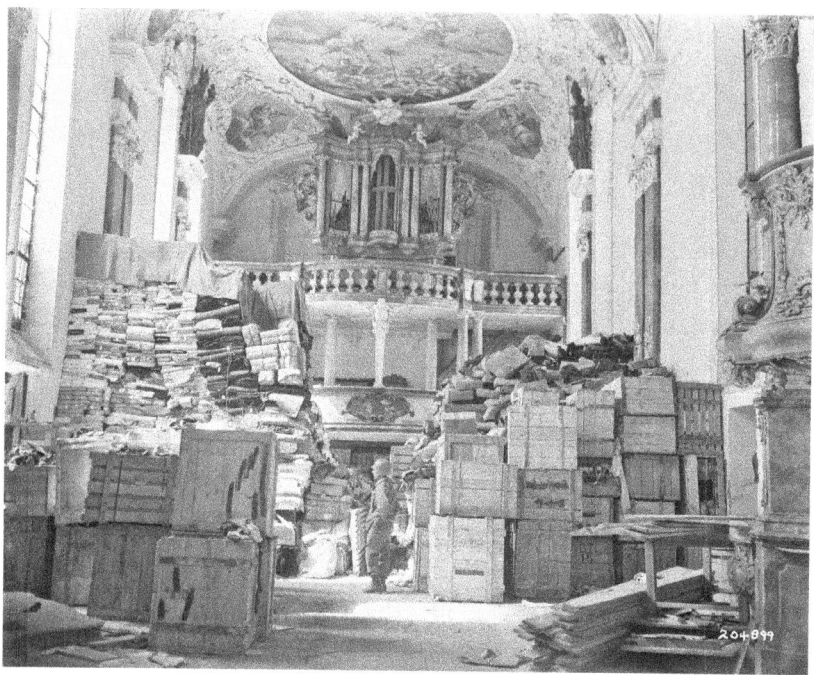

American soldier with cultural stash at a church turned German repository in Ellingen. Courtesy United States National Archives and Records Administration (RG 111-SC-204899).

jeep prompted some minor inconveniences when American soldiers flocked around them, seeking coffee and doughnuts.[89]

En route to Füssen, they stopped at a Carthusian monastery in Buxheim, following another tip from Valland. They spoke to American guards posted at the site, who believed they were merely protecting some French dry goods. The monuments officers soon discovered, in fact, that one room contained seventy-four cases of art. Rorimer immediately recognized "DW" stamped on some of them, for the French Jewish collector David David-Weill. The monastery also was sheltering dozens of German civilians. Rorimer found a priest, thirteen nuns, and twenty-two children living among a vast stash of paintings, sculpture, furniture, and tapestries.[90] "The corridors were stacked with Renaissance and eighteenth-century furniture—good, bad, indifferent." Some objects were carefully packed; others had been stored haphazardly. The floor of the chapel "was covered about eight or ten inches thick with rugs and tapestries," some of which, he later recalled, were "Rothschild textiles taken from the walls and floors I had found denuded in their Paris and country homes."[91]

Rorimer was stunned by the quality of works at Buxheim: "There are few museums in the world that could boast a collection such as the one we found here. Works of art could no longer be thought of in ordinary terms—a roomful, a carload, a castle full, were the quantities we had to reckon with." The initial list he and Skilton drew up included 158 paintings—with six Bouchers; four Watteaus; seven Fragonards; four Davids; two works each by Delacroix, Goya, Gainsborough, and Renoir; and one each by Vlaminck, Guardi, Murillo, and Greuze. Rorimer secured additional guards for the monastery and ordered all the refugee civilians to find shelter elsewhere.[92]

Rorimer questioned two elderly German men who managed the monastery. Their discomfort at speaking to an American officer was obvious, and they offered little information. More helpfully, they led him to Martha Klein, an art restorer from Cologne. Her husband, Otto, also was a restorer, and the couple were temporarily living and working in a two-room suite in the monastery, with their child and other family members. At the time, Otto was hospitalized at Memmingen, so Martha was continuing the restoration work on her own. As Rorimer glanced through the restored pieces, a small but exceptionally good painting caught his eye. It was a Rembrandt, Martha explained, found in a bank vault in Munich. Rorimer ordered her to cease all restoration work immediately. As he later recalled, "the Allies could assume no responsibility for turning Tintorettos into Titians, or satyrs into harmless beasts of the forest." He then asked to see records of all the paintings the Kleins had restored. Martha gave him two binders filled with lists of artworks, and he noticed that only the most coveted works were being restored. When he asked about other repositories, she confirmed the location of sites already known to the MFAA, and that the mine near Alt Aussee in Austria was the largest.[93]

Rorimer's next stop with Skilton was the elaborate Neuschwanstein castle near Füssen, so fairytale-like it later became the model for Disneyland's Sleeping Beauty Castle. But under the Nazis, Neuschwanstein became "a picturesque, romantic and remote setting for a gangster crowd to carry on its art looting activities."[94] The chief custodian of the castle led the officers through the labyrinthine building, up dizzying staircases and through multiple locked doors. Finally, they entered rooms filled with art, much of it plundered from France. Newly constructed racks held paintings, tapestries, fine furniture, two large chests of Rothschild jewels, and around one thousand silver pieces from the David-Weill collection, among others. Art libraries of Paris collectors were stashed with rare manuscripts. Among the German-owned works were some thirteen hundred paintings from Munich museums, and the private collections of the Bavarian Wittelsbach family. Also of tremendous value were filing cabinets with records of 203 private collections from France, eight thousand photo negatives, and catalog cards detailing nearly twenty-two thousand confiscated items. Unable to remove any materials at the time, Rorimer secured the doors with sealing wax and an antique Rothschild seal, and told the guards no unauthorized individuals should enter the storage spaces. They dutifully obeyed, such that when Captain Rose Valland finally reached the castle, even she was barred from entering.[95]

Rorimer faced an altogether different kind of challenge at the Heilbronn salt mine. The Germans had discovered that salt mines offered underground protection from air raids, with stable temperatures around fifty degrees and humidity near 60 percent—excellent conditions for the conservation of art. There were twenty square miles of mineable salt at Heilbronn, with around ten thousand square yards used for art storage, some spaces reaching ninety feet high.[96] But there was a significant problem. Combat operations had disrupted electricity to pumps in the mine, and water from the Neckar River was seeping into the cavities, rising to storage areas that held famed stained glass windows from the Strasbourg Cathedral, and German-owned archive collections and works of art. Rorimer consulted with the mine's vice-director and Charles Kuhn to devise a plan: the mine elevator and skips would remove the water, an estimated three million gallons. Following a several-week water removal operation, the MFAA recovered the stored cultural property intact.[97]

Another important repository was in a copper mine near the city of Siegen, about 130 miles northwest of Heilbronn. Stout knew the mine was an important repository and suspected it held precious objects from the Aachen Cathedral, including a bust of Charlemagne believed to contain a portion

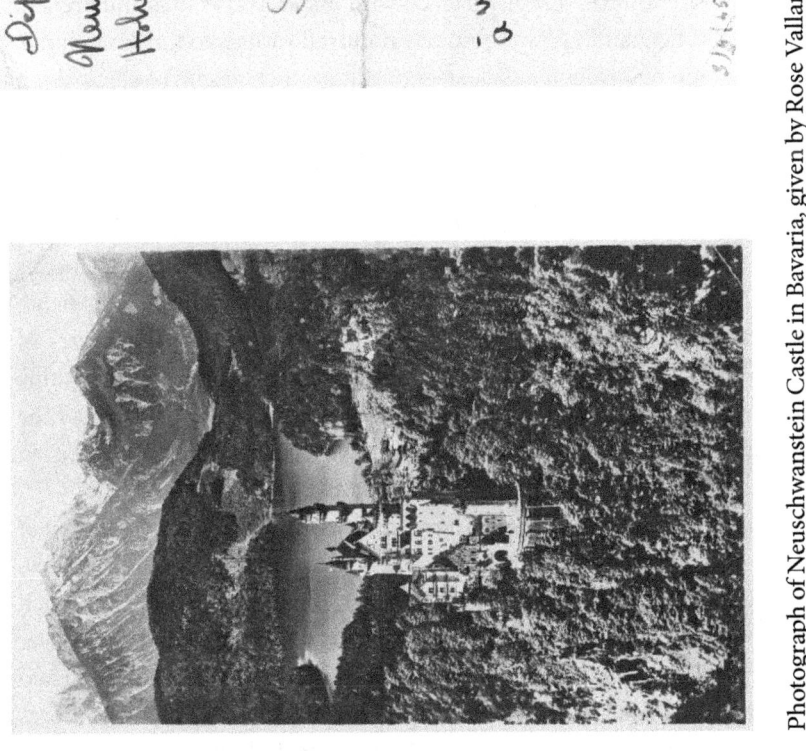

Photograph of Neuschwanstein Castle in Bavaria, given by Rose Valland to James Rorimer in the spring of 1945. It appears she wrote on the back of the photograph twice, the second time, in August 1945, in friendship and gratitude. Archives of American Art, Smithsonian Institution.

of the emperor's skull, the alleged robe of the Virgin, and jewel-encrusted medieval crosses. Allied forces had been notified of the mine's contents as they advanced toward the city, and Stout and Hancock arrived on April 2, accompanied by vicar Stephany of Aachen.[98] The area was still an active war zone. German resistance from that morning had ceased, but light shelling from the enemy continued around them. Navigating around fallen wires and other debris, the men drove up a hill to the mine. They entered the main passage, around half a mile long, and found it packed with frightened civilians. A foul stench permeated the muggy air. Stout believed that he and Hancock were the first Americans the Germans had ever seen, eyeing them with warily with an "attitude of fear and hate." Hancock heard whispers, "Amerikaner! Amerikaner!" as mothers called for their sons and daughters, having absorbed Nazi propaganda that American soldiers would happily kill German children.[99]

The mine passage did not lead to the repository, so Stout and Hancock tried another entrance, this one packed with displaced persons and French, Russian, and Belgian POWs. About one hundred yards into the damp mine, carefully stepping through a slick layer of sludge, they reached a single door. They opened it and found a brick-walled room, about two hundred by thirty feet with a twelve-foot vaulted ceiling, lined with wooden racks that held some five to six hundred paintings—masterpieces by Rembrandt, Rubens, Delacroix, Fragonard, Van Gogh, Cézanne, Cranach, and Hals. There were around one hundred sculptures, plus cases of two hundred miscellaneous works. Many of the pieces were from German museums in the Rhineland. The vicar, to his great relief, found several cases holding the treasures of Aachen. Yet all of the men were dismayed to find that conditions in the mine were far too damp for delicate artworks. Mold was growing on many of the paintings, and moisture had blanched the varnishes. Stout instructed an Allied captain to post guards until the evacuation could begin.[100]

At the Merkers mine in central Germany, which later would fall just east of the boundary between the American and Soviet occupation zones, soldiers of Patton's Third Army made a spectacular discovery: the Third Reich gold reserves, along with hundreds of precious artworks from the Kaiser Friedrich Museum in Berlin and the Kunsthistorisches in Vienna, evacuated belatedly as the Allies closed in on Hitler. They found stashed music scores and costumes from the Berlin opera. A more morbid discovery was chests full of gold teeth, presumably extracted from Holocaust victims. The gold bullion attracted the attention of top brass, and on April 12, Eisenhower, Bradley, and Patton inspected the mine together, pausing to glance through a row of stored paintings.[101] With Soviet troops advancing toward Berlin, and potentially Merkers, SHAEF ordered an immediate evacuation of the mine contents to Frankfurt, well inside the eventual US zone.[102]

The MFAA assigned Stout to oversee the transfer of art from Merkers. Sorting through hundreds of items, he was startled to see the famed Egyptian bust of Nefertiti sitting in an open case. Many other items had been hastily evacuated without packing cases. He received a work party of German prisoners, but no packing materials. Soldiers fortuitously had discovered around a thousand sheepskin coats stashed in a nearby mine, meant to protect troops on the Eastern Front. Instead, Stout and the team of prisoners wrapped them around German art treasures. Stout struggled to keep the men on task as they worked through a sleepless night, while navigating a stream of salt water in the main mine shaft. Thanks to the importance of the gold bullion evacuation, SHAEF prioritized transportation in this instance, and thirty-nine ten-ton trucks hauled the artworks to Frankfurt. The convoy was maneuvering through a combat area and had a full armed escort, with a few aircraft flying overhead for additional security.[103]

A more macabre discovery awaited at Bernterode, north of Merkers and also just east of the eventual border of the Soviet-occupied zone. The cache contained a wide variety of Prussian items evacuated from Potsdam: tapestries, rare books, around one hundred paintings, and military standards. In a separate room were four caskets, one of them festooned with a wreath, and swastika-bearing red ribbons. The makeshift shrine also contained two crowns, two swords with gold and silver sheaths, a scepter, and an orb. To Hancock, summoned to inspect the repository, the scene looked like a "modern pagan ritual." Labels on the caskets had an oddly childlike quality, secured with Scotch tape and bearing names scrawled in red crayon: Field Marshal von Hindenberg and his wife, and King Frederick William I of Prussia and his son, Frederick the Great. The paintings, including Watteau's *Embarkation for Cythera*, appeared to have been hastily stashed.[104] Given the immense evacuation effort required, Hancock requested assistance from the skilled and patient Stout.[105] With a work crew of French

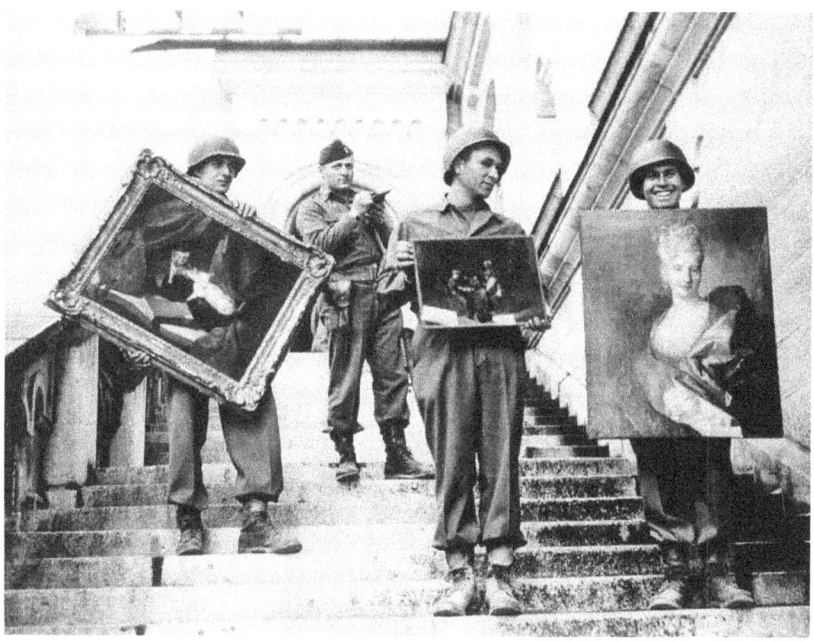

James Rorimer, at top, with American soldiers and recovered art, Neuschwanstein Castle, 1945. Photo by Universal History Archive / Universal Images Group via Getty Images.

laborers, they spent four days evacuating the mine, transferring the works of art first, then the caskets, saving for last the heaviest one holding Frederick the Great, at an estimated twelve hundred pounds. They finished the work on VE Day.[106]

Meanwhile, Rorimer spent May 8 in Berchtesgaden, a small town in the Bavarian Alps near the Austrian border and, in his words, the "playground of Nazidom." In mountains above the town in the Obersalzberg were Hitler's Eagle's Nest and his mountain residence, the Berghof, along with homes owned by Göring and Bormann, and an SS training school. The top Nazi leadership—Goebbels, Himmler, Speer—all had regularly gathered in the mountain resort, but they had long since fled. When Rorimer arrived, accompanied by Calvin Hathaway, he found victory-fueled pandemonium. French troops had entered Berchtesgaden ahead of the Americans and raised the tricolor above the Eagle's Nest. They also succumbed to looting and vandalism, leaving empty picture frames in tunnels under the Nazi leaders' residences.[107] Rorimer later was somewhat sympathetic to bad French

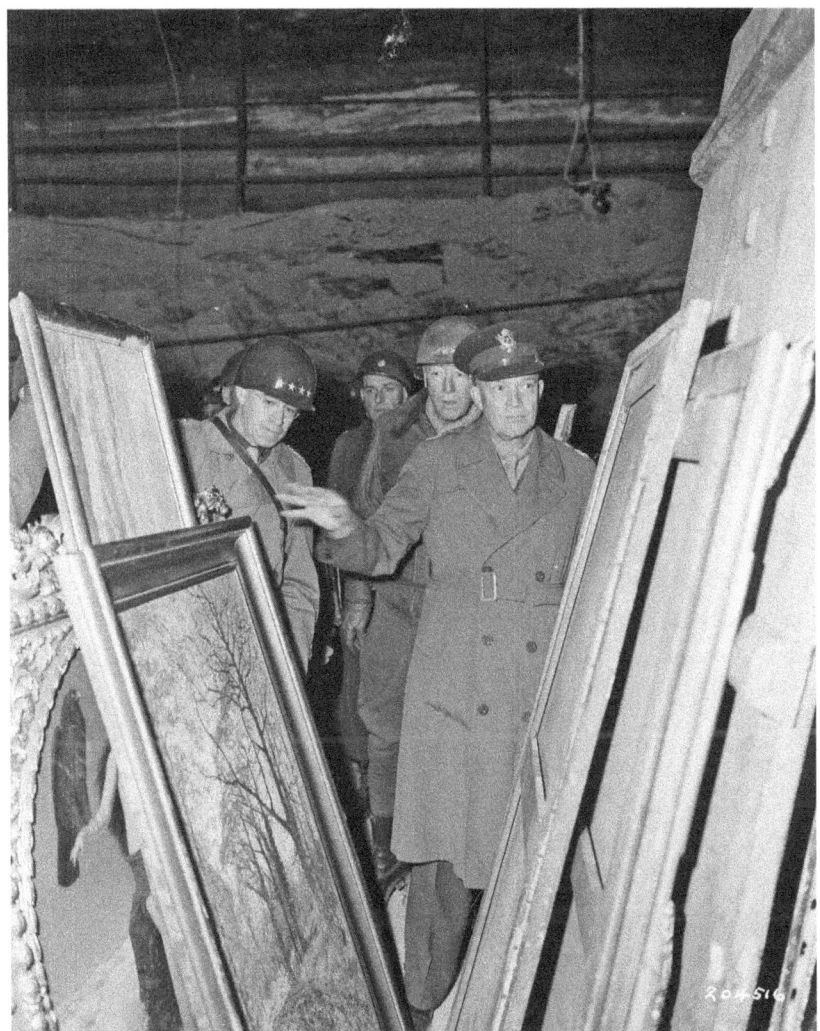

Generals Bradley, Patton, and Eisenhower examine paintings at the Merkers mine, April 1945. Courtesy United States National Archives and Records Administration (RG 111-SC-204516).

behavior after four years of brutal occupation—"we could understand it"—but noted aptly at the time that the looting was "wasteful and stupid."[108]

Of greater immediate concern to Rorimer was the location of Göring's art collection. The Reichsmarschall had been unceremoniously detained at the Seventh Army interrogation center near Augsburg, and Rorimer prepared questions that investigators could use at the right moment, when Göring was willing to talk. On the night of May 13 and 14, a French officer, Captain A. Zoller, employed a time-honored tactic: he drank with him. Once loosened up, Göring effusively shared details about his art acquisitions, all above board, of course, and amassed with noble intentions, for the planned museum at Karinhall. He had loaded the art on his special train, and on April 15 headed for Berchtesgaden. On Bormann's orders, the SS arrested him eight days later and halted the train cars in tunnels near the town. Unbeknownst to Göring, the cars had been separated and some were pilfered by local townspeople. German authorities unloaded the other cars and transferred the objects to a yet unfinished cement shelter in the woods—a site wholly inadequate for the conservation of delicate artworks. An American intelligence agent happened to learn about the cache during an interrogation of the engineer who built the structure, prompting a company of US engineers to recover the works, already wet from condensed moisture.[109] A nearby hotel in the city of Unterstein became a small collecting point. The items, as Göring had boasted, might well have formed the core of a fine national museum—Rembrandts, Bouchers, a Tintoretto from Florence, a Van Ostade from Amsterdam, a Memling from Belgium, and a sixteenth-century wooden statue of the Magdalene known as *La Belle Allemande*, negotiated in a lopsided "exchange" with French national museums.[110]

While officers sorted through the Göring cache at Berchtesgaden, another great challenge awaited at the Alt Aussee salt mine in Austria. The US Third Army arrived on May 8, encountering no Austrian resistance, and Posey and Kirstein reached the mine a week later. If the intelligence provided by Bunjes, Lohse, and other German operatives was accurate, they were on the cusp of finding much of Hitler's Linz collection. As they approached the mine, Kirstein later recalled, "a hive of wild rumors buzzed about the entrance: the mine had been blown; we could see nothing; there was no use trying to enter."[111] In fact, the mine and its precious contents had escaped destruction, but narrowly. In March and April 1945, high-level Nazi officials, including Hitler himself, had issued contradictory directives regarding the mine's contents. As the Allies pressed toward Berlin from east and west, Hitler ordered a scorched-earth policy, as reflected in the so-called Nero Decree of March 19, 1945, calling for the destruction of bridges, roads, and factories to prevent their use by the Allies. He also ordered the sealing of the Alt Aussee mine entrance. In early April, August Eigruber, a zealous Gauleiter of the

Upper Danube region, oversaw the positioning of six unexploded American bombs in a mine passage for imminent detonation, outside the art storage area. An explosion of that magnitude might not only seal the entrance, but also destroy the tunnels and provoke a flood, imperiling the stored works of art. Yet there is evidence that Hitler wanted to preserve the artworks. He specified in his will, drawn up during his final days in the Berlin bunker, that he hoped the Linz museum project would come to fruition. On May 1, moreover, a day after Hitler's suicide, a document issued by Martin Bormann's aide indicated that Reich authorities should prevent the Soviets from seizing the artworks, while keeping the pieces intact. In the confusion of competing directives and the collapse of the Reich, the Austrian mine managers sought permission to remove the larger bombs. They received it from Austrian-born Gestapo leader Ernst Kaltenbrunner, who had fled from Berlin to Alt Aussee. On May 5, the miners detonated smaller explosives to seal the mine entrance.[112]

Posey, an architectural engineer by training who had assisted in the evacuation of the Merkers mine, estimated it would take one to two weeks to clear the debris and reach the mine cavity. But with the miners' assistance, he and Kirstein were able to enter the first chamber the next morning. A former ERR employee led them through a narrow passageway and opened two padlocks on an iron door. When they stepped into the chamber they saw resting on cardboard boxes, unwrapped, eight panels of the Ghent Altarpiece. As the light from their flickering lamps shone in the painted jewels of the crowned Virgin Mary, Kirstein later recalled a kind of serenity: "Calm and beautiful, the altarpiece was, quite simply, there."[113] They also found four panels of Dierik Bouts's altarpiece from Louvain, works by Watteau, Gerard ter Borch, Van Ostade, and, lying on an old mattress, Michelangelo's Madonna sculpture from Bruges. Posey oversaw a swift inventory of the mine's contents and requested assistance from Stout, known among the MFAA as the best officer to oversee the most important evacuations. Stout arrived on May 21 and noted the following estimates from the inventory: 6,577 paintings, twenty-three hundred drawings and watercolors, 954 prints, 137 pieces of sculpture, 129 pieces of armor, seventy-nine baskets of objects, 484 cases "thought to be archives," seventy-eight pieces of furniture, 122 tapestries, 181 cases of books, and 1,200-1,700 cases "apparently books or similar."[114] All told, it would be the largest and highest-quality cache found by the MFAA.

By June 15, Stout estimated the massive evacuation would take another six weeks, prioritizing the removal of highest value works.[115] But the US government had a different timetable. Allied forces were still a hundred miles inside the projected Soviet zone, and Stalin refused to convene the Allied Control Council until all forces withdrew to agreed upon boundaries. On June 18, President Truman instructed the army to withdraw to the US zone by July 1, taking with it the plundered works currently under American control. The affected area encompassed mines in Thuringia, including Merkers, while Stalin's designs for Austria were unclear. In the meantime, Stout was forced to intensify the evacuation effort, assisted by monuments officers Thomas Carr Howe and Lamont Moore.[116]

As at Merkers, the officers used sheepskin coats to protect the works of art. Stout also devised packing "sausages," which consisted of thick cloth found in one of the mine chambers, wrapped in lace fabric and tied with string.[117] Stout finessed the packing process to a science: waterproof, thick green paper once procured by the Wehrmacht to defend against gas attacks was placed on the side bars and floor of a 2.5-ton truck, topped by a layer of felt and the packing sausages. Each truck could hold around 150 medium-sized paintings, plus several sculptures. Convoys of six trucks transported the works to the Munich collecting point more than a hundred miles away, with two armored trucks as front and rear guards.[118] Stout spent several days packing up the Bruges Madonna, which emerged from the mine heavily padded and "trussed up like a ham." He inspected the system of ropes and pulleys used to lift the precious sculpture onto a mine train and said with a smile, "I think we could bounce her from Alp to Alp, all the way to Munich, without doing her any harm."[119] Joking aside, the evacuation of the Belgian national treasure, along with the Ghent Altarpiece, had to be flawless. The crew spent most of an entire day removing those two masterpieces.[120] The evacuation continued past the July 1 deadline, as negotiations over the Austrian zones continued. Eventually, Alt Aussee ended up in the US zone. By July 19, the MFAA had evacuated eighty truckloads with 1,850 unpacked paintings, 1,441 cases of artworks, eleven large sculptures, thirty pieces of furniture, and thirty-four cases of textiles, with more pieces left to pack up.[121]

While the vast majority of recovered objects were found in the western occupation zones of Germany and Austria, and the Soviets never joined the MFAA, several monuments officers secured hundreds of works from the Soviet zone and eastern Europe. The indefatigable Rose Valland played a leading role in these missions. During her first trip to the Soviet zone in the spring of 1946, she traveled clandestinely to the site of Göring's former hunting lodge, Carinhall, which was destroyed on his orders as Allied troops closed in on Berlin. She found two sixteenth-century stone lions that stood at the lodge entrance and ensured their repatriation to France.[122]

The French organized additional missions in eastern Europe, thanks to the Quadripartite Procedure for Restitution of April 8, 1946. Valland again led a mission in eastern Germany accompanied by French Army Museum expert Bernard Druène, launching a long process of identifying and claiming

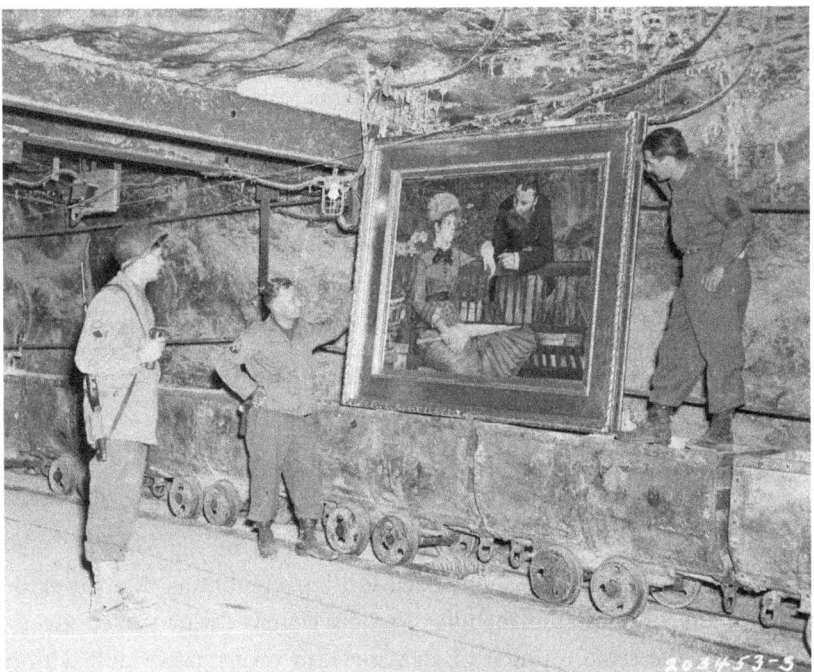

American soldiers with Edouard Manet's *Wintergarden* from the National-Galerie in Berlin, evacuated by the Germans to the Merkers mine for safekeeping. Courtesy United States National Archives and Records Administration (RG-111-SC-203453-5).

items stolen from the museum.[123] In December 1946, CRA member Philippe Gangnat led a mission to Czechoslovakia and identified 850 works stored in the partially burned Nikolsburg castle, concluding that the fire had destroyed other French objects.[124] In February 1947, the French established a "permanent" mission in Soviet-occupied Germany, and in December, Valland inspected works at the Seisenegg castle near Amstetten in the Soviet zone of Austria. ERR documents shared by the Americans allowed her to prove French ownership of 309 cases of items, mostly lower-value furniture, tapestries, and decorative items, some of which came from the David-Weill collection.[125] In 1949, Valland inspected items at the Heidecksburg castle near Rudolstadt in Thuringia, where she identified paintings and tapestries from France, as well as cannons, flags, and other items from the Army Museum.[126] Identifying works, however, did not necessarily lead to repatriation, and in May 1949 she bitterly noted "the Soviets' determination not to return anything."[127] Still, by June 5, 1950, France had received 742 items from the Soviet zone in Germany, including East Berlin, and 450 cases from the Soviet zone of Austria, compared to 615 items from the British zone.[128] In November 1950, Valland reported that the Soviets had "found" several seventeenth- and eighteenth-century French cannons from the Army Museum, precisely where French cultural officers had identified them. The Soviets, she wrote sardonically, had finally "decided to give them to us."[129] Despite these victories, Valland lamented in November 1955 that French missions in eastern Europe did not have the relative ease of access they enjoyed in the western zones.[130]

Art Crimes as War Crimes

As the MFAA recovered works from hundreds of repositories, they also gathered intelligence about Nazi looting operations. Met director and Roberts Commission member Francis Henry Taylor played a central role in the establishment of an American investigative unit within the OSS to track the flight of cultural assets and individuals involved in Nazi art plunder. With the support of James Murphy, head of the OSS Counter-Intelligence Branch (X2) in Washington, and David Bruce, head of the OSS in London, the Art Looting Investigation Unit (ALIU) was established in November 1944. Because of the US army's unwillingness to provide officers who would operate outside of SHAEF command, Taylor suggested recruiting naval officers and tapped into a network of the East Coast elite in the art world.[131] He recommended three art historians and naval reserve officers as primary investigators: James Plaut of the Fogg Museum (who headed the unit), S. Lane Faison of Williams College, and Theodore Rousseau, a former assistant curator at the National Gallery of Art. Plaut aimed not only to facilitate restitution, but also to encourage the inclusion of art plunder in war crimes charges against the Nazis and their collaborators.[132] In March 1945, Lord William Finlay, British representative to the United Nations War Crimes Commission, similarly proclaimed at a meeting of the Vaucher commission that art looting should be considered a war crime.[133]

In May and June 1945, Plaut and Rousseau questioned seven hundred art dealers, curators, museum directors, and others tangentially involved in Nazi art looting; Faison joined the effort in July. The investigators created a list of twenty-one major operatives and between June and September, detained them all for questioning at the US Judge Advocate General's Interrogation Center near Alt Aussee.[134] The center actually was a villa with ornate exterior décor. One evening when Howe joined Plaut and Rousseau for an elegant dinner, he observed Göring's dealer and advisor Walter Andreas Hofer, one of the detainees held for interrogation, pacing in the garden outside. The ALIU questioned Hofer for weeks, while he displayed a prodigious but selective memory of individual transactions, recalling artists, titles, and prices.[135] Other individuals detained and questioned at Alt Aussee included dealers Bruno Lohse, Karl Haberstock, Walter Bornheim, and Gustav Rochlitz; museum officials Hermann Voss, Robert Scholz, and Ernst Buchner; and Gisela Limberger, Göring's personal secretary. At Neuschwanstein, Plaut questioned Günther Schiedlausky, a German art historian who had served the ERR in Paris and was held by the US Seventh Army.[136] From this wealth of information, the three investigators each produced a highly detailed Consolidated Interrogation Report: Rousseau focused on the Göring collection, Faison on the Linz collection, and Plaut on the ERR. Dutch intelligence officer Jan Vlug contributed a report on the Dienststelle Mühlmann. The ALIU also produced thirteen Detailed Interrogation Reports on the principal actors, and a final report, all sent to OSS Counter-Intelligence, the Roberts Commission, and the UN War Crimes Commission.[137]

Other Allied investigators contributed to the growing intelligence on Nazi art plunder. The head British investigator was art historian, collector, and Wing Commander Douglas Cooper. In Paris, he discovered crucial documentation produced by Schenker International Transport, detailing numerous wartime shipments from France to Germany. The records, a treasure trove for investigators, included the names of French dealers and German buyers, descriptions of objects, and transaction dates. Cooper also investigated Swiss dealers who had traded Nazi-looted art, such as Theodor Fischer, and shared with French officials his intelligence on works in Switzerland from the Kann, Rosenberg, and Wildenstein collections.[138]

Among French investigators, Rose Valland interrogated key German operatives. She interviewed Haberstock for several days and gleaned detailed information on individual transactions, tracing several French-owned works. She also questioned Voss on works purchased in France for the Linz collection. "Strange as it sounds," she noted, "he remembered nothing." She conceded that Voss truly might not have remembered specific transactions, having succeeded Posse as director of the Linz project.[139]

Valland was more skeptical about Hildebrand Gurlitt's alleged lapses in memory, certain that he must have remembered his own wartime art purchases in France.[140] When interrogated by Allied investigators, Gurlitt denied collaborating in Nazi plunder and crafted a clever story about his alleged precarious status in the Third Reich as a second-degree *Mischling* (partial Aryan), with a Jewish grandmother. He also claimed that most of his own collection and ownership records had been destroyed by Allied air strikes in Dresden. The investigators doubted his carefully constructed story but lacked proof of his involvement in illicit transactions. American authorities kept him under house arrest for three years in Aschbach while investigations continued.[141] But before evidence surfaced against him, the OSS ceased interrogations as the United States prepared to transfer sovereignty to the Germans. Like so many other dealers who had served the Nazis, Gurlitt thus escaped prosecution. He was released in 1948 and went on to serve as director of the Westphalian Kunstverein in Düsseldorf. Works in his sequestered art collection returned to him in batches, beginning in 1950 with eighty-one paintings and thirty-seven drawings, including Max

Beckmann's *The Lion Tamer*, sold under duress by German Jewish dealer Alfred Flechtheim in 1934, and Max Liebermann's *Two Riders on the Beach*, relinquished in a forced sale to the Nazis in Breslau by Jewish collector David Friedmann.[142]

Given Valland's acrimonious wartime interactions with Bruno Lohse at the Jeu de Paume, she was highly motivated to help bring charges against him. Following extensive ALIU interrogations, in January 1948 the United States extradited him to France, where he appeared before a military tribunal. Writing from Berlin before the trial, Valland asked the judge to question Lohse about transactions related to several items purchased in France on Göring's behalf—paintings by Roelant Savery and Pieter Brueghel, a Govaerts confiscated from the Unger collection, and Gobelin and Aubusson tapestries. Lohse had proven cooperative with the ALIU and had responded to other such requests while detained at the Cherche-Midi prison. He hand-wrote testimony, for instance, that he may have seen a certain Cranach painting, *Hercules and Omphale*, but could not confirm details without seeing the picture.[143] In the end, the French military tribunal acquitted him and he was released on August 3, 1950. Apparently unfazed by several years of detention, he promptly tried to claim five paintings from France that, in his view, had been erroneously restituted to the country and were among works under consideration for the state custodianship. Writing from Berlin in June 1951, Valland petulantly told her colleagues in Paris that if they wanted to return paintings to "a man who is in part responsible for most of the losses from our artistic patrimony," they might as well claim from him all objects still missing from France. The Schloss collection would be a good place to start, she suggested, as the family had lost most of the 284 works Lohse had negotiated for Germany.[144] US officer Lane Faison also was perturbed by the whole affair, but in contrast to Valland wondered whether Lohse had a just claim. In response, Valland proposed to her colleagues with some irony that the French could "restitute" the pictures to the American MFAA and let them deal with the matter, but surmised that the charismatic Lohse had swayed Faison.[145] All told, Lohse's activities can be traced to at least thirty-one works selected for the French custodianship.[146] To Valland's chagrin, once he was a free man he reestablished his art dealership in Munich and, prudently, rarely spoke about the war.[147]

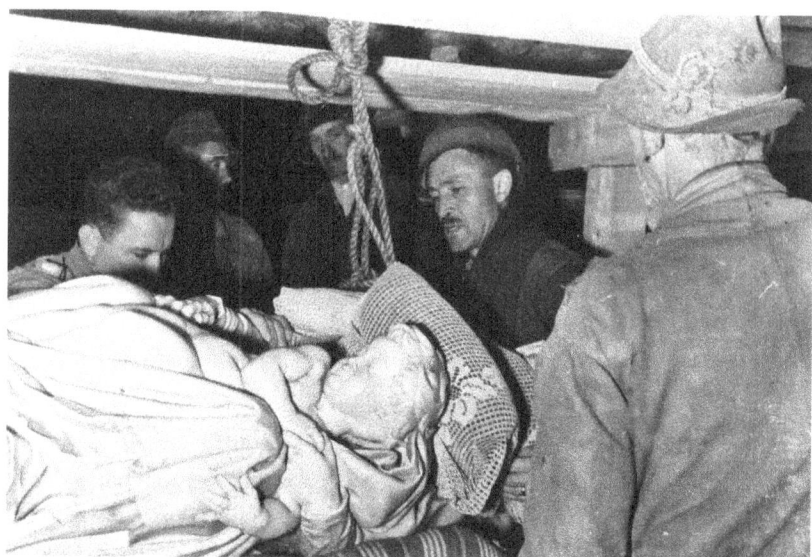

In the Alt Aussee mine, George Stout (center) oversees protection and removal of Michelangelo's Madonna sculpture, stolen by the Germans from the Church of Our Lady in Bruges. Courtesy United States National Archives and Records Administration (RG 239-PA-1-7).

When the Nuremberg Trials began in late 1945, the charge of "plunder of art treasures" was included in the cases against Göring and Alfred Rosenberg. Their eventual conviction, at least to some degree, was informed by their role in art looting, fulfilling one of Plaut's central aims for the ALIU. But they were the only two principals charged; the rest, like Lohse, were able to reestablish their museum careers and art dealing within a few years.[148]

3
Negotiating Cultural Restitution

The heroic recovery of Nazi-looted art from castles and salt mines was only the first phase in a long restitution process. As thousands of cultural objects flowed into MFAA collecting points, the Allies negotiated demands for compensation and in-kind assets from Germany. Talks repeatedly stalled, as the four occupying powers had incompatible objectives stemming from their distinct historical experiences with the enemy. The French, while recognizing the excessive demands placed on Germany after the First World War, aimed to secure a wide range of industrial, transportation, and cultural assets, including the replacement of lost art with works from German public and private collections. They envisioned a protracted period of international cooperation and embraced their own leadership role representing the interests of smaller Allied countries, including the Netherlands and Belgium. In contrast, top US officials opposed saddling Germany with onerous restitution obligations, a view eventually supported by the British, and aimed to transfer management of recovered assets to the Germans as soon as possible. The Soviets increasingly focused on seizing assets from their own zone, without cooperating in the international restitution effort. These competing objectives prevented quadripartite agreements and the creation of an international restitution organization, leaving the occupying powers in control of cultural restitution from their own zones. By end of the western occupation in 1955, the liberated countries, represented most forcefully by France, had failed to receive cultural replacements from German art collections. The breakdown of international cooperation at the end of the war thus strengthened national government control over recovered works claimed as cultural heritage, in the formerly occupied countries of western Europe, as well as former Reich territories of West Germany and Austria.

Wartime Diplomacy, 1943–45

As the only despoiled country in western Europe with an occupation zone in Germany, France held a unique position among the Allies. Amid broader reparations negotiations, French officials advocated for in-kind restitution of lost artworks with equivalent pieces from German collections.[1] They believed the Inter-Allied Declaration of January 1943 had provided a framework for a multilateral restitution process that would compel Germany to replace lost works of art, an idea also supported by Belgian and Dutch diplomats. In this line of thinking, the enemy had ravaged the artistic patrimony of the occupied countries, and postwar settlements must make those nations culturally whole. While the French pursued this bold objective, they were forced to accept their junior status relative to the United States, Britain, and the Soviet Union, whose leaders ultimately would determine future settlements.[2]

Allied planning for postwar control over German territory began in a series of wartime conferences attended by the Big Three powers. At the Moscow Conference in October 1943, foreign ministers Anthony Eden of Britain and Vyacheslav Molotov of the Soviet Union and US Secretary of State Cordell Hull agreed to the formation of a European Advisory Commission (EAC) to issue recommendations on the anticipated surrender of enemy states and occupation of German territory. Headquartered in London, the EAC convened delegations from the three Allied countries and allowed France to join in November 1944. The commission drafted a brief surrender document to be presented to Germany and provided a basic institutional framework for the Allied occupation with zonal boundaries. A military governing body, the Allied Control Council (ACC) would oversee the partition of Germany, initially envisioned as three occupation zones controlled by the United States, Britain, and the Soviet Union. The three Allies ratified plans for the ACC at the Yalta Conference in February 1945. They also allowed France to join the council and carved a French occupation zone from the original US and British zones.[3]

In this early phase of negotiations, the French-backed effort to secure in-kind restitution from German collections fuelled heated debate. The idea had circulated during the war among representatives of the exiled governments of Belgium, Greece, Luxembourg, the Netherlands, Norway, Poland, Czechoslovakia, Yugoslavia, and the French Committee of National Liberation (CFLN). These countries established the Inter-Allied Committee for Study of the Armistice, which on September 14, 1943, produced one of the first reports calling for the replacement of lost works of art.[4] In this plan, enemy states would repatriate to formerly occupied countries all plundered artistic, historic, scientific, educational, and religious objects, and they would replace items that could not be restituted; national governments would manage any unclaimed assets.[5] This last provision would allow states to benefit from the art recovery process, even though the vast majority of fine art lost from these countries had been privately owned, disproportionately by Jewish collectors and dealers.

The armistice committee report also foresaw that asset restitution would be calculated according to German economic potential, but negotiated separately from the broader realm of reparations.[6] The issue of whether art restitution should count toward German reparations would continue to stymie quadripartite settlements over the next few years. The French advocated including art in reparations demands, an idea the Soviets initially accepted, whereas Britain and the United States favored separating the two obligations.[7]

In contrast to French demands, top US military and civilian leaders advocated allowing Germany to rebuild without the burden of heavy reparations and restitution obligations.[8] Below these highest-ranking officials, some cultural advisors and civil servants believed that works of art constituted a special category of assets extrinsic to German economic reconstruction, and could be demanded from the enemy. In July 1944 a US inter-departmental committee recommended allowing replacement of "works of art and other cultural treasures, these exceptions being justified by the peculiar importance attached to those categories of goods."[9] The Roberts Commission initially endorsed this position, several months prior to the MFAA discoveries in the repositories. Had Belgium lost the Ghent Altarpiece, for instance, the commission advocated replacing it with the equivalent in Flemish paintings "belonging to public or private collections in Germany." At the same time, the commission recognized that demands for replacement should not "make a cultural desert of Germany itself."[10]

While debates over these central principles continued into early 1945, officials representing France, Belgium, and the Netherlands, still partially occupied, developed their own restitution principles, reiterating demands for German replacement of lost artworks with equivalent pieces. In their view, all occupation-era transactions with the Germans had contributed to national duress through distorted currency rates and a clearing account system that enabled the enemy to import goods from the occupied territories through deficit payments. By the end of the war, Germany had accumulated clearing deficits of RM 4.9 billion in Belgium, 8.5 billion in France, and 10 billion in the Netherlands.[11]

For these countries, securing works of art from Germany would be a form of cultural reparations. On February 12, 1945, members of the education and foreign ministries of France and the Benelux countries proclaimed that all items lost from the national cultural patrimony, whether stolen or purchased by the enemy, must be restituted or replaced with equivalent pieces.[12] The delegates also proclaimed the Allies' right to seize works from German public or private collections to ensure in-kind replacement. The Belgian delegates, for example, drew up a list of works from German collections that together would constitute an acceptable replacement for the Ghent Altarpiece.[13] For American diplomats, the demands went too far, threatening the integrity of German art collections. Eventually, west European efforts to secure cultural replacement failed amid broader reparations negotiations.[14]

Another key question was whether the Allies would create an international commission, beyond the MFAA, to organize the massive art restitution effort.[15] The British Macmillan Committee reported to Foreign Secretary Anthony Eden in September 1944 that such an international body was a *sine qua non* of the envisioned restitution process: "... it is essential that it should derive its power from the national Governments concerned [and] should be created at the earliest possible moment so that it can advise the Allied Governments during the period of military control and, in the meantime, under direction prepare a program of restitution of loot and stolen material."[16]

Drawing on these ideas, British and American cultural experts issued proposals for an international commission. The British delegation to the EAC proposed an inter-Allied body that would facilitate the claims process for identifiable works found in enemy countries, with binding decisions overriding national government authority.[17] The American Roberts Commission endorsed the concept, but believed such a body should be administered by the United Nations, with authority to advise occupation zone commanders and assert trusteeship over German cultural resources.[18] Like demands for restitution in kind, however, these proposals raised thorny questions about the sovereign control of property and were rejected by higher authorities. As Eden put it, "We regard these governments as solely responsible for the treatment of property within their own borders."[19] Richard Law of the British Foreign Office similarly argued that an international body would lack authority to review ownership claims of works taken from Allied countries, and only local courts could determine the validity of wartime transactions.[20]

Eventually, top officials in all four occupying countries rejected proposals for an international restitution commission. The French opposed granting such a body the power of trusteeship, while British and American authorities feared it could lead to intelligence leaks and civilian interference in military operations. Most important, the Soviets wanted full control over cultural property in their zone and rejected all plans for an international body charged with cultural restitution.[21] The idea continued to resurface over the next several years but never came to fruition, leaving the national governments ultimately in control of cultural property repatriated to their territories.

The German surrender on May 8, 1945, led to another round of talks in July and August, as the war in the Pacific continued. Allied leaders gathered in the Berlin suburb of Potsdam amid significant leadership changes. Harry Truman had assumed the US presidency after the death of Roosevelt on April 12, and Labour Party leader Clement Attlee replaced Churchill during the conference. The French still were excluded from this new iteration of the Big Three, to De Gaulle's great chagrin.[22] Truman and other officials who toured Berlin's surroundings were shocked by the vast destruction and only gradually learned the full extent of German suffering. Truman established his headquarters in the suburb of Babelsberg, in a villa that had been requisitioned by Soviet soldiers a few months earlier. He learned years later that the soldiers had raped the home's female residents in front of their entire family.[23]

While absorbing various dimensions of European trauma, Truman had two central but competing goals at Potsdam. First, he aimed to assert US authority in Germany. At Yalta, Roosevelt and Churchill had acknowledged Soviet dominance in Poland and eastern Europe, but Truman was not about to negotiate away American interests in Germany.[24] Second, Truman intended to extricate the United States from the occupation as quickly as possible, a goal that became more pressing in the following months. After the Japanese surrender, the American public wanted its government to focus on domestic concerns. In October 1945, a mere 7 percent of voters believed foreign policy was a greater priority.[25]

One of the key accomplishments of Potsdam was the creation of entities that would negotiate peace settlements and administer the occupation of Germany. The Allies established a Council of Foreign Ministers charged with drafting peace treaties with Germany's allies—Italy, Bulgaria, Romania, Hungary, and Finland—and with Germany itself once it had established an autonomous government. They confirmed plans for the ACC as defined at Yalta, and the French were allowed to join the first council meeting on July 31, 1945.[26] The council aimed to promote denazification, economic reconstruction, and the reintegration of Germany into the international community. Yet competing visions also emerged from Potsdam: Germany would remain a unified country with a federal system, but each occupying power was allowed to extract reparations from its own zone. Moreover, the western Allies would transfer to the Soviet zone 15 percent of industrial assets that were not vital to reconstruction in exchange for food and raw materials, and an additional 10 percent that did not require compensation from the eastern zone, reinforcing the economic division of Germany.[27]

In negotiations leading up to Potsdam and during the conference itself, the Big Three powers failed to agree on the very definition of restitution, let alone a procedure to transfer assets. The Soviet view was closest to the French at the time: it allowed for a broad definition of restitutable assets, including goods plundered or created during the occupation, and allowed for replacement in kind of unique cultural objects. The Americans argued for a limited scope of restitution to include only religious and cultural objects, while crediting the value of any additional restituted assets—industrial, vehicular, railway—toward Germany's reparations obligations.[28] The British, for their part, held a view in between the Soviets and Americans, allowing the restitution of non-cultural assets, so long as reconstruction goals were met, and the replacement in kind of cultural objects. These differences among the Allies persisted at Potsdam, while the occupying powers continued seizing assets in their respective zones.[29]

Over the next few years, it became clear that liberated countries would never secure a broad restitution of assets from Germany, including in-kind equivalents of lost artworks. By early 1948, in the context of US financial support through the Marshall Plan, French economic experts and diplomats believed that a thriving, prosperous Germany was in their national interest, and pursued economic cooperation within a European framework and under French leadership.[30] Amid this remarkable Franco-German reconciliation, the MFAA repatriated to western Europe thousands of items found in Axis territories.

Cultural Repatriation, August 1945–December 1947

Crowds had hardly dispersed from the Allied victory parades when cultural officials in the liberated countries grew restive waiting for the return of their national treasures. Shortly after the German surrender, Belgian art historian and MFAA officer Leo Van Puyvelde went so far as to lead a convoy of twenty-five trucks to Alt Aussee to retrieve the Ghent Altarpiece himself. American MFAA officers there, rather perplexed by Van Puyvelde's exceptional zeal, turned him away empty-handed.[31] But they heard his message: the liberated countries must receive key national treasures as tokens of goodwill—soon. The US cultural advisor to General Eisenhower, John Nicholas Brown, proposed allowing the restitution of several highly symbolic masterpieces to formerly occupied countries, an idea that had been endorsed at Potsdam. As a result, on September 3, 1945, Van Puyvelde finally had the satisfaction of attending a restitution ceremony in Brussels alongside Prince Regent Charles to welcome back the Ghent Altarpiece; Michelangelo's Madonna sculpture returned to Belgium soon afterward. In early May 1946, the Poles received their magnificent Veit Stoss altarpiece, a crucial piece of Polish cultural heritage from St. Mary's basilica in Krakow.[32]

In the several months following Potsdam, the four occupying powers established separate approaches to restitution that endured throughout the occupation period. A Directorate of Reparations, Deliveries and Restitutions (RDR) was created within the ACC and the four military governments oversaw operations within their own zones. In the US zone, some five hundred cultural repositories had been located by September 1945, and the Office of Military Government, United States (OMGUS), was not willing to wait for Allied agreements to begin repatriating assets. Deputy Governor General Lucius Clay issued instructions to allow the repatriation of industrial, agricultural, and transportation equipment to liberated countries, as well as identifiable cultural objects stolen or purchased by the Germans. American MFAA officers led by Major Bancel LaFarge established four collecting points in the US zone. In the northern section, a center in Marburg quickly filled with objects found in surrounding areas. In Munich, James Rorimer helped establish the Central Collecting Point (CCP) for plundered art in a former Nazi administration building. The CCP also held works of art found in the US occupation zone in Austria, including the massive Alt Aussee repository. A museum in Wiesbaden mostly held works that had been evacuated from German museums or seized from residents in Germany, and the Offenbach collecting point housed books, archives, and Judaica. MFAA officers created a property card for each object, determined the country of origin whenever possible, and organized repatriation deliveries. In the fall of 1945, the three western zones allowed missions of art experts from liberated countries to investigate plundered assets and submit claims on behalf of their governments. American officers launched repatriation procedures, and by the end of the year, regular shipments of cultural objects were flowing back to the liberated countries.[33]

In the British zone, the investigation and restitution of plundered assets was overseen by the Control Commission for Germany-British Element. Plundered objects discovered in the British zone were transferred to a collecting point at Schloss Celle near Brunswick. Many of these pieces had been evacuated from German museums, though caches also contained works plundered from Jewish collections.[34] The recovered cultural property included some two thousand church bells requisitioned by the Germans across Europe and found in Hamburg scrap yards. An estimated fifty thousand bells had been shipped to the Third Reich, most of them recycled into bullet casings and other weapons.[35] British MFAA officers headquartered in

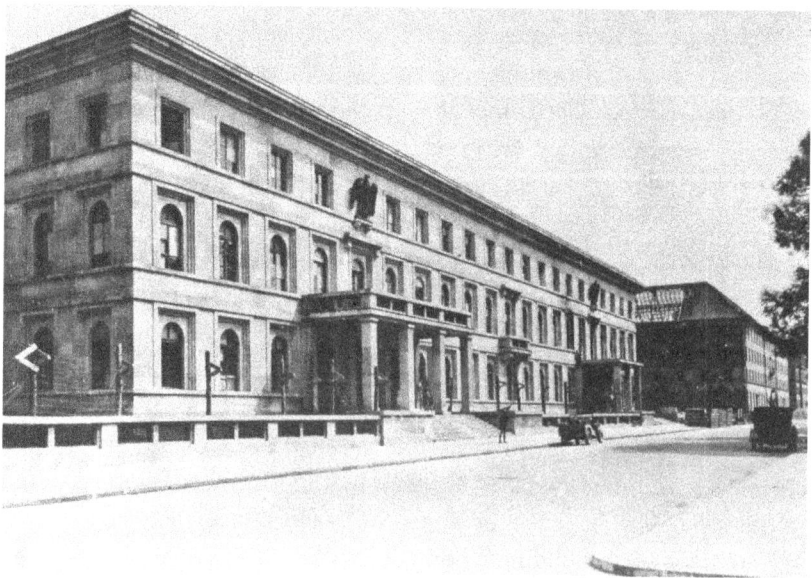

Main entrance to the Munich Central Collecting Point, formerly the Nazi Party headquarters. Courtesy United States National Archives and Records Administration (RG 260-MCCP-1-36).

Bünde fielded restitution requests by priests, local officials, and townspeople eager to recover their religious and sonic heritage.[36]

In the French zone, a Directorate of Reparations and Restitutions was established in Baden-Baden in September 1945, overseen by the economy and finance administration of the military government. The office maintained communication with the RDR in Berlin to carry out inter-Allied directives, established reciprocity agreements with other formerly occupied countries, and oversaw recovery missions in the other zones. In 1946 Rose Valland became head of the fine arts section of the French Group Control Council in Berlin and maintained regular contact with cultural authorities in Paris. The French contingent in the MFAA grew to fifteen experts by July 1947, including painter Jean Rigaud, archivist and curator André Chamson, inspector of historic monuments Jacques Dupont, and writer and museum inspector Pierre-Louis Duchartre.[37]

The situation was altogether different in the eastern zone, and the western Allies grew increasingly skeptical of the Soviets' willingness to restitute cultural assets. During EAC negotiations, the Soviets had supported only general administrative agreements that would not hinder their ability to seize assets in their zone, and offered no restitution plans.[38] In the meantime, they set about securing "trophy art" found in German repositories, and by the end of 1945 had seized assets from 4,339 German factories, businesses, and other enterprises.[39]

Months went by as the Allies continued to debate basic restitution principles. In numerous meetings between July and November 1945, various Allied bodies including the EAC (dissolved at the end of Potsdam), the Council of Foreign Ministers, and the Coordinating Committee of the AAC (CORC) had been unable to agree on a definition, and the Soviets refused to allow the shipment of goods from their zone without established parameters. A reparations conference held in Paris from September to December 1945 established the Inter-Allied Restitution Agency (IARA), which convened delegates from eighteen countries claiming compensation from Germany, as debates over asset restitution were mired in broader reparations negotiations.[40]

US General Clay attempted to break the stalemate in November 1945 by presenting a proposal to the CORC that struck a compromise between the French broad definition of restitutable property, and the restricted definition advocated by the United States and Britain. The Soviets by then also had shifted to a more limited view of restitutable assets, as they seized property in their zone and focused on securing reparations from Germany.[41] Clay's proposal led to an interim agreement in December 1945, which limited restitution to well-known and easily identified objects, while allowing the program to broaden the range of applicable cultural assets as the Allies developed procedures and created a restitution infrastructure. In the repatriation phase, art experts from the countries of origin would submit claims and receive objects on behalf of governments, not private individuals or entities. National governments would then manage the restitution process to private owners.[42]

Despite the interim agreement, quadripartite negotiations were doomed to fail, as the art restitution effort countered Soviet designs to retain objects seized by the Red Army. In July 1946 the western Allies agreed on a common cultural restitution framework, in which the governments of liberated countries would distribute lists of missing objects and request the assistance of customs officials in neutral countries to prevent exports of plundered items. The lists would be distributed internationally to art dealers, curators, and other specialists who might identify recently acquired pieces or those surfacing on the global art market.[43] Eighteen months later, the US embassy in Moscow invited the Soviet Union to join the effort, along with the governments of Austria, Belgium, Bulgaria, Czechoslovakia, Denmark, Finland, Greece, Hungary, Ireland, Italy, the Netherlands, Norway, Poland, Portugal, Romania, Spain, Sweden, Switzerland, and Yugoslavia.[44] In a terse and entirely predictable response, the Soviet Ministry of Foreign Affairs rejected the agreement, which was "concluded a year and a half ago without the knowledge of the Soviet Government and which affords special rights to the United States of America and Great Britain in comparison with the countries whose territory was occupied by Germany."[45] Without specifying the "special rights" enjoyed by the United States and Britain, the Soviet response reflected a deepening divide between east and west.[46]

Meanwhile, negotiations stalled over the issue of cultural restitution in kind. On July 9, 1946, the CORC adopted a text drafted by American representatives that outlined five categories of replaceable objects: the most important masterpieces in painting, engraving, and sculpture; masterpieces in the applied arts and anonymous works representative of national art; historical artifacts; rare and historic manuscripts and books; and objects significant to the history of science. By September 23, however, General Clay opposed distributing information on these defined categories to the liberated countries and argued that broader restitution negotiations would solve the problem of cultural losses. The abrupt reversal of the American position dismayed French officials, amid tensions in the field among MFAA officers from the two countries. According to Richard Howard, LaFarge's successor as head of the MFAA in the US zone, some American officers distrusted their French counterparts and considered them "constant thieves" who claimed objects without clear French provenance.[47]

Despite American opposition, the French continued to pursue restitution in kind from Germany. The 1947 *Répertoire des biens spoliés*, the French army's official list of property removed from the country during the war, flagged items of "undeniable cultural value" with an asterisk. If these items were never found, the French would demand compensation "from Germany's Art treasures."[48] Yet even some French art experts were troubled by the prospect of demanding works of art from German collections. In early 1947 the Musées Nationaux asked curators to submit lists of works in German collections that might complement their holdings. The head curator of the national museum at Versailles, Charles Mauricheau-Beaupré, dutifully provided a list of pieces: from the Museum of Decorative Arts in Berlin, a sitting room piece with gold décor and a label in French, "the Queen's boudoir"; from the Sanssouci palace in Potsdam, gold vases created for Madame de Pompadour from Boucher drawings; and Louis XIV's rifle at the Zeughaus in Berlin.[49] At the same time, Mauricheau-Beaupré attached a note to the director of French museums, Georges Salles, expressing "how distraught I am by measures that resemble the displacement of people. Such a precedent, no matter how well-intentioned, is no less dangerous."[50] Marcel Aubert, curator of sculpture at the Louvre, also conveyed mixed feelings. He proposed receiving German examples of medieval and Renaissance objects that "we are missing," such as works by Tilman Riemenschneider, Veit Stoss, Adam Kraft, and Peter Vischer from museums in Cologne, Munich, and the Kaiser Frederick museum in Berlin. At the same time, Aubert realized the danger of pushing the demand for replacements too far. The Sanssouci palace, he argued, held numerous examples of French sculpture that would be "a significant enrichment" for the Louvre, but "their arrival in France would have an unpredictable moral and diplomatic impact."[51]

Among British officials who opposed the principle of restitution in kind was Geoffrey Webb, who worried about a potential "drain of works of art out of Germany."[52] Many plundered items found in the British zone had been purchased by German museums or private individuals, raising thorny ownership questions: Would German private buyers be compensated if works purchased "in good faith" were repatriated to countries of origin? How would the Allies prevent arbitrary decisions about which works were removed from Germany? Given the uneven distribution of works among the occupied zones, with a high concentration in the US zone, how would the liability of restitution in kind be allocated? Webb proposed at the very least that replacement only be granted to works of art above a defined value, based on prewar appraisals. It would be impossible to replace objects at the other end of the value spectrum, he predicted, such as numerous lower-quality furniture pieces stolen in France.[53]

The American Roberts Commission also had changed its view on the feasibility of restitution in kind, partly due to cultural property issues that had emerged in US-occupied Japan amid restitution claims from Korea. The MFAA in East Asia aimed to protect the Japanese seizure of cultural objects, in contrast to repatriation efforts in Europe.[54] The US State Department encouraged the commission to pass a resolution to "strengthen the hand" of American diplomats "in keeping Japanese cultural objects out of reparations." In its final meeting on June 20, 1946, the commission recommended that "cultural objects belonging to any country or individual should not be considered or involved in reparations settlements growing out of World War II." In the words of Secretary Huntington Cairns, proposals to allow cultural replacement in kind were "dead at the moment," and the resolution passed unanimously.[55]

In the end, the Allies failed to reach an agreement on cultural replacement and from February 1947, each zone commander determined the merits of demands on a case by case basis.[56] The RDR for the British and American zones, fused into a bizone on January 1, 1947, announced on July 23 that only the zone commander, delegating responsibility to the RDR and MFAA, had the power to define a work of art and admit restitution, "whether or not the element of duress had been proved." The commander maintained the right to reject claims in cases where an object was found to have been "legitimately acquired from an occupied country during the period of the occupation."[57] To the liberated countries, the bizone policy appeared to contradict the 1943 Inter-Allied Declaration, which had nullified plunder by the enemy and "transactions apparently legal in form, even when they purport to be voluntarily effected."[58] The bizone thus lacked a clear policy toward works of art purchased by German museums and individuals, one of the dilemmas Webb had identified more than a year earlier.

US General Clay later explained that he had opposed the concept of cultural replacement, as it was difficult to prove that a valuable object had been lost in Germany. Even if such proof existed, "it was still impossible to determine what item of similar value should be offered in replacement." He saw wide-ranging implications of such a policy, given the powerful symbolism attached to a nation's cultural treasures. Trying to impose such a significant transfer of cultural objects, in his view, might go so far as to "prevent the creation of democratic government." The German people, he argued, would not understand a policy that removed their cultural heritage and "was akin to the Hitler policy which we condemned."[59]

Those lofty ideas contrast starkly with Clay's actions at the end of 1945, when he approved the shipment of 202 paintings from Berlin museums—two from the German National Gallery and the rest from the Kaiser Friedrich Museum—to the US National Gallery. Clay claimed to have been "disturbed by the possible future of Berlin" and did not wish "to return these masterpieces under such conditions."[60] Most American MFAA officers heard in Clay's argument for "safekeeping" the echoes of Nazi plunder and bitterly opposed the measure. The selected works included paintings by Vermeer, Rembrandt, Memling, Dürer, Botticelli, Rubens—highly valuable works that were widely considered part of the German cultural patrimony. On November 7, 1945, twenty-four of the thirty-five American MFAA officers in Germany signed a protest initiated at the collecting point in Wiesbaden, where many German-owned works were held. Known as "Wiesbaden Manifesto," the petition recognized the solemn military obligation of US officers "to the nation to which we own allegiance," while emphasizing "further obligation to common justice, decency, and the establishment of the power of right, not of expediency of might, among civilized nations." Signatories included Walker Hancock, Edith Standen, Walter Farmer, and Thomas Carr Howe. James Rorimer was one of three US officers in Germany who endorsed the sentiment but did not "feel at liberty to sign any statement."[61] By that time, George Stout was serving the MFAA in Japan and was unable to sign the protest, but he expressed solidarity shortly after receiving a copy.[62]

Despite MFAA opposition, the 202 paintings were shipped to Washington, D.C., at the end of 1945 and kept in storage at the National Gallery to avoid controversy. By the spring of 1948, the State Department recommended showing the pictures to the American public before they returned to Germany. An initial five-week exhibition at the National Gallery was an enormous success with some 1 million visitors, prompting a wider US tour to art museums in New York, Philadelphia, Boston, Detroit, Chicago, Cleveland, Minneapolis, San Francisco, Los Angeles, St. Louis, Pittsburgh, and Toledo. In all some 10 million people viewed the pictures and, thanks to a bill sponsored by Senator William Fulbright, entrance proceeds raised several hundred thousand dollars for UNICEF to protect German children from tuberculosis.[63] The paintings were shipped back to Wiesbaden in 1949 but did not return to Berlin until 1955. Their new home was the Dahlem Museum in West Berlin, as the Kaiser Friedrich Museum and National Gallery sat across the Iron Curtain in East Berlin.[64] Clay and other US authorities may have always intended to return the paintings to Germany, but in this instance, many Germans believed the Americans had controlled German heritage in ways far too similar to the Nazis' policies, the very perception Clay had wanted to avoid.

Some cultural officers of the smaller liberated powers also resented the weight of US decisions. Dutch proponents of cultural replacement, like their French counterparts, were disappointed by American and eventually British opposition to restitution in kind. In November 1946, the head of the Dutch Art Property Foundation, A. B. de Vries, informed the head of the

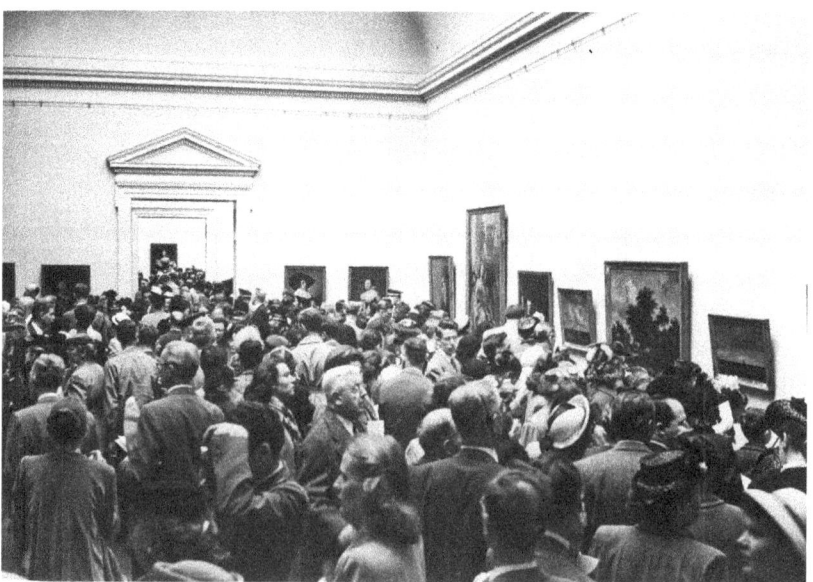

German paintings on display at the National Gallery in Washington, D.C. Courtesy of National Gallery of Art, Washington, D.C., Gallery Archives.

French Commission for Art Recovery (CRA), Albert Henraux, that several American officials had rejected proposals for replacement during a recent meeting in Berlin. De Vries noted with some sarcasm that, of course, the Americans and British wanted restitution to be carried out "as efficiently as possible by the duped countries themselves."[65]

Despite tensions and power struggles among the western Allies, the repatriation effort proceeded at a remarkable pace. By the end of 1947, American authorities had discovered 1,498 repositories in the US zone alone and had repatriated 1.7 million books and works of art. France had received more than half a million cultural items, Belgium more than 20,000, and the Netherlands more than 330,000 pieces, close to the same amount also sent to the Soviet Union.[66] As cultural repatriation continued over the next two years, the western Allies faced another diplomatic tangle: restitution under a sovereign West Germany.

Toward German Sovereignty, 1947–49

After the initial repatriation of thousands of works of art in the first two years of the restitution effort, each military government conserved objects that remained in the collecting points while planning for the eventual restoration of German sovereignty and, potentially, German control over the restitution process. Differences in objectives among the western Allies persisted, with the Americans aiming to end the occupation and extricate themselves from the entire business of restitution. The French, in contrast, planned for a longer occupation and period of international cooperation before transferring restitution responsibilities to the Germans. The lack of a tripartite agreement led to the creation of three different military laws in the three western zones, plus a fourth law for the western sectors of Berlin. On November 10, 1947, the United States enacted Military Law no. 59, which addressed "internal restitution," or assets acquired by the Nazis from citizens and non-citizens in Germany "for reasons of race, religion, nationality, ideology or political opposition to National Socialism."[67] It provided for a Central Filing Agency that would receive documented claims through December 31, 1948. In cases where the Restitution Agency was unable to mediate an "amicable settlement," the claim would be referred to the German court system, and cases could be appealed to a US military government Board of Review.[68] Also on November 10, 1947, the French military government enacted similar measures in its zone through ordinance 120, allowing claims for an eighteen-month period. It provided for restitution tribunals in courts of first instance with a head judge and two associate judges, one of whom would be a survivor of Nazi persecution, as designated by the *Land* justice minister.[69] The British issued their own Military Law no. 59 on May 12, 1949, drawing heavily on the US law and, in turn, the AAC used the British law as the basis for a restitution law in the western sectors of Berlin.[70]

Each of the three western military governments also faced the challenge of determining the fate of so-called heirless Jewish assets. Traditionally, heirless assets had reverted to state control, as they did in formerly occupied countries that received works of art from the MFAA. But for American, French, and British authorities and Jewish organizations, this solution was morally and politically unjustifiable in the case of Jewish assets from the German *Länder*, and each of the Western powers designated successor organizations to serve as trustees of heirless assets and to distribute the recovered property to Jewish communities.[71] In June 1948, the US military government gave this authority solely to the Jewish Restitution Successor Organization (JRSO), founded in New York in 1947. Jewish Cultural Reconstruction (JCR), also created in New York the same year, became the cultural branch of the JRSO and distributed heirless objects.[72] The JRSO also served the three western sectors of Berlin beginning on May 9, 1951, and in all distributed some half a million books, Torah scrolls, and ceremonial objects to the Jewish diaspora: 40 percent in the United States, 40 percent to Israel, and 20 percent to other communities around the world.[73]

There were fewer heirless cultural objects in the British and French zones, where negotiations focused on other forms of communal assets, such as buildings, cemeteries and plots of land, and compensation to Jewish communities. The Jewish Trust Corporation (JTC) was established in the British zone in 1950 to distribute assets and settlement funds, and the French established a branch two years later.[74] Initially intended to serve Jewish communities outside Germany, the successor organizations also negotiated with new Jewish communities inside Germany, composed in part by foreign Holocaust survivors, to distribute heirless communal assets and compensation for indemnification claims.[75] Altogether, by 1957 the successor organizations had acquired assets worth some DM 300 million.[76]

The United States, meanwhile, aimed to extricate itself from restitution procedures and transfer authority to the Germans. The director of the US military government in Bavaria, Murray van Wagoner, informed

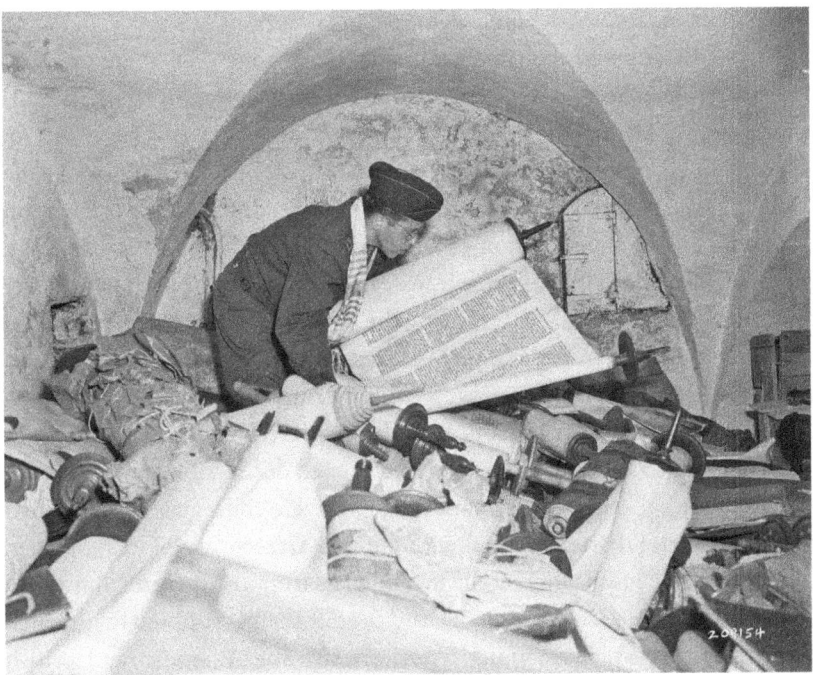

Chaplain Samuel Blinder examines a Torah scroll, one of hundreds stolen from across Europe. Courtesy United States National Archives and Records Administration (RG 111-SC-209154).

Land Minister President Hans Ehard on August 3, 1948 that "in light of the increased participation of Germany in its own affairs," responsibility for several categories of cultural property in the Munich collecting point would be transferred to Bavaria at the end of the month. The objects included privately owned German property, to be restituted by the *Land* government, and assets owned by German public entities, including art museums. Works formerly owned by the Prussian state (dissolved by the Allies in February 1947), the German Reich, and Nazi officials were "to be held in sacred trust" by Bavaria until a new German government established proper legal distribution of the assets, "in accordance with Control Council and Military Government laws and directives." All works found to be property of Jewish individuals and entities would continue to be held at the Munich collecting point "for further disposition by the Military Government," but other cultural objects and archives would "become a German responsibility." Van Wagoner considered this transfer of responsibility an important moment in German reconstruction. Repair to bomb-damaged art museums was proceeding and curators had resumed their activities, providing hope that "these priceless objects can again be placed on display for the benefit and enjoyment, and cultural enlightenment of the people."[77]

As planned, responsibility for conservation of works remaining in the Munich collecting point transferred to the Bavarian minister president on August 31, 1948. Conservation of works in repositories in other *Länder* in the American zone similarly was transferred to the corresponding minister president.[78] In a step further removing the United States from the restitution process, the American Reparations and Restitutions division announced at a meeting of heads of foreign missions in Karlsruhe on August 11, 1948, that asset restitution from the US zone would end on December 31.[79]

These unilateral US decisions alarmed French occupation authorities, including Rose Valland, who dramatically reported to colleagues in France that the Americans and British were abandoning the art recovery effort altogether. In response, Jacques Jaujard convened officials from the French Ministry of Foreign Affairs, National Museums, and the CRA, and proposed that French authorities take over remaining repositories in the American and British bizone and oversee restitution from all three western zones. Addressing the interests of France and other liberated countries, Jaujard believed such a measure was necessary to maintain the right to restitution of stolen works and to oversee objects that would be temporarily placed under German control. Attendees showed remarkable confidence that American officials would back such a measure. Albert Henraux of the CRA noted that an unnamed "American delegate" had reassured him the United States would support the proposal. A M. Jeannel from the Ministry of Foreign Affairs believed British support would follow, as "the British point of view always ends up aligning with that of the United States."[80]

The quixotic idea went nowhere, but the French continued to denounce the American transfer of restitution responsibility to the Germans. On September 18, 1948, French chargé d'affaires Armand Bérard explained to the US State Department that the American decision appeared to signal the abandonment of restitution efforts. The transfer would "sanction the most odious theft," as the objects were "the artistic patrimony of the various victims of German aggression." No cultural assets, he argued, should be transferred to the Germans until French authorities had reviewed inventories of the items. The French government requested that the US government issue urgent instructions to General Clay to delay the transfer at least until after the end of the restitution period on December 31.[81]

To the Americans, French fears were wildly overblown. The US State Department reassured the French embassy that objects subject to restitution claims would remain under American control. The restitution deadline of December 31, moreover, only applied to non-cultural property, a distinction assumed to be understood by French authorities in Germany.[82] The US government thus saw no reason to provide an inventory of items. The State Department also regretted that the French government would question the US restitution effort, which had been widely praised and already restored thousands of items to France.[83]

American reassurances failed to placate Valland, who remained the most outspoken critic of US policy and repeatedly urged higher French authorities to defend the cultural interests of France and other liberated countries. In March 1949, she identified two key areas of concern: the fate of seized collections once held by Nazi leaders, and works of middling quality that were still unidentified in the collecting points. Among the Nazi collections, some pieces acquired by Hitler, Göring, Martin Bormann, and other top officials had been repatriated to claimant countries. But Valland believed additional works of French provenance remained in the collecting points.[84]

US authorities were well aware of the ownership complexities surrounding these pieces. In March 1948, Robert Murphy in the Office of the Political Advisor for Germany had informed the State Department that works formerly owned by Hitler and Baldur von Schirach, along with 90 percent of Göring's collection, were at the Munich collecting point. Most of the pieces were considered "restitutable" under US Military Law no. 59 or external restitution claims, but Murphy estimated "a fair amount" would remain in the collecting point. Some 2,500 paintings from the Linz collection presented a particular challenge, as they had been collected from both Germany and Austria, and the United States had no clear plans for their eventual disposal.[85]

For Valland, the Nazi-owned art provided the best hope for replacement in kind, as the United States and Britain continued to oppose restitution from German art collections, and she advocated distributing the items among liberated countries in proportion to wartime losses. She had learned that American MFAA officers were preparing a proposal to transfer the Göring hoard to German officials, on condition that it would be dispersed among various German museums and would not be known as "the Göring collection." Distributing the Nazi-owned objects to German museums, Valland argued, would legitimize Nazi art policy. Some German curators, she noted without identifying them, had told her they had no desire to take over stewardship of the Göring items.[86]

Beyond the Nazi collections, questions remained about thousands of other ownerless works that remained in the collecting points. American proposals lacked any kind of enforcement mechanism to ensure ownership research and restitution would continue under German control. The head of the French mission in the US zone, J. L. Bonet-Maury, feared it would be

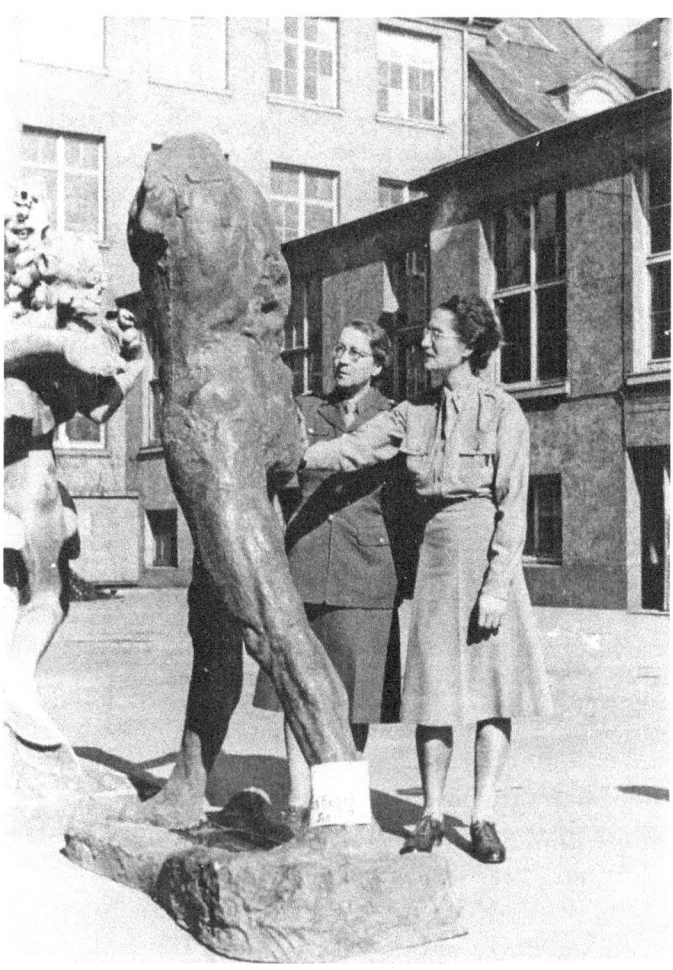

Rose Valland (left) and Edith Standen examine sculptures at the Wiesbaden Collecting Point. Archives of American Art, Smithsonian Institution.

impossible to require the Germans to restitute the items, even though the German government technically would become merely a guardian of the assets and not the full property owner.[87]

Nonetheless, American plans advanced with the imminent fusion of the three western zones. On May 18, 1949, the State Department summarized the progress of external restitution of all types of assets to that point and issued recommendations for the transfer of responsibility to Germany. The report underscores persistent differences in Allied positions and indicates how little the Allies knew about one another's restitution activities, even in the British and American bizone. The United States had determined in 1947 that "claims must arise from some element of dispossession [and that] property removed as a result of a transaction essentially commercial in character does not meet this standard and is not eligible for restitution," a shift away from the 1943 Inter-Allied Declaration. The Americans believed the British followed this approach.[88] According to the British RDR, however, the United Kingdom had widened its perspective of restitutable property since August 1948 to allow restitution when the enemy had exploited wartime circumstances to purchase works of art. British Foreign Office instructions, moreover, specified that items considered part of a nation's cultural patrimony were restituted, whether they had been stolen or purchased by the enemy.[89] Compared to US policy, the shift in the British approach better suited the demands of the liberated countries to restitute works of art sold during the occupation. But far more works had been recovered in the US zone.

There was also a lack of information on the transfer of items from western zones to the eastern zone under Soviet control. Amerian officials reported that up to the fall of 1947, the Soviets had "manifested only passing interest in restitution." Soviet claims received in the US zone often contained insufficient information, and when the Americans authorized the release of assets, the Soviets repeatedly failed to organize a restitution mission. From the Soviet perspective, the United States had violated international agreements by holding assets from the Baltic states. In March 1949 Soviet Marshal Sokolovsky accused American authorities of sabotaging restitution efforts, and he requested permission to inspect German factories and museums in the US zone for Soviet assets. Clay denied the charges and blamed the Soviets' own failure to cooperate.[90]

American officials also criticized the French for refusing to engage in interzonal exchanges pursued by the United States and Britain, and failing to communicate restitution statistics and their intended claims deadline.[91]

A French proposal from April 1949 also revealed differences in the two countries' visions for restitution after trizonal fusion. The French text would have created a restitution service in each of the western *Länder*, redefined restitutable property to include assets for which Germany had not provided an "economic equivalence," allowed restitution in kind for assets that had remained in Germany by order of the zone commander, and continued Allied missions in the western zones.[92]

American authorities rejected all of these French demands, as OMGUS aimed to end the restitution program with the establishment of a new government in Germany, and found it highly unlikely that additional repositories with significant assets would be discovered. According to the State Department, the Allied High Commission—the civilian successor to the ACC—would retain oversight of restitution operations and delegate responsibilities to Allied entities in the *Land* capitals. The State Department recommended all Allied restitution activities cease on March 31, 1950, allowing Germany to assume responsibility for cultural restitution.[93]

In an annex to the State Department report, cultural advisor Ardelia Hall acknowledged that the restitution of cultural assets "is today and will probably remain for many years one of the troublesome problems arising from World War II." She emphasized the importance of rejecting French claims to replacement in kind:

> Any replacement requiring the seizure of works of art belonging to another country has so many undesirable aspects that it has been generally renounced in modern times. The French view conflicts with accepted principles of respect for the cultural heritage of all peoples and is inconsistent with the program for the recovery of missing objects of art.[94]

According to Hall, UNESCO and the International Council of Museums (ICOM, established in 1946) would be appropriate bodies to maintain lists of lost cultural objects. ICOM could create a consolidated list of objects lost in all countries, and an international convention by ICOM, UNESCO, the UN nations and Germany would be satisfactory.[95] While acknowledging the long-term challenges presented by cultural restitution, Hall believed the international community might continue facilitating the repatriation of plundered works of art. "For the first time in history," she wrote in August 1951, "restitution may be expected to continue for as long as works of art known to have been plundered during a war continue to be discovered."[96]

Hall's optimism emanating from Washington, far away from the occupation zones and collecting points, contrasted starkly with Rose Valland's growing disillusionment in Berlin.

Restitution under the Federal Republic of Germany, 1949-52

In the broader Cold War struggle playing out in Berlin, the airlift led by the United States and Britain wore down Stalin's resolve and he lifted the blockade on May 12, 1949. A victory for the western Allies, the nearly yearlong standoff had helped convince western Europeans to pursue collective security under American leadership through the North Atlantic Treaty Organization (NATO), established in April 1949. Many Germans in the western zones who had been reluctant to divide their country felt a greater urgency to do so in response to Stalin's aggression in Berlin. A parliamentary council met on September 1, 1948, in Bonn and elected Konrad Adenauer as president. The council drafted a constitution that came into force on May 23, 1949, establishing the Federal Republic of Germany (FRG).[97] While the western Allies maintained occupation forces through the next six years, high commissioners headquartered in Bonn replaced the military governors and maintained control over key policy areas, including restitution, foreign policy, defense, and trade.[98]

Rose Valland continued to serve the restitution effort in this new phase of the Allied occupation. In September 1949 she defined three objectives: the reorganization of French cultural restitution services, continuation of French research missions in other Allied zones, and cooperation with a German restitution committee backed by the support of the Bonn government.[99] Working with colleagues in the French reparations and restitutions division in July 1949, she spearheaded the reorganization of French cultural restitution services under the French high commissioner. The new Service for the Return of Works of Art (SROA) headed by Valland had offices in West Berlin and in Baden-Baden, where the French continued to manage a collecting point and archive center.[100]

In her new capacity, Valland fostered positive relationships with other cultural officers and helped ensure restitution to German museums.[101] On September 9, 1949, a meeting of MFAA officers from the three western zones and a new German art restitution commission seemed to signal renewed international cooperation, with greater German involvement. The German commission convened six curators and museum directors from the three western zones—including Franz Graf Wolff Metternich, now a regional director in the British zone.[102] According to Valland, the Germans showed "sincere willingness to ensure the honest liquidation of the Hitler regime's plunder" and considered it in their interest to prevent the loot from entering German museum collections.[103] Some of the American officers, in her view, appeared to be biding time between the departure of General Clay and the arrival of the American High Commissioner, John McCloy. Restitutions from the US zone had all but ceased, following Clay's directives, but some American MFAA personnel remained in place and had expressed solidarity with Valland, hoping to continue the mission. With the change in American military leadership and the German commission in place, she saw an opportunity for renewed restitution operations.[104]

Valland's hope for more robust international cooperation was short-lived, as higher authorities from all three western countries aimed to cease operations, close the collecting points, and transfer restitution responsibility to the Germans. The French restitution mission in the US zone was dissolved in October 1949, and three months later, British restitution services announced a deadline of March 31, 1950, for claims processing in the UK zone.[105] American authorities aimed to close their collecting points in 1951 and redeployed Monuments Men Thomas Howe and Lane Faison to oversee the closures at Wiesbaden and Munich, respectively.[106]

Toward the end of 1950 a contentious debate emerged between French and American authorities over the fate of works of art recovered from Nazi repositories in Austria. Like Germany, Austria had been divided into four Allied occupation zones. The eastern Soviet zone surrounded Vienna and the Austrian capital was divided into five sectors, one for each of the occupying powers, plus an international zone at the city center.[107] The US zone contained the massive Alt Aussee mine, and by then the MFAA had transferred most of the objects to the Munich collecting point. Although masterpieces such as the Ghent Altarpiece and Vermeer's *Astronomer* had been repatriated, thousands of works from Nazi collections found in Austria remained in Munich.[108] Valland had learned from "an absolutely reliable source" that the United States planned to transfer works to Austria.[109] The pieces would be received by MFAA officers in the US zone, but Valland feared the objects would be promptly transferred to the Austrian government.[110]

The plan had been developed by US occupation authorities in Frankfurt, not by the MFAA, and Faison also was shocked to learn of the planned transfer of works to Austria. The news, Faison later recounted, "took my breath away," as "there was no proof that these works had been acquired in Austria."[111] He saw great irony in the fact that most of the works found at Alt Aussee had previously been evacuated from Munich for safekeeping. A German reporter with *Abendzeitung* picked up the story and wrote a scathing article in August 1951, prompting a brief public relations flap. "Wires were buzzing between the offices of the High Commissioner in Frankfurt and the Land Commissioner in Munich," Faison later recalled, and that the latter "got me on the phone in a rage and tore me apart."[112] For these officials, the problem was not the plan, which moved forward, but the embarrassing news leak.

Valland repeatedly tried to convince higher French authorities to oppose the transfer of art to Austria. "It is unacceptable," she argued to the French RDR, "that Austria, like Bavaria, become the beneficiary of plunder by Rosenberg, Göring or Hitler, while despoiled countries have not received the original or equivalent that was stolen from them." She suggested that French diplomats renegotiating occupation terms with British and American counterparts in London could require a clause forbidding the transfer of Nazi collections without an Allied agreement.[113]

Valland's frustration was compounded by news in late May 1951 that the Wiesbaden and Munich collecting points would close on June 15. She learned of the closures once again by chance—from a source in Wiesbaden, most likely Thomas Howe. She felt "brutally confronted with unexpected decisions" by American officials, for whom all that mattered was how fast one could "put the key under the door and leave." With the imminent closures, all objects still in the collecting points would be given to the former enemy: "Nazi spoliation thus will end up enriching the Germans and probably the Austrians."[114]

American oversight of the collecting points lasted a bit longer than expected, until August 1951. Valland met with Faison and other American officers in Munich shortly before the end of US operations and observed staff packing up some thirteen hundred works of art for shipment to Austria. She appreciated the understanding displayed by her American MFAA colleagues, but made a last ditch attempt to stop the shipment. In a small victory, Valland convinced the Americans to hold around one hundred objects from the collection of the former police prefect of Berlin, Ditter von Dittersdorf, with possible French provenance. Separately she admitted to French authorities she was not "absolutely convinced of the value of the pretext given to maintain control over these paintings." She also noted "nervousness" in the German artistic community over the shipment of art to Austria and the potential for negative press in German newspapers. "It's possible," she mused, "that the Americans are more sensitive to German displeasure than French protests!" Nonetheless, Valland argued, the French had a duty to oppose the transfer of Nazi-owned works to Austria on behalf of despoiled French owners as well as the Germans, who would see in this operation "a denial of the principles on which we have based all of our restitutions."[115]

Despite Valland's persistent opposition, on January 18 and 22, 1952, 967 works from Nazi collections were shipped from the Munich collecting point to the Neue Residenz, a Baroque palace in Salzburg. According to a statement by the US State Commissioner for Bavaria Oron Hale, American authorities in Austria would hold the works "pending the establishment of satisfactory arrangements for further identification and just determination as to their ultimate disposition."[116] Writing in the *College Art Journal*, Ardelia Hall euphemistically called the objects "residual works of art" and a mere 3.5 percent of the twenty-seven thousand pieces recovered from Austrian repositories. Some thirteen thousand works had been repatriated to Allied countries, she explained, while 8,500 other pieces were restituted to private German owners, and 3,600 had been identified as property of the German federal government.[117]

French officials had mixed reactions to the transfer. Valland, naturally, was outraged and argued that Austria "abusively" claimed to be a victim nation of the Third Reich.[118] But some of her compatriots were less alarmed. G. H. Pommery, head of the Office for Personal Property and Interests (OBIP) delegation in Austria, planned to inspect the paintings once they were unpacked and believed that "legitimate restitution rights of property owners will be maintained until the end." He considered Valland's fears "unfounded" and preferred to "stick to facts." Neither the Americans nor the Austrians, in his view, would question the French right to continue claiming works of art shipped to Austria.[119]

Soon afterward, however, that right to restitution seemed to slip further away when the United States remitted some two thousand other Nazi-owned pieces to Bavarian authorities. Most of the pieces had belonged to Nazi officials—Hoffmann, Schirach, Göring, Frank—whose descendants were living in Bavaria. After the distribution to Austria and Bavaria, American occupation authorities transferred the remaining two to three thousand objects from Nazi collections to the German federal government. According to Valland, the most competent American personnel, apparently a reference to Faison and Howe, had been sent home and remaining authorities were merely wrapping up operations.[120]

Behind the scenes other French officials echoed Valland's view and recognized that they had reached a turning point. One OBIP representative, a M. Amphoux, wrote in his personal notes, "The principle of restitutions has been maintained, but in fact a page has turned. No official means to take back works of art from the current holder."[121] By the end of 1952, there were no illusions that the French and other liberated countries could claim pieces from Nazi art collections for restitution in kind. For Valland, 1952 also was a year of personal transitions, as she stepped down as head of the SROA and returned to the National Museum administration in Paris, becoming head of the Service for the Protection of Artworks (SPOA). In this new role, she developed a program to protect objects in the event of nuclear war, a sign that Europe had entered a new strategic era, and continued to manage French art claims from West Germany. She provided information to potential claimants, facilitated the restitution of archives from the Federal Republic, and in 1962 worked with the TVK in Munich to restitute two sculptures from the Seligmann collection. The same year, Valland also managed eighty new French claims for compensation from Germany.[122] In 1960 she published memoirs on her wartime experiences resisting the Nazis at the Jeu de Paume. Her account ends in 1945, omitting nearly all of her more politically sensitive restitution efforts in Germany.[123]

The End of the Allied Occupation

By the early 1950s, the western Allies had political, diplomatic, and economic reasons to end restitution operations. Key leaders—French Foreign Minister Robert Schuman, French Economic Advisor Jean Monnet, American Secretary of State Dean Acheson, and West German Chancellor Konrad Adenauer—pursued a vision of European prosperity with West German cooperation.[124] For Adenauer, this meant scaling back restitution demands from the FRG. As historian William Hitchcock puts it, "the Germans would not commit themselves to the West until the West demonstrated its goodwill toward the Germans."[125] In this more cooperative spirit, western Europe reached a milestone in April 1951 as foreign ministers from France, West

Germany, Italy, Belgium, the Netherlands, and Luxembourg signed the Treaty of Paris creating the European Coal and Steel Community.[126]

At the same time, negotiations to end the occupation of West Germany stalled over the issue of rearmament. The Bonn accords of May 1952 envisioned the creation of a European Defense Community, in which West German forces would be integrated into a European army. The idea had been proposed by French Prime Minister René Pleven in October 1950 but faced significant criticism from the French press and public, and in August 1954 was rejected by the French parliament. Another round of negotiations eliminated the common defense plan and allowed West Germany to join NATO. The Paris Treaties signed on October 23, 1954, came into force on May 5, 1955, ending the western occupation of Germany.[127] However, the western Allies maintained influence in deciding legal disputes over restitution through Supreme Restitution Courts, one in West Berlin and one to replace restitution tribunals overseen by the three powers in each of the western zones, in Rastatt, Herford, and Nuremberg. In Berlin and in each division, a judge from a neutral country presided over an equal number of Allied and German justices.[128]

Following terms of agreements elaborated by the western Allies, the FRG established institutions to continue restitution processes. In February 1952, the West German government created the *Treuhandverwaltung von Kulturgut* (Fiduciary Administration for Cultural Assets, or TVK) in the foreign affairs ministry to oversee the conservation and restitution of works remaining in the collecting points. With the end of the occupation, the FRG established the *Bundesamt für äussere Restitutionen* (Federal Office for External Restitutions) under the finance ministry. From 1952 to 1962, the TVK continued to carry out ownership research using ERR lists of plundered art, some sixty thousand property cards and five thousand photographs created at the US collecting points, 143 declarations of art acquisitions in France by German collectors, and MFAA and intelligence reports from the early postwar years.[129]

This research continued amid growing West German resentment toward Allied restitution polices. Internal claims pitted Jewish former owners against current non-Jewish and German property holders, and the latter mobilized to protect their property rights and seek compensation for restituted assets, especially real estate. Many Germans associated restitution legislation and the JRSO with excessive de-Nazification policies imposed by the Allies. Compensation measures were less controversial, as they involved the German state rather than individual property owners. In the early 1950s the FRG negotiated directly with the state of Israel and the Conference on Jewish Material Claims against Germany (Claims Conference), and in 1952 agreed to pay the latter DM 450 million.[130]

The international restitution effort ceased with the end of the western Allied occupation in 1955. The failure of the Allies to establish an international restitution commission left national governments in full control of repatriated works, with the ability to exploit ownerless works as they saw fit. The finest of these pieces were worthy of the great art museums of France, the Netherlands, and Belgium. While these governments failed to receive cultural replacement in kind from Germany, they appropriated scores of orphaned objects to restore each nation's cultural heritage.

4
Recovered Art as French Patrimony

In the summer of 1946, a small museum located in the Tuileries garden in Paris once again held hundreds of Nazi-looted artworks. Whereas the Germans had inventoried the loot at the Jeu de Paume during the occupation, this time the works were displayed at the Musée National de l'Orangerie, an architectural pendant to the Jeu de Paume, to celebrate the Allied art recovery effort. The Orangerie, home to Claude Monet's famous water lily panels, hosted an exhibition of 283 repatriated pieces—Vermeer's *Astronomer*, Chardin's *Soap Bubbles*, a Vigée Le Brun portrait of Marie Antoinette, and paintings by Watteau, Fragonard, Delacroix, Boucher, Cézanne, Monet, Matisse, Rembrandt, and Van Gogh, as well as numerous decorative objects. The show drew record crowds for the small museum. In the few months these works were displayed together, a total of 122,399 visitors enjoyed the exhibition, making it one of the most successful shows held to that point at the Orangerie.[1]

The exhibition catalog features a preface by the president of the CRA, Albert Henraux, who proclaimed that "efforts to reconstitute the national patrimony were not in vain."[2] Yet the catalog fails to mention a crucial point: most of the plundered artworks had been owned by Jews. The early postwar notions of a restored French *patrimoine national*, the nation's cultural heritage, illustrates a tension between universalist conceptions of nationwide loss wrought by the Nazis and their collaborators, and the particular loss of life and property by Jews in the context of the Final Solution.[3]

Under the Germans, France had lost many more works than had Belgium and the Netherlands, and after the war it managed the largest stash of repatriated pieces, while consigning the smallest percentage to museums and other state entities. By the end of 1950, France had recovered more than 61,000 works of art, of which some 45,000—roughly 74 percent—had been restituted to private owners.[4] Still, by the end of the 1940s the French government held thousands of ownerless objects that were worthy of public art museums, embassies, and other government buildings. Between 1949 and 1953, a committee of experts in several government divisions reserved some

2,100 objects for public use, or around 3 percent of all recovered works and 13 percent of ownerless objects.[5]

In the context of disillusionment over Allied reparations and restitution negotiations, the cache of unclaimed art created an opportunity for France to enhance state art collections during a period of economic reconstruction, when it would have been impossible for the state to purchase comparable works on the international art market. France, like Belgium and the Netherlands, also held extensive archives on German plundering operations that could have been used to trace the unclaimed objects to rightful owners. According to cultural property norms of the time, however, government agencies only processed claims; they were under no obligation, legal or ethical, to search for rightful owners. And amid the return to republicanism, French Jews no longer constituted a distinct legal minority and thus did not benefit from legal measures that might have recognized their particular losses. While liberated from Vichy's antisemitic policies, Jews in early postwar France faced obstacles in the restitution of all manner of plundered assets—real estate, household effects, books, and art collections.[6] The dispossession of Jews wrought by the Nazis and their collaborators thus continued, in some cases into the twenty-first century.

The Restitution of Private Art Collections

As combat continued in the Low Countries in the fall of 1944, France, the Netherlands, and Belgium all established national art recovery commissions. According to Michel Florisoone, a curator at the Louvre and head of administration in the CRA, the French commission shared a threefold aim with the other national and international cultural agencies: the protection of cultural objects, recovery of works looted by the Nazis, and the "reconstitution of national heritage."[7] Florisoone's definition emphasizes the importance of heritage and national patrimony, without specifying restitution to private owners, even though they were the primary victims of Nazi plunder, and public art collections emerged from the occupation largely intact. Notions of public and private ownership thus were indistinct in the concept of *patrimoine national*, allowing the state to become the steward of unclaimed items.

Members of the French CRA began meeting informally in September 1944, two months before the entity was officially created.[8] An administrative order defined the commission's two primary goals: to study problems posed by the recovery of art taken from French territory by the enemy or under its control—phrasing that included Vichy collaboration with the Nazis—and managing claims and information about these objects from public entities or French nationals.[9] The commission fittingly established its headquarters at the Jeu de Paume museum, where the ERR had inventoried and sorted the looted collections from western Europe. At the urging of the National Library director and Buchenwald survivor Julien Caïn, the commission's purview expanded in June 1945 with the creation of a section devoted to the recovery of books, archives, and manuscripts.[10]

Jacques Jaujard initially headed the CRA, but with his promotion to director general of arts and letters, the task shifted to Albert Henraux, curator of the Condé museum in Chantilly and president of the Friends of the Louvre advisory organization. Florisoone managed administrative operations and other members included René Huyghe, head curator in the Louvre Department of Paintings, and Georges Salles, Jaujard's successor as director of national museums.[11] Rose Valland served as secretary but attended only the first three meetings from September to December 1944, as she joined the French art recovery effort in Germany as a captain in the French First Army. Eventually, she headed the fine arts division in the French section of the ACC in Berlin and played a key role in the restitution process, for France and other formerly occupied countries. Also central to the French recovery effort was museum inspector Pierre Louis Duchartre, who represented the CRA at the Central Collecting Point in Munich.[12]

The postwar fine arts administration and CRA benefited from the prestige of members who had joined or supported the Resistance, including Jaujard, Huyghe, and Valland. Most CRA members had been civil servants under the Vichy regime, but operated in the middle strata of the bureaucracy, untainted by the accommodations of German demands by Jérôme Carcopino and Louis Hautecoeur, and the more strident cultural collaboration pursued from April 1942 by Carcopino's fascist successor, Abel Bonnard.[13] This continuity in personnel eased the French administration's transition to the art recovery process. Valland, in particular, harnessed her extensive knowledge as a witness to Nazi looting operations, documented in photographs and extensive notes she had compiled on plundered private collections and the destination of art convoys.[14]

After the MFAA repatriated plundered artworks to France, the largest and most prestigious Jewish collections, once the most obvious targets for Nazi looting, returned to their owners with the fewest complications. Elite collectors and dealers held the required ownership documentation for many items—sales receipts, insurance policies, wills, contracts for exhibition loans, and photographs of their galleries and decorated homes. Curators working for the CRA were already familiar with many pieces from the great private collections; no one doubted, for instance, that Vermeer's *Astronomer* belonged to Edouard de Rothschild. Stamps and seals on the back of paintings confirmed rightful ownership, as did servants who had worked among the objects and dusted museum-quality furniture. German archives recovered by the Allies helped validate information in the claims, along with Rose Valland's notes on wartime German shipments from the Jeu de Paume.[15]

Most of the art looted from France had been owned by a handful of Jewish families, some of whom had sought refuge in the United States during the war. More than ten thousand pieces came from the Rothschild, David-Weill, Kann, and Seligmann families alone. The Wildenstein and Paul Rosenberg families also lost hundreds of works each. As a result, this elite group of large collectors and gallery owners, making up only 5 percent of despoiled collectors, owned 75 percent of the plundered art. French authorities returned thousands of works to members of the Rothschild family—1,300 to Maurice de Rothschild, including 256 paintings and drawings, more than one thousand objects to Alexandrine, and three hundred to Edmond. The Seligmann family recovered nearly seven hundred objects, including 188 paintings and drawings; the Stern family, five hundred.[16]

Beyond the most prestigious collections, the task of restitution became much more complicated. Aiming to reach owners who were not so directly connected to the national arts administration, the CRA publicized the claims process in newspapers and radio broadcasts. Claimants were instructed to submit several copies of a detailed inventory of plundered items, a description of the circumstances of the theft, and proof of ownership. The commission created two index cards for each claimed object, organized first by artwork category (painting, sculpture, drawing, tapestry, decorative object), then by subcategories of the artist and claimant. Between 1944 and 1949, the CRA processed 2,289 claims for some eighty-five thousand objects.[17]

The CRA submitted information from the index cards to the French Reparations and Restitutions office in Germany, which issued a ten-volume report on Nazi plunder of a wide range of assets, the *Répertoire des biens spoliés*. Published between 1947 and 1949, the *Répertoire* detailed the loss of industrial materials, agricultural machinery, railway cars, horses, and works of art. Volume II provided lists of paintings, tapestries, and sculpture with an index of artists; volumes III and IV listed furniture and decorative art, respectively.[18] Aiming to facilitate identification of objects that ended up on the art market or in foreign collections, French and American occupation authorities distributed the volumes on cultural assets to museums, galleries, and customs officials in their own countries, and in Germany and Austria.[19]

By September 1944, the CRA had recruited thirty-eight specialists to review claims, including experts from the Louvre, the National Museum of Antiquities, the National Library and the National Archives. In the next six years, the corps of French specialists serving the CRA and the MFAA grew to around one hundred art experts.[20] After reviewing claims to repatriated items, the CRA sent copies of successful dossiers to OBIP in the Ministry of Foreign Affairs, which initiated restitution procedures to private owners. For works still held in collecting points in western Germany, OBIP submitted claims to the MFAA and oversaw restitution to individuals once the objects were on French soil.[21] Works found in neutral countries, a haven for Nazi assets, required international agreements. One such agreement, reached by Switzerland on one side and by France, Britain, and the United States on the other, allowed French owners to claim stolen works found on Swiss soil until December 31, 1947. The results were meager. Paul Rosenberg, Alexandrine de Rothschild, and Raoul Mayer recovered a handful of pieces through the agreement, and by January 1950, France had recovered a total of thirty-nine objects,[22] likely a mere fraction of the works in Switzerland plundered from French collections.

The CRA panel rejected claims on several grounds, such as insufficient proof of ownership, sales or transfers of property that fell outside the purview of the CRA, or evidence of voluntary sales to the enemy.[23] In some cases involving voluntary sales, the CRA granted restitution to the seller upon payment of the sale amount to the French treasury. The extent of coercion in these transactions, however, was often ambiguous in available records. For instance, the commission required a claimant to a Watteau painting from the Thiebault-Sisson collection, *Portrait de l'acteur Poisson*, to cede RM 100,000 in German treasury bonds held at the Dresdner Bank in Berlin. Another claimant of a Guardi painting, *The Crucifixion*, from the P. W. Leuner collection, was required to pay the sale price of Ff 100,000.[24]

At other times, the French government required payment for the recovery of items that clearly had changed hands through forced sales. One such case involved a Goya painting, *Portrait of Don Manuel Garcia de la Prada*, once owned by Jewish collectors John and Anna Jaffé. The couple were British citizens who had enjoyed retirement on the French Riviera, and for fifty years entertained guests in a sumptuous villa on the Promenade des Anglais in Nice. Generous benefactors to numerous charities, they amassed a well-known art collection with paintings by Rembrandt, Turner, Constable, and Guardi. John died in Nice in 1934, and with Anna's passing in March 1942, the French Commissariat for Jewish Affairs seized all of the Jaffé property—the villa, quality furniture, jewels—and sold the art collection at auction in July 1943. A Monsieur Dutey purchased the Goya picture and promptly resold it.[25] After the war, the painting returned to France, but restitution was complicated by the fact that in 1930, John had bequeathed it, along with a picture each by Guardi and Rembrandt, to the National Gallery in London. An ownership struggle ensued between the National Gallery and the Jaffé heirs, and in November 1947, a Paris tribunal ruled in favor of the latter, finding that Anna as sole heir had bequeathed the pictures to her descendants—a niece and three nephews.[26] The Goya painting was finally restituted to Jaffé heirs in November 1951, but the government required a payment of Ff 48.486, the "amount received with the sale of this work by order of the General Commissariat for Jewish Affairs."[27] The passive voice in the decision obscures who exactly had "received" the amount. A central principle of the CRA, as articulated by Florisoone in January 1950, was that "no restitution fee should be paid by owners." Yet the state apparently determined that the heirs had received compensation for the sale.[28]

As for the number of works repatriated to France, in January 1950 Florisoone compiled the best data on the first four years of the recovery effort, figures he updated later that year in June and November.[29] He provided the following statistics:

Table 4.1 Location of works repatriated to France by 1950

Germany and Austria	58,477
Italy	10
Switzerland	39
Belgium	4
France	1,895
Czechoslovakia	808
Total	61,233

Table 4.2 Restitution to owners of repatriated works

From Germany, to:	
Individuals (includes 1,600 pieces of David-Weill family silver)	33,509
Musée de l'Armée (Army Museum)	1,444
Domaines (includes porcelain, damaged during transport from Buxheim)	3,080
OBIP, Strasbourg	583
Austria	4,973
France	1,762
Italy	9
Belgium	3
Switzerland	20
Czechoslovakia	58
Total restituted works	**45,441**
Other items held by French government	
Objects found in France and not claimed, transferred to Domaines	383
Objects transferred to Office of French Museums	1,333
Total restituted and government-held objects	**47,157**

Table 4.3 Items liquidated by French government

Repatriated (61,233) minus restituted and state-held objects (47,157). Includes:	14,076
Frames without artistic value given to Domaines	1,800
Canvases and frames given to Entraide charity	200
Works left by Germans at Jeu de Paume, transferred to Domaines	3,580
Various objects without artistic value transferred to OBIP between May 1947 and July 1949	202
Objects handed over to restitution services of OBIP March 20, 1945	20
Objects transferred from CRA to OBIP 1 January 1950 (figure from November 1950 addendum)	8,298

Source for tables 4.1, 4.2, 4.3: Florisoone, "La Commission de Récupération Artistique," January 1950, AN AMN O 30-438; Florisoone, "Addendum au Rapport sur la Commission de Récupération Artistique: Tableau numérique des œuvres récupérées et des œuvres restituées," n.d.; addendum cover letter from Henraux to Jaujard, June 7, 1950, AN AMN 2MM6.

As one might expect in a report on thousands of objects, there is a good deal of ambiguity in Florisoone's numbers. A "piece" or "object" could be one silver object or a set, such as a tea service; it could refer to a masterpiece or a low-quality fauteuil. In an apparent inconsistency, the January report indicates that 3,580 pieces were left by the Germans at the Jeu de Paume but only 1,895 objects were found in France, the latter figure confirmed in the June addendum. Also unclear is the "restitution" of 3,080 damaged objects—porcelain and ceramics—recovered from the Buxheim monastery and transferred to the Domaines state property agency. Florisoone indicates that twenty pieces were transferred to "restitution services," most likely a reference to lower-quality furniture that did not qualify as "works of art" and were managed by another office charged with processing claims for household items and musical instruments.[30]

The Mattéoli Commission report published in 2000 uses Florisoone's numbers from 1950 to indicate the total number of objects repatriated to France (61,233),[31] though nearly five hundred additional items were recovered in 1950 and 1951. Rose Valland also reported two convoys from Germany in January and July 1952, without specifying the number of repatriated objects. The total number of recovered pieces thus most likely falls between sixty-one thousand and sixty-two thousand items.[32] Given that claims for 107,566 objects and assemblages were submitted to the CRA by March 22, 1947, the recovery rate of plundered works may be as low as 57 percent—meaning roughly half the works plundered from France were destroyed during the war or were dispersed in unknown locations.[33]

With millions of art objects, books, and archive collections traversing the European continent, some items were bound to disappear. Even the head of the CRA, Albert Henraux, worried he had misplaced a painting. In February 1952, he contacted Florisoone about an inquiry by British MFAA officer Douglas Cooper, who claimed to have entrusted to Henraux a small, fourteenth-century painting, *Head of Christ Crucified*, sometime in 1945. According to Cooper, Henraux had placed the painting in his office closet in the Jeu de Paume. Henraux remembered nothing about the painting, but found Cooper's claim plausible, admitting, "I am increasingly losing my memory." With the help of a few museum staff members, Henraux searched CRA offices and correspondence for signs of the missing painting, to no avail. Florisoone suggested that Henraux ask Cooper for the receipt, "which you surely gave him."[34] The correspondence ends there, with the head of the CRA awkwardly caught in a case of missing painting.

Some art collectors who successfully recovered objects expressed gratitude by donating pieces to the Louvre and other museums. In September 1945, Henraux announced that Madame Richard Thalmann had donated to the Louvre a black lacquer Louis XV chest of drawers stamped by seventeenth-century cabinetmaker Jacques Dubois. Paul Rosenberg donated thirty-three paintings and two drawings to provincial museums and promised the Louvre additional donations.[35] Inspired by the exhibition of repatriated works at the Orangerie in 1946, art critic Waldemar George suggested that David David-Weill and Maurice de Rothschild ought to consider donating works to American museums in gratitude toward the kindred Republic that had ensured the safe return of the masterpieces from the former Reich.[36] Though such largesse did not extend across the Atlantic, the Louvre did enjoy additional donations from owners wishing to express "gratitude to the state": fifteen gold and silver pieces from David-Weill, paintings by Murillo and Hubert Robert from Victor Lyon; a Gainsborough portrait from Robert de Rothschild, a Houdon bust from the descendants of Arthur Veil-Picard, and a Van Eyck portrait from those of Edouard de Rothschild.[37]

Despite these restitution success stories, the process was not always seamless. Jewish-owned works held by the Vichy regime, in an acquisition scheme carried out by some of the same civil servants who served the postwar arts administration, created additional legal entanglements as owners anxiously waited to receive their assets.

The Restitution of Sequestered Collections

One challenge faced by the provisional government was management of items sequestered from Jewish and Masonic collections during the occupation, and the forty-nine pieces selected from the Schloss collection.[38] The men who remained in the civil service from Vichy and into the postwar arts administration—Jacques Jaujard, René Huyghe, and Germain Bazin—did not attempt to follow through on the wartime acquisition efforts; with the provisional government's nullification of spoliation laws in November 1944,[39] the works were no longer considered "ownerless." However, the state's temporary possession of the collections greatly complicated the restitution process. The new director of national museums, Georges Salles, oversaw the legal transfer of ownership, a process that took months—to the despoiled owners' great frustration.

A series of ordinances in 1944 allowed the restitution of assets acquired by the French government during the occupation. An ordinance of August 9 reestablished the rule of law under the Republic and nullified antisemitic legislation enacted by the Vichy regime; another promulgated on October 16 invalidated spoliation committed "by the enemy and under its control"; a third measure from November 14 created procedures to restitute property still held by provisional administrators, but postponed for future legislation the management of assets that had been liquidated or acquired by the state, including the sequestered art collections.[40]

In the meantime, Salles tackled the legal complexities surrounding the sequestered collections. The case of Jacques May was most easily solved. This collection of eighteenth-century paintings, furniture, and decorative objects had been selected by curators for the Versailles palace. For several months after the Liberation, May had received no information about his collection, and he grew increasingly suspicious of French cultural authorities. He demanded the immediate return of his *ancien régime* objects. Salles was caught in legislative limbo and unable to restitute sequestered objects without further legislation. But he saw a loophole in the May case, as the French state had not paid for the objects. Salles consulted with the Domaines state property agency, while May continued to endure unpleasant mail and telephone exchanges with museum office staff. He finally received his collection in July 1945.[41]

By February 1946, the arts administration had received restitution claims for the Bois and Weiller collections and for four Rothschild collections, owned by Maurice, Robert, Edouard, and Henri. Jacques Jaujard, having been promoted to director of arts and letters, drafted the retrocession order for the Council of State with a revisionist justification for sequestration. Whereas during the occupation, Louvre curator René Huyghe had aimed to "fill gaps" in the museum's collection,[42] Jaujard now described the wartime acquisition as a way to shield certain private collections from German looting; the works' "artistic value made it necessary to keep them in France."[43] The Council of State granted retrocession by early April 1946 and the owners recovered their collections over the next few years; Maurice de Rothschild waited until April 27, 1949.[44]

The case of Elie-Joseph Bois was the most complex among the sequestered collections, as competing claims among his descendants delayed restitution. In the early twentieth century, Bois had enjoyed a successful journalism career in Paris, culminating in his appointment in 1914 as editor in chief of the moderate daily *Le Petit-Parisien*, one of the most important French newspapers at the time. Bois frequented the Parisian cultural and literary elite, and his artist friends included Vlaminck, Derain, Dunoyer de Segonzac, and Chagall. Feeling threatened as German troops advanced toward Paris in June 1940, he resigned from *Le Petit-Parisien* and fled with his wife—his third marriage—to London, at age sixty-two. The Vichy regime stripped his citizenship in September 1940 and seized his assets in Paris. He continued writing in London for British newspapers, gave lectures, and in 1941 published *Les Malheurs de la France* (*Truth on the Tragedy of France*). In a letter to his sister Marie and his younger son Léonce, he wrote in July 1940, "If my words can reach Léonce, my little Marie, tell him my mind often searches for him.... I left to serve my fatherland, and rest assured I will make you all proud. I have faith the day will come when you are able to join me."[45] He became ill after hiding in a cellar during an air raid alert and died on April 27, 1941, without knowing that his older son had been "slaughtered by the Germans," according to fellow writer Robert Christophe.[46]

Meanwhile in Paris, during Bois's final days, the Direction des Musées was examining his sequestered art collection to determine which pieces would be worthy of French national museums. It contained coveted items, including a dozen engravings by Dunoyer de Segonzac, seventeen framed drawings by Luc-Albert Moreau, and an album of ten Matisse lithographs. Curator Pierre Ladoué requested these works for the Musée national d'art moderne (MNAM) on May 15, 1941, and a decree from December 31, 1942, indicates that Ff 39,000 francs had been paid for the "definitive acquisition" of the objects. In July 1944, just weeks before the Liberation, Jaujard confirmed to Ladoué that the pieces had been acquired for the museum.[47]

Once the purchase was invalidated by postwar legislation, the education ministry approved restitution to Madame Blayo Bois on April 4, 1946.[48] Several Bois heirs, however, jointly contested her claim. Bois's first two wives, his younger son Léonce, and the widow of his older son filed a lawsuit arguing that Elie and Madame Blayo Bois had negotiated a prenuptial agreement in 1936. However, a civil court found the agreement applied to personal effects such as clothing and jewelry, not the assets jointly used by the spouses in their homes, such as art and furniture. Léonce and Madame Blayo Bois reached an agreement in July 1953 that the former would receive the twelve Dunoyer de Segonzac engravings. In the end, the Direction des Musées transferred ownership of all the pieces to her on July 28, 1954.[49]

Salles and his colleagues hoped the Ff 66 million previously authorized for the sequestered collections and additional art purchases would be maintained in the budget. According to a law of June 16, 1948, the Direction des Musées could recover the value of assets restituted to victims of spoliation, with interest. OBIP thus initially credited the museum system's account with Ff 68,690,466, mostly in treasury bonds. However, since the postwar staff argued that the office merely had served as the custodian of the Jewish assets, and not truly acquired them, the government's central accounting office withdrew the funding. In April 1953, the museum office restored the Ff 68 million credit to the treasury, again mostly in treasury bonds.[50]

As for the forty-nine paintings from the Schloss collection selected for the Louvre by curators Huyghe and Bazin, the rightful owners faced a different series of bureaucratic and legal entanglements. The Schloss heirs had remained in France and maintained their citizenship under the Vichy regime. Thus in legal terms, the paintings were not sequestered, ownerless assets; the government had negotiated a deal with Göring to select the best pieces. Legislation on sequestered assets did not apply to these paintings, and Huyghe, having doggedly attempted to acquire them for the Louvre since the late 1930s, hoped to secure a donation or purchase agreement from the heirs.[51]

Soon after the Liberation, Salles met with one of the Schloss descendants, Madame Prosper-Emile Weil, née Juliette Schloss, to discuss a possible donation to the Louvre. In a follow-up letter drafted by Huyghe in November 1944, Salles explained that the Louvre had tried to protect the most famous paintings in the collection from German theft, as well as lesser-known works with research value for art historians and students. A few weeks later, the Schloss family attorney, Max Gonfreville, informed Huyghe that his clients would keep the Louvre in mind if they decided to sell some pieces, but in the meantime, they categorically rejected the proposed acquisition and wanted their paintings back—immediately.[52] Faced with the reality that the Louvre would not acquire the Schloss pieces, Huyghe wrote to Salles, "I deeply regret [the heirs] did not feel the need to recognize through a kind gesture that the Louvre had saved the principal masterpieces of their collection. But given the circumstances, there is nothing else we can do."[53]

Legal issues remained, however, as Salles tried to determine whether he or the CRA held authority to restitute the paintings. He reported to the CRA in February 1945 that the heirs were demanding restitution "in an imperious fashion."[54] Bureaucracy delayed restitution for another year and a half, until

July 26, 1946.⁵⁵ Germain Bazin later claimed in his memoirs that the Schloss paintings were "immediately [*aussitôt*] returned to their owners after the Liberation,"⁵⁶ omitting the government's efforts to keep them.

While those works eluded the Louvre for the time being, Huyghe secured two Rembrandt paintings, *Portrait of Titus*, once owned by Catherine the Great, and *Landscape with a Chateau*. In 1942, wine merchant Etienne Nicolas had sold them to German dealer Karl Haberstock for sixty million francs, a payment issued by the German embassy. Nicolas had acquired them in 1935, taking advantage of the Soviet government's sale of works from the Hermitage. The wartime sale to Haberstock was by no means carried out under duress. Nicolas was a savvy businessman, unaffected by exclusionary laws, and took advantage of German willingness to pay exorbitant prices for Rembrandts. Eventually, the MFAA found the paintings in the US zone in Germany and returned them to France. In a meeting on September 27, 1945, the CRA discussed whether it was required to restitute paintings to an individual who had freely sold them to the Germans during the war. Jaujard argued that since the Americans had repatriated works voluntarily sold to the Germans, the CRA should sequester them without initiating restitution to Nicolas. Other commission members deemed it more prudent to seek an official donation agreement, which it secured from Nicolas in 1948.⁵⁷

As with all donations, the acquisition of the two Rembrandts required approval by an advisory council. On December 2, 1948, Huyghe presented the paintings to the council and emphasized the importance of the landscape painting, as the Louvre lacked this dimension of Rembrandt's oeuvre—phrasing that recalls his earlier aim to fill a regrettable "gap" with the Rembrandt landscape from the Schloss collection.⁵⁸ The council, once again headed by David David-Weill, unanimously approved the acquisition and a few weeks later, the committee of Musées nationaux curators thanked Henraux for "the active role he played in this magnificent result benefitting national museums."⁵⁹

The Nation's Patrimony

With the end of the occupation, the museum office had another opportunity to secure "ownerless" works—objects recovered from Germany that had not been restituted to private owners. A proposal to acquire the works for state collections was floated by the provisional government within months of the Liberation. In March 1945, Education Minister René Capitant sought approval from the finance ministry to purchase for French museums any recovered objects that had not been restituted within three years. He envisioned a special credit, outside the usual museum budget that would enable the state to exercise a right of first refusal on unclaimed works that normally would be sold at public auction—the same mechanism used toward sequestered collections during the occupation. Capitant believed this solution would "effectively defend the wealth of French collections and our national patrimony."[60]

In the end, French law allowed the Direction des Musées to become the custodian of the chosen pieces without fully acquiring and purchasing them. An ordinance from April 21, 1945[61] allowed the Domaines agency to transfer property that was not restituted to private owners within two years after the end of the war. Given complexities in the recovery and claims process, the government extended the deadline twice, in August 1945 and October 1947, and continued accepting claims.[62] The September 1949 decree that dissolved the CRA also provided for two selection committees charged with choosing the finest works of art and books to be held in trusteeship by the French state.[63] In reality, the art committee already had been operating informally for more than a year. Henraux informed Salles in June 1948 that the committee was "charged with selecting works of art taken or purchased by the enemy or its intermediaries during the occupation," and that "for whatever reason could not be restituted to a legally recognized owner." The works would be transferred to the Direction des Musées, "in accordance with legal measures regulating the devolution of sold or looted mobile assets" for which "legislation authorizes allocation." Henraux expected the selection process would "significantly enrich our patrimoine national,"[64] setting in motion state appropriation of unclaimed Nazi plunder.

The education ministry appointed a fifteen-member art selection committee, which met eight times between 1949 and 1953. The members included Jaujard, who served as president as Director of Arts and Letters; Salles, as vice president; Henraux, representing the CRA; curators from the Louvre, National Museum of Modern Art, and the national museum in Algiers; the director of the national furniture administration (*Mobilier national*); the inspector general of provincial museums; and representatives from the justice, finance, and foreign ministries.[65] The committee defined its top priorities. Most important were high-quality objects worthy of the Louvre and national museums. Next, members sought signed and dated works by second-tier masters, also suitable for museum collections. Of lower importance, but still useful, were intriguing or rare pieces, which could be held in reading rooms of the Louvre or stored for possible future display. The committee would also consider pieces for historical museums and provincial museum collections, and finally items that would decorate French embassies, ministries, and other government buildings.[66]

The meeting minutes contain no discussion of the objects' potential Jewish provenance, and no proposal for more thorough ownership research. Committee members assumed that many items under consideration had been sold to the enemy, not stolen from Jewish-owned homes, bank vaults, or repositories. In the meeting on December 21, 1949, members concluded that among several hundred paintings evaluated that day, "most if not nearly all" had reached Germany through the Paris art market.[67] While this perspective may have seemed to justify the committee's task, the MFAA and CRA had not carried out nearly enough provenance research to conclude with certainty that the items had not been stolen, nor to determine the extent of duress in the case of sales.[68]

The meeting minutes do convey remarkable efficiency, as the relevant curatorial departments evidently had chosen the pieces well in advance. During the December 1949 meeting, for instance, the committee selected 562 paintings in fifty minutes. And many were—or were believed to be—masterpieces: Boucher, *The Fountain*; Ingres, *Portrait of "Father Desmarets"*; Monet, *Cliff at Fécamp*; Delacroix, *Vase of Flowers on Console*; Veronese, *Leda and the Swan*; and Tiepolo, *Alexander and Campaspe in the Studio of Apelles*. In less than an hour, the committee had chosen works that alone would constitute a small world-class collection of European paintings. The committee believed they were selecting several other prestigious works that with further research would prove less valuable: a Manet landscape and Goya portrait, the attribution of both works later designated "anonymous"; *Virgin and Child* by Cranach the Elder, later determined to be "in the style" of Cranach; *The Martyrdom of Saint Laurent*, by Antoon van Dyck, eventually attributed to Jan Boeckhorst.[69]

The committee assumed that most of the unclaimed works would not be claimed for restitution as, it was believed, they had been sold to German buyers in Paris. Research carried out by the Mattéoli Commission and published in 2000 confirmed this perspective, estimating that at least 65 percent of selected objects had been purchased during the occupation.[70] Yet like the postwar officials who selected the pieces, the Mattéoli Commission

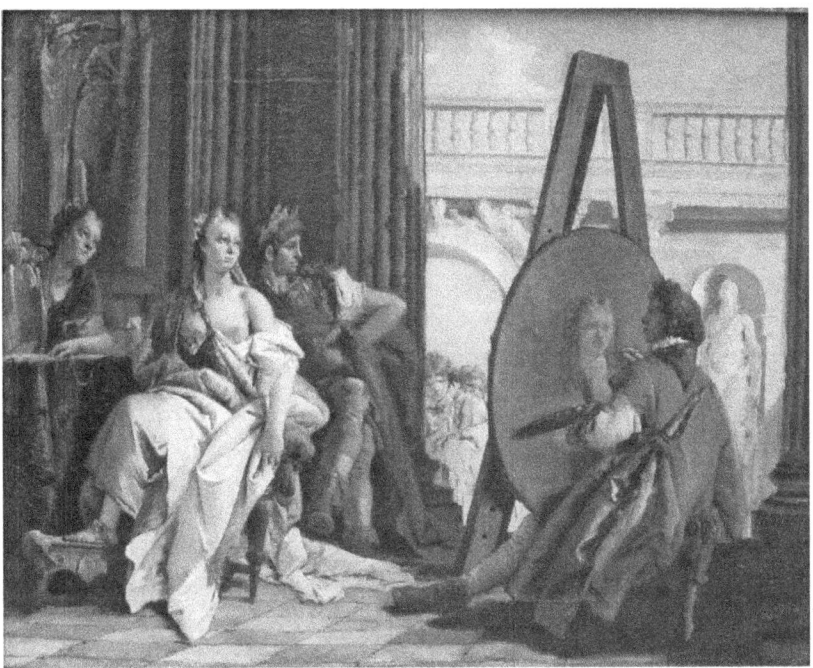

Giovanni Battista Tiepolo, *Alexander the Great and Campaspe in the Studio of Apelles* (c. 1740), selected by the French committee. Restituted to heirs of Federico Gentili di Giuseppe in 1999. Courtesy of the J. Paul Getty Museum, which purchased the painting in 2000.

also did not adequately address under-duress sales. According to French law, an individual could not doubly benefit from a wartime sale—interpreted in the early postwar years to have been carried out according to ordinary law—and postwar restitution.[71] The state, however, could hold the objects in trusteeship in the interest of the *patrimoine national*. Correspondence and reports indicate the selected objects were "entrusted" (*confiées*) or "assigned" (*affectées*) to the Direction des Musées, and that museums "accepted" them into their galleries.[72]

In March 1950, additional museum quality pieces "assigned" to the National Museum of Modern Art included Gleizes, *Landscape*; Léger, *Woman in Red and Green*; Matisse, *Landscape, the Pink Wall*; Utrillo, *House of Berlioz*; Maillol, *Three Graces*.[73] A forty-five-minute meeting on March 28, 1952, reaped ninety-six objects, including sixty-one paintings (Boucher, *The Forest*; Cranach the Elder, *Saint Peter* and *Saint Paul*), sixteen drawings (one each by Delacroix, Tiepolo, Boucher, Meissonier, and Goya), and six tapestries (Aubusson manufacture, *Biblical Scene: The Victory of David*).[74] Committee members were careful to identify any work that might be a forgery, defined as an object "that was conceived and produced for trade purposes with the intention of selling it as an authentic piece in all aspects." A sub-committee identified forgeries and retained the highest-quality pieces for educational purposes, and authorized destruction of lower-quality copies to prevent illicit sales.[75]

By 1954 the selection committee had chosen some two thousand items for distribution to art museums, embassies, state palaces, and other public buildings.[76] Instead of fully acquiring the objects, the French state remained a custodian, cataloging the works in a special inventory and continuing to accept restitution claims. Curators grouped the art into fourteen categories, the best known of which is "Musées Nationaux Récupération" (National Museums Recovery, MNR). Today the acronym is commonly used to refer to all works in the custodianship, though it initially referred to fifteenth to early twentieth-century paintings, or roughly half of all chosen objects. Other codes were RP (twentieth-century paintings), RFR (fifteenth to nineteenth-century sculpture), AGRR (Greek and Roman antiquities), and MAR (East Asian objects).[77]

But did all the chosen objects truly belong in France? As the MFAA transferred millions of books and objects across Europe, invariably lacking adequate personnel and resources, it made mistakes and granted some dubious claims. A group of fourteen paintings that were "repatriated" to France actually belonged in Belgium, and six of them had been selected for French museums. The French museum office acknowledged the error and in 1953 transferred the pictures to the Belgian government, which also had assembled a selection committee for its museums. Among the pieces, the Belgian committee considered placing a four-panel polyptyque in a royal museum, but ended up selling all of the items at auction.[78]

Another dubious repatriation involved a small Matisse painting, *Landscape, the Pink Wall* (1898), designated an MNR in December 1949. Depicting a hospital in Ajaccio, the picture had been owned by Harry Fuld Jr., a German Jew who fled to Switzerland in 1937 and left behind an art collection packed in crates. The Nazis confiscated the collection and the Matisse painting ended up in the hands of SS officer Kurt Gerstein, a fervent Christian and engineer who specialized in decontamination techniques. In 1941 Gerstein was assigned to the Nazi Hygiene Institute, and the following year

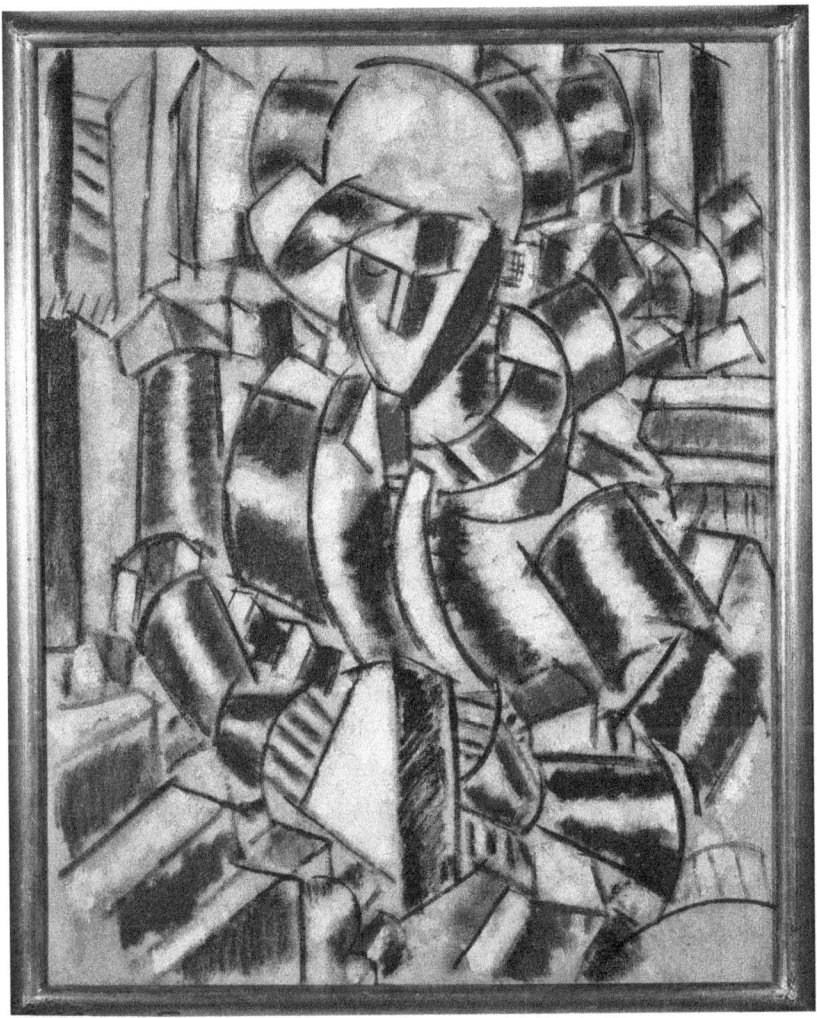

Fernand Léger, *Woman in Red and Green* (1914). Confiscated by the Nazis from the Paris gallery of Paul Rosenberg in 1941. © 2022 Artists Rights Society (ARS), New York / ADAGP, Paris. Bridgeman-Giraudon / Art Resource, NY.

the SS enlisted him to deliver large quantities of Zyklon-B gas to Auschwitz and other death camps. He was thus an eyewitness to the Final Solution, having observed other atrocities, such as the mass killing of Jews in Belzec in August 1942. In the final days of the Third Reich, Gerstein surrendered to French authorities near Stuttgart and offered information on atrocities committed by the Nazis. He claimed to have opposed Nazi genocide from within the SS, a perspective confirmed by historian Saul Friedländer.[79] Yet his French captors were unmoved and detained him in Paris at the Cherche-Midi prison for complicity in war crimes. In July 1945, he hanged himself in his cell.[80]

Meanwhile, back in Germany, MFAA officers found the Matisse painting in the US zone among Gerstein's other assets. They saw a French customs stamp on the back of the frame from 1914, when Fuld's father had purchased it in Paris, and transferred the painting to Baden-Baden. It was displayed in various French museums, most recently at the National Museum of Modern Art in Paris. In 2008, while researching the MNR pieces, German historian Marina Blumberg identified the painting as part of the Fuld collection.[81] From there, the research took a circuitous path to a rightful owner, showing the complexity of restitution several decades after Nazi plunder. Fuld had died in Switzerland in 1963, leaving his entire estate, for unknown reasons, to a woman named Gisela Martin, about whom little is known. Martin died in Switzerland in 1992 and bequeathed her estate to Magen David Adom UK, a British charity supporting medical services in Israel. After Blumberg identified the painting, the French cultural ministry released it to the charity in 2008. In February 2010, Magen David Adom sold the Matisse to the Jewish Museum in Frankfurt.[82]

The selected pieces that had been purchased by dealers working for Göring, Hitler, and other top Nazi officials raised other ownership questions. In the 1950s the West German TVK discovered flaws in some MFAA repatriation decisions, and in 1957 it demanded restitution of two paintings and five Gobelins tapestries. One of the paintings was a sixteenth-century panel *Virgin with Grapes* (MNR 436), at the time attributed to Flemish artist Jan Gossaert, later defined as a Flemish school work in the style of Quentin Metsys, and held by the fine arts museum in Troyes. The Rose Valland Database provides a rather vague ownership history: the painting was purchased in Frankfurt in the nineteenth century, next acquired by Otto Voigtländer in Leipzig, followed by M. Bornheim in Munich, and then purchased by a M. Schmitz, who offered it to Göring in November 1938 or January 1939. No detail in any of this known sales history indicates the MFAA should have transferred it to France. At the time it was recovered, the MFAA in Munich—and Valland—relied solely on the testimony of Hofer, Göring's primary art advisor, who claimed it had been purchased in France.[83]

The other painting claimed by the Federal Republic was *Virgin Adoring the Child* (MNR 250), at the time attributed to Botticelli but later identified as an anonymous Italian school piece.[84] The MFAA property card contained conflicting information: either the painting had been purchased in 1940 "on the Paris market" or acquired by a Count Ingenheim near Meissen in July 1939. The evidence was much clearer that it ended up on the Linz museum inventory as item 1081/776. Based on the limited information available, the MFAA transferred the painting to France and the selection committee reserved it for the Louvre.[85]

In the case of the contested Gobelins tapestries, Valland pointed to the postwar testimonies of German experts, including art historian Walter Borchers, who had worked for the ERR in Paris and asserted that the works had been purchased in France. Two of the tapestries (OAR 24, OAR 25) were part of the Indies series (*série des Indes*), well known by experts at the time, depicting Indigenous peoples of South America, and exotic flora and fauna. The three others, from the Hunts of Maximilian series (OAR 15–17), had been purchased by Josef Angerer of the Berlin dealership Quantmeyer und Eicke on behalf of Göring in May 1938. MFAA officers had found all five tapestries at Berchtesgaden in 1945 and sent them to the central collecting point in Munich; they were transferred to France four years later. In 1957 the TVK contested the restitution and argued the tapestries should have remained in Germany, as Göring had purchased them prior to the war. Valland responded that American MFAA officers knew the sales history when they transferred the tapestries to France in 1949, and according to the 1954 Paris accords, only the discovery of new evidence could reverse restitutions. Since the Germans were relying on US information on property cards from 1949, she argued, they had no basis to overturn the restitution.[86]

For Valland, this dispute was not only about keeping these particular objects on French soil. She strongly opposed the German claims in principle, which could potentially throw into question other restitutions to France. She saw a need to "put a brake on German claims,"[87] and the TVK eventually dropped its claims to the two paintings. The Flemish school picture remained in Troyes, while the Baron Gérard Museum in Bayeux received the Italian school painting. Negotiations continued over the tapestries until 1961, with West German recognition of French ownership, on condition that the French drop claims to two other items, described on the Ministry of Culture's Rose Valland MNR database simply as "an ancient head and a Baldun Grien."[88]

All of these negotiations served Valland's goal to defend the French cultural patrimony.

The French government created the custodianship as a temporary measure, and French curators wondered how long they would serve as mere caretakers before the objects were legally acquired by the state. The September 1949 decree had instructed the Direction des Musées to provide an inventory of selected works to victims of looting or spoliation "until the end of a claims period," without defining a statute of limitations.[89] In November 1949, the Direction des Musées drafted a proposal to establish a three-year limit on claims, but it was not enacted. Florisoone tried to settle the matter again in October 1951 with another proposal for a three-year claims limit, approved by an inter-ministerial restitution committee.[90] In addition, the transfer of property required an act of parliament, which the education ministry repeatedly failed to secure in 1951, 1952, and 1953. In 1954, the cultural administration submitted another draft bill to an advisor in the education ministry that would have required OBIP to remit ownerless works of art and books to public museums and libraries. Upon the transfer, the objects would become state property, though the government would continue to accept restitution claims through 1979, thirty years after the dissolution of the CRA. However, an education ministry official, M. J. Pernot, saw no need for new legislation, as the period of thirty years suited the relevant statute of limitations already in force under French law. Exasperated by Pernot's response, Florisoone complained to Salles, "the refusal to review this draft bill is preventing us from considering these objects our property." The failure to implement a statute of limitations, he argued, was delaying the transfer of objects to embassies, ministry buildings, and the *Mobilier national*, including decorative pieces that had been collected precisely for this purpose.[91]

In December 1956, Louvre curator Germain Bazin expressed a similar view to Salles, arguing that the unclear legal status of the chosen objects created a "dangerous" situation, in which French national and provincial museums risked losing them. Bazin situated this dilemma in the broader context of ongoing French control of the Sarre region of Germany and the transfer of steel assets to the FRG. He worried that works of art similarly could be transferred to Germany. If French museums were forced to relinquish the selected pieces, Bazin predicted "an emotional reaction throughout France," with repercussions for parliament members whose districts lost the coveted objects.[92] In the end, Bazin and other curators were forced to accept the uncertain legal status of the MNR objects, as no statute of limitations on claims was ever established. The temporary custodianship thus became permanent.

Some of the selected objects were quickly claimed by private owners. The decree of September 30, 1949 had provided for the public exhibition of all chosen pieces, which were displayed at the Chateau de Compiègne national museum, about forty miles northeast of Paris, from 1950 to 1954. According to the Mattéoli Commission report, the fine arts administration had chosen this rather remote location because it had sufficient space.[93] The public was invited to view the exhibition Monday through Saturday, 10am to 12pm and 2 to 5pm.[94] Several collectors identified their property at Compiègne. On June 12, 1951, Henry Schloss reviewed the display with his lawyer and an appraiser, and angrily chastised the museum staff for not publicizing the exhibition, prompting their reassurances that notices indeed had been published in French newspapers. After this heated exchange, Schloss regained his composure, studied the pieces, and ended up recognizing one of his paintings: MNR 420, a landscape attributed to Rubens. It was returned to him later that year, along with MNR 011, a painting by Basaiti, *Virgin with Child and Saint John*, confirmed as his property following additional research by OBIP, and MNR 726, a Franz Hals painting, *Portrait of an Old Woman*.[95] The same year Paul Rosenberg received MNR 191, *Flowers* by Courbet. A total of nine works were restituted to private owners from 1951 to 1954, followed by only seventeen over the next forty years. As time went on, the number of claims decreased as the temporary custodianship became the status quo.[96]

Enriching Museum Collections

The MNRs and other selected pieces created an opportunity to enhance collections in the prestigious French national museums as well as smaller institutions throughout the country, known as provincial museums (*musées de province*). The Vichy regime had extended central state control over several hundred local and regional art museums in 1941, a measure validated by the provisional Republic in 1945.[97] After 1949, the government used the MNRs to bolster public museum collections throughout France.

The actual distribution of objects elicited fierce debate among curators. All were aware of a clear hierarchy: the Louvre was given top priority to house the most important works up to the modern period, while the top modernist pieces, roughly beginning with the rise of Impressionism, were allocated to the national modern art museum in Paris. An object was available for provincial museums only after curators at the Louvre, MNAM, and other national museums had declined it. The general inspector for provincial museums, Jean Vergnet-Ruiz, consulted with national museum curators to determine the distribution of each piece. In October 1949, for instance, national museum curators declined a bust of the eighteenth-century German composer Glück (item RFR 13), at the time attributed to sculptor Jean-Antoine Houdon, but the selection committee agreed to keep it for a provincial museum. The bust had been purchased in France in 1942 by German dealer Hildebrand Gurlitt for RM 12,000, on behalf of the Wallraf-Richartz-Museum in Cologne. It was then stored at the Langenau chateau in the Rhineland-Palatinate, which became part of French occupation zone. The MFAA repatriated it to France, where the selection committee chose it for French museums in October 1949. Earmarked as "in storage" for the Louvre, it has been housed at the municipal museum of Soissons since 1953.[98]

Louvre curators oversaw the distribution of works created up to the modernist period. In November 1950, Germain Bazin sent to Vergnet-Ruiz a list of works chosen for the Louvre that were "unavailable" to provincial museums. Notes next to some items indicated they might be distributed to the provinces, but Bazin emphasized, "this doesn't mean we have abandoned these paintings. On the contrary, we are still considering them."[99] For instance, Bazin initially planned to reserve a painting by Boudin for the Louvre, as the museum lacked examples of the artist's Antwerp period, but the picture eventually went to Grenoble. The Louvre also would keep *The Merchant's Quay at Rouen* by Corot (MNR 155), in his view "one of the most important pieces of the recovery effort," not only for display at the Louvre but also for a possible exchange with a foreign museum; talks were already underway with the Rijksmuseum in Amsterdam. It is not clear whether Bazin meant a permanent exchange, as opposed to a loan, as the former option only would have been feasible if the Louvre had legally acquired the painting. In the end, curators allocated the painting to the fine arts museum in Rouen, where it remains today.[100]

Curators at the MNAM oversaw the distribution of modern pieces throughout France. Head curator Jean Cassou, previously dismissed from the museum by the Vichy regime for leftist political activities, had joined a resistance network based at the Musée de l'Homme that also included Boris Vildé and Paul Rivet. Cassou survived arrest, a year of imprisonment, and several months at an internment camp at Saint-Sulpice du Tarn, and was reinstated at the MNAM in October 1945. Two years later, he edited a collection of documents on German looting of Jewish-owned artworks and libraries, with a preface condemning antisemitism and plunder committed by the Nazis and Vichy.[101] Soon afterward, he selected some of the recovered objects for the MNAM. In October 1950, Cassou explained to Vergnet-Ruiz that the museum had rearranged a room devoted to Utrillo and Valadon, and that two recovered Utrillos filled "one of our most significant gaps, as our Utrillos cut a rather sorry figure compared to our Valadons." Cassou's colleague Bernard Dorival echoed these sentiments to Vergnet-Ruiz: "You know how much this artist [Utrillo] is under-represented at the museum, and the extent to which we needed to improve this ensemble. These two works arrived just in time to satisfy our wishes; you will understand that above all, we want to keep them and I'm sure you will allow them to stay with us."[102] Cassou was willing to relinquish one Utrillo: "I can leave for a provincial museum *Village Street under Snow*," which ended up at the Toulouse-Lautrec museum in Albi, before being transferred to the MNAM. "I want to keep the Gleizes," Cassou continued, "as the Minister wants it for one of his apartments," and finally, "I'm creating a Léger room as important as our Picasso, Matisse and Braque rooms, and I'd very much like to keep the recovered Léger." Showing some magnanimity toward provincial museums, he made "no claim to the *Composition* by Picabia," nor the "*Three Nymphs* by Maillol and *Assia* by Despiau," noting they were "two major works."[103]

National Museum curators also used the MNR pieces to prompt exchanges with provincial museums. Although the Louvre, Versailles, and the MNAM could simply "accept" the chosen works, provincial museums were required to exchange works from their collections to receive higher quality MNR pieces; the national museums would benefit either way. Bazin suggested that Vergnet-Ruiz create a list of all works in the provinces that could be used in exchanges with the Louvre, "no strings attached."[104]

After months of haggling, Vergnet-Ruiz made it clear to Bazin he was losing patience with the short shrift given to provincial museums, prompting the Louvre curator to reply, "I could respond in the same tone . . . but that approach wouldn't advance the joint task we are pursuing, which up to this point we were carrying out in perfect agreement." Bazin reminded Vergnet-Ruiz that they were discussing only an initial distribution. Louvre curators were keeping a large number of paintings so they would have the time to examine the full array of available pieces in "our collections"—indicating his view of the Louvre's at least de facto possession. With recovered pieces entering the Louvre collection, other paintings held by the museum would be available for distribution to provincial museums. Bazin viewed the current situation as a unique opportunity to reorganize collections in a way that would benefit all French museums: "It is not at all my intention, I can assure you, to enrich the Louvre museum at the expense of provincial museums." He wondered if Vergnet-Ruiz believed the reorganization "should occur at the expense of the Louvre." Defending the retention of nineteenth-century paintings for possible exchanges, Bazin found it perfectly reasonable to use recovered works for this purpose. It was "impossible, or at least very difficult, to use recently donated pieces in exchanges," as benefactors often expressly gave works to the Louvre.[105] Vergnet-Ruiz agreed that recovered works should be used in a general reorganization of the Louvre's collection, but not at the expense of all other art museums. "Otherwise," he said, "the art recovery would in reality only serve the Louvre."[106]

In the end, the two curators facilitated numerous exchanges between the Louvre and provincial museums. Bazin allowed the transfer of two MNRs— a Guardi and an Ingres—to Toulouse in exchange for another Guardi he wanted for the Louvre.[107] Vergnet-Ruiz also managed wish lists of curators in the provinces, aiming to reinforce the collections' existing strengths. Curator Robert Mesuret in Toulouse, for example, had quite specific requests. He wanted an eighteenth-century painting measuring around 2.2 x 2.3 meters; a sculpture by Charles Meynier, "ancestor of the mayor"; and a "fairly audacious" modern painting. The closest the administration came to these criteria was MNR 314, an allegory of justice or *Venise Tronant*, once believed to be a Tiepolo, now attributed to Salvator Francesco Fontebasso.[108] In a separate case, Vergnet-Ruiz convinced the mayor of Cognac to accept an exchange: if the mayor would release a painting of Grenoble to that city, Cognac would receive two MNRs by Cranach constituting an Adam and Eve pendant, which would complement other sixteenth-century German paintings already in the Cognac collection.[109]

Some of the selected objects went to the National Fine Arts Museum in Algiers, which housed a significant collection of French and "Orientalist" art—Delacroix, Pissarro, Gauguin, Monet, Renoir—along with important works by Italian, Dutch, and German artists. Although the "national" museum was established in 1930, it was overseen and financed not by the Réunion des musées nationaux in Paris, but by authorities in Algeria.[110] The museum was eligible for recovered artworks nonetheless, and French Governor General Marcel-Edmond Naegelen and Curator Jean Alazard made a strong case that museum should receive items, to compensate for a history of neglect compared to collections in the metropole.

Alazard attended the first selection committee meeting on October 27, 1949, and was able to secure for his museum two clay objects and three Maillol statues (*Woman, Young Girl* and *Desire*).[111] In Naegelen's own wish list sent to Salles, most likely drafted at least in part by Alazard, the governor emphasized the importance of museums in Algeria to the education of a "a young and vibrant people, distanced from metropolitan art centers" that were "several hundred years old and only accessible to a privileged few"— those able to travel to the metropole. He wanted Algerian museums to prioritize the works of foreign artists "to offer a fairly complete perspective of the evolution of French art" while maintaining "the seductive character of Mediterranean museums." He attached a list of thirty-three recovered works that would "complete existing collections," including Tiepolo, *Alexander and Campaspe in the Studio of Apelles*; Van Goyen, *Landscape*; Géricault, *Ancient Chariot Race*; Breughel, *Flowers*; Renoir, *Portrait of a Woman*; Toulouse-Lautrec, *Coquelin in Cyrano*; and Degas, *Portrait of Colonna Romano*.[112] Florisoone concurred and wrote to Vergnet-Ruiz, "it would be beneficial, for all sorts of reasons, to favor the Algiers museum."[113]

An order from December 18, 1952 authorized the fine arts museum in Algiers to house sixteen MNR paintings, including a Delacroix, a Van Goyen, two fifteenth-century Italian school paintings, a sixteenth-century Dutch school painting, and a seventeenth-century French school painting.[114] Altogether, the fine arts museum in Algiers received at least twenty-nine recovered objects, which also included a bas-relief and two sculptures by Maillol, a Joos de Momper painting, and six illustrated pages from *Wonders of Creation* by Zakariya al-Qazwini, a thirteenth-century Persian scientist. The distribution was short-lived, however, due to the war of independence. By 1962, all of the art recovery items, except for a few antiquities, were repatriated to France and distributed to the Louvre and provincial museums.[115]

Back in the metropole, other selected pieces enabled the Musées nationaux to reorganize works by Italian artists. Vergnet-Ruiz and other curators aimed to regroup the so-called Campana collection, some 600 fourteenth- and fifteenth-century Italian paintings acquired by the Roman Marquis Giampietro Campana in the 1840s and 1850s. Campana had inherited Rome's central pawn broking institution, the Monte di Pietà. Having facilitated loans to the papal government, he was knighted by Pope Gregory XVI and developed a passion for collecting art and archeological artifacts.

Campana became a member of major Italian learned societies and used his wealth to spearhead philanthropic projects. He also was corrupt and in 1858 was sentenced to twenty years in prison for embezzlement. The papal state, then under Pius IX, confiscated his vast art collection and sold it to buyers across the globe: 84 sculptures and pottery pieces went to the Victoria and Albert Museum in London; 767 statues, frescoes, and vases to the Hermitage in Saint-Petersburg; and in June 1861, 11,835 artifacts, paintings, and pottery were purchased for the French state by Napoléon III.[116]

After the Second World War, French curators developed plans to regroup the paintings from the Campana collection, which by 1976 ended up at the Petit Palais in Avignon. Previous histories of the collection, including one on the Petit Palais website,[117] fail to mention a key detail: Vergnet-Ruiz reorganized the collection through provincial museum exchanges with MNR paintings. In May 1952, he told Florisoone he supported the proposal to regroup the Campana works, at the time planned for the Louvre, but was adamant that he must receive MNR pieces in exchange: "I cannot and should not exchange works without equivalent compensation."[118]

As a result of the Campana exchanges, MNR 586, a seventeenth-century Dutch painting by Philips Wouwerman, *Annunciation to the Shepherds*, went to Bergues; MNR 841, a seventeenth-century French school painting, *Portrait of an Old Woman*, went to Laon; MNR 231, attributed to Stanislas Lépine, *The Seine*, went to Caen; MNR 40 by seventeenth-century Flemish artist Lucas Franchoys went to Le Puy; and MNR 701, *The Temptation of Saint Anthony* by seventeenth-century Flemish artist David Teniers, went to Montargis.[119] An exhibition at the Louvre from May to July 1956 displayed forty-five Campana paintings in a show with 168 Italian primitives. In the catalog's introductory text, Florisoone assured visitors the dispersed collection would "soon be brought together again to benefit one of our most artistic provincial cities," and art historian André Chastel advocated grouping the works together in Avignon. The wish was fulfilled twenty years later, largely due to MNR exchanges.[120]

Sales of Less Worthy Objects

The selection committee declined roughly thirteen thousand lower-quality works of art, more than six times the number of chosen objects. OBIP transferred the rejected pieces to Domaines, and they were sold at auction in Paris between 1950 and 1953.[121] Many were lower-quality furniture and household items—beds, tables, chairs—and would hardly qualify as works of art. The Mattéoli Commission studied lists of the sold objects and was able to identify only 1,527 pieces. Among them, however, were quality works, such as Lancret's *The Marshall of Luxembourg's Wife and Family*, and Van Ostade's *Tavern Interior*, sold in March 1951 for Ff 3.2 million and Ff 705,000, respectively, as well as Corot's *Garzano—Goatherd and Village*, sold three days later for Ff 3.9 million, today at the Phillips Collection in Washington, D.C.[122] In some cases, authorities had identified a rightful owner, such as a piece depicting scenes of Nuremberg belonging to one Hermann Arnstein, but sold the objects in the absence of a claim. Other owners had not responded to mailed notices about their identified property. French authorities did not attempt to determine whether the owners had been deported or otherwise forced from their homes during the occupation. One auctioned statuette of Saint Sebastian was later found to have belonged to Maurice de Rothschild and the state compensated him,[123] an indemnity more easily secured by influential collectors with more extensive ownership documentation.

The Domaines office exhibited the objects prior to sales and its *Bulletin officiel* publicized descriptions of some items and illustrations for the most valuable pieces. There was no indication of the objects' likely Jewish provenance. By June 15, 1953, the Domaines agency had collected Ff 96,120,000 from these sales and OBIP estimated the total would reach Ff 100 million by September 1954. Even considering these were "old" French francs with an exchange rate of roughly Ff 350 to one US dollar, prior to revaluation of the franc in 1960, the sales generated significant revenue for the French treasury.[124] Restitution officials believed the proceeds provided just compensation to France. Rose Valland boasted in 1954 that through these auctions, "the French state recovered a good portion of the funds it had been forced to give to the enemy."[125]

Other observers at the time were more critical of the sales. Some journalists and art experts were well aware the pieces up for sale had been subject to wartime looting or spoliation. The press also questioned the authenticity of certain pieces, illustrated by controversy surrounding a soup tureen reportedly created by Thomas Germain, an eighteenth-century French silversmith known for elaborate rococo designs. Experts disagreed as to whether it truly was the work of Germain and the Domaines agency, following standard practice, put it up for sale in December 1952 without guaranteeing authenticity. One dubious appraiser quipped, "I don't want to get soaked in this tureen."

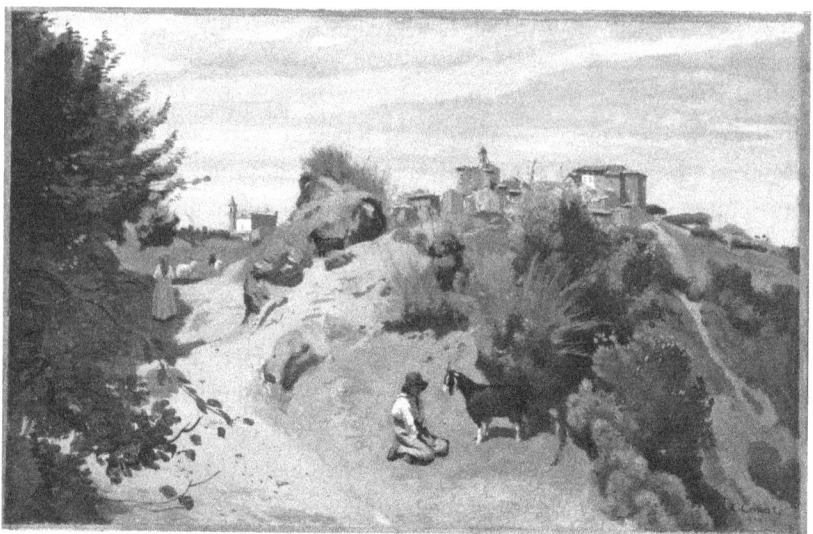

Jean-Baptiste-Camille Corot, *Genzano* (1843). Oil on canvas, 14 ½ x 22 ½ in. The Phillips Collection, Washington, DC. Sold by the French state and acquired in 1955.

The item sold for more than four million francs.[126] Many other buyers were willing to gamble, and as long as buyers coveted the spoils, the Domaines agency facilitated deposits to the French treasury.

The OBIP office closed in 1953, the foreign affairs and finance ministries having determined that the office had achieved its objectives. There was consensus across several government divisions that the art custodianship was serving an important cultural mission. The lauded *résistante* Rose Valland boasted in 1954 that works "purchased during the occupation of France, the most beautiful ones, such as paintings by Rembrandt, Delacroix, de La Tour entered our national collections"—though "entered" here does not mean fully acquired by the state, as the objects remained on a separate inventory.[127]

At the same time, Valland questioned recurring proposals to establish a statute of limitations on claims to the MNR objects, preferring to continue accepting them. In 1965, the director of French museums, Jean Châtelain, explained to her that one had to think about not only the individuals who had experienced traumas of the past, but also "those who live today, and those who will come after them, year after year." For the latter, "who are the future, we must forget the past . . . however moving the past may be." He suggested relaunching research into the collection if it contained major works. Otherwise, "let's leave the pieces available to the living, which does not at all diminish the respect we owe the dead."[128] Works by Picasso, Monet, and Courbet surely qualified as major, but there was no effort to pursue additional research. Valland's responsibilities included managing the archives related to wartime art looting and spoliation, and she could have spearheaded the effort. But the French state was under no legal obligation to search for rightful owners, and the museum office held no sense of ethical responsibility to pursue provenance research on objects seized from Jewish victims of Nazi and Vichy persecution. Valland accepted the norms of the time and remained a defender of the French *patrimoine*. She was, above all, a patriot and loyal civil servant. While she may have harbored mixed feelings about the custodianship, she was among those in the government who preserved it, along with nine hundred boxes of archives on art plunder in France.

5
National Heritage in the Netherlands

In the wake of war, famine, deportations, and Nazi exploitation, the recovery of Dutch cultural heritage symbolized the restoration of the nation as a whole. The postwar government organized several public exhibitions of masterpieces that had survived multiple transfers to German repositories and the circuitous route back to the Netherlands. One show, "Recovered Art Property" (*Herwonnen Kunstbezit*), was held at the Mauritshuis from March to May 1946. The 257 pieces were organized by artistic school—Dutch, Flemish, French, and Italian painting—and by categories of porcelain, glass, jewelry, and fine furniture. Paintings on display included highly coveted works by European Masters—Frans Hals, Van der Heyden, Van der Neer, Rembrandt, Ruysdael, Jan Steen, Van Dyck, Rubens, Cranach the Elder, Tintoretto, Watteau, Boucher, and Fragonard.[1] Another *Herwonnen Kunstbezit* show with 172 objects was held at the Centraal Museum in Utrecht from June to September 1946, almost entirely with different pieces. It featured many of the artists shown at the Mauritshuis exhibition, with drawings by Boucher, Fragonard and Watteau, fine sculpture, furniture, medieval gold pendants, majolica pottery, and other decorative objects.[2] From December 1946 to January 1948, forty-nine paintings also went on tour in the United States in a show entitled "Paintings looted from Holland." They were shown at thirteen institutions that had contributed personnel to the MFAA, including the Albright Art Gallery in Buffalo, Yale University, Smith College, and the Palace of the Legion of Honor in San Francisco. In the foreword to the exhibition catalog, Dutch MFAA officer Alphonsus "Phonse" Vorenkamp paid tribute to his MFAA colleagues: "Holland is deeply grateful to America." The paintings by masters such as Van Goyen, Ter Borch, Van der Heyden, Rembrandt, and Steen were "only a handful of works taken from the enormous collection of returned loot—a few flowers from a large bouquet." The exhibition would be held at a limited number of galleries, he explained, as "the anonymous lenders would like to get their treasures back." However, at least one painting—a Rembrandt, and perhaps the show's most prestigious piece—had not been claimed by a rightful owner. Listed for the American tour as *The Peahens* (*De Pauwen*), the picture likely is item NK2346 in the state Art Property Collection, today housed at the Rijksmuseum.[3] These spectacular shows in the early postwar years celebrated the return of Dutch national heritage and the American role in the recovery effort, while eliding questions about rightful ownership.

Art losses reported to the Dutch government totaled twenty thousand items, valued in 1947 at 150 million guilders, based on prewar prices.[4] Compared to France, a much smaller percentage of works repatriated to the Netherlands were restituted to private owners. Recovery statistics remain incomplete, but a US report indicates that by the end of October 1949, the MFAA had released 5,004 objects to the Netherlands from the Munich collecting point.[5] In June 1952, the head of the Office for Reparation Payments and Restitution of Property (HERGO), Jolle Jolles, reported with unfortunate imprecision that the Netherlands had received four thousand

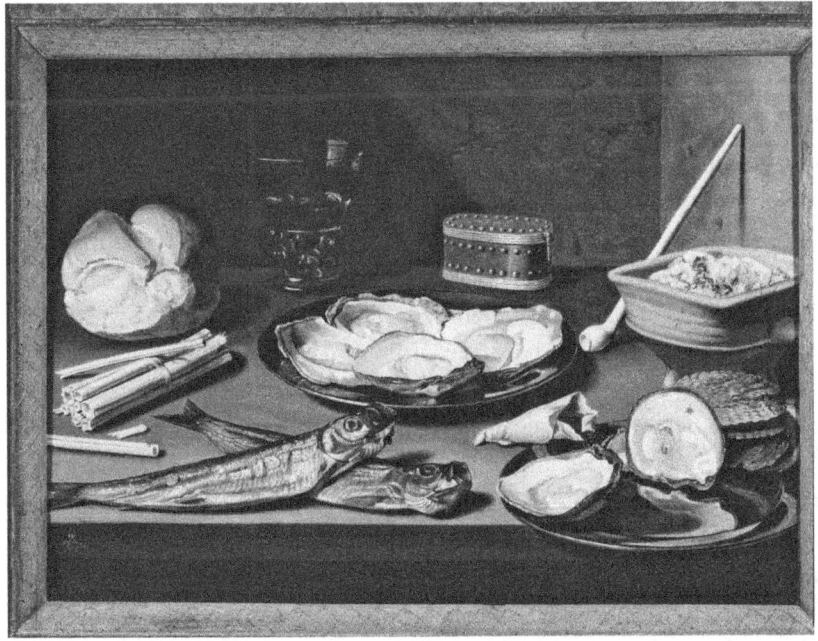

Floris Gerritsz van Schooten, *Still Life* (1625). Courtesy of Frans Hals Museum, Haarlem, purchased with the support of the Rembrandt Society and Fonds J-P de Man. Photograph by Arend Velsink.

paintings, four hundred rugs, thousands of furniture and decorative pieces, plus several thousand additional objects from collections known to have been sold to the Germans (Mannheimer, Gutmann and Lanz).[6] By July 1950, the Netherlands had restituted 111 furniture pieces, 146 applied art objects, 118 paintings, nine drawings, and two rugs; an additional 352 paintings were restored to owners by 1953,[7] a much smaller proportion compared to the roughly 75 percent of works restituted in France in the same period. Among the unclaimed pieces in the Netherlands, more than four thousand objects became part of the Dutch Art Property collection by the early 1950s.[8]

Several factors hindered art restitution in the Netherlands. Survival itself was a key factor, and compared to France and Belgium, Jews in the Netherlands suffered the highest deportation and death rate.[9] Moreover, the agency charged with art restitution, the Dutch Art Property Foundation (*Stichting Nederlands Kunstbezit*, SNK), was plagued with mismanagement and corruption, and often served the state's interests to the detriment of claimants. As historian Gerald Aalders puts it, "The management of the SNK can be summarized in two words: boondoggle and chaos."[10] The Ekkart Committee similarly reported in 2001 that the art agency's approach to restitution was "legalistic, bureaucratic, cold and often even callous."[11]

Assessing restitution policy beyond art collections, legal historian Wouter Veraart sees a stark contrast between French and Dutch approaches. Whereas restitution in republican France was considered "a necessary step within project of re-establishing legality and rule of law," he argues, the Netherlands displayed "extreme pragmatism" and viewed restitution as just one step of many in postwar reconstruction aimed at bolstering the Dutch economy. The French "expended considerable efforts to make sure Jewish owners were really getting their assets back," according to Veraart, while the Dutch administration "clashed with interests of the post-war Jewish community." He concludes that "on the whole, the restored French Republic did its duty."[12]

Factors other than republican notions of the rule of law explain the higher restitution rate in France. Most important, a high percentage of looted art came from a limited number of easily identified Jewish collectors and dealers who survived the war.[13] In contrast, there were fewer such large Jewish collections in the Netherlands and the most significant ones—Goudstikker, Mannheimer, Gutmann—had been sold to the enemy and were not automatically restitutable under Dutch law. The approach of both governments to unclaimed works of art was, in fact, remarkably similar, and prolonged the Nazi-era dispossession of Jewish victims and their descendants.

The Repatriation of Dutch Cultural Assets

During some of the darkest days of the occupation, the Dutch government in exile began planning the anticipated restitution of seized assets. At the end of 1942, civil law professor Jannes Eggens oversaw a committee of legal experts and civil servants, including two Jewish members, who prepared decrees aimed at reestablishing a Dutch legal framework for property ownership. The decrees stemmed from the notion that the Nazis had so thoroughly disrupted legal relations in the Netherlands, postwar judges would need to review property cases with some flexibility, using standards of reasonableness and equity, rather than a strict rule of law, and assessing cases more as arbitrators than jurists.[14]

The Dutch government in London issued two key legislative texts on September 17, 1944. Decree E100, on the reestablishment of legal relations provided a framework for the restitution of seized assets and allowed the creation of a central restitution agency, the Council for the Restoration of Rights (*Raad voor het Rechtsherstel*). The council was an umbrella organization that would eventually include four divisions: real estate, securities, an administrative agency (*Nederlands Beheersinstituut*) to oversee asset transfers including works of art, and a judicial division. The first three divisions made binding restitution decisions that could be appealed to the judicial division. The ability of the council to decide cases outside the usual Dutch court system reflected Eggens's belief that an extraordinary legal process was necessary to reverse the extraordinary damage to Dutch property rights inflicted by the Nazis. Yet Decree E100 granted the judicial division wide latitude in restitution decisions on a case-by-case basis, using a standard of "reasonability" that was unpredictable, and often favored current owners. For many unsuccessful claimants, the decisions appeared capricious and unjust. The council's departments operated until 1967, with the exception of the securities department, which continued to process claims until 1971.[15]

The second measure issued on September 17, 1944 was decree E93, which nullified 423 orders and decrees of the German administration, including antisemitic legislation. However, transactions based on German legislation, such as the Aryanization of art dealerships, were not necessarily declared null and void; presiding judges would review each case.[16] In addition, the Enemy Property Decree (E133) of October 20, 1944, proclaimed that the assets of enemy states and subjects in the Netherlands would be controlled by the Dutch state. This measure allowed the postwar government to control assets of the Liro repository, falsely portrayed by the Germans as a bank branch, where Jews collectively had been forced to deposit investments, jewelry, works of art, and other assets during the occupation.[17]

The Dutch government issued these key restitution policies toward the end of 1944, as the war continued on Dutch territory. Southern Dutch regions were liberated along with Belgium in November 1944, but the northern provinces were forced to endure war and occupation for several more grueling months, including the brutal "Hunger Winter." The weekly calorie rations for Dutch civilians in some areas fell below the daily rations allotted to SHAEF soldiers, with a devastating impact on children and the elderly. An estimated sixteen thousand people starved to death due to disruptions in the distribution of food and fuel.[18] With the German surrender in the Netherlands on May 5, 1945, the Dutch finally could celebrate. In Amsterdam, a British correspondent reported, "We have been kissed, cried on, hugged, thumped, screamed at and shouted at until we are bruised and exhausted. The Dutch have ransacked their gardens so that the rain of flowers which falls on the Allied vehicles is endless."[19]

Once the liberation euphoria had subsided, the challenges of reconstruction were immense. The war and occupation had taken a tremendous toll on the civilian population and decimated the Dutch economy. Finance minister Piet Lieftinck was the man chiefly responsible for overseeing the economic recovery, and his challenges were legion: the infrastructure of roads, bridges, and canals was badly damaged; the Rotterdam Blitz of May 1940 had almost entirely destroyed the port city's historic center; the Nazis had exploited Dutch producers and funneled resources to the Reich; and liberation had closely followed the devastating Hunger Winter. In these dire circumstances, the interest of national economic reconstruction overrode those of any single ethnic or religious group, including Jewish survivors and heirs. Toward the end of 1945, as Allied representatives prepared to meet in Paris for the reparations conference, Dutch authorities estimated wartime losses in material and moral terms. "The Netherlands," they maintained, "suffered more on account of the war than most, if not all, other occupied European countries," adding, "the case of the Netherlands is therefore exceptional and special,"[20] a proposition that surely rang hollow to other delegates, not least the Poles. They claimed a total Nlg 25.7 billion from Germany, including an estimated Nlg 640 million guilders in lost cultural property, jewelry, diamonds, and precious metals—Nlg 200 million for lost paintings alone.[21] In compiling these figures, the Dutch had drawn on the

1943 Allied Declaration and affirmed they understood "looted property" to mean, according to international law:

> ... all goods by their nature fit for restitution, which the enemy, his agents or his subjects, by favor of their occupation of the whole or of part of the Netherlands, have removed from the country's national patrimony as it existed before the occupation, either directly by acts of transfer or of dispossession, or indirectly by purchases or by transactions effected by means of payment which were created, imposed or extorted by the enemy due to the occupation.[22]

Purchased artworks, therefore, were subject to repatriation along with stolen assets.

Over the course of Allied negotiations between Potsdam in July 1945 and the Paris conference of 1947, it was increasingly clear to Dutch authorities they could not expect reparations payments from Germany, especially given US opposition to saddling Germany with heavy financial obligations. In this international context, Lieftinck viewed restitutions as a way to bolster the financial interests of the Dutch nation as a whole, at the expense of Jewish claimants who had lost assets due to antisemitic persecution and the Holocaust.[23]

Dutch authorities entrusted the task of art restitution to the SNK, jointly overseen by the education and finance ministries. The foundation staff members were selected for their cultural expertise and included curators, museum directors, art historians, and artists. A charter for the foundation drafted in June 1945 summarized the organization's mission: to assist "all activities relating to art treasures, libraries, and archives that are or were in enemy possession, and to engage in all related activities in the broadest sense of the word," in accordance with instructions issued by "competent bodies."[24] In April 1946 the charter was amended in a few key ways: it specified that the SNK would manage objects with "cultural significance," the "enemy" could refer to a state or individual, as defined by decree E133, and the foundation explicitly assumed responsibility over works "whose owner is unknown."[25]

A seven-member board of directors appointed by the ministries of education and finance oversaw SNK operations. D. C. Roëll, director of the Rijksmuseum, was named chairman by the education minister, and Jan Gerrit van Gelder, acting director of the Netherlands Institute of Art History, served as secretary. The SNK guidelines also stipulated that the foundation's administrative costs would be borne through associated assets; thus, claimants were required to pay fees to cover costs in the recovery and restitution process. The organization initially had a Foreign Affairs Department to manage objects found abroad, co-directed by Van Gelder and art historian Ary Bob de Vries, and a Home Department for assets found within the Netherlands. The latter division transferred to the Beheersinstituut in August 1948.[26]

De Vries was an ardent but controversial administrator. A Jewish expert in sixteenth- and seventeenth-century Dutch painting, he was forced to relinquish his position at the Rijksmuseum after the German invasion, and in 1943 he fled to Switzerland. He then joined the exiled Dutch government in London, where he represented the Netherlands on the Vaucher Commission.[27] Once back on the continent, De Vries joined the MFAA at the rank of major and divided his time between field work in Germany and office work in Amsterdam at SNK headquarters, in the former Goudstikker premises at Herengracht 458. Although his ardor to recover Dutch cultural patrimony earned him respect in the art world, it also rankled British and American MFAA officers. His disregard for restitution procedures, moreover, eventually led Dutch authorities to charge him with fraud, and he was forced to resign in July 1948.[28]

Far less controversial was Phonse Vorenkamp, a Dutch art historian who had been teaching at Smith College in Massachusetts since 1926, described by Howe as "a little man with gray hair, shrewd gray eyes and steel-rimmed spectacles."[29] While teaching at Smith, the Dutch scholar had befriended Francis Henry Taylor, then director of the Worcester Art Museum, who said the two were "thrown together constantly." Vorenkamp was on sabbatical in the Netherlands during the German invasion of 1940 and fled to Italy, where he boarded a ship to the United States. Once back at Smith College, he helped Dési Goudstikker store sixteen paintings from her late husband's collection on campus for the duration of the war, and again took a teaching leave to serve in the US army from 1942 to 1943.[30] Vorenkamp confided to Howe that as a private in the US army, he had trouble understanding his drill sergeant's orders, and earned such retribution that he considered changing his first name from Alphonsus to "Latrinus."[31]

Vorenkamp and Taylor, who became the Met director in 1940, again had an opportunity to work together in the art conservation effort during the war. While Taylor served on the Roberts Commission, Vorenkamp prepared maps of Holland for the American Council of Learned Societies that were later used by the MFAA. He was an ideal candidate for the division and Taylor recommended him to the Dutch education minister "in the highest terms." In May 1945, Vorenkamp joined the Dutch art recovery team at the rank of lieutenant colonel and was appointed chief liaison officer to the Netherlands at the Munich Central Collecting Point.[32] Vorenkamp thus had the unusual experience of serving both the US and Dutch armies and excelled as an MFAA field officer. He served the SNK until late 1946 and briefly returned to Smith College. He was appointed director of the Boymans Museum in Rotterdam in 1947, and two years later became director of the Museum of Antiquities in Groningen.[33]

Assisting the recovery effort in the western district of the US zone, Dutch Lieutenant Hans Jaffé worked as a liaison officer in the Heidelberg headquarters, and like De Vries had been forced from a position during the occupation due to his Jewish origins. A professor of modern art history at the Nieuwe Kunstschool in Amsterdam, Jaffé had fled to Lucerne in 1942.[34] According to Howe, Jaffé was "intelligent and industrious" and as successful as Vorenkamp in investigating looted Dutch collections: "Jaffé didn't reap so rich a harvest, but that was only because there was less loot in his territory."[35]

In the summer of 1945, the SNK board of directors confirmed in their first meeting that domestic and foreign operations would "be performed for the benefit of the Dutch State."[36] For recovery work in the former Reich, "militarized" members of the SNK (MFAA officers) would work with the Office of the General Commissioner for Dutch Economic Interests in Germany (CGR). The board discussed general guidelines for the SNK, which at this early stage included the distribution of unclaimed works of art for museums and other public institutions. Objects that had been freely sold to the enemy would become state property, and selected pieces would be provided to Dutch museums, ministries and public palaces, embassy buildings, and consulates, and other Dutch institutions abroad. Claims for repatriated items would be allowed for a set period of time, after which they would revert definitively to the state.[37] Vorenkamp found this last point misleading and suggested a clarification: "the stolen property reverts to the state only if it has been clearly shown that the owners are no longer present."[38] The exact meaning of "present" was unclear, but the board did not pursue the idea. The board revised these guidelines several times but delayed adopting them, an early missed opportunity to clarify the foundation's procedures.[39] Nonetheless, the guidelines from 1945 remain useful in providing insight into Dutch perspectives on art restitution and appropriation, and illustrate plans within weeks of the liberation to display unclaimed works in state museums, palaces, and other buildings.

Meanwhile, the MFAA was recovering significant artworks from the Netherlands that were held in Nazi repositories. The officers located items from the Mannheimer collection in Vyšší Brod, Bohemia. Goudstikker paintings had been stashed in salt mines near Alt Aussee, Austria, and were among the works in Göring's collection at Berchtesgaden. Items from the Lugt and Lanz collections, not Jewish-owned, also were found at Alt Aussee.[40] In mid-October 1945, Thomas Howe met with the US ambassador in The Hague, Stanley Hornbeck, and discussed a possible ceremony to welcome the first shipment of art to the Netherlands. Hornbeck, who according to Howe "looked more like a successful businessman than a diplomat," scoffed at the idea. "We've had too damn many celebrations and ceremonies in this country already. We need more hard work instead of more holidays. It's very nice about the pictures coming back, but steel mills and machinery would be a lot more welcome." After hearing the ambassador's reaction, Vorenkamp told Howe, "We would not expect your ambassador to arrange a ceremony. That is for us to do. It is for us to express our gratitude to General Eisenhower." A few weeks later, Dutch officials hosted a modest luncheon at the Rijksmuseum attended by LaFarge and Hornbeck. While "only the simplest food was served," they laid out a table setting worthy of the venue, with fine silver, porcelain, and crystal.[41]

The first art shipment arrived at Amsterdam's Schiphol airport from Germany the same day, without great fanfare, and the next morning Vorenkamp escorted Howe to the Rijksmuseum to examine the paintings. Some had been culled to represent the finest tradition of Dutch painting and were mostly seventeenth-century masters. Among the pieces were four Rembrandts, including *The Peahens*, the aforementioned NK2346, which Howe had inspected at the Alt Aussee salt mine.[42] After viewing these works, Howe was able to enjoy an exhibition at the museum entitled "The Return of the Old Masters" featuring 140 paintings that had been held for safekeeping in Dutch underground shelters during the war, with six Vermeers, seventeen Rembrandts including *The Night Watch*, and nine works by Frans Hals.[43]

Numerous convoys from Germany followed, transporting thousands of objects of varying quality. Paintings continued to flow from Munich. From Offenbach, the Dutch received books, Judaica, and the libraries of the International Institute for Social History, Freemason lodges, and the Portuguese Jewish community.[44] By late spring 1946, the Dutch MFAA team had helped repatriate to the Netherlands more than nine hundred paintings, some two thousand sculptures, numerous tapestries and high-quality furniture, porcelain, and decorative objects. SNK facilities took in recovered Judaica and books from the Rosenthaliana library at the University of Amsterdam, the Ets Haim library from the Portuguese-Jewish synagogue complex, and Freemason lodges.[45] In August, Vorenkamp reported that "5 percent of the looted objects quantitatively had been returned, but that qualitatively about 80 percent were back." The Netherlands received twenty-four shipments of some 4,700 cultural objects by the end of the year, plus five thousand crates from the archival depot at Offenbach.[46]

The Dutch faced greater frustration receiving works of art from the British zone, where according to Dutch records, 6,200 objects from the Netherlands had been sent—though it was unclear how many remained in the zone after the war.[47] The delay was due in part to discussions in the Foreign Office about whether the British would repatriate objects that had been sold to the enemy. In March 1946, an exasperated De Vries reported to British MFAA officer Christopher Norris that no works had been repatriated from the British zone: "I wonder whether a final decision in favor of the looted western countries will ever been [sic] taken. If not, which I never would be able to understand, we could as well close our shop. In itself, I would not mind that very much, but Holland would in that case really be duped," especially, he pointed out, since the Dutch could not expect reparations from Germany.[48] By April 1947, 425 Dutch claims had been submitted for some three thousand objects in the British zone, of which 250 had been released to the Netherlands.[49]

The British MFAA officers, for their part, admonished the Dutch for issuing incomplete reports and trying to thwart repatriation procedures to secure works on their own. In November 1946, British Major Anne Olivier Popham met with De Vries and Dutch officer C. J. N. Deirkauf in the Bünde office, a conversation she summarized as a "long discussion over the same old ground, about slowness of restitution and necessity for Dutch investigations." Popham offered encouragement but reminded the Dutch officers that they must coordinate their efforts with the MFAA and fully report all findings. With a touch of snark, she added that De Vries and Deirkauf then left the meeting and feasted on "100 oysters" in the officers' mess hall.[50] Tensions between the British and Dutch MFAA continued over the next several months, as the Bünde office complained about a lack of detail in the reports of Deirkauf and other Dutch officers, and informed De Vries that two high-quality chairs most likely from the Netherlands had been taken from the St. Annen museum in Lübbeck without the proper documentation. Norris, who replaced Geoffrey Webb as head of the British MFAA in July 1946, explained to De Vries that "the precedent was an exceedingly vicious one" and urged him to "take a strong line" with his officers. De Vries promised to address these issues with Deirkauf and, perhaps less convincingly, assured Norris that the Dutch would effectively carry out restitution procedures.[51] Among items successfully restituted to the Netherlands were some three hundred church bells of great symbolic and religious value to Dutch communities, especially in smaller towns.[52]

Artworks Found and Lost

As the recovery process was underway, the SNK gathered documentation from individuals who had lost art during the war, even in cases of voluntary sales. A Dutch decree from July 24, 1945, required registration forms from anyone in the Netherlands who had sold or transferred ownership of objects during the war to the enemy—a state entity or private individual. The initial deadline just a few months later, on October 15, proved far too short, and Dutch authorities ended up processing the forms through the early 1950s. Registration forms accumulated quickly as the first convoys of objects began arriving from Germany, and the limited staff at times failed to make connections between the documents and the works of art. In some cases, there were two sets of forms related to the same piece: a claimant's form, and an SNK form indicating unknown ownership. Compounding the confusion were works of art mistakenly sent to the Netherlands from the German collecting points, and lists of objects from Liro with scant information. Multiple "landscape," "Madonna and Child" pictures, and common scenes of daily life from a given time period could be easily misidentified when seen in isolation from the artist, date, exact measurements, and provenance information.[53]

The Dutch also were slow to create a legal framework for art restitution and the state appropriation of ownerless objects. The SNK operated for a year and a half without official guidelines, despite repeated efforts of certain members to define the legal status of cultural assets. On December 17, 1945, Willem van Elden, an attorney on the SNK board of directors, drew up a memorandum defining such legal principles in light of the reparations conference underway in Paris. The Dutch, he emphasized, understood "looting" to include theft and illegal requisition as well as "any form of sale, regardless of whether it was effected by an administrator or by the original owner acting under greater or lesser pressure, or was done by the latter on a completely voluntary basis." More simply put: "All of the property taken out of the Netherlands by Germans is considered 'looted.'" The SNK received repatriated cultural property for "the Dutch people," and once the works were on Dutch territory, they were subject only to Dutch government regulations. When receiving works of art from collecting points in Germany, SNK representatives signed a receipt, which stated in English that they took possession of the items "as custodians pending the determination of the lawful owners thereof." The objects would "be returned to their lawful owners within the territorial jurisdiction of said Government, as they may appear."[54] As in France and Belgium, the burden was on owners or heirs "to appear" with proof of ownership; searching for them was beyond the SNK's purview.

Van Elden defined four categories of recovered art. The first were objects "stolen or illegally acquired without payment or any compensation," whose owners were known and generally speaking must be restituted.[55] The other three categories involved sales to the enemy: objects sold "without the original owners' involvement, by persons appointed by the Germans to administer the original owners' property,"[56] as through the Aryanization of Jewish art galleries; pieces sold by the owners themselves "acting under greater or lesser pressure," meaning some measure of duress; and those sold by owners voluntarily. The category of voluntarily sold works, for which no rightful owner came forward, presented an opportunity for the Dutch government. Article 113 of decree E100 allowed the state to sell such assets for "a purpose to be specified by the Crown" or to purchase them for public use: "if the State wishes to acquire the objects, then it must first buy them." Through some budgeting and public accounting maneuvers, the proceeds could be deposited to the national treasury "by direct exchange."[57]

Even as Van Elden attempted to establish legal principles for the SNK, he recognized the difficulty in determining "known" and "unknown" owners: ". . . this is not so much about knowing where the item originally came from; rather, the question is how the original owner lost possession of it." In the event of competing claims, the SNK would refer claimants to the judicial division of the Council for the Restoration of Property Rights. The council, according to Van Elden, was the appropriate body to settle contested ownership claims, not the art experts in the SNK.[58]

Van Elden had identified some thorny legal issues, but the foundation took more than a year to approve its own restitution guidelines.[59] Adopted in January 1947, the guidelines defined the conditions in which the foundation would grant restitution. The identity of owners must be clear, along with a demonstrated involuntary loss, with no competing claims by other individuals, and no reason to expect future competing claims. In cases with some evidence of cooperation by owners, as in sales, the SNK would determine whether the loss was due to duress or "improper influence" of the enemy.[60]

For some claimants, evidence that one had bilked the Germans might be considered a kind of resistance activity. Even the forger Han van Meegeren earned the sympathy of many Dutch people during his trial for fraud in 1947, as he had managed to fool Göring and Miedl with his phony "Vermeer," *Christ with the Adultress*.[61] American MFAA officer H. Steward Leonard recounted Göring's reaction when Leonard told him during an interrogation in August 1946 that his precious Vermeer was a fake. The Reichsmarschall ranted about the dishonesty of dealers and, as Leonard's MFAA colleague Bernard Taper put it, "looked as if for the first time he had discovered there was evil in the world."[62] From the Dutch perspective, selling an authentic Vermeer to Göring would have been a far greater crime than duping him with a forgery.

Whether rightful owners had lost their works of art through theft or sales, they were required to pay fees to get them back. Most owners who had provided proof of ownership and had successfully demonstrated "involuntary loss" were forced to pay 2.75 percent of the works' estimated value to cover administrative, transportation, and insurance costs. In some cases, the SNK exempted claimants from this fee; collector Frits Lugt, for example, received an exemption for his "contributions to Dutch cultural life in the past and present."[63] Overall, however, the fee placed a financial burden on claimants, and Vorenkamp predicted in 1946 that many rightful owners would relinquish claims to avoid paying it.[64]

In some cases, the state offered individuals the opportunity to purchase pieces after their restitution claims had been denied. But the conditions and possibilities for purchases varied, reinforcing a sense among many claimants that the process was unpredictable and unjust.[65] Even in cases of forced sales, rightful owners were required to buy back their objects from the state at the wartime price. This policy served reconstruction efforts, as the postwar Dutch central bank held some six billion devalued

Reichsmarks that had flowed into the Netherlands after April 1941, when the Germans created an open currency market. The Reichsbank refused to reabsorb its own unconvertible marks and German purchases were made with devalued guilders. The postwar Dutch state thus aimed to regain some of the financial assets lost in these German transactions by requiring payment for the recovered works of art. Wealthier owners bought back objects with an air of anti-Nazi patriotism, as the victims of forced sales, and could expect to make a profit in subsequent transactions. Less fortunate owners, such as cash-strapped heirs who never received proceeds from wartime sales, were forced to seek loans or relinquish their claims altogether.[66]

The Dutch state benefited further by appropriating high-value, unclaimed works of art for public museums and other buildings, and selling less prestigious works at auction. At a meeting of the SNK board of directors, De Vries pointed out that the MFAA was repatriating works of art to the Netherlands because the Allies believed the objects were part of the Dutch "*patrimoine culturel national*"—using French terminology for cultural heritage. "But as soon as they [the artworks] cross the border," he added, "they come under the authority of the Beheersinstituut as items of an unknown owner."[67] Several thousand pieces remained under the management of the Dutch state for various reasons: claimants lacked sufficient proof of ownership; the owners had perished in death camps; survivors or heirs did not have proof of ownership, could not pay restitution fees, or were not even aware the state held items that were rightfully theirs; or the MFAA had mistakenly sent the objects to the Netherlands.[68] In all, the Dutch government became the custodian of several thousand repatriated, ownerless artworks—a tremendous cultural opportunity that coincided with the acute economic demands of postwar reconstruction.

The SNK determined that significant portion of the unclaimed objects had been sold voluntarily to the enemy and were subject to state appropriation. One such case involved the collection of Otto Lanz, purchased by Hans Posse for the Linz museum project through the Dutch and Jewish dealer Nathan Katz. Before the war, Lanz's widow, a Swiss citizen, had allowed the Rijksmuseum to hold a substantial array of Italian Renaissance paintings, furniture, and ceramics. The MFAA recovered the items at Alt Aussee, along with works from the Lugt and several other Dutch collections, and returned them to the Netherlands in 1945[69]—a boon for Dutch officials, though eventually they were willing to sell off part of the Lanz collection. The Frederik

Muller auction house in Amsterdam sold some paintings and furniture pieces from the collection on behalf of the government in March 1951, while others remained in the Dutch custodianship.[70]

The SNK held a narrow view of what constituted forced sales and determined that certain transactions were voluntary, though research several decades later would prove they had been conducted through antisemitic coercion. The fate of the Fritz Gutmann collection illustrates the injustice of early postwar cultural property norms. The MFAA repatriated some two hundred Gutmann pieces to the Netherlands, and two heirs, son Bernard and daughter Lili, submitted restitution claims for the objects purchased by Haberstock. On July 1, 1952, the Council for the Restoration of Property Rights instructed the SNK to release the pieces to the Gutmann heirs, on the condition they pay the sale price to the state, as the wartime transactions were deemed voluntary:

> ... the Council, in assessing the reasonableness of this intervention, also takes into account that the State, in recovering items originating from private collections and transported to Germany during the occupation, must be deemed to have done so with a view to restoring those items to their original owners, on the understanding that the restitution should not lead to an enrichment of said owners, which entails that they should refund to the State any compensation they might have received.[71]

Bernard and Lili, in their thirties at the time, were in no position to make such a large payment, and the objects remained in the Dutch custodianship for fifty years—until Fritz and Louise's grandsons sued for restitution and the government reconsidered the case in the early 2000s.[72]

In some cases, owners negotiated with the Dutch state and received compensation and restitution of certain objects while relinquishing claims to other pieces. For instance, at the end of the war Dutch authorities found some seven hundred Goudstikker objects on the gallery premises and seized them as enemy property. The MFAA also located a few hundred pieces in Germany and Austria, including those purchased by Göring, and repatriated them to the Netherlands. Goudstikker's widow, Dési, returned to Amsterdam in 1946, with a little black notebook that Jacques had been carrying in his jacket pocket on the night of his fatal accident. The notebook contained typed details of each piece the couple had left behind—artist, title, dimension, and provenance history. Despite her insistence that she had opposed the sales to

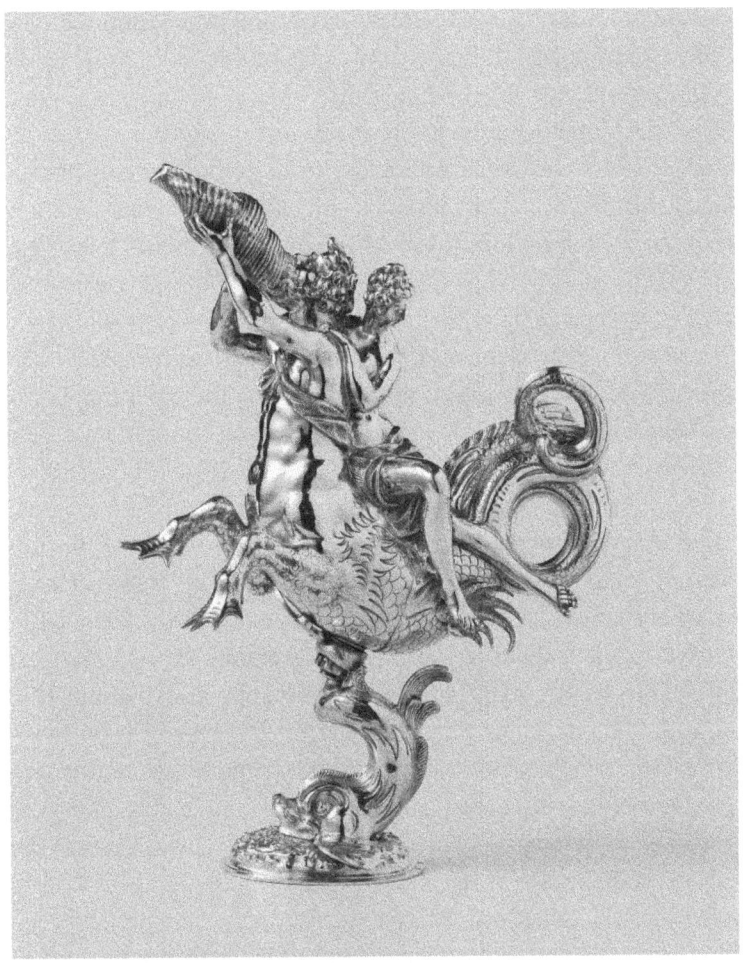

Johannes Lencker, *Ewer in the shape of a triton and a nereid* (c. 1620), selected by the Dutch state. Restituted to heirs of Fritz Gutmann. Courtesy of the Rijksmuseum, which purchased the item in 2003.

Miedl and Göring, the council determined the transactions carried out by dealership employees were voluntary.[73]

For several years, Dési negotiated with the Dutch state to regain the family assets. In the meantime, she married her American lawyer in 1950, and she and Eduard took his surname, Von Saher. According to a settlement reached August 1, 1952, Dési received the funds that remained in the account protected by Miedl, though the value had depreciated by one half. She used the funds to purchase the real estate and some 160 works from the gallery's stock. She also was given the opportunity to purchase the "Göring works" at the 1940 sale price, but was running short on funds and motivation to continue the legal battle. Still, she did not formally renounce her rights to the paintings, of which the Dutch state sold at auction some seventy pieces and distributed the rest to public museums and other government buildings.[74] More than two hundred Goudstikker objects remained in the Dutch custodianship by the late 1990s, when Eduard's American widow, Marei von Saher, resurrected the family's claim.[75]

The case of the Fritz Mannheimer collection also was complex. After the war, the MFAA repatriated most of the objects to the Netherlands, where officials believed Mannheimer's widow could not claim rightful ownership, as the sale had been used to pay her late husband's debts. Dutch authorities also claimed for the Netherlands several pieces that had been returned to France, leading to negotiations in Paris among representatives of the two governments and Mannheimer's widow, Jane, who by then had married American industrialist Charles Engelhard, had taken his name, and was living in New York. She was granted restitution of four pieces: a painting and etching by Fragonard and a painting each by Myervelt and Chardin.[76]

Even with this agreement, a comedy of errors in 1948 nearly foiled efforts to ship the objects to Engelhard, illustrating how many things could go wrong in the restitution process. The pieces were still being held in France when De Vries was charged with corruption and arrested. Given the uncertainty of affairs in the Netherlands, the French postponed the shipment. Engelhard contacted the US embassy in the Netherlands, which attempted to hasten the shipment. In August 1948, the new head of the SNK and director of the Rijksmuseum, D. C. Röell, made arrangements for French authorities to send the objects to the American embassy. The cases were indeed delivered to the embassy building, but with no addressee, no accompanying documents, and only a partially legible stamp indicating they had been packed by an art shipping firm in Paris. The cases were stashed away for several weeks, unbeknownst to American diplomats who had taken up the matter on Engelhard's behalf. An embarrassed official, Glion Curtis, finally contacted her in early December and reassured her that the cases had been stored in a dry, secure location and had sustained no visible damage. The shipment was arranged through American Express and Engelhard confirmed receipt by telegram: "PAINTINGS ARRIVED SAFELY TODAY MANY THANKS BEST WISHES FOR THE NEW YEAR JANE ENGELHARD."[77] She promptly sold

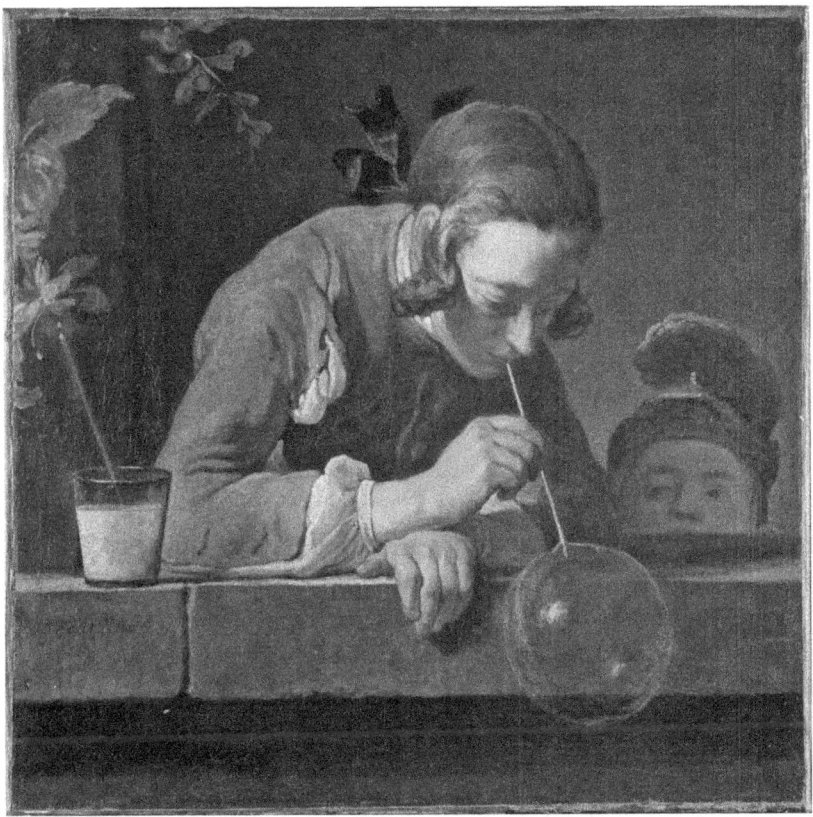

Jean Siméon Chardin, *Soap Bubbles*, ca. 1733–1734, restituted by the Dutch state to the widow of Fritz Mannheimer. Sold to Wildenstein, New York. Courtesy of the Metropolitan Museum of Art, which purchased the painting in 1949.

the Chardin picture, *Soap Bubbles*, to Wildenstein, New York, which in turn sold it to the Metropolitan Museum of Art, where it remains today.[78]

Enriching Dutch Museums

Works of art from the Lanz, Goudstikker, and Mannheimer collections were among thousands of unclaimed objects that remained in the custody of the SNK. In the summer of 1946, the foundation's board of directors recommended convening an advisory commission that would help select works of art from this cache to complement existing museum collections.

The president of the Rembrandt Association, E. Heldring, served as chairman, and other members included Jan Gerrit Van Gelder, director of the Mauritshuis; Jan Karel van der Haagen from the education ministry; D. C. Röell, director of the Rijksmuseum; and industrialist and collector D. G. van Beuningen,[79] whose role on the commission was complicated, due to his sale of 527 Old Master drawings from the Koenigs collection to Posse. The fate of the drawings would remain unknown until 1990, when Russian journalists determined they had been seized from Dresden by the Red Army and were in the Soviet Union.[80] But in the mid-1940s, when Van Beuningen was serving on the museum advisory commission, the drawings were still missing. He also remained an important benefactor of the Rotterdam museum, renamed the Museum Boijmans Van Beuningen in 1958, following the bequest of his private collection.[81]

The commission held its first meeting on August 23, 1946, and discussed the distribution of some twelve hundred objects, including five hundred paintings. Van der Haagen noted the view of some Dutch people, including members of the finance ministry, that recovered assets should be sold to raise funds that would benefit "the common good." He pointed out that some works would indeed be sold at auction, and the commission should only distribute those worthy of Dutch public ownership. Heldring countered that the first cull had already taken place, separating works to be sold and kept. The commission's objective, in his view, was "to recommend that a considerable quantity be retained in public ownership as the nation's cultural property." At the same time, commission members recognized that others in the government might choose to sell rather than distribute the objects, most likely a reference to finance minister Lieftinck. They thus agreed for "tactical reasons" to issue opinions on the allocation before seeking approval from other ministries. Van der Haagen proposed the distribution could be in the form of a loan to museums, creating "a semi-official situation" that was likely to endure.[82]

Van Gelder compared the task ahead of them to assets divided in an inheritance; most likely, no beneficiary would be entirely satisfied with the outcome. Yet the process was bound to enhance the most prestigious collections. Van Beuningen argued pointedly, "it is of utmost importance to make the great museums more glorious than they already are. This is what must be the focus of all attention first and foremost."[83] Special attention thus was given to larger museums in the Randstad region of Amsterdam, Rotterdam, The Hague, and Utrecht. At the same time, the commission also aimed to bolster the collections of smaller or so-called provincial museums, which according to Van Gelder had been neglected by the state and treated like "poor relations." The commission also considered the distribution an opportunity to compensate museums that had sustained loss or damage during the war.[84]

The commission invited museum directors to submit a "wish list" of recovered objects based on a catalog of enemy property provided by the SNK. The guidelines specifically invited such lists from museums in Arnhem, Dordrecht, Eindhoven, Groningen, Haarlem, Leiden, and Maastricht, reflecting the body's aim to distribute pieces beyond the nation's most prestigious museums.[85] In September 1946, the SNK board of directors confirmed the importance of responsibly supplementing existing collections: "this must not be a case of throwing money around; rather, the various museum boards will have to present arguments, based on the museum's program, about why they support a particular choice."[86]

To help museum directors create their wish lists, many of the ownerless paintings were displayed at the Rijksmuseum in April 1947. In a speech welcoming the directors, Heldring pointed out the objects' uncertain legal status and emphasized that the SNK would loan them to museums, at least initially: "As soon as a statutory arrangement has defined the legal status of this recovered art property" it would be possible to "undertake definitive acts" of distribution. Once museums acquired "actual ownership," however, they, like private claimants, would be expected to pay 2.75 percent of the works' appraised value to compensate the government for incurred expenses.[87] The fee was not actually imposed, as Finance Minister Lieftinck later argued it could only apply when restitution was made to former owners or their legal successors, and the state had acted as custodian of assets, not when the foundation transferred assets to another public entity; funds to cover any operating expenses would need to come from the regular state budget.[88] Heldring reassured directors from less prestigious museums by adding, "We consider it very important that the provincial and smaller museums receive their share of the recovered art property." He encouraged directors "to provide grounds for requesting each piece; in particular, please state to what extent the requested painting fits in with the framework of the respective museum." Restitution claims were still in process for some pieces, Heldring explained, such as objects from the Goudstikker collection that were "grouped together in the last gallery." Museum directors were free to include the pieces on their wish lists, "but you should keep in mind that a decision about the possibility of assigning them cannot be made until later." Heldring concluded by wishing the museum directors "a pleasant day in these galleries, which at least partly make up for the wrong inflicted on us by the enemy during the years of occupation."[89]

Museum directors then lobbied to secure pieces for their collections. Staff at the Stedelijk Museum in Amsterdam identified works by several artists that would fill "gaps" in the collection, including two paintings by Van Gogh, and one each by Kokoschka, Daumier, and Monet.[90] Some museum directors sought the support of powerful patrons. Anton Frederik Philips, former head of the Philips multinational best known for manufacturing light bulbs, endorsed the wish list of Edy de Wilde, director of the Van-Abbe Museum in Eindoven. Philips believed the works would give the public an excellent educational experience.[91] In other cases, historical connections to a given city and the location of depicted scenes helped determine the distribution; Groningen received works from the northern Netherlands while the commission deemed Maastricht suitable for paintings from southern regions. The commission also considered a former owner's connections to a given museum; thus it declined a request from the Mauritshuis for two paintings from the Koenings collection, sending them instead to the Boijmans museum in Rotterdam.[92] Local community dedication to the arts also made a difference. Van Gelder, who took the lead role in the distribution process, advocated prioritizing Roosendaal in the North Brabant region, which had "virtually no art collection" but "very great" interest in establishing one among local authorities, the clergy, and the broader public. A group of particularly motivated individuals in Roosendaal formed a cultural association to promote the initiative. Van der Haagen suggested a better location might be Roermond, "where a museum exists that has a good gallery with skylights." Van Gelder disagreed, as "Roermond has not made contact. There appears to be no interest there. This is in sharp contrast to the enthusiasm experienced in Roosendaal."[93]

Rijksinspector Scheurleer also advocated sending pieces to Curaçao and Suriname: "Since Curaçao is currently a very important oil center frequented by many foreigners, I think it is a national matter to ensure that the palace is presentable. In my opinion, the paintings provided on load here should thus be of rather good quality." Governor Struycken had specific ideas for paintings for the main government building: he preferred landscapes, still lifes, and interiors approximately 100 to 110 cm long with the frame. Struycken also requested furniture, though the threat of termites led Scheurleer to recommend "a hard type of wood (teak). I could probably help him with two benches and a similar chest (17th or 18th century)." The Rijksinspector also recommended reserving paintings for a government building and museum in Paramaribo.[94]

The commission issued an initial distribution list in October 1947, and the SNK board of directors approved it a month later, acknowledging the provisional nature of the recommendations given the uncertain legal status of the ownerless works.[95] Museum collections would be enriched first, then pieces would be available to build a state collection of furniture, art, and decorative objects for government offices, embassies, and other public buildings.[96]

While distribution plans were made, the SNK continued to accept claims on repatriated objects. In 1949 and 1950, the recovered works of art were exhibited at public museums, including the Rijksmuseum, on so-called viewing days, to allow potential claimants to examine the recovered objects for at least one month. Newspapers announced the exhibitions, which were open to claimants who had filed official restitution forms reporting a theft, confiscation, or forced sale. The SNK also provided claim forms at the exhibitions. By July 1, 1950, the viewing days had generated a few hundred new claims in the following categories:

Furniture	35
Applied art objects	206
Rugs	149
Paintings	86
Drawings	8

The viewing days did not significantly bolster restitutions,[97] as they did not change the key impediments to restitution: fees imposed by the SNK, the inability of claimants to provide indisputable proof of ownership, and a lack of knowledge among survivors and heirs that the state held assets that were rightfully theirs.

In all, the Netherlands created a custodianship for more than four thousand recovered objects that were distributed to museums, public buildings, and the new State Art Objects Collections Service. The state collection included prestigious works by Frans Hals (*Portrait of a Man*), Jacob van Ruisdael (*Watermill, Wooded Landscape, Rocky Landscape with Waterfall*), Jan Steen (*The Expulsion from the Temple, Cockfight in a Tavern, A Peasant Wedding*), Gerard ter Borch (*Portrait of a Woman, Interior of an Attic-Room, Interior with Soldiers Playing Cards*), Lucas Cranach the Elder (*Madonna and*

Child with the Infant St. John the Baptist, Venus and Amor), and Cornelius Troost (*The Maternity Visit, The Doctor's Visit, Portrait of a Man and Boy*).[98] Yet Dutch officials continued to debate principles of rightful ownership.

Debating Rightful Ownership

Throughout the selection process, advisors to the SNK and the members themselves questioned the legality of the custodianship. One report from September 1946 put the question in blunt terms: By what right can the state control recovered works of art? If rightful owners were always easily identified, there would be no legal issue. In reality, the author acknowledged, the rightful owners often were not clear, and typically the state would be required to sell the assets to third parties within a reasonable time frame. Yet, there were cases in which the state wished to keep items for public use.[99] Operating under the assumption that the vast majority of unclaimed pieces had been voluntarily sold to the enemy, De Vries and other SNK officials wondered whether German buyers or Dutch sellers might be able to claim the repatriated objects. French terms pepper the meeting minutes, in which the SNK members agreed that the Allies were pursuing the restoration of "*patrimoine national culturel.*" At the same time, the expropriation of assets from German buyers was "not a very attractive way to treat items claimed by the Netherlands."[100] According to one proposed measure, if no rightful owner had come forward after one year, the item would "definitively" revert to the state, which could either sell it to a third party or keep it for public use.[101] This proposal with an exceedingly short claims period never came to fruition, fortunately for claimants, and the legal limbo continued.

In October 1946, the Dutch justice minister requested advice from the Council for the Restoration of Rights on the legal status of a wide range of recovered assets. The council appointed a legal commission on December 11 made up of three attorneys: W. J. Belinfante, L. O. van der Plas, and J. Woudstra, of the justice, finance, and economic affairs ministries, respectively. In its final report, the legal commission argued that the state could not claim the assets based on decree E100 applicable to assets found within the territory of the Netherlands, nor according to decree E133, which applied to enemy property of residents within the kingdom. The Dutch state had a stronger claim based on international law. From this perspective, the Allies had transferred the assets to the Netherlands from the former Third Reich to benefit the Dutch nation, and the state "is free to dispose of [the assets] as it sees fit." The government had responsibilities of "fiduciary ownership" and served as "custodian" for claimants in the Netherlands. When assets were not successfully restituted, the state could claim them by appropriation. According to the commission, no new legislation was necessary to regulate state ownership of assets recovered from Germany.[102]

Apparently unsatisfied with the commission's report, De Vries sought further advice from C. Heyning of the CGR. In an analysis issued on January 5, 1948, Heyning determined that the commission's report failed to provide a clear legal basis for state ownership of repatriated objects. In his view, the commission had merely advanced several theories to justify absorbing the items for public use, none of which appeared tenable. Heyning concluded that "*a right of ownership on the part of the state is generally nonexistent with respect to the recovered items.*"[103]

From this central premise, Heyning identified potential legal issues that could surface during the appropriation process. German wartime buyers might claim recovered objects, a possibility the SNK hoped would be prevented in a final treaty with Germany.[104] Another question: Would other Allied governments hold the Dutch state liable for the public sale of items declined by the commission? How would the state respond to claims that might surface? The claims period was due to expire July 1, 1948, a deadline that likely would be extended. If the state were found to be "the possessor in good faith," the statute of limitations on such claims would be a period of three years after the loss, a deadline that would have passed in nearly all cases. Heyning doubted that good faith could be assumed, however, "since the presumption of wrongful loss of possession is obvious." If the state were not acting in good faith, the statute of limitations would extend to thirty years. Heyning further argued that the state's claim to ownership was weakened by the fact that the SNK had not notified potential owners about the claims process. Given all these factors, Heyning recommended that the SNK create new guidelines for the definitive government acquisition of repatriated objects, to be approved by the council and the education and finance ministries.[105]

The fate of repatriated cultural assets also was an economic issue. In the summer of 1948, SNK officials aimed to prevent the sale of museum-quality pieces. They pointed out that MFAA officers from various Allied countries had not worked to recover works from German repositories and salt mines only to see the objects sold at auction in the home countries. They argued that such sales would put the Netherlands out of step with other victimized countries in western Europe, though in reality, officials in France and Belgium also were planning sales of unclaimed, lower-quality items.[106]

The issue became particularly acute in discussions over the creation of a national furniture collection akin to the French *Mobilier national*. Dutch officials had discussed proposals for such a program in the 1930s, but they had stalled with the outbreak of war. During the art restitution process, the new stock of ownerless art and furniture helped revive the idea. By August 1948, the proposal had broad support in the Council of Ministers, but Lieftinck opposed it due to more urgent reconstruction priorities. An internal finance ministry memo argued that given the dire financial position of the nation, it would be irresponsible to set up a *Mobilier national*, invoking the French term, and the art should be sold with proceeds benefiting the national treasury.[107] By November, Lieftinck's position had softened and the State Art Collections Service (*Dienst voor Rijks Verspreide Kunstvoorwerpen*) was established in 1949, constituted in part with recovered objects.[108]

But Lieftinck created other difficulties for the SNK, positing that repatriated assets "whose original owners have not come forward or for which restitution claims cannot be recognized" become the responsibility of the finance ministry, not the SNK or the Beheersinstituut. He pointed to Royal Decree no. 112 from 1841, which designated the finance ministry as the administrator of state property. His ministry, he argued, should make decisions about which objects could be included in the national collection, with the advice of the SNK.[109] Increasingly, the finance ministry did play a key role in the management of the art custodianship, as reflected in the appointment of Jolle Jolles, director of HERGO in the finance ministry, to succeed De Vries in October 1948. In another important shift, custody of the artworks was transferred to HERGO on July 1, 1950.[110]

The state also benefited from sales of less coveted objects, ranging from tchotchkes to pieces from the renowned Goudstikker, Mannheimer, and Lanz collections.[111] In August 1950, Jolles reported that "719 paintings were sold at auction, 18 paintings were sold in direct sales, 120 carpets and an unspecified number" of furniture and applied art objects were sold at a total value to that date of Nlg 51,667.76.[112] However, the total revenue amount collected through 1953 was much higher—at least Nlg 2 million. Government reports and correspondence provide limited information on the sale of

Jewish-owned items, but objects from the Mannheimer collection alone generated Nlg 1.5 million.[113]

Controversy within the SNK

Just as the SNK was determining the legal status of ownerless objects and making plans to distribute the best pieces to museums, the foundation was destabilized by the arrest of De Vries in July 1948. He had authorized the restitution of thirty-two paintings to Nathan Katz, the dealer who had earned a visa to Switzerland through the Lanz collection sale to Posse. De Vries and Katz were on good terms while both were in Switzerland during the war, a rapport that appears to have clouded De Vries's judgment in restitution decisions. Other Dutch officials believed that sales facilitated by Katz, such as Göring's purchase of Rembrandt's *Portrait of Saskia* from the Ten Cate collection, were voluntary and the objects should have remained in the custody of the Dutch state. Once Katz had received the pictures, he shipped ten of them to Switzerland and sold the *Saskia* Rembrandt to Swiss industrialist and collector Emil Bührle, who himself had purchased works looted from the Paul Rosenberg collection through the Theodor Fischer gallery in Switzerland. The controversy over De Vries's handling of the Katz case forced him to step down as SNK director in July 1948, during the investigation.[114]

De Vries's arrest prompted expressions of solidarity from former MFAA officers abroad. Writing to Paul Coremans in Belgium, Thomas Howe expressed sympathy for De Vries: "The consensus of opinion seems to be that there is a good deal of dirty politics involved and that the only fault on Bob's part was, without realizing the possible consequence, in being too lenient with a certain dealer regarding the restitution of certain pictures. I feel so badly about the whole affair...". Coremans concurred: "His professional mistake can only be minimal and Dutch justice has gone too far in borrowing methods worthy of the Gestapo. His friends are all on his side."[115] De Vries eventually was cleared of charges due to insufficient evidence, a decision confirmed on appeal in April 1951. But the public relations damage had been done, as reflected the following month in a damaging *De Telegraaf* headline: "Chaos at the Art Property Foundation: Fraud, Black Money and Poor Administration."[116]

A less public example of SNK mismanagement involved Monuments Man Phonse Vorenkamp, who received an unspecified "small painting" through irregular procedures. Members of the SNK board were caught off guard in September 1948 when questioned by Dutch authorities about the gift. After learning they lacked authority to offer such a gift, the board members sought retroactive approval from the ministers of education and finance.[117]

Dutch or French Patrimony? Complexities of Inter-Allied Restitution

A restitution dispute between France and the Netherlands in the early 1950s reveals the complexities of inter-Allied restitution when two countries aimed to receive the same items. The dispute originated in the purchase of artworks in the Netherlands in 1942 and 1943 by Kurt Martin, the German head of Strasbourg museums after the Third Reich's annexation of Alsace. Martin was a highly respected art historian and former director of the Staatliche Kunsthalle, an important fine arts museum in Karlsruhe, about fifty miles northeast of Strasbourg. Martin was not a Nazi party member and throughout the annexation period maintained a remarkably positive rapport with Hans Haug, the former head of Strasbourg museums, whom the Germans had aimed to expel from the administration in early 1941 for "Francophilia." Intervening on behalf of Haug, Martin helped convert the expulsion order into an authorization for voluntary departure, enabling Haug to serve as director of the French national museum repository at the Cheverny chateau, which held works evacuated from the Louvre.[118] Martin remained in touch with Haug during the annexation period and consulted him when considering art acquisitions for Strasbourg museums.[119]

Haug, who regained his position in Strasbourg after the war, never doubted the legality of purchases made by Martin in the Netherlands. He knew Martin to be exceedingly cautious with acquisitions, verifying provenance and working only with established dealers. When air raids threatened the security of the art collections in 1944, Martin evacuated objects to the Heilbronn and Pfullendorf mines—repositories that ended up in the American and French zones, respectively. American authorities repatriated the objects in their zone to the Netherlands while Rose Valland sent those in the French zone to Strasbourg.[120]

On March 15, 1946, Dutch MFAA officer Hans Jaffé visited Strasbourg and presented Haug with a list of fifteen paintings and decorative objects purchased by Martin for the city's museums in devalued Dutch guilders—a form of spoliation as defined by the 1943 inter-Allied declaration and ACC directives on wartime sales to the enemy. But were the purchases truly "German"? Haug's initial reaction to the Dutch claim, as expressed to Albert Henraux of the French CRA, focused on moral issues: "I don't understand why, no matter the regime under which the museums of Strasbourg operates, affairs always turn against them." Air raids in August and September 1944 had rendered the galleries "among the most brutally damaged of French museums" and according to Haug, they deserved "some generosity." Given the Allies' view that the German annexation of Alsace was illegal under international law, Henraux referred to the case to French Ministry of Foreign Affairs.[121]

In the meantime, Haug gathered more information on the circumstances of the purchase and the funds used, in part by contacting Martin, who was once again head of Staatliche Kunsthalle, having been cleared for service by French de-Nazification authorities. Haug had helped to rehabilitate Martin and informed Henraux that the German curator's "attitude during the *entire* war was, from a personal and professional standpoint, beyond reproach."[122] Martin supplied Haug with details on the transactions, from which Haug drew several conclusions: the Strasbourg museums were not German at the time of the purchase, as the annexation had violated international law; the acquisitions were made using Alsatian funds that supported the German civil administration; Martin had moved the works further into German territory only because the repositories were the closest with available storage space and offered the best protection against air raids; the purchases were similar to those carried out in peacetime and were fully voluntary sales at the Boer, Bachstitz, and Hoogendijk dealerships[123]—all of which, however, actually traded in confiscated art during the occupation, raising questions about the works' provenance. Martin claimed to have believed that Germany would lose the war and the works would remain in Strasbourg. In 1947, the French OBIP determined the purchase was not a form of spoliation and was carried out with Alsatian funds. In the French view, the works thus should remain in Strasbourg.[124] The French position disregarded a complicating factor: funding of the German civil administration came in part from Alsatian contributions, and in part from funds raised from the public sale of despoiled assets.[125]

The dispute waned until Haug traveled to the Netherlands in 1949, prompting Jolles of the SNK once again to demand the works held in Strasbourg. OBIP, in turn, reiterated its findings from 1947, and Haug threatened to demand objects purchased by Martin for Strasbourg that had been repatriated to the Netherlands. The affair abated again until February 1950, when the French embassy in The Hague claimed a Pissarro painting, listed as *Garden at Pontoise*, on behalf of Maurice de Rothschild. The picture had been looted by the Germans from the chateau d'Armainvillers, and then was part of an exchange of works between Göring and the Kröller-Müller museum in Osterloo, facilitated by the German dealer Hans Lange in 1940 or 1941. Göring offered the museum several French Impressionist paintings, including the looted Pissarro, and in return received three paintings by Baldung Grien, Lucas Cranach the Elder, and Barthel Bruyn, which were later recovered by the MFAA and repatriated to the Netherlands. The Dutch refused to restitute the Pissarro to Rothschild, as the French had not returned the works in Strasbourg purchased by Martin. From the French perspective, the two cases were entirely separate and unrelated, as the Pissarro had been stolen, while the works in Strasbourg had been purchased in a "normal" manner. According to Michel Florisoone of the CRA, "there cannot be any link or interdependence between them. They are not of the same nature or character." The Pissarro, he argued, must be returned to France "unconditionally."[126]

The Dutch disagreed. Martin's purchase, they reasoned, was only possible because of the German elimination of the currency border in 1941, which had left the Netherlands with worthless German marks. Göring's avarice thus had led to "a real impoverishment of the Dutch patrimony." According to the Dutch, both were cases of German spoliation—in France, the victim was an individual (Rothschild) and in the Netherlands, an entire nation. Once the French fulfilled the Dutch claim to works from Strasbourg, they argued, they would restitute the Pissarro, as the Dutch had already recognized Maurice de Rothschild's rightful ownership.[127]

The French continued to press for the unconditional restitution of the Pissarro, perhaps buoyed by the Baron's promise to donate the painting to the Louvre if the French government helped him recover it.[128] Finally, in the spring of 1954 Dutch authorities allowed Valland to secure the Pissarro for Rothschild, and as promised, he promptly donated it to the Louvre.[129] Negotiations over the Strasbourg objects continued into the summer, when the annexation of Alsace was again at the center of public debate in France, in anticipation of the trial of Alsatian soldiers who had participated in the Waffen-SS massacre at Oradour-sur-Glane during the German retreat of June 1944. In this highly politicized context, the French embassy asked the

Dutch Ministry of Foreign Affairs to consider "the unusual conditions of the acquisition of paintings by an Alsatian museum during the occupation." As illustrated by the Oradour trial, the French diplomats argued, "the solution to problems in Franco-German relations in Alsace must take into consideration the particular sensitivity of a region that felt the cruel military and political repercussions of the most recent conflicts." Just as the Dutch government had acknowledged Maurice de Rothschild's rightful ownership of the Pissarro, the French asked to maintain the status quo for the works purchased by Martin—Strasbourg would keep its objects and the Dutch would keep those repatriated by the Americans.[130] Finally in October 1954, the Dutch foreign ministry accepted the French position and dropped its claim to the Strasbourg objects.[131] In this inter-Allied agreement, the Dutch relinquished legal arguments that had equated Nazi theft from an individual (Rothschild) and the sale to Martin, and accepted French moral arguments that Alsace had earned the right to keep some of the purchased items, owing to the German exploitation during the annexation. Neither side at the time investigated whether the Dutch dealers who sold the objects to Martin had obtained them in voluntary sales. Despite French confidence in Martin's probity, it remains worth investigating whether Nazi persecution ended up enriching museum collections in both countries.

From SNK to the Netherlands Art Property Collection (NK)

De Vries's arrest in July 1948 disrupted the productivity of the SNK, as its personnel sought long-term employment elsewhere. Jolles took over as director in October while also serving as head of HERGO, and he attempted to improve efficiency by reorganizing the administration and reviewing unresolved cases. He found that "virtually nothing had been done in recent years in the area of returning art works to the original title holders [and] many letters had gone unanswered for months." The storage of recovered works in air-raid shelters in Zandvoort and Heemstede "was organized appallingly. Many art objects suffered greatly from this storage." For works that already had been distributed to museums, there were no loan agreements, and proof of transfer of furniture for public buildings often was missing.[132] By March 1950, Jolles and Scheurleer reported a return to order, with the organization of correspondence, use of loan agreements, and creation of detailed inventories of pieces held by the SNK. The nine-member staff and four temporary employees appeared to enjoy a boost in morale, carrying out its duties "with great dedication," despite a demanding workload.[133]

The custody of ownerless pieces transferred to HERGO in July 1950, then to the education ministry two years later. The SNK was dissolved in November 1952 and since then, the ownerless works have been classified as the Netherlands Art Property Collection (*Nederlands Kunstbezit-collectie*, or NK). Some items were placed on display in museums, others went to embassies and other public buildings abroad, and some remained in storage. The information gathered by the SNK remained in the finance ministry archives, separating the art collection and relevant documentation. Over the next forty-five years, no effort was made to review the foundation archives systematically and connect the information with data from other government offices.[134] In the meantime, the central task of Dutch art experts as defined by Van Beuningen in 1946 had been achieved, making the great Dutch museum collections all the more glorious.

6
Restoring Belgian Artistic Heritage

In November and December 1948, Belgian cultural officials, following the example of their French and Dutch counterparts, staged an exhibition of recovered works of art to celebrate the nation's cultural patrimony and express thanks to the western Allies for their commitment to the restitution effort. Visitors to the Palais des Beaux-Arts in Brussels viewed Michelangelo's *Madonna* and works by Memling, Van der Weyden, Lucas Cranach the Elder, Ferdinand Bol, and Jacob Jordaens, as well as examples of fine porcelain, incunabula, and rare books. According to the exhibition catalog, the display was a sign of MFAA success: "the presence of works of art, like the ones on display in these rooms, represent, at once, the most eloquent and most palpable evidence of fruitful work carried out together."[1] In the end, this international cooperation most benefited the Belgian state.

Through the transnational efforts of the MFAA, the heads of national restitution committees kept one another apprised of Allied policy and were aware of national restitution policies. As in France and the Netherlands, Belgian authorities saw an opportunity to expand state collections with unclaimed furniture and works of art.[2] The latest research indicates that Belgium recovered 1,155 objects, of which roughly 10 percent were restituted to rightful owners. The remaining 90 percent benefited the Belgian state through auction proceeds or distribution to Belgian public art museums, embassies, ministry offices, and other government buildings. These institutions absorbed 639 objects of which at least 305 items were Jewish-owned. Only four of these "items" were paintings. The Royal Museums of Art and History in Brussels received a total of 292 objects, mostly archeological artifacts, Asian and Middle Eastern antiquities, gold and silverworks, and bronzes. Also in Brussels, the Jewish Museum received one lot of 460 books in Hebrew.[3] Though the Belgian case involves fewer masterpieces than in the cases of France and the Netherlands, it nonetheless reveals dominant attitudes toward repatriated and ownerless works of art that had been sold to the enemy. The Belgian state appropriated the highest-quality items as a way of securing cultural reparations and bolstering national collections. It also exposes administrative shortcomings, a narrow view of restitutable assets, and a persistent lack of political will to pursue thorough, systematic research on appropriated Jewish cultural property. Belgian policy thus prolonged the mishandling of cultural assets well into the twenty-first century.

Toward Political Stability, 1944–51

The Allies secured the territory of northern France by mid-August 1944 and faced little German resistance as they pushed into Belgium. American forces crossed the border on September 2, and a British armored division reached Brussels the next day. A second British division arrived at the key port city of Antwerp on September 4, while Canadian and Polish divisions moved along the North Sea coast toward Bruges. Tank and motorized units kept up their steady advance, pausing to acknowledge the cheers of elated Belgian onlookers, as Martin Conway puts it, "rather in the manner of the *peleton* of a cycle race."[4] After ten days, the Allies controlled nearly all of Belgian territory.[5] As a slower second wave of Allied forces advanced through the territory, the lack of German resistance enabled enthusiastic celebration—crowds pouring into city streets and public squares, women climbing on tanks, all waving flags and toasting the demise of the Germans.[6]

Once the jubilant crowds had dispersed, Belgian authorities faced tremendous challenges, as the occupation had left the country economically depleted and politically divided. The Germans had deported King Leopold and his new wife in June 1944, holding them first at Hirschstein near Dresden, then in the village of Strobl, Austria, where they were liberated by American forces on May 7, 1945.[7] After the war, the royal couple remained in exile in Switzerland because of controversies over the king's wartime association with the enemy. There was no Belgian equivalent of Charles de Gaulle to rally the masses and create even an illusory sense of national unity. The strength of the nation-state had been called into question thrice over, due to a humiliating defeat in 1940, exploitative occupation, and liberation by foreign armies.[8]

Ministers who had served the exiled government in London, led by presumed prime minister Hubert Pierlot, arrived inconspicuously at an airfield near Brussels on September 8. Navigating a chaotic post-liberation environment, they were quickly forced to grapple with the proclaimed sovereignty of the absent king. On Pierlot's second day back in Belgium, two senior legal officials presented the minister with a political testament written by Leopold in March 1944, anticipating his own forced exile. He claimed that all wartime agreements between the ministers in London and Allied authorities lacked his approval and thus were invalid. He also denounced the ministers' wartime criticisms of the monarchy, arguing they had damaged royal prestige and national honor, and he demanded just "reparations" for this repeated disparagement. Faced with Leopold's defiance, the ministers reviewed their options and agreed to ignore the testament. Instead of recognizing Leopold's authority, they offered a regency to the king's younger brother, Prince Charles. It was a shrewd political move, as Charles had remained distant from Leopold's entourage and conveniently lacked charisma, to the point of appearing ill at ease in public. He displayed little of his brother's political ambition, and the ministers gambled he would be a compliant figurehead. The two reassembled houses of parliament approved Charles' regency on September 20, and Pierlot begrudgingly accepted the role of prime minister, which he held until February 1945, through a long winter of food and fuel shortages as the war continued against Germany.[9]

Meanwhile, Leopold was still waiting to recover the throne from Prince Regent Charles. After being liberated by US forces near Salzburg in May 1945, he emigrated to Switzerland and waited for negotiations over his return to Belgium. He retained support among many Flemish Belgians, devout Catholics, and the French-speaking upper class, but most leftist and middle- to lower-class French speakers saw him as incompetent or even collaborationist. In March 1950, a popular referendum produced a slim majority in favor of the king's restoration. His return to Belgium in July 1950, however, prompted violent protests that deeply divided the nation. In July 1951, Leopold finally abdicated in favor of his twenty-year-old son, Baudouin. This crisis in the monarchy at first glance appears to reflect opinion of a fundamentally changed Belgian society in the wake of war and occupation. Yet debates over Leopold's restoration actually fell along traditional political lines of right and left, and this essential framework in Belgian politics remained a source of stability into the 1970s.[10]

Claiming a National Heritage

The repatriation of cultural assets from Germany and Austria thus occurred in a paradoxical period of simultaneous upheaval and continuity in Belgian authority. Among the key figures in the art recovery process was art historian and curator Leo Van Puyvelde. Trained as an expert in Flemish literature at the Catholic University of Leuven, he was an auto-didact in the field of art history and developed internationally renowned expertise in medieval, Renaissance, and seventeenth-century Flemish painting. In 1927, he was appointed head curator at the Royal Museums of Fine Arts in Brussels, where he established an art conservation laboratory, and in the 1930s he taught as a visiting professor in Paris and Algiers, and in the United States at Princeton, Harvard, and Yale.[11]

When the war began, Van Puyvelde was among the Belgian elite who fled to Britain. King George VI invited him to examine pieces in the British royal collection, which enabled him to publish studies on Flemish and Dutch drawings during the war. He also served multiple roles in the Belgian government in exile, including general director for fine arts. From the spring of 1944, he also served as the Belgian representative to the Vaucher Commission, and in July headed a new office in the education ministry meant to protect Belgian cultural patrimony and spearhead art restitution from Germany.[12]

In this last capacity, Van Puyvelde led the Belgian effort to compile lists of cultural objects removed by the enemy, and he provided contact information for local experts across the country who could assist MFAA officers in the field. After the Liberation, he joined the Belgian military mission at the rank of lieutenant colonel.[13] The widely respected senior scholar and curator, who had only completed occasional Sunday drills in Brussels during World War I, made a less convincing senior military officer. Van Puyvelde arrived home sporting his colonel battle dress, an entertaining sight to some colleagues.[14]

As the arts bureaucracy expanded under Van Puyvelde's leadership, he soon faced administrative competition in a broader Belgian effort to recover from Germany a wide range of lost assets: industrial and military equipment, vehicles, trains, and ships. Belgian officials considered compensation from Germany crucial to economic recovery, whether in the form of reparations, restitution, or the transfer of comparable assets. In November 1944, the Pierlot government created the Office for Economic Restitution (*Dienst Economische Recuperatie*, DER/*Office de récupération économique*, ORE). The DER was charged with several tasks: identifying Belgian assets in Germany and Austria; ensuring conservation by third party holders; researching owners or rightful heirs; and facilitating restitution, compensation, or the liquidation of recovered goods. On January 16, 1945, it was also charged with creating a general inventory of enemy assets found in Belgium.[15]

In the grand scheme of reparations and restitutions, the department prioritized the recovery of non-cultural assets. In 1945 alone, Belgium received 126 naval vessels from Germany, and by 1952, 211 factories had been transferred to Belgium, helping the country re-establish the production of heavy metals, chemicals, textiles, and petroleum. Between 1945 and 1952, the DER oversaw financial compensation totaling BFr 567,368,388, of which 429.223.299 came from industrial materials, and the value of German ships reached Bfr 132,813,797.[16]

The DER also established a cultural office charged with recovering and restituting works of art, apart from Van Puyvelde's service. The DER office was headed by a twenty-four-year-old soldier and university graduate, Raymond Lemaire, who served as a liaison to the MFAA in the US zone. Assisting Lemaire was Franz Baudouin, a renowned scholar of Flemish baroque art. Still a young man at the end of the war, Lemaire would later earn a doctorate in archaeology and art history and became a major figure in postwar Belgian conservation.[17] But by 1945, he had merely shown promise as an art history student. Van Puyvelde, in contrast, already had an international scholarly reputation and had located displaced objects in Germany, Austria, and within Belgium, including some fifty paintings found at the Ecole Militaire and other storage sites in Brussels.[18]

An unproductive rivalry thus developed between the services headed by Van Puyvelde and Lemaire. The senior scholar continued to act as if he were the head of the Belgian art recovery operation, while the DER accused him of insubordination and barred his access to repositories.[19] On February 5, 1947, the head of the DER, Monsieur Reul, reported that Van Puyvelde's service had repeatedly sent unauthorized representatives on mission to Germany and Austria, and had inappropriately contacted Allied authorities to secure the repatriation of objects. According to Reul, such actions violated the authority of the DER and his office could not be held responsible for the fate of assets transferred to Van Puyvelde's division, including restitution to parties other than rightful owners.[20] The scholar's actions also prompted scolding from the education minister, Herman Vos: "Such incidents will only slow down progress in the reconstitution of the cultural patrimony, for which you are responsible." Any mission to Allied occupied zones, the minister emphasized, were to be authorized in advance only by the DER.[21] Asset restitution was further stymied by the scattering of relevant German archives among several

Belgian offices: the DER held ERR documents, while BTG records were at the Sequestration Office, and papers from the German Quartering Office (*Quartieramt*) were held by the Requisition Service. Belgian restitution thus suffered from a lack of coordination and communication among these various agencies.[22]

Moreover, Belgian restitution and compensation policy undermined the interests of foreign Jews, who constituted around 90 percent of the Jewish population at the time of the invasion. The government Property Custodian Office (*Dienst van het Sekwester*) held assets of German and Austrian Jews as "enemy property," which became restitutable in 1947 only with proof of non-enemy status. In addition, laws promulgated in 1945 and 1947 allowed compensation for significant losses only to Belgian nationals. Compensation to other Jewish war victims was delayed until the German Federal Restitution Law (*Bundesrückerstattungsgesetz*, or BRüG) of 1957.[23]

According to the Belgian Study Commission, at least 885 Jewish-owned objects were sent to Germany and Austria. These can be grouped into three categories: those looted by the ERR in Belgium, works sent by German authorities to the ERR in Cologne, and objects seized by the BTG and the Paris branch of the ERR. The first category contained 249 objects, of which twenty-eight were recovered by American and French MFAA officers. Among twelve despoiled families, only two recovered their assets: Hugo and Elisabeth Andriesse (twenty-four canvases and two tapestries) and Eric Lyndhurst (two paintings). Among 351 works from Jewish collections sent to ERR authorities in Cologne, no pieces were recovered. In the third category, the BTG and the *Sonderstab Bildende Kunst* of the ERR in Paris had seized 285 objects, of which two hundred returned to Belgium—193 from the American zone and seven from the French capital. Only thirty-four of these paintings were returned to two Jewish families: twenty-eight to David and Jacob Reder, and six to Robert and Alice de Bauer.[24] Overall, only 7 percent of plundered Jewish artworks were restituted to rightful owners.[25]

In addition to the recovery of fine art, the DER secured 4,568 church bells that had been seized by the enemy for recycling into armaments.[26] It also recovered archives with symbolic importance plundered from Eupen-Malmédy, a largely German-speaking region that had been annexed by the Third Reich and was restored to Belgium after the war. In broader terms, however, the DER missed an opportunity to pursue the restitution of seized Belgian archives and libraries—the primary focus of ERR looting in Belgium. Instead, the DER focused on the visual arts due to the prestige and value of these works, especially high-quality paintings, and the greater likelihood of identifying owners. The Germans seized some 56,000 books from Belgium, yet only an estimated 1.2 percent of plundered library materials were restituted to rightful owners.[27]

Recovered Works on Display

By the summer of 1948, the DER began phasing out the art recovery service and planning the next phase of cultural property management. Lemaire met with the head of fine arts, Lucien Christophe, on August 19, and the two discussed transferring cultural responsibilities from the DER to the fine arts administration in the education ministry at the end of the year. The ministry was already in the process of distributing ownerless books to Belgian libraries, and it developed a similar plan to select quality works of art for museums and public buildings. Second-rate pieces would be transferred to the property division of the finance ministry (les Domaines) and sold at public auction.[28]

Lemaire also wished to exhibit the works of art recovered from Germany and Austria, following the example of such shows in France, the Netherlands, Italy, and Poland. Lemaire envisioned two separate exhibitions: the first would be a "public and spectacular" show at the Palace of Fine Arts, displaying the greatest masterpieces recovered with identified rightful owners—whether they were Belgian institutions, such as the Saint Bavo cathedral (the Ghent Altarpiece) and St. Peter's church in Leuven (Dieric Bouts's *The Last Supper*), or private owners such as the Andriesse and Reder families. The second show would be a closed exhibition of works whose owners had not been identified, designed to allow Belgian curators to choose pieces suitable for public art museums, including Savery's *Hunting Scene*, Jan Brueghel's *River Landscape*, an *Eve* by Lucas Cranach the Elder, and Jordaens's *Neptune and Amphitrite*.[29]

Lemaire's exhibition plans sparked a quick negative reaction from the fine arts administration. Curators believed the DER was overstepping its responsibilities by asserting too much control over the selection of works for the public exhibition and determining which pieces would be acquired for Belgian museums. In response, the DER allowed several fine arts experts to view the recovered pieces with Lemaire, a concession that did not allay the curators' concerns. One fine arts official wanted to ensure that Van Puyvelde's service, and not the DER, was credited with recovering works displayed in the "spectacular" exhibition, though several works mentioned—the Dieric Bouts panels from Leuven, the Michelangelo Madonna—actually were located by American and French MFAA officers. More perceptively, the fine arts official questioned the purpose of the confidential display of ownerless art: either the works were still subject to legal proceedings, and there was no reason for curators to consider acquiring them, or they could be acquired by the state and the DER should simply transfer them to the education ministry, which would oversee the distribution. Lemaire created further distrust during the tour by telling his secretary there was no need to note the curators' opinions, leaving the impression that their visit was merely a token gesture, meant ultimately to further his own personal ambitions.[30]

Another fine arts official, O. Van Mulders, proposed the creation of a committee led by Lemaire that would bring together several curators and academic art experts to select works for the public exhibition. He recommended including Paul Fierens, an expert on modern painting at the University of Liège; Edmond de Bruyn, an expert in Italian painting; Monsieur Van Becelaere, assistant curator at the Royal Museum of Fine Arts in Antwerp and an expert in Flemish art; and E. Langui, head of the foreign exhibitions service in the fine arts office. Mulders also encouraged the education ministry to demand that the DER transfer all non-restitutable works to its care and suggested the ministry should not move too quickly to auction off the works not chosen for museums, given the "paradoxical" plan to sell works of art when they could be used to adorn public buildings that lacked appropriate décor.[31]

Christophe took Mulders's advice and convened a commission that would help select works for the exhibition and edit the show catalog.[32] Yet on November 4, nine days before the show was to open, Christophe learned that the DER had entirely disregarded the commission and organized the show and the accompanying catalog without consulting the fine arts office. Compounding his frustration, the education ministry had endorsed the show without Christophe's knowledge, and all he could do was recommend that the minister and his staff silently protest the exhibition premiere through their conspicuous absence.[33] The exhibition was carried out as planned at the end of 1948. The DER touted the show as a "crowning achievement" of the cultural service, made possible by Lemaire's "enthusiasm and tenacity."[34] The catalog preface described fruitful cooperation between the DER and art recovery experts in the education ministry—a nod to Van Puyvelde and his colleagues.[35] And representatives from the two divisions did collaborate as plans developed to distribute much of this patrimony to state museums and other public buildings.

Enriching Belgian Museums

Having taken control over the art recovery process, the DER then sought a solution for managing the cache of unclaimed items, which in the words of Reul "must be considered state property." Reul had determined that all the objects under consideration were sold to enemy buyers during the occupation in "regular transactions," and had been "restituted by Allied occupation authorities since they came from the Belgian cultural patrimony."[36] He proposed that the education ministry would first select works for state collections, to "enrich our cultural patrimony." The DER would then transfer the remaining items to the Domaines state property agency in the finance ministry, which would sell them at auction.[37] For the fine arts office, which had been granted only a small budget for purchases amid broader reconstruction priorities, the deal was a boon. However, the state-run museums could not simply obtain the artworks cost-free, a benefit that would have violated public finance laws. As a result, the education ministry was required to purchase the selected objects from Domaines, including buyers' fees normally paid at public auctions. Christophe in the fine arts office reassured the education minister, Camille Huysmans, that he would secure "reasonable prices" by mutual agreement with the finance ministry.[38] His office would circulate lists of the pieces to museum curators and ask them to submit requests for items that would complement existing collections. In the event that cities vied to acquire the same pieces, the education ministry would serve as arbiter.[39]

By the end of June 1949, a committee of curators had selected sixty-eight paintings worth just over Bfr 4 million. For the provincial museum in Liège, the committee selected Lambert Lombard's *Lamentation of Christ*; for the Rubenshuis in Antwerp, a painting attributed to Corneille de Vos, a landscape by Lucas Van Uden, and Frans Snyders' *Statue of the Virgin Surrounded by Flowers*; for the Jordaenshuis in Antwerp, five paintings by Jacob Jordeans; for Tournai, *The Holy Family* from the school of Rogier Van der Weyden. The commission also selected a landscape by Van Goyen for an eventual exchange with the Netherlands.[40] By mid-November, the value of selected items had grown to BFr 5.3 million, an amount budgeted to a Domaines account and defined as "restitutions from Germany."[41] In a request to the finance ministry for the special funding, fine arts official Van Mulders recognized the creative public accounting involved, reassuring the finance ministry "this is a fictional operation with no real cost to the State."[42] After months of bureaucratic inertia, responsibility for the items transferred from the DER to the fine arts office on December 11, 1950. With a list of the 112 selected pieces, the two divisions agreed on the primary objective: "to enrich our museum collections."[43]

The last page of the list contains an additional eight paintings chosen by the committee that for the time being remained under the authority of the DER, including works with the highest estimated value among the selected pieces: two panels by Memling depicting the Annunciation, originally the rear wings of a triptych, for Bfr 300,000; and one painting each by Van der Weyden (Bfr 300,000) and the Master of Saint Veronica (Bfr 250,000).[44] The pictures were from the collection of Emile Renders, a non-Jewish Belgian banker and collector of early Flemish art who had sold twenty paintings to Göring in 1941. Ten pieces were recovered by the DER, including the eight pictures selected by the committee. After the war, Renders claimed he had been forced to sell the paintings under duress and sued the Belgian state for restitution. The case was still pending in December 1950 during the selection process.[45]

Leading up to the war, Renders had earned some notoriety in the Belgian art world by teaming up with painter and restorer Joseph van der Veken, whose techniques included entirely painting over canvases. Critics' suspicions about this extensive "restoration" were confirmed several decades later by x-ray technology that revealed multiple layers of brush strokes. In 1927, Renders displayed his collection at the Burlington House in London, and a German scholar of northern Renaissance art, Friedrich Winkler, questioned the authenticity of some pieces. The collector generated further controversy in the 1930s by arguing that Hubert van Eyck, long believed to be the brother of Jan van Eyck and co-author of the Ghent Altarpiece, actually never had existed, despite the name on the Altarpiece frame. Some influential observers found Renders's theory plausible, including German art historian and curator Max Friedländer and Belgian expert Jacques Lavalleye, but it remained a minority viewpoint.[46]

Renders thus already had earned critics in the Belgian cultural administration by the time he claimed to have sold his paintings to Göring under duress. In a statement to Allied authorities on June 28, 1945, Renders reported that Hofer and a Dutch dealer named W. Paech had visited him in September 1940, inquiring about the sale price for his collection. He responded that he was "a collector and not a dealer," but he would accept no less than $450,000 dollars in gold. Five days later, Miedl and another agent working for Göring visited him and offered Bfr 10 million—roughly RM800,000 or $320,000 (around $5.6 million in 2020 dollars[47]), which he promptly refused. Renders then learned the Devisenschutzkommando had frozen his collection and he was forbidden to dispose of it without German authorization, which he believed was "beyond any doubt a maneuver coming from Göring." Discussions over the form of payment continued, and in January 1941, Renders told Miedl he would only take coined gold, "knowing that the German Reich does not allow exports of gold" and believing "it was the only way to escape Göring's exactions."[48]

Was Renders truly being forced into the sale, as he claimed, or was he stalling to secure the best possible deal? While the extent of duress is unclear, Göring grew impatient by March 1941 and ordered Miedl to reach a final agreement, that would be "satisfactory for both sides." The Reichsmarschall issued a threat directly to Renders: if negotiations failed again, he would "unfortunately be compelled to withdraw my offer and then things would go their normal way, without my being able to do anything to impede it."[49] This additional goading prompted Renders to negotiate the deal with Miedl. The collector later claimed to have received a "compulsory price fixed by Göring, say eleven millions [sic] of francs, in Belgian and Dutch paper money," two currencies that were "depreciating at the time; that sum was less than half the value of my collection," to which he had devoted "half a century of work, research and study."[50]

After the war, the MFAA recovered six Renders pictures from Göring's collection in Munich, and four others in a repository of the Witzig Bank in Lenggries. Dutch MFAA Captain Jan Vlug, also an ALIU investigator, believed that ten works from the Renders collection were taken by Miedl to Spain. This assessment was based on interrogations of Hofer, Paech, staff members at the Goudstikker firm in Amsterdam, and Miedl's chauffeur, who drove the art-filled car on the first leg of Miedl's escape to Breda. But the MFAA located only the ten paintings found in Germany.[51]

The DER held the repatriated pictures while gathering documents from Renders and Allied investigators. A DER official, A. Rossignol, instructed Belgian MFAA officer and conservator Paul Coremans to allow Renders to view the pictures, and informed Renders he would be able to examine "the works of art belonging to your collection."[52] Rossignol assured Coremans he was not favoring Renders's claim by granting the collector this access, but was merely giving him "harmless satisfaction given his age" while the DER waited for American documents.[53] An analysis most likely produced by American investigators indeed cast doubt on Renders's version of the story. Using interrogations of Hofer and Miedl, questioned separately and in detail, the investigator found that Renders was paid in securities, not paper currency, a transaction that required the intervention of Göring, as the Belgian stock exchange was closed at the time. Renders's claims of duress were further weakened by the fact that he offered his sculpture collection to Göring under the same conditions. Göring rejected the offer, given complications in the proposed transaction. The investigator found that Renders "appears to have been driving a hard bargain rather than 'resisting for six months,'" and doubted the collector's story: "Like many other collaborationists converted by the Allied victory, he is probably trying to have his cake and eat it too."[54]

The Belgian government also questioned Renders's claims of duress and continued to hold the ten recovered paintings. Renders responded with a lawsuit, but a Belgian court ruled against him in July 1949 based on Belgium's three-year statute of limitations on stolen mobile property, and the ACC resolution of January 1946 that allowed states to recover assets sold voluntarily to the enemy. Renders lost again on appeal in 1951, and the fine arts office took possession of the paintings the following year.[55] Eight were distributed to Belgian museums: the two Memling panels went to the Groeninge Museum in Bruges, the Van der Weyden to Tournai, and one each by the Master of Baroncelli and the Master of Saint Veronica to Antwerp. The Royal Museums in Brussels received the Massys, a Pietà by the Master of Hoogstraten and *Crucifixion* by an unknown Flemish painter. The other two works most likely were sold at auction by the state.[56]

DER reports contain a significant amount of ownership documentation on works believed at the time to have been sold voluntarily. A table created in 1951 with columns for provenance and buyer includes sales by Renders and a Lagrand—most likely Maurice, a Belgian antiquarian who collaborated with Mühlmann's office in The Hague.[57] The list also includes the widow of collector Michel Van Gelder, whose mansion in Brussels had a room of works by Jacob Jordaens, indicating she had sold pieces to Göring, the "Linz museum," and the Dorotheum in Vienna.[58] Other entries indicate the provenance only as "Belgium" or "Palais des Beaux-Arts," site of an auction house in Brussels during the occupation. One indicates a Frans Snyders painting, *Crown of Fruit around a bust of Ceres*, from a "private collection" initially was acquired by the Dorotheum in Vienna, then reserved for the Linz collection.[59] In other cases, the buyers were German museums in Cologne (item B2, then attributed to Van der Weyden, and most likely the *Salve Regina* triptych by an unknown artist, inventory number 663 at the Museum of Fine Arts in Tournai[60]) and Düsseldorf (twelve pieces of porcelain allocated to the Royal Museums of Art and History in Brussels).[61] Among likely Jewish-owned items, two were confiscated by the ERR: item A287, Jan Denens, *Vanitas*, currently inventory number 5054 at the Royal Museum of Antwerp; and P27, a Chinese piece, *Stork*, allocated to the Royal Museums of Art and History in Brussels.[62]

The number of objects distributed to Belgian museums continued to grow in the early 1950s. As one DER official put it, "there is no doubt the fine arts department had among the most favorable conditions to enrich the cultural patrimony of our country."[63] In May 1953 the Belgian state received fourteen paintings that the MFAA had erroneously shipped to France. A list of transferred works contains little information about the pictures, which included a four-panel polyptyque by the Master of Nuremberg, *Descent of the Holy Spirit*; a sixteenth-century Swiss panel, *Christ before Pilate*; David Teniers's *Still Life*; Coecke Van Aalst's (most likely Aelst) *The Holy Family*; and Jan Fyt's *Still Life with Dog*.[64] The DER recognized the works' value to "the national artistic patrimony" and aimed to "make them available for museums that could enrich their collections." Rossignol suggested to Lemaire, now artistic advisor to the education ministry, that the museums could acquire them using "the same conditions as in the past."[65]

A few months later, on September 22, a committee of experts reviewed the fourteen paintings from France. They determined that only one was worthy of the royal museums—the sixteenth-century *Christ before Pilate*—but they recommended acquiring the rest for provincial museums. The cost of the paintings plus a group of engravings destined for the Cabinet d'Estampes, including fees and repatriation costs, was BFr 114,591.10.[66] Having been through this exercise before, Christophe dismissed the significance of these expenses and reported to the finance ministry that the process "does not involve any real budgetary charge."[67] This time, however, the rather cavalier approach did not sit well with finance inspector J. L. Caris, for whom the proposal was not simply a numbers game. The mission of the DER, he explained, was conservation and restitution, not the liquidation of sequestered assets. Caris advised against providing a special credit for the acquisition and

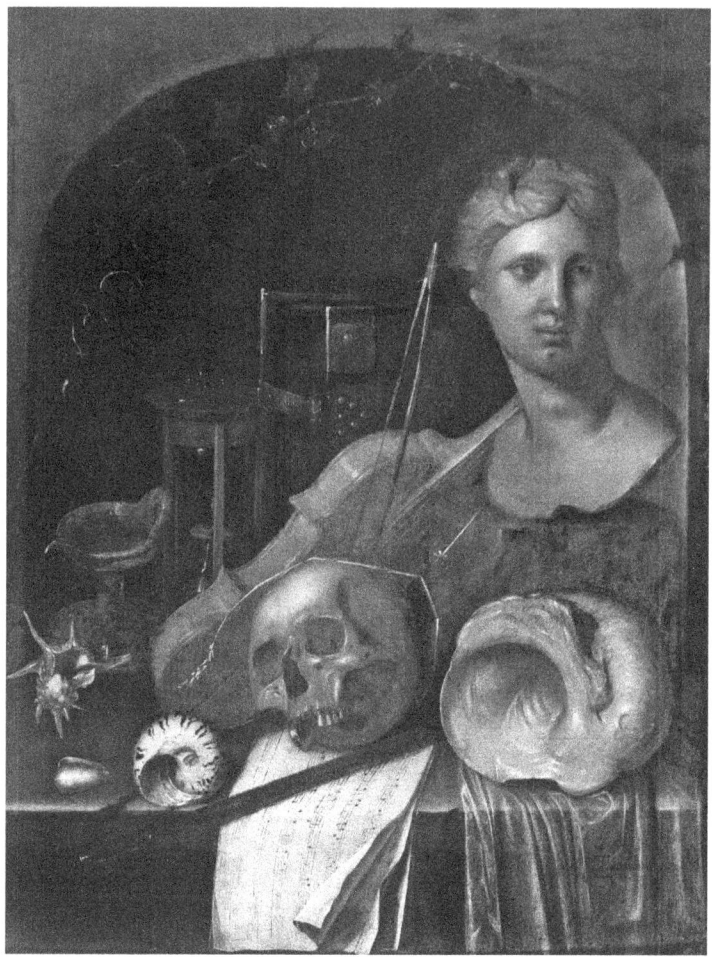

Jan Denens, *Vanitas* (seventeenth century), selected by the Belgian state. Courtesy of the Royal Museum of Fine Arts, Antwerp.

instead preferred to include it in the regular 1954 fine arts budget, or to create a subsidy for provincial museums, where most of the works would be distributed.[68] Christophe continued to advocate for the special credit, arguing that the regular budget of the fine arts office had already been exhausted on expenses such as planned purchases of sculpture and paintings and a quadrennial exhibition in Liège. If the works were sold at auction, Christophe warned, they might fetch a paltry sum of Bfr 40,000 to 50,000. The minister would need to decide whether "the goal of cultural promotion will take priority over savings, or vice versa."[69] In this instance, the government chose not to invest in the recovered paintings and sold them all at auction on December 22, 1954.[70]

The Distribution of Museum-Worthy Objects

The Belgian government's new supply of high-quality pieces inevitably led to lobbying among curators and debates about the proper distribution to royal and provincial museums. The city of Tournai, birthplace of Rogier van der Weyden, hoped to acquire the painter's *Virgin and Child* from the Renders collection. The curator of the local museum urged Christophe to include Tournai in the distribution, emphasizing the damage done to the city during the war and a tremendous reconstruction effort by the local population. "The granting of several works, including a Rogier," he proclaimed, would "reward" the townspeople and give them a much-needed boost in morale.[71] Similarly, an assistant mayor for the fine arts in Liège, Paul Renotte, underscored his institution's losses at the end of the war. On September 7, 1944, the museum was damaged when a German tank filled with dynamite exploded nearby. As Renotte put it, Liège had "a right to reparations." Plus, he pointed out, the museum had fewer Old Master works compared to other museums in the country, at a time when it aimed to expand its holdings by artists from the Meuse region and the southern Netherlands.[72]

The deputy mayor of Antwerp likewise made a case for the Rubenshuis, the artist's former home that had been purchased by the city in 1937 and had been restored with local funding. It first opened to the public as a museum in 1946 but still was not "adequately decorated." Most of the works it held were on loan from the Plantin-Moretus museum, which itself would reopen the following year, and the Antwerp municipal budget would not allow art acquisition for the time being. The city thus would welcome some paintings by Rubens's contemporaries and associates.[73]

In February 1951, the power of distribution lay with a committee composed of several curators and art experts representing the Royal Museums of Fine Arts in Brussels and the Royal Museum of Fine Arts in Antwerp. Christophe presided over the meeting and explained that some sixty works would be divided into three groups: those selected for the Royal Museums in Brussels, for the Royal Museum in Antwerp, and for all other institutions. The Brussels and Antwerp delegations drew lots to determine which would choose first (Brussels), and then took turns selecting objects. Within an hour, each delegation had chosen eighteen paintings; the rest would be distributed to provincial museums or put in storage. The meeting minutes contain no details as to why certain works were chosen, but the speed with which decisions were made—an average of less than two minutes per painting—suggests the delegations had studied the list of available works in advance and determined their preferred pieces.[74]

Committee members chose eighteen works each for the Royal Museums in Brussels and Antwerp. Works for the former included a landscape by Jan Brueghel the Elder, Jacob Jordaens's *The Martyrdom of Saint Lawrence*, and Roelandt Savery's *Stag Hunt*. For the Royal Museum in Antwerp, the committee chose eighteen pieces, including a Van Goyen landscape, a Madonna by Jan Gossaert, an Eve by Lucas Cranach the Elder, along with Jacob Jordaens's *The Fruit Saleswoman*, and a painting plundered by the ERR, Jan Denens's *Vanitas*.[75] At the end of the selection process, all parties reportedly were "perfectly satisfied" with the distribution. Baron Descamps made a point of thanking Christophe for the methodical and courteous manner in which the process was carried out, prompting the other attendees to follow suit.[76]

Separately, thirty-nine works were reserved for the Royal Museums of Art and History, including Veit Stoss's *Two Young Chevaliers*, several pieces of Meissen and Tournai porcelain, and six Ming vases. Twenty-eight objects were acquired by the fine arts administration for distribution to local museums and historic sites. Works selected for royal museums were added to each institution's official inventory, while items reserved for local museums, historic sites, and other public entities were listed on the inventory of the fine arts administration.[77] The Belgian state thus shifted from custodian to owner of the recovered cultural assets.

For the works allotted to provincial and local museums, the earlier lobbying efforts of lower-level officials paid off. The fine arts office drew directly from their letters when explaining the distribution of works: Tournai ended up receiving two Van der Weyden paintings, including the Renders piece; Liège obtained eight paintings, and the Rubenshuis in Antwerp received four paintings by the master's contemporaries. A few cities had not requested artworks but benefited from the largesse of the fine arts office. The Wuyts-Van Campen and Baron Caroly museum in the city of Lier, for instance, was in Christophe's words "a pretty and well maintained little museum" in an attractive area for tourists, and thus deserved two paintings—a

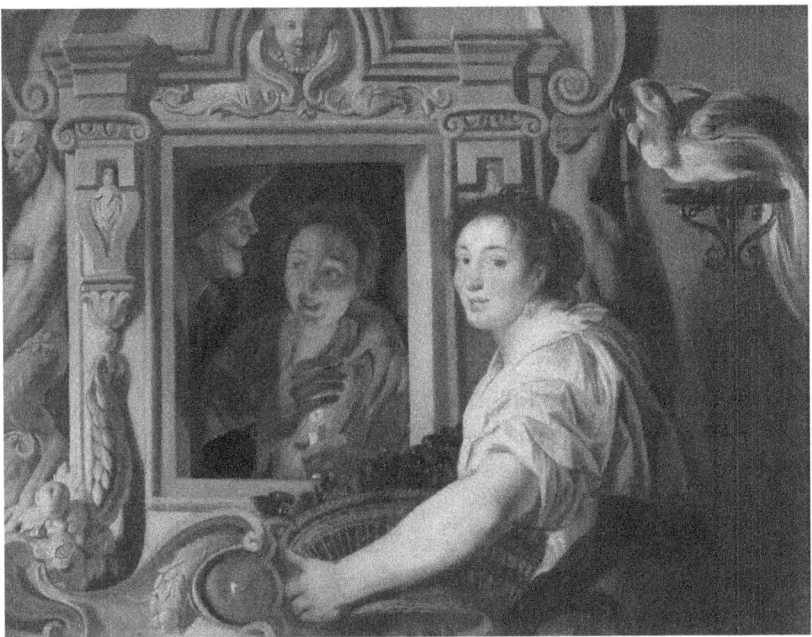

Jacob Jordaens I, *The Fruit Seller* (seventeenth century), selected by the Belgian state and today at the Royal Museum of Fine Arts, Antwerp, inv. No. 5049. Photograph by Hugo Maertens, courtesy of Collection KMSKA — Flemish Community.

seventeenth-century portrait of a man, and Jacob de Backer's *Last Judgment*.[78] The office of the education minister, Pierre Hamel, also benefitted from the acquisition, at least temporarily. Four paintings went to the ministry, including a painting each by Van der Weyden, Brueghel the Younger, and Streek (first name unspecified). The pictures replaced less prestigious works that were redistributed to museums.[79]

Liquidating Less Worthy Objects, 1948–54

While cultural officials were choosing works suitable for Belgian art museums, they also sold lower-quality pieces at auction and deposited proceeds into the national treasury. As in France and the Netherlands, Belgian authorities operated with the understanding that the pieces had been freely sold to Germans, and asserted the state's right to liquidate ownerless assets by invoking the Inter-Allied Declaration of 1943. Sales of lower-value art were meant to mitigate Belgian losses incurred through the German clearing system and thus became a form of indirect reparations, providing a small fraction of the millions of francs the Belgians believed were owed to them from Germany.[80] The sale of sequestered assets was nothing new, and had been codified in civil law. According to article 713 of the civil code, any asset without a present owner—either because an identified owner is absent or no owner is identified—belongs to the state, and is subject to public sales through the Domaines state property agency. In the fall of 1945, Domaines operations were reorganized due to the influx of mobile enemy assets, including works of art, and other sequestered property.[81]

Between 1948 and 1954, the Belgian Domaines agency held six public auctions of ownerless artworks and quality furniture, with sales totaling more than BFr 3.3 million, of which an estimated BFr 1.5 million came from Jewish-owned property (see table 6.1). The sold objects constituted 35.8 percent of works recovered from Germany and Austria.[82] The auctions were held at the Palais des Beaux-Arts, which oversaw the transfer of artworks to the auction site, publicized the auctions, and produced the catalogs. The auction house received a 10 percent commission plus additional fees for an

Table 6.1 Public sales of ownerless cultural assets at Palais des Beaux-Arts (PBA), Brussels, in BFr

Sale date	Gross sales	PBA 10%	PBA, DER fees	Remitted to Belgian Treasury	Estimated value of Jewish property
December 30, 1948	522,835	52,283.50	1,170	469,381.50	522,835
January 30–31, 1950	2,184,790	218,479	10,100	1,956,211	961,307.60
May 21, 1951	24,000	2,400	65	21,535	5,000
June 21, 1951	24,150	2,415	0	21,735	19,725
November 5, 1952	47,170	4,717	0	42,453	22,936
December 22, 1954	500,450	50,045	15,340.10	435,064.90	3,200
Total	3,303,395	330,339.50	26,675.10	2,946,380.40	1,535,003.60

Source: Commission d'étude (Belgium), Les biens des victimes, annex 9, "PBA: Vente aux enchères (1948–1954)," 33.

estimated total of around 25 percent of sales revenues. It transferred the net proceeds to the Domaines agency, which itself absorbed 15 percent, and the remainder was deposited to the treasury. The auction catalogs provided no indication these were cultural assets recovered from Germany and Austria, with likely Jewish provenance.[83]

The first two sales, in December 1948 and January 1950, were the largest of the six and contained the highest value objects. Domaines failed to invite members of the Jewish community to examine the objects before the sales, but several highly motivated despoiled collectors studied the catalogs in advance and successfully identified their property. Mathematics professor Alfred Errera claimed stolen pieces in 1948, as did an Ebstein, Rosenberg, and Natengel; in 1950, heirs of dealer Léon Seyffers-Kresstein secured five canvases, and a W. Katz claimed a Koekkoek painting. The DER pulled the objects from the sales and restituted them, but only after collecting processing fees from the claimants. In a few rare instances, the state compensated claimants who identified their assets after sales. In May 1950, one person claimed a piece of furniture that had been sold in December 1948. The DER compensated the sale price, BFr 1,200, but demanded BFr 264 in handling fees.[84]

Members of the fine arts administration learned of the first auction in December 1948 only shortly before the event. The sale included 297 lots, mostly furniture, sculpture, porcelain, *faïencerie*, horloges, and crystal and ivory pieces—all described by Rossignol at the DER as ranging from high-quality furniture to "*bibelots*" (knickknacks).[85] Altogether the auction generated Bfr 522,835 in sales, of which Bfr 469,381.50 went to the Belgian treasury.[86] The Belgian study commission for Jewish assets later determined that all of the objects in this sale had come from the BTG and ERR, and thus concluded that all the property had been Jewish-owned. Though this may be true for most objects, the sale also included furniture from another state enemy of the Nazis—the Grand Orient Masonic lodge on rue de Laeken in Brussels.[87] The head curator at the Royal Museums of Art and History, Lavachery, secured from the auction two pieces known to have been seized from the Grand Orient lodge—a sixteenth-century sculpture of Saint Sebastian for Bfr 10,000, and a calvary for Bfr 15,000.[88] DER documents contain no evidence of attempted restitution to the lodge.

Christophe asked a fine arts representative, Mademoiselle Berryer, to attend the first auction. She recounted that the auctioneer, a Monsieur De

Mul, began the session in typical fashion by explaining how the auction would proceed. He added, however, that several lots had to be removed, some claimed by private owners and others by the fine arts administration, which had intervened at the last minute, "as it often does." During the sale of sculpture, a well-known collector from Antwerp, a Monsieur Stuyck, sat in the front row, intent on purchasing the Grand Orient Saint Sebastian claimed by the fine arts office. When he learned it had been pulled from the sale, Stuyck protested to De Mul, "Why didn't you tell me two days ago?" The auctioneer retorted, "I only found out about it ten minutes before noon," adding it was "a bureaucrat's whim!" The rest of the attendees, according to Berryer, seemed to accept the government's right of first refusal, and there were no further protests. There was also no mention that the piece had belonged to the Masonic lodge before the war.[89] Berryer reported that overall, most attendees thought it was "perfectly natural" that in a sale organized by the state, the fine arts office would "be permitted to claim some pieces."[90]

Even Lavachery, the curator who secured the two pieces from the Grand Orient lodge, was upset by the sale, having learned of it, he recalled, "almost by accident." He was further distressed to learn about the sale of objects found in a repository in Neder-over-Heembeck, abandoned by the Germans. The works included statues and furniture that might have suited his museum, and other sold items could have decorated austere government offices and Belgian embassies abroad. The Belgian state, he argued, could have "a warehouse of furniture to fulfill these needs," akin to the French Mobilier national. Instead, the Belgian finance ministry "saw fit to sell off pieces that would work perfectly well" to build this stock, and curators were not given adequate time to identify museum worthy pieces. Lavachery showed some concern that the objects might have rightful private owners, including dispossessed Jews, by pointing out that Alfred Errera had identified several pieces of furniture plundered from his home by the Nazis. However, Lavachery used this case to illustrate threats to state interests, not the plight of Jewish victims. He recommended that an attorney for the education ministry review legislation to allow the state "to own the goods it holds" to prevent the finance ministry from selling assets that could be used by the government.[91] A few weeks later, the education minister himself, Camille Huysmans, also was troubled to learn that the DER planned to allow the sale of some objects displayed in the exhibition of recovered objects. He was incredulous that the Belgian state would "put on the auction block high quality works of art . . . without the slightest concern for the interests of museums [and] the enrichment of our national artistic patrimony."[92]

By the second sale, held on January 30 and 31, 1950, the selection process of works for Belgian museums was in place. This auction was the largest of the six, with 491 lots, and many of the sold items had been recovered from German warehouses in Brussels. The sale generated total revenue of Bfr 2,184,790 with an estimated Bfr 961,307.60 coming from Jewish-owned assets.[93] A commentary in the weekly political magazine *Pourquoi Pas?* yields insight into public buzz surrounding the sale. In a lightly satirical tone, the reporter describes great excitement surrounding the auction, an important cultural event for Bruxellois that also drew Dutch, British, and American buyers. A newcomer to the scene, the author happened to sit next to a veteran collector—a stroke of good luck, "the god of journalists." The informed collector pointed out they were only seeing the dregs of the recovered works, as the state had chosen some two hundred paintings for national museums. Puzzled, the journalist observed, "We have here works we took back from the Germans because they were stolen from us. Inevitably, if they stole them, they stole them from someone. So why aren't we returning them to their respective owners?" The knowing collector explained that individuals who proved ownership could receive their art back, but not all rightful owners were claiming the recovered pieces. The Germans used Belgian funds to purchase the works, so the claimants were required to pay the sales amount to the state. In evident sarcasm, the collector then explained the long process of research carried out by the DER, which had examined in detail all public and private sales concluded during the occupation, plus extensive research in Germany and Austria, carrying out lengthy investigations that were part brain teaser, part crime puzzle. The recovered works absent from the auction would soon be in Belgian art museums. In the end, the collector explained, "It's not the individual who was despoiled, but the Belgian community," thus the state was merely recovering what it was owed. The journalist wondered about the German buyer who had purchased art in good faith; didn't that owner become despoiled in the recovery process? "Bah!" retorted the collector, "The Krauts . . . I don't worry too much about them." The two men watched items flow across the auction block one by one, selling at unusually high prices. Buyers seemed to have "lost their sense of proportion," as if German purchasing alone had inflated the objects' value. In the future, the journalist wondered, would mere German esteem for a work of art automatically double or triple its value? Such a trend would give "the critical eye of

Krauts bizarre reliability," suggesting one should "no longer talk about the bad taste of the Teuton or barbarity of Germans! Or should we! . . ."[94]

In some cases, state appropriation was even more deliberate than the journalist had supposed. Some art sales proceeded despite available documents that listed the owners' names. Belgium received three paintings by "Dubois, Bastien, and Permeke" with provenance information indicating they were part of the Alfred Errera collection. In the absence of a claim, the state sold them at auction in January 1950.[95] Recovered assets owned by German Jews in Belgium also became property of the Belgian state. For instance, Robert von Wassermann and his mother, Alice von Taussig, were German Jews deported to Auschwitz from Brussels. Robert escaped, but Alice did not.[96] ERR documentation indicated the seizure of goods from "the Wassermann home, Brussels," which prompted the MFAA to return eleven Persian rugs to Belgium. Given Wassermann's German citizenship, Belgian authorities considered the rugs enemy assets and sold them in the second DER auction. He failed to recover his mother's plundered assets, which also were sold. The sequestration of Wassermann's assets was lifted in April 1952, too late to prevent the sales, and he received neither restitution nor compensation for the lost family assets.[97]

Sales declined precipitously in subsequent DER auctions, reaching Bfr 24,000 at each sale in May and June 1951. The catalog from the latter event advertised the public sale of antiques, paintings, and art objects, with no mention of the works' provenance. Seventeenth-century paintings included Théodore Rombouts, *Return of the Prodigal Son*, signed and dated 1631; a picture in the style of Rubens, *Fortuna*; and a presumed portrait of Caspar Netscher attributed to Jan van Noort. Among modern paintings were two signed pieces by Victor Simonin, *Still Life* and *Winter Landscape*. Art objects included Delft porcelain, crystal, old and modern tapestries and furniture, and Chinese and Japanese porcelain.[98] The sale on November 5, 1952, generated total revenue of Bfr 47,170, with twenty-three lots including Richard Kaiser, *Summer Landscape*; Carl Riser, *Snowy Landscape*; and a sixteenth-century French school sculpted wood piece, *Saint Catherine*.[99] Revenues jumped again on December 22, 1954, to Bfr 500,450, due to the sale of pieces recovered from France and declined by the education ministry. Of seventeen lots, thirteen were works recovered from France, two from the Netherlands—a Jacques d'Arthois landscape and a painting by Abel Grimmer, listed as *Peasants Attacked (Paysans attaqués)*—and two Jewish-owned pieces recovered by Van Puyvelde: a painting by Euphrosine Beernaert, a female

Dutch painter internationally renowned in the 1870s, *Cows at the Trough*; and a Eugène Plasky landscape. Each of the last two paintings sold for Bfr 1,600.[100] The Belgian state purchased several items at auction that had not been chosen in advance for museums: the Royal Museum of Art and History acquired the two pieces from the Grand Orient Masonic lodge, plus a piece of gothic furniture, and a Flemish school statue of the Madonna for a total of Bfr 51,000; and the Royal Museums of Fine Arts in Brussels acquired one painting each by Albert Servaes, Albert Saverys, and Lovis Corinth for a total of Bfr 20,000.[101]

Enemy Assets: The Case of Joachim von Moltke

The sale of objects declined by the fine arts commission led to an important lawsuit filed by German Count Joachim von Moltke, a former Kunstschutz officer who had purchased pieces in Belgium during the occupation. A descendant of Helmuth von Moltke, head of the German general Staff prior to the First World War, Joachim had a doctorate in art history and specialized in seventeenth-century Dutch painting. His older brother, Helmuth James Graf von Moltke, was a founding member of the Kreisau Circle resistance network and was executed for his role in the July 1944 attempted assassination of Hitler.[102]

Joachim was not so clearly an anti-Nazi resister. With the occupation of western Europe, von Moltke was called up to serve in the Kunstschutz in Belgium under General von Falkenhausen and, in his own words, "oversaw private collections in accordance with the German organization for art protection." In 1942, he was redeployed to Russia, then in 1944 to Norway, where he was interned at the end of the war.[103] After his release, he was appointed in June 1946 to serve as a cultural expert in the Schleswig-Holstein government, in the British occupied zone. He held the position for two years and also became director of the Schleswig-Holstein Landesmuseum. In 1948, von Moltke emigrated with his family to South Africa, where he became an art history instructor at the University of Cape Town.[104]

According to information gathered by French and Belgian officials, von Moltke largely avoided political entanglements during the occupation and carried out his assigned duties in the Kunstschutz to protect historic buildings from damage in military operations and billeting of soldiers. He also later claimed to have assisted the French, Belgian, and Norwegian resistance, though he had arrived in Norway when the tide of the war clearly had turned against Hitler. As he was leaving the country in 1946, he prudently gathered character references from members of the Norwegian resistance. One Norwegian officer, Major Vilhelm Evang, asserted in 1946 that Norwegian authorities considered von Moltke "wholeheartedly anti-Nazi," as he had served as a liaison between Theodore Steltzer, an anti-Nazi German officer in Norway, and his own brother Helmut and other resistance members in Germany, and met regularly with the head of Milorg, the Norwegian resistance organization. According to Evang, von Moltke "never revealed military secrets" and "despite his party affiliation, did his best to help the Norwegian resistance, and risked his life opposing the Nazis." Very similar language appears in another statement by the bishop of Oslo, Jacques Mangers.[105] In addition, the Count of Montblanc credited von Moltke with preventing the billeting of German soldiers in his chateau, a Belgian historic site in Ingelmunster, and securing the release of his son from a Gestapo prison.[106]

Von Moltke also secured a reference from British MFAA officer Ewan Philipps, who wrote in 1947 that the count "is considered to be of the highest moral character and personal integrity." Philipps believed von Moltke was "a man in whom the fullest confidence can at all times be placed. He is of very considerable education and culture and of broadly liberal opinions." Belgians, Philipps continued, spoke of von Moltke's "character and conduct in their country during the German occupation in the highest terms," and the German officer was "said to have been instrumental in saving works of art in Belgium from loss and destruction."[107]

At the same time, von Moltke played an intermediary role between Belgian art dealers and German buyers, raising suspicions that he personally profited from the booming art market. For instance, he attempted to secure the Renders collection for the Wallraf Richards museum, but Göring's interest in the paintings foiled his plan. He more successfully helped a Frau Langenhob purchase a collection of Sèvres porcelains from a dealer in Brussels, and facilitated the sale of an eighteenth-century silver pitcher from Gallery Raphael to a buyer in Berlin. He also personally took advantage of the opportunity to purchase art in occupied Belgium, and French soldiers discovered several newly acquired pieces in his requisitioned villa in Baden-Baden. These works included a painting by Rubens, *Head of a Woman*, valued at Bfr 343,000; a canvas by Courbet depicting a fort on a rocky cliff, purchased at auction in Brussels on November 24, 1941; Signac, *Fishing Port*, purchased at the same auction as the Courbet; and two color lithographs of the Palais des Etats-Généraux and the Place Royale in Brussels. In addition, the home contained an eighteenth-century map of Silesia, with a Belgian dealer's stamp on the frame, and a library of academic art history books.[108]

The von Moltke case reveals some distrust between French and Belgian MFAA officers. A Belgian officer on mission in the British zone reported to Lemaire in February 1947 that French authorities had decided to allow von Moltke to keep artworks he had purchased in France during the war, thanks to his resistance activities. A British MFAA officer, Major Lionel Perry, recommended that the Belgians similarly reward von Moltke's conduct by allowing him to keep purchased objects. Stunned by the suggestion, Lemaire asked Henraux of the French CRA to explain "the motives that prompted French authorities to take such a generous stance." Although Henraux had not dealt with a claim from von Moltke, he aimed to quash rumors about French generosity: as a matter of principle, he saw no reason to link "the looting of French artistic patrimony" with "a reward for service to the Resistance," adding that purchases during the occupation were a form of looting.[109] Nonetheless, Perry again asserted in October 1948 that the French government had declined to claim items acquired in France by several Germans who had been known to protect French interests, without specifying the objects or Germans.[110]

The Belgians chose to claim items from von Moltke's collection. The MFAA repatriated the objects to Belgium, in accordance with ACC directives. According to the DER, the count's purchases were a form of looting, to which "our artistic patrimony and that of other occupied countries fell victim."[111] From South Africa, von Moltke accepted Belgian control over all the pieces except the Rubens, the most valuable painting he had left in Baden-Baden. He had purchased the picture in February 1941 from a Jewish dealer in Brussels, Léon Seyffers, who later was deported and perished at Auschwitz.[112] The lawsuit failed to address the dealer's fate or the possibility that he conducted the sale under duress, as both sides presumed that Seyffers had received a fair sum of Bfr 250,000. Von Moltke had used the Belgian-German clearing system and paid a total of RM 21,221 to the Deutsche Verrechnungskasse (German Clearing Office) in Berlin. He also claimed to have paid in part with Dutch florins, though MFAA documents suggest most of the payment was made in Reichsmarks.[113] According to Belgian authorities, the heirs of Seyffers did not claim the picture after the war because they believed he had received a fair price in the sale.[114]

The Rubens was among the pieces reviewed by the selection commission, but members determined it was a second-rate canvas, perhaps not even an authentic Rubens, and it was sold in the auction of January 30, 1950, for Bfr 50,000.[115] As von Moltke could not claim it from the new owner, he sued the Belgian state for compensation rather than restitution, a total of Bfr 900,000: 250,000 for the true value of the painting, 500,000 to mitigate the fluctuation in the Belgian currency since March 1941, 50,000 in damages for removal of the right to enjoy the painting, and 100,000 in moral damages.[116]

The Belgian RDR mission in Düsseldorf sought the opinion of Rose Valland, at the time head of the Art Recovery Service in Berlin. "This case is absolutely clear," she argued, and the Belgians were "directly applying decisions of the Control Council." Von Moltke, she explained, used his position of influence to acquire works of art in occupied territories, and therefore those countries had a right to claim the objects, no matter how he had obtained them. She considered the lawsuit a "personal battle" waged by von Moltke, who had mobilized his connections to Konrad Adenauer and staff at the Cologne museum to sway Allied authorities in his favor. Yet von Moltke could not simply create laws, "despite the vehement claims expressed from the depths of his African retreat." She concluded by expressing solidarity with the Belgian RDR and French willingness to cooperate whenever possible.[117]

The case worked its way through the legal system over the next three years, ending on April 29, 1954, with a tribunal decision against von Moltke on several grounds: the Belgian court did not have the right to challenge the 1948 British decision to restitute the painting to Belgium; a measure negotiated among the Allies and the FRG on August 31, 1951, stipulated that no former owner in Germany could claim works restituted to liberated countries; the Belgian state had a right to manage the painting as it saw fit, including the right to sell it; a law of September 19, 1945, banned exporting it; and the Belgian RDR was fulfilling a mission to reintegrate into the national artistic patrimony a work that was removed by the enemy and replaced by a payment through a clearing account—a form of commercial plunder. Moreover, the court ordered von Moltke to pay a total of Bfr 7,730 in legal fees to the Belgian state.[118] He did not appeal the decision.

The von Moltke case put to test ACC directives and Belgian law related to enemy assets, confirming the right of governments to control assets repatriated to their territories. The court's decision in the government's favor came roughly a month before the Bonn accords of May 26, 1954, which prompted a new round of discussions about Nazi-era cultural assets in the

FRG. In October 1955, the DER submitted to the West German Federal Office for External Restitutions (*Bundesamt für aussere Restitutionen*) a list of 1,564 paintings, sculpture, and tapestries that had been stolen or purchased by the Germans in Belgium, and were still missing. Yet the DER failed to contact descendants of Holocaust victims, and no new research was undertaken on the Belgian or German side. Between 1955 and 1962, not a single cultural object was restituted. In 1967, the DER was dissolved by royal decree and merged with the Commercial Office for Provisioning to create the Belgian Office for Economy and Agriculture.[119]

Not all the former owners of appropriated works of art were Jewish, as the drawn-out lawsuits filed by Renders and Moltke indicated, but according to the Belgian study commission nearly half of the selected pieces, some three hundred items may have been owned by victims of antisemitic persecution.[120] The government carried out no further ownership research until the 1990s, when the heirs of Holocaust victims, the press, and the broader public began to question the right of states to hold recovered Jewish assets.

7
Contested Patrimony

In the fall of 2002, Simon and Nick Goodman traveled with their elderly aunt Lili to the Dutch city of Rijswijk. Their destination was the storage facility for the Netherlands Institute for Cultural Heritage (ICN). The massive repository located in a modern business park held some fifty thousand works of art. It was not a space for tourists, nor were the Gutmann descendants in the Netherlands for typical sightseeing. Once inside the building, the visitors went through security screening and put on laminated badges. They were greeted by the repository director, Rik Vos, and the head of collections, Evert Rodrigo, who led them through a series of long hallways. They swiftly passed by rooms filled with all manner of art objects—sculptures, drawings, decorative pieces, and racks neatly lined with paintings. The group descended several floors to a vast windowless room the size of a warehouse, "bunkerlike" with brick walls, as Simon recalled, and temporarily transformed to re-create the opulent interior of an art collector's home. Softening the floor was a large, dark brown Savonerrie carpet, once in the dining room of the Gutmann mansion. Tapestries and paintings hung on the wall. Tables and shelves teemed with Meissen plates and bowls, bronzes, and silver-gilt Renaissance cups. They were all pieces from the collection of Fritz and Louise, plundered by the Nazis, and the Dutch state had recently approved the restitution of 255 items to Nick, Simon, and Lili.[1] According to Simon, this warm welcome by the Dutch officials followed decades of refusal to acknowledge Nazi theft and forced sales, "the greatest robbery in history, all swept under the rug." But the family's claim was not, in the end, about acquiring art, he said; "it was primarily about justice."[2]

This particular restitution story had a happy ending, sixty years after the plunder. Following the flurry of restitutions in the early postwar years, Nazi loot continued to circulate through auction houses, private collections, and museums. On the whole, curators, dealers, and museum directors asked few questions about objects' histories when acquiring and trading works over the next five decades, and the global art market continued to disperse the assets.

Acceptance of the status quo shifted only in the mid-1990s, amid growing awareness of the history and postwar legacy of Nazi art looting.

Restitution and Compensation through the 1980s

By the mid-1950s, art restitution efforts had waned in western Europe. Victims of Nazi plunder and their heirs faced numerous obstacles in their continued search for lost objects. Many claimants lacked requisite sales or insurance documentation and fell short of the burden of proof required by national governments. Some works of art with unclear authorship were difficult to identify, as official inventories commonly repeated vague titles, such as "Dutch landscape" or "Madonna and Child." In the private art market, civil codes protected good faith purchasers, and postwar governments lacked the political will to enact reforms.[3] Dealers and auction houses defended the confidentiality of business transactions, while private collectors failed to cooperate in investigations over lost art. For many survivors and heirs, the legal costs of pursuing restitution added up quickly and made drawn-out claims prohibitively expensive. In this environment, most potential claimants gave up the search for their families' lost art.[4]

Having returned to France in 1953, Rose Valland continued to oversee claims from West Germany as head of the SPOA. But art restitutions were increasingly rare. In 1962 one painting held by the Louvre—MNR 249, a fifteenth-century Italian painting of Saint George—was returned to Paul Jonas.[5] In all, only two other works from the custodianship were restituted to individuals between 1955 and 1994: the front of an ancient sarcophagus (MND 1966) restituted to P. L. Weiler in 1966, and a bronze reduction of *The Thinker* (RFR 056) to the heirs of Fritz Todt in 1979.[6] Restitutions from the Dutch and Belgian custodianships were similarly rare. By 1992, twenty-four Old Master paintings in the Dutch NK had been returned to rightful owners, but there is no evidence of Belgian restitutions from the 1950s to 1990s.[7]

By the late 1950s, there was a widely held belief that victims' claims had been fulfilled, a perspective reinforced by restitution and compensation agreements negotiated by the western Allies, the state of Israel, and the FRG. In May 1952, the western Allies made the continuation of asset restitution an important condition of West German partial sovereignty in the transitional treaty. This agreement, however, applied only to objects taken to West

German territory, including West Berlin. As a result, most of the successful claimants were German citizens whose assets had been recovered in western Germany. The Allies also required the FRG to provide compensation for lost assets, estimated at the time by Allied experts at DM 5 billion. German Ministry of Finance officials, some of whom had also helped implement antisemitic policies under the Third Reich, successfully defended the financial interests of the state and limited this liability to DM 1.5 billion.[8]

Compensation agreements expanded further with negotiations involving the FRG, Israel, and the Conference on Materials Claims against Germany (Claims Conference), an umbrella body representing the interests of twenty-three diaspora organizations. West German Chancellor Konrad Adenauer was well aware that his goal of achieving a position of stature for the FRG among western allies would require some measure of official contrition for the crimes of the Holocaust, backed by the compensation of victims.[9] On March 12, 1951, the state of Israel demanded reparations from West and East Germany for a sum of at least $1.5 billion, to assist in the resettlement of 500,000 European Jews in Israel. Underscoring the moral and legal dimensions of such a settlement, the Israelis argued that "the establishment of equal status for Germany in the community of nations is unthinkable as long as this fundamental measure of restitution has not been met."[10] The German Democratic Republic never responded, but Adenauer offered reassurance to the Jewish people through a speech to the Bundestag on September 27, 1951, acknowledging that under the Nazis "unspeakable crimes were committed which require moral and material restitution [*Wiedergutmachung*]."[11] Extensive talks brokered by American diplomats resulted in the Luxembourg Agreement of September 1952, by which the FRG agreed to pay DM 3.45 billion in goods and services to Israel, including DM 450 million to the Claims Conference for the compensation and resettlement of Holocaust survivors outside Israel. These payments allowed West Germany to avoid restituting assets taken from territories occupied by the Third Reich.[12]

The FRG again expanded compensation with the Federal Restitution Law (BRüG) of 1957, which compensated Jewish victims in former Nazi-occupied territories across Europe. Yet as with previous agreements, it applied to goods taken to West Germany or West Berlin and required recipients to hold citizenship in a country that diplomatically recognized the Federal Republic, in effect barring claims from victims under Soviet domination in eastern Europe.[13] Subsequent laws allowed compensation for the loss of furniture and household items looted by the Möbel-Aktion, but these lower-value items often were not inventoried by the Germans and owners commonly lacked the requisite ownership records.[14] In all, the Federal Republic provided compensation to individual survivors of Nazi political, racial, and religious persecution—mostly Jews—in the amount of DM 40.4 billion by 1971, and DM 77 billion by 1986.[15]

While restitution of art plundered during the Nazi era slowed, the impact of decolonization beginning in the 1950s prompted an expansion of international law meant to protect both movable and immovable cultural property. The United Nations Educational, Scientific and Cultural Organization (UNESCO) headquartered in Paris took a leadership role in this area, and administered the 1954 Hague Convention for the Protection of Cultural Property in the Event of Armed Conflict. The convention includes a wide definition of cultural property—architectural monuments, works of art, books, manuscripts—with a central criterion that the property should be "of great importance to the cultural heritage of every people."[16] At the time, the United States and United Kingdom refused to ratify the convention because of its potential restrictions on military operations in the event of nuclear or conventional war. The Soviet Union ratified it in 1957; the United States did so much later, under the Obama administration in 2009, and the United Kingdom in 2017.[17]

In 1970 UNESCO also coordinated the first significant international effort to prevent the illegal trafficking of art in peacetime, through the Convention on the Means of Prohibiting and Preventing the Illicit Import, Export and Transfer of Ownership of Cultural Property. Newly independent states primarily drove this initiative, aiming to restore cultural heritage plundered by imperial powers. European delegations insisted on non-retroactivity, limiting the measure's impact.[18] UNESCO then expanded preservation efforts to immovable property with the 1972 World Heritage Convention for historic monuments, archeological sites, and natural heritage.[19]

These agreements reflect a good faith effort by the international community to protect artistic heritage in the wake of destruction in the Second World War, and in the context of decolonization. Adherence, however, was repeatedly stymied by powerful national interests, the persistent prioritization of military necessity, and a lack of enforcement mechanisms. UNESCO measures, moreover, remain state-centric and fail to address individual claimants' efforts to recover stolen art, such as Nazi plunder.[20] Similarly, a Code of Ethics for Museums adopted by the International Council of Museums (ICOM) in 1986 demonstrated global awareness of the need for professional standards and best practices, but at the time did not have a significant impact on provenance research on Nazi-era art held by museums.[21]

An Awakening in the 1990s

The collapse of communism prompted new investigations into property losses across the European continent during and after the Second World War, attracting the attention of journalists, scholars, and the broader public. In the United States, Cold War realpolitik gave way to moral concerns about the incomplete compensation of Holocaust victims and their descendants. The fiftieth anniversary of the end of the war further led to national commemorations, public debates about belated justice for Holocaust survivors, and the declassification of archives related to wartime plunder.[22]

In the mid-1990s, influential books on Nazi art plunder reached public audiences beyond the ivory tower. In 1994 American writer Lynn Nicholas published the seminal book *The Rape of Europa*, drawing on first-hand accounts by former MFAA officers, including interviews with some of the last surviving members, and research in US and French archives. The following year Paris-based journalist Hector Feliciano published *Le Musée Disparu*, translated into English in 1997 as *The Lost Museum*. It was the first book-length study of works in the French custodianship, commonly known under the rubric Musées Nationaux Récupération, or MNR. At the time, French archives related to art plunder and spoliation were still classified, so Feliciano studied documents in the US national archives, such as reports by American MFAA officers and French intelligence agents.[23] Historian Jonathan Petropoulos brought scholarly rigor to the field with the 1996 publication of *Art as Politics in the Third Reich*, followed by numerous books and articles.[24]

These publications coincided with investigations into Nazi plunder beyond works of art. In the spring of 1995, Itamar Levin, deputy editor of an Israeli business newspaper, published a series of articles on heirless, dormant accounts of Holocaust victims still held by Swiss banks. The story was not entirely unknown; members of the Jewish and banking communities had long been aware of it. But at that moment, Levin's reporting provoked a new kind of outrage, and the international news media seized upon the story with unprecedented vigor, as did the World Jewish Congress and American attorneys. The following year three class action lawsuits, open to American and foreign plaintiffs, were filed in a Brooklyn federal court against Credit

Suisse, the Union Bank of Switzerland, and the Swiss Bank Corporation. Investigations then extended to gold assets held in Swiss banks that the Nazis had plundered from the central banks of occupied countries, and had extracted from the teeth of Jewish victims at the death camps. The suit led to a settlement of $1.25 billion.[25] American lawyers filed additional class action lawsuits against German corporations that had used slave and forced labor under the Nazis—giants of German industry including Daimler Benz, Volkswagen, Bayer, and Siemens. In a complicated settlement involving eight national governments, German industry agreed in 1999 to pay $5.2 billion to Jewish and non-Jewish laborers.[26] Additional class action lawsuits filed in US courts targeted six major European insurance companies who continued to hold the policies of Holocaust victims. In August 1998 the companies formed the International Commission on Holocaust-Era Insurance Claims (ICHEIC) to reach an agreement with American regulators, the state of Israel, the World Jewish Restitution Organization, and the Claims Conference. The ICHEIC reported in March 2007 that it had disbursed $306 million to forty-eight thousand Holocaust survivors and their heirs, amid criticism that the agreement gave too much power to insurance companies to determine the validity of claims, in amounts far below the 2003 estimated $15 billion face value of the policies.[27]

Domestic politics in the United States under the Clinton administration, and the key role played by influential donors and advisors, helped to spur investigations into plundered Jewish assets held by American institutions.[28] In April 1998, US Senator Alfonse D'Amato sponsored a bill to create a Presidential Advisory Commission on Holocaust Assets in the United States, a measure that passed Congress with unanimous support and was promptly signed by Clinton. The twelve-member commission was charged with investigating assets of Holocaust victims that may have been held by the federal government, private individuals, private entities, or non-federal government entities.[29]

Like the reports of study commissions established in France, the Netherlands, and Belgium, the US advisory commission carried out important research on the Nazi plunder of various assets, including art and other cultural property, gold, and financial assets. Among proposals in the final report, issued in December 2000, was the recommendation that the federal government promote restitution from all private and government entities, preserve archival records, and pursue Congressional legislation "that removes impediments to the identification and restitution of Holocaust victims' assets."[30] Despite these well-intentioned proposals, produced at the cost of $2.7 million, some critics charged that the commission failed to meet basic objectives, such as establishing a database of Holocaust-era assets in the United States. It also failed to address the collaboration of American industry and private corporations with the Nazis.[31]

As the US advisory commission was conducting this research, delegates from across the globe convened in Washington, D.C. in December 1998 for a Conference on Holocaust-Era Assets. Heading this initiative was Stuart Eizenstat, US special representative of the president and secretary of state on Holocaust-era issues. Eizenstat was well known in this area of diplomacy, as he had helped to negotiate earlier agreements with Swiss banks and German corporations.[32] In the realm of Holocaust-era art, representatives from forty-four countries agreed on a set of eleven non-binding principles, popularly known as the Washington Principles, while recognizing that "among participating nations there are differing legal systems," and "countries act within the context of their own laws." With these caveats, the delegates agreed, in repeated conditional phrasing, that art plundered by the Nazis should be identified and publicized in an effort to "locate" pre-war owners and their heirs. Related records and archives, moreover, should be opened to researchers. In the event that rightful owners could be identified, steps should be taken to achieve "a just and fair solution," but with the understanding that each case must be evaluated separately. National governments also were "encouraged to develop processes to implement these principles," especially involving alternative dispute resolution.[33] Despite the limitations of non-binding principles and uneven compliance, including in the United States, the Washington Conference achieved a milestone international agreement calling for systematic provenance research on artworks held in private and state-run museums, and transparent publication of data.

Russia's actions were contradictory. It endorsed the Washington Principles but earlier in 1998 had enacted a federal law proclaiming that cultural property displaced to the Soviet Union after the war and remaining on Russian territory provided compensation for the plunder and destruction of cultural valuables by Germany and its allies. The law aimed to protect the interests of the Russian Federation in disputes with foreign governments through adherence to principles of reciprocity, and Russian intransigence regarding this "trophy art" was evident in ongoing disputes with other countries.[34] The Netherlands, for instance, had sought information from the Soviet Union on the collection of 527 Old Master drawings formerly owned by Franz Koenigs, which had ended up in a castle outside Dresden at the end of the war. The Soviets remained silent about the fate of the drawings in their possession, but in 1987 the German Democratic Republic repatriated thirty-three pieces to the Netherlands. In October 1992, the Russian Minister of Culture Evgenii Sidorov announced that some three hundred of the drawings were indeed still located in Russia. This acknowledgment led to the formation of a Dutch and Russian commission that studied 307 pieces in the Pushkin State Museum in Moscow, followed by an exhibition of the drawings in October 1995. The Russian government, however, continued to block Dutch restitution claims, while Ukraine restituted 139 of the drawings in 2004.[35] Russia also repeatedly rejected German claims to thousands of items seized by the Red Army, including a collection of gold and archeological artifacts known as Priam's Treasure, and a Bronze Age cache of eighty-one gold objects in the Treasure of Eberswalde, continuing to view the spoils as restitution in kind for cultural damage inflicted by the Nazis.[36]

Other international agreements followed the Washington conference. In October 2000 the Council of Europe organized the Vilnius International Forum on Holocaust-Era Looted Cultural Assets. Thirty-eight countries sent delegations, including Russia and the United States, and approved a declaration that extended good intentions from the Washington Principles.[37] Discussions continued in June 2009 with the Holocaust Era Assets Conference held in Prague, at the time seat of the European Union presidency, attended by representatives from forty-six countries, including Russia. Stuart Eizenstat again headed the US delegation. The gathering led to the Terezin Declaration of June 30, 2009, which addressed a wide range of issues related to Holocaust-era assets: the welfare of Holocaust survivors and other victims of Nazi persecution, immovable property, Jewish cemeteries and burial sites, Nazi-confiscated and looted art, Judaica and Jewish Cultural Property, archival materials, and "Education, Remembrance, Research and Memorial Sites." In the realm of plundered art, the declaration mostly reaffirmed the 1998 Washington Principles, urging "all stakeholders to ensure that their legal systems of alternative processes, while taking into account the different legal traditions, facilitate just and fair solutions with regard to Nazi-confiscated and looted art, and to make certain that claims to recover such art are resolved expeditiously and based on the facts and merits of the claims and all the relevant documents submitted by all parties."

It further encouraged governments to "consider all relevant issues when applying various legal provisions that may impede the restitution of art and cultural property, in order to achieve just and fair solutions, as well as alternative dispute resolution, where appropriate under law."[38]

The Washington, Vilnius, and Prague conferences all contributed to a new international paradigm, in which approaches to restitution shifted from adherence to traditional legal instruments to procedures that would allow a greater moral concern for victim groups, through mechanisms such as alternative dispute resolution. Yet a tension emerges in this new paradigm, as art fundamentally is property and concerned entities, whether governments or private institutions, cannot entirely abandon principles of legal ownership. Cases in which an entity retains the right to continue holding claimed objects may leave a public perception that claims are not being dealt with fairly, and that justice has not been achieved.[39]

There is good reason for claimants and an informed public to doubt the goodwill and probity of art-retaining entities, as restitution claims had been thwarted for several decades after the end of the war, including the works held by western European governments.

The French MNRs: Rhetoric versus Reality

By 1980 a mere twenty-nine of the more than 2,100 pieces in the French custodianship had been restituted, with no additional restitutions through 1993.[40] The holdings of the Musées de France even expanded by twenty-eight paintings in June 1994, when France signed an agreement with Germany that allowed the repatriation of works that had been discovered in the city of Magdeburg, formerly in the German Democratic Republic. Among the repatriated pieces, a Monet painting captured the attention of the French news media, as Helmut Kohl ceremoniously handed it to François Mitterrand during a Franco-German summit in Mulhouse.[41] Mitterrand expressed "exceptional gratitude" and considered the repatriation a sign of friendship between the two countries. Lest curators worry that other paintings might be pulled from their museums in a kind of restitution contagion, he emphasized the unusual circumstances of the transfer and downplayed the artworks' national significance. Works of art in European Union museums, he observed, would increasingly be seen as common cultural heritage: "All of us, walking here or there, opening the doors of a museum in Europe will feel at home."[42]

Yet the paintings were not merely French or European heritage; some easily could be traced to rightful owners. The Musées de France quickly identified the provenance of seven pictures, which therefore never received the official MNR designation. Heirs to the Raphaël collection received two paintings each by Corot, Henri-Edmond Cross, and Henri-Joseph Harpignies, while a Gauguin painting was restituted to Rothschild descendants. The twenty-one remaining works, including the Monet, entered the custodianship.[43]

Little did French officials know they were in the calm before a storm of public controversy surrounding the MNRs. Feliciano published his polemical book soon afterward, and French media quickly echoed his criticism of inaction by the Musées de France regarding potential Nazi plunder in its care. Under director Françoise Cachin, the Musées de France responded to the bad press organizing a conference in November 1996 that addressed the fate of artworks plundered in France during the war. Feliciano was among the presenters, a significant gesture by the Musées de France, along with Lynn Nicholas and French art historian Laurence Bertrand Dorléac. However, the program above all highlighted the wartime resistance activity of the French museum administration, featuring talks on Jacques Jaujard and Rose Valland, and failed to address adequately the government's inaction with regard to the MNRs.[44] Louis Amigues, director of archives at the Ministry of Foreign Affairs, greatly exaggerated the organization and accessibility of spoliation archives, claims that would have rung hollow to anyone familiar with Feliciano's work.[45]

Undeterred, Feliciano continued to expose the bad faith of the Musées de France. Writing in *Le Monde* he and fellow journalist Philippe Dagen revealed a scathing report issued by the Cour des Comptes, the French government accounting office, on the government's mismanagement of the MNRs. The office had distributed the report confidentially in January 1996 to the state budget office, the Musées de France, and the Ministries of Justice and Culture. According to the report, the museum administration had "failed to meet its obligation to publicize" the status of unclaimed works and had not adequately pursued provenance research. The report denounced this "troubling situation" that stretched "for almost fifty years without alarming anyone, including the Direction des Musées de France." Feliciano and Dagen ran the story with a sensational headline: "Museums hold nearly two thousand works stolen by the Nazis during the Occupation."[46] The headline is misleading, as many MNR objects had been sold, not stolen—a point the authors make in the article. But such press coverage intensified public debate over the controversy.

Meanwhile, the French government was developing plans to study the history and legacy of looting and spoliation writ large during the German occupation. In early February 1997, Prime Minister Alain Juppé invited former Resistance activist and deportee Jean Mattéoli to head a study commission investigating German and French confiscation of Jewish assets. Researchers would determine whether public entities in France continued to hold the assets and would recommend the proper course of action.[47] Commission members included eminent historians such as François Furet, Claire Andrieu, Antoine Prost, and Annette Wieviorka and archivist Caroline Piketty, assisted by a team of researchers who were divided into several working groups.

The resulting multi-volume report published in 2000 examined the fate of movable and immovable Jewish assets, financial spoliation, art looting, the confiscation of apartments, aryanization of businesses, and the confiscation of goods at French internment and transit camps, including Drancy, Pithiviers, and Beaune-la-Rolande. The work of the Mattéoli Commission, as it is commonly known, was in many ways a kind of national *mea culpa* and an important official acknowledgment of French spoliation under the Vichy regime. It led to the creation of the Commission for the Compensation for Victims of Spoliation (Commission pour l'indemnisation des victimes de spoliations, CIVS), which by September 2019 had issued some thirty-five thousand indemnity recommendations, for a total of more than €536 million. More than forty-three hundred dossiers involved claims for fine art, of which 310 were compensated for a total of more than €50 million.[48]

Despite important progress made by the Mattéoli Commission, the examination of art looting and the MNRs was woefully inadequate. The general report proclaimed that in contrast to assets spoliated by the Vichy regime, art plunder was "a German affair."[49] The oversimplified dichotomy of German theft and French spoliation allowed the report to avoid a critical examination of the French sequestration of Jewish assets with the intent to enrich the national patrimony. The elision cannot be blamed on a lack of access to relevant archives. The coeditor of the volume on art looting, Isabelle Le Masne de Chermont, at the time oversaw archives of the National Museums that documented French wartime efforts to acquire the works from Jewish collections permanently.[50] Analysis of works still held in the custodianship showed a startling lack of thorough provenance research. The report indicated that 10 percent of the objects likely had been plundered, 65 percent had been purchased in Paris during the war, and the provenance was unknown for 25 percent. Regarding the purchased art, moreover, the report failed to acknowledge the need for in-depth research to ascertain the persecution of Jewish owners and whether the works had been sold under duress.[51]

In its defense, the working group on art looting and the MNRs lacked the time necessary to carry out extensive provenance research, as the government aimed to publish the entire commission's final report promptly manner. But even after the publication of the Mattéoli Commission report, the Musées de France continued to avoid this important work for another fifteen years. French policy evolved slowly in the early twenty-first century, even amid rhetoric from the Musées de France of alleged openness and transparency.

Sales under Duress: The Gentili Collection

In July 1999, the Court of Appeals in Paris awarded restitution of five MNR paintings to the heirs of Federico Gentili di Giuseppe, a Jewish Italian businessman who died of natural causes in Paris in 1940.[52] It was a landmark case that revealed a new interpretation of sales under duress during the occupation, following decades of litigation.

Gentili di Giuseppe, born in 1868, was a prominent businessman and official representative of the Italian Ministry of Finance in Paris. Between 1910 and 1940, he had amassed a collection of several thousand books and several hundred paintings, with a particular predilection for eighteenth-century Italian masters. His four-thousand-square-meter apartment on avenue Foch was tastefully decorated with eighteenth-century French furniture. He died a widower on April 20, 1940, and left the estate to his adult children, Marcello and Adriana. Marcello, an astronomer, served in the French army and in June 1940 was demobilized in southern France. When the Germans occupied the French capital, he secured a position at the Pic du Midi Observatory in the Pyrenees. Adriana fled Paris with her three children and managed to catch the last ship from Bordeaux to London, where her husband Raphaël Salem was serving in the French army. When the Salem family learned that their home in the posh sixteenth arrondissement had been requisitioned by the Germans, they fled to Canada and spent the duration of the war in the United States.[53] They were then subject to a Vichy decree enacted on July 23, 1940, depriving Jewish emigrants of citizenship rights and allowing the confiscation of their property. Marcello was unable to reach Paris because of a German order of September 27, 1940, banning the return of Jews who had fled the territory of the occupied zone.[54]

With Marcello and Adriana both living outside Paris, a creditor named Julien Giraud sought to recover ninety thousand francs from Federico's estate, arguing that the heirs had shown "absolutely no interest" in the matter. On October 29, 1940, a judge in the Civil Court of First Instance granted Giraud's request for a provisional estate manager, a M. Moulin of the Compagnie Générale Française de Crédit.[55] This timing is important. Moulin assumed authority to manage the Gentili assets before the creation of the Commissariat Général aux Questions Juives in March 1941, a point later used by the French government to argue that the liquidation of Gentili's estate was not an act of antisemitic persecution.[56] Following an inventory and appraisal of Gentili's personal property, Moulin oversaw the sales carried out between March and June 1941 at the Hotel Drouot.[57] Agents in Göring's employ purchased five paintings: *The Visitation* by Moretto da Brescia, *The Holy Family* by Bernardo Strozzi, *Alexander and Campaspe at the Studio of Apelle* by Tiepolo, *Cardplayers by a Fire* by Alessandro Magnasco, and *Portrait of a Woman* by Rosalba Carriera. The sale generated higher than expected proceeds of Ff 4,776,289, credited to the estate.[58]

After the war, the MFAA recovered the five pictures from Göring's collection and repatriated them to France. In the absence of a claim from the heirs, who were unaware of the paintings' fate, the French selection committee reserved them for public use.[59] Adriana returned to Paris in 1950 and during a visit to the Louvre was shocked to see the Tiepolo hanging near the Mona Lisa, along with the Moretto da Brescia and Strozzi.[60] She filed a restitution claim with OBIP, which was rejected by an interministerial committee in June 1951 on the basis that the 1941 sale was voluntary and not the result of antisemitic spoliation.[61]

Pursuing the restitution of other family assets, the privileged Salem family was fortunate to regain their home but faced difficulties recovering valuable furniture and decorative objects. Their inventory of lost items included "18th-century porcelain from Saxony," "Louis XV chair in natural wood, reupholstered in velvet," "a Louis XVI-era box with carved gold," "Louis XV-era clock in porcelain and gold," "two Louis XIII chairs in natural wood." The restitution service deemed these brief descriptions inadequate in June 1950 and requested additional information to process the claim. Adriana replied tersely that she had already provided color photographs and nine copies of the lists to French services. The records end there, with no indication that the family ever recovered the valuable furniture.[62]

In 1954 a cousin of the Salems, Attorney Marcelle Kraemer-Bach, reopened the case of the three MNR paintings with a letter to then Minister of National Education, Jean Berthoin. Madame Salem, she argued, without question had been a "victim of state spoliation," and the sale of the three paintings carried out by agents of the justice system thus should be nullified.[63] In the absence of new evidence supporting the claim, the French administration again rejected it on the basis that the 1941 sale had been carried out according to ordinary law, with the approval of Marcello. The government argued that the replacement of the initial estate manager by a provisional administrator of the CGQJ in June 1942 was further evidence of the sale's legitimacy.[64]

Kraemer-Bach continued to pursue the case on behalf of the family and in 1961 visited the office of Rose Valland, who reiterated the government's position that the sale had been voluntary and was carried out according to French civil law. In response to the government's continued intransigence, Kraemer-Bach proposed a more moderate solution: the loan of one painting during the lifetime of Adriana and Raphaël Salem. Valland found the request reasonable and trusted the goodwill of Raphaël, owing to his stature as a mathematics professor at the Collège de France. She also found the solution politically wise, as it would definitively end the family's continual claims, and do so in a favorable circumstances.[65] However, the Director of French Museums Henri Seyrig rejected it, prompting a new suggestion from Kraemer-Bach that the frames of each of the three paintings carry a small plaque indicating "former collection of Gentili di Giuseppe." Valland herself denied the request, considering it analogous to self-serving patronage plaques. Yet the whole matter made Valland uneasy. She believed the museum administration would win any case brought by the family, but urged the Louvre "to bring an end to these incessant claims."[66]

The Gentili heirs then dropped the lawsuit for thirty-seven years, until the more favorable political climate of the late 1990s. In March 1998, Federico's grandchildren—Marcello's daughter Christiane and Adriana's sons Daniel and Lionel and daughter Emmanuele—filed a lawsuit against the Louvre museum and the French state, asking the government to nullify the 1941 sale and award restitution of all five identified paintings, plus damages. A Court of First Instance dismissed their claims, but it also rejected the government's argument that the statute of limitations had expired. The heirs appealed, and in a momentous decision, the Court of Appeal of Paris ruled in their favor, granting restitution of all five paintings.[67]

A key shift in the Court of Appeal ruling was the determination that the absence of Marcello and Adriana in Paris in 1940 was, in fact, due to "exorbitant common law measures laid down against Jews after 16 June 1940," even though these measures preceded the creation of provisional administrators under the CGQJ. The court further found that the heirs' presence in Paris from June 1940 to April 1941 "would have allowed for the inheritance operations to reach quite a different conclusion."[68] The decision marked a shift in legal notions of under-duress sales, acknowledging the fear of persecution among Jews in France from the earliest days of the occupation. The appeals court decision was all the more extraordinary given that it allowed the heirs to benefit from both the 1941 sale and restitution, an award that more than made the family legally whole.[69]

Claiming a Monet Water Lily: The Rosenberg Collection

Amid official rhetoric promoting transparency and research on spoliation in 1999, another restitution was forced upon the Musées de France by the heirs of Paul Rosenberg. At issue was MNR 214, a Monet water lily painting (*Nymphéas*, 1904) housed since 1960 at the fine arts museum in Caen, Normandy. In late 1998, just as the imminent Washington Conference on Holocaust-Era Assets was garnering significant international press, the Rosenberg heirs identified the painting at an impressionism exhibition at the Museum of Fine Arts, Boston. The Rosenberg family swiftly submitted a formal claim to the French government, eliciting a clumsy public statement from Françoise Cachin professing ignorance as to whether the painting had been stolen or purchased from Rosenberg.[70] The picture had been in high demand for impressionism exhibitions abroad and was next due to go on loan at the Royal Academy of Arts in London. Instead, the French government withdrew it from the London show and shipped it back to France while it considered the Rosenberg family claim.[71]

The Musées de France then finally carried out the provenance research that should have connected the picture to the Rosenberg family decades earlier. Researchers determined that the Germans most likely had stolen it from the Rosenberg family home in Floirac on September 15, 1940, and carted it off to the German embassy in Paris. From there it was shipped to Berlin for the collection of foreign minister Joachim von Ribbentrop. It likely was among works by Manet, Ingres, and Fragonard found as a result of investigations in the British occupied zone in October 1945, in which interrogators learned quite by accident that works of art had been sent from the foreign ministry to a farm in Schleswig-Holstein. Owners of the Paulsen shipping company in Hamburg reported that an army vehicle had delivered the pictures the previous April, without giving the company any further instructions. Some of the paintings were found in a Paulsen cellar; others had been stashed in a Ribbentrop hideaway.[72]

At various points in the art recovery process, French officials failed to connect the painting to Paul Rosenberg, even though it was listed in the 1947 *Répertoire des biens spoliés*. The Monet painting appears as item number 5280 with the exact dimensions and rightful owner, Paul Rosenberg, flagged with an asterisk as among the missing pieces of "undeniable cultural value," and "an outstanding class."[73] Thus even a painting considered part of the French patrimoine with a known owner could elude proper identification. The minutes of the fourth selection committee indicate that "Monet, L'Etang aux nymphes [sic]" was chosen for public use on December 21, 1949, as MNR 214. The committee selected more than five hundred objects that day, including 250 paintings by French artists.[74] Given the thousands of pieces being processed by the CRA with limited staff, there were bound to be errors. Compounding potential confusion and misidentification, Monet had created numerous water lily paintings.[75] At the same time, the system was fraught with institutional conflicts of interest. The officials selecting works for French museums, including curators Michel Florisoone, René Huyghe, German Bazin, and Jean Vergnet-Ruiz, had an interest in appropriating high-value, unclaimed works without thoroughly investigating their ownership histories. In this case, the fine arts museum in the city of Caen was the primary beneficiary, and it held the water lily painting from 1960 until it was returned to the Rosenberg family.[76]

During the restitution ceremony on April 29, 1999, symbolically held at the Jeu de Paume Museum, Minister of Culture Catherine Trautmann said there would always be a "lingering mystery" as to why French officials had not identified it as a work from the Rosenberg collection after the war. The Jeu de Paume had displayed it, and according to Trautmann, Rosenberg was frequently invited to the postwar exhibitions and "should have at least been familiar with the catalog of the Jeu de Paume in 1952 featuring the painting." A case in point was an MNR painting by Courbet allocated to the Louvre in 1949, which "having revealed itself" to be the property of Rosenberg was restituted two years later. In the case of the water lily painting, the Musées de France finally had been able to prove Rosenberg's ownership, Trautmann explained, thanks to a combination of recent discoveries: a photograph from the Rosenberg archives, a stock number from records from the Rosenberg gallery that appeared on the back of the painting, and the use of infrared technology, which revealed a partially hidden number on the back of the canvas corresponding to a Monet piece known to have been in the Ribbentrop collection. This case, Trautmann added, showed the complexity of provenance research, and willingness of the Musées de France to work through challenges and "achieve legitimate restitutions."[77]

Trautmann's statement was disingenuous at best, as this display of "goodwill" had been forced upon the Ministry of Culture by the Rosenberg claim. Descendant Marianne Rosenberg, granddaughter of Paul, finds the statement "a perfect embodiment" of the attitude of the Musées de France at the time that the descendants bore the responsibility for locating objects and pursuing restitution. According to her, the family was able to claim the Monet painting "totally by happenstance." The heirs had more information than many other descendants, as Paul was an art dealer and kept inventory records of every item, including artists, dates, and exact measurements. Even armed with this documentation, Marianne Rosenberg points out, descendants living in France and the United States could not be expected to locate all of the family's items, especially in the fifty years after the war, before the internet age, when crucial ownership information was sealed away in classified archives.[78] The Rosenberg heirs were among those fortunate enough to identify some pieces, and they sold the Monet water lily painting for an estimated $20 to $25 million.[79]

In the years following the publication of the Mattéoli Commission report in 2000, the French government failed to carry out systematic provenance research on the MNRs. Yet the press continued to cover the story, and in January 2013, French senator and historian Corinne Bouchoux spearheaded a report that was highly critical of the government's management of the items. As a result of growing public pressure and amid press coverage of George Clooney's film *The Monuments Men*, the Ministry of Culture finally intensified provenance research efforts in 2014, enlisting the assistance of genealogists to trace objects to increasingly distant heirs.[80] The research led to some progress, as eight works were restituted from 2015 to 2017. But more could have been done, as an internal French government report acknowledged in early April 2018. Minister of Culture Audrey Azoulay had commissioned the report, written by David Zivie of the cultural heritage administration. Zivie correctly criticized the French government's continued "inefficiency and a lack of ambition" to determine rightful ownership of the objects. The report led to the creation of yet another task force in the fall of 2018 to intensify research efforts.[81] In 2019, the number of restitutions spiked to thirty-five, the most in one year since at least 1951.[82] In early 2022, the French parliament voted unanimously to return fifteen artworks plundered from Jewish owners and held by the French state. The works included a painting by Gustav Klimt acquired in 1980 and forcibly sold by an Austrian collector in 1938, and a picture by Marc Chagall that entered French national collections in 1988 and was held at the Centre Pompidou.[83] In another striking measure, both houses of parliament voted unanimously in 2023 to facilitate the restitution of works plundered from Jewish owners, without requiring a separate deaccession law in each case.[84] It appeared the tide had turned with a resounding recognition that French museums held works as a result of Nazi-era spoliation that should be given to rightful owners.

Yet complications remained in other cases, especially when the plunder involved spoliation by the Vichy regime. In May 2021, the Commission for the Compensation of Victims of Spoliation (CIVS) granted the return of twelve works held by French museums to the heirs of Armand Dorville, a French Jewish lawyer who died in July 1941, in southern France. The Vichy regime appointed a provisional administrator to oversee the sale of 450 artworks from the Dorville collection in June 1942, including twelve pieces purchased by the French state. Louvre curator René Huyghe represented the Louvre at the sale, ensuring that some pieces would enter the museum collection. By early 2020, the Louvre had recruited art historian Emmanuelle Polack to study works acquired by the museum during the war, and she helped identify ten pieces from the Dorville collection. Although the CIVS allowed the return of the twelve pieces in 2021, as Dorville heirs had not been able to benefit from proceeds of the sale due to antisemitic persecution, the Commission determined that the 1942 auction was not a forced sale. Descendants were outraged by the interpretation of Vichy spoliation and litigation ensued over other works from the Dorville collection that remained in French museums.[85]

Confronting the Past in the Netherlands

Compared to the French government, Dutch cultural officials were initially far more proactive in carrying out provenance research and granting restitution of NK works in response to controversy in the late 1990s. The Dutch government, like the French, launched an extensive investigation in 1997 into the wartime plunder of Jewish assets, and the nature and extent of postwar restitution and compensation. It created four committees to study distinct asset categories: gold; financial assets, including bank accounts, stocks, and insurance policies; goods once held by the Liro robber bank and sold in 1968 to employees of the Ministry of Finance; and artworks in the NK collection.[86]

The group of art researchers was popularly known as the Ekkart committee after its chairman, Rudi Ekkart, director of the Netherlands Institute for Art History. The Dutch government charged the committee with assessing whether provenance research should be conducted on the entire NK collection, based on preliminary research on about a hundred works of art. Researchers were to determine whether information on despoiled owners could be found in records of the Netherlands Institute for Art History, the Institute for War Documentation, and archives of the Dutch Art Property Foundation (SNK), and whether additional research was needed on objects with known prewar owners, such as works in the Lanz and Mannheimer collections.[87] In a separate initiative, museum directors in the Netherlands also initiated a self-study of works acquired by Dutch museums between 1940 and 1948, as a number of these items were of "partly obscure, sometimes identifiably questionable provenance."[88] With the cooperation of the ICN and financial support from the Ministry of Education, Culture, and Science, researcher Eelke Muller compiled the data in a 1999 report, with guidelines for Dutch museums on current holdings, acquisitions and loans.[89]

After nearly six months of research, the committee determined that the ICN held in custodianship a total of 3,723 objects and that national museums housed 473 items, for a total of 4,196 works of art. Those of known provenance were removed from the pilot study, initially found to be eighty-four from the Lanz collection, 173 from the Mannheimer collection, and thirty-seven from the Koenigs collection of drawings. The committee created a database for known information on NK items and divided the objects into four categories: painting and drawings, prints and reproductions, ceramics, and other applied works of art. It pulled a random sample of one hundred works in the ICN custodianship, proportional in size to each of the four categories, plus thirteen works from the national museums, for a total of 113 objects. Researchers compiled a dossier for each object and submitted 113 separate reports. It was the first systematic research in the Netherlands that compared data from SNK records, still held by the finance ministry, with those held by the ICN under the Ministry of Education, Culture and Science.[90]

The committee published an initial pilot study in April 1998 and reported that researchers had been able to determine a complete wartime ownership history on thirty of the 113 works of art. They had gathered limited information on 38 objects, and no provenance details on forty-five items. Even in cases with complete ownership histories, ambiguities often remained in SNK records as to whether works had been confiscated or sold, and the degree of coercion in sales. Based on this initial study, the committee concluded that "further research is urgently needed in order to clarify existing uncertainties as much as possible," and should encompass the entire NK collection. "Without further research," the report warned, "the Netherlands Art Property collection will remain shrouded in a veil of secrecy with regard to the origins of the individual objects" and "there can be no assurance that individual questions from possible former owners or their descendants will be dealt with effectively." This research would be pivotal in tracing pieces to rightful owners.[91]

Based on the Ekkart Committee's recommendations, in 1998 the Dutch government created the Origins Unknown Agency (Bureau Herkomst Gezocht, BHG), which over the next six years carried out more extensive provenance research on all items in the NK collection. The Dutch government fully adopted recommendations issued by the committee in three phases: an intermediate report in April 2001 on private property, recommendations on art dealerships in January 2003, and final recommendations published in December 2004.[92]

In the 2001 report, the Ekkart Committee confirmed the findings of the other Dutch study groups that "legal restitution was characterized by a strictly bureaucratic approach without any flexibility and turning a blind eye on the exceptional position and interests of the victims." Similarly, it concluded, "we must describe the way in which the Netherlands Art Property Foundation generally dealt with problems of restitution as legalistic, bureaucratic, cold and often even callous."[93] The report summarized government policy as of March 2000, according to which settled cases would remain closed but allowed the state to examine new claims or new facts related to past claims. "The concept of *new facts*," the authors argued, should "be given a broader interpretation than has been customary so far" to include information obtained from recent provenance research. This new approach also would allow the reconsideration of postwar decisions issued by the Council for the Restoration of Property Rights, due to "changed (historic) views of justice and the consequences of the policy adopted at the time."[94]

The committee also granted claimants the "benefit of the doubt" in a few key areas, including the assertion of sales under duress. The SNK restitution guidelines from 1946 had stipulated that "there must be no doubt as to the involuntary nature of the loss of the property," and documents must affirm that "the original owners did not lend their co-operation to the loss of the work or works of art belonging to them." The Ekkart Committee found that the SNK had reached restitution decisions based on this "rather narrow definition of the term 'involuntary loss of property.'" It recommended that all art sales by Jewish individuals in the Netherlands after May 10, 1940, be treated as forced sales, "unless there is express evidence to the contrary."[95] This reformulation thus crucially gave claimants the benefit of the doubt.

The recommendations also addressed the repayment of sales proceeds in cases where owners had sold works of art and received payment from a buyer or through a postwar settlement with the Dutch government. Postwar policies requiring payment to recover objects sold under duress, according to the committee, "can only be described as extremely cold and unjust," as many owners had used the funds to flee the country and escape persecution. In many cases, the authors noted, sellers did not have access to the proceeds. They concluded that claimants should be given the benefit of the doubt and bear no administrative costs. In cases where restitution would require partial or full repayment of proceeds, the amount would be adjusted according to a price index, "for the sake of equality before the law compared to those who did buy back their property." This measure would also prevent "extra profits being gained now by those who at the time very consciously opted for money instead of restitution of works of art."[96] In cases where restitution applications were denied, the committee allowed the repurchase of art by owners who did not previously use the opportunity.[97]

The state's more liberal approach also extended to proof of title, in recognition of the fact that in many cases owners lost such documents during the war. The benefit of the doubt, the committee advised, "should be given to the private person and not to the State," and restitution should be granted if title has been proven with "a high degree of probability." At the same time, the authors preserved a central principle applied by the SNK, that "there must be no mutually inconsistent claims submitted and there should be no reason to suppose that such claims will be entered in the future."[98] The committee further recommended that researchers examine whether a work changed hands involuntarily more than once during the war, potentially leading to multiple claims that would need to be resolved through arbitration or the court system.[99]

The Ekkart Committee recommendations signaled a significant shift in the government's position on claims to works in the NK collection and created the need for a separate body that would review applications. In November 2001 the state secretary for education, culture, and science established an independent restitution committee (Restitutiecommissie) to assess claims as an alternative to litigation. Given provisions in Dutch civil law that had blocked legitimate claims in the past, such as short statutes of limitations and protections of ownership title for good-faith purchasers, the government aimed to develop a more policy-oriented approach, beyond the legal system.[100] The restitution committee also developed procedures for alternative dispute resolution by offering binding opinions and mediation related to private or state-owned works of art outside the NK collection, such as items held by regional or municipal governments, and foundations. For these decisions, the restitution committee used a more narrow standard of "reasonableness and fairness" in determining rightful ownership.[101]

In January 2003, the Ekkart Committee issued an additional set of recommendations related to art dealers.[102] In cases of outright theft, Jewish and non-Jewish art dealers or their heirs had a right to restitution, and the government was to interpret evidence of theft of confiscation "in a magnanimous way." With regard to Jewish dealers, moreover, "the threatening general circumstances must be taken into account."[103] Sales declared voluntary by the dealer or direct representatives would be interpreted as such by the government, "unless other clues clearly contradict the correctness of this qualification." Involuntary sales were defined as transactions with the enemy or convicted Dutch collaborators that were carried out "under threat of reprisal." Also included in this definition were agreements that provided passports or safe conduct to the dealer, and sales by Aryan trustees not appointed by the dealer, unless the dealer "fully benefited from the sale," or the dealer, heirs, or their appointed representative "explicitly renounced" restitution rights after the war.[104]

In its final set of recommendations in December 2004, the Ekkart Committee emphasized the temporary nature of the government's more liberal restitution policy. Initially, the committee recommended that the government continue to accept claims under the new policy for a period of two years, a time frame that was later extended to June 30, 2015.[105] The committee also clarified that claims from foreign private individuals should be dealt with in the same manner as those by Dutch citizens, whereas claims from a foreign government should be addressed through bilateral consultations.[106] Works in the NK collection found to have belonged to Jewish owners with a "high degree of certainty," they stated, should be displayed to the public with a plaque indicating the known provenance. Moreover, the state should donate a sum equivalent to the works' estimated value to Jewish cultural charities, along with an indexed percentage of proceeds from public sales of unclaimed art through 1952.[107] Finally, the committee recommended that all research compiled by the Origins Unknown Agency be conserved in the Dutch National Archives and be made available to all interested parties and researchers, in accordance with laws protecting the right to privacy.[108] The impact of this more liberal approach to art restitution, which remained in effect until 2012, is evident in the claims to works in the Fritz Gutmann and Jacques Goudstikker collections, each one leading to the restitution of more than two hundred objects.

Sales Reconsidered: The Gutmann Restitution

In the fall of 1994, Los Angeles resident Nick Goodman received a shipment of his father's papers from Germany. His father, Bernard, had passed away unexpectedly while swimming in the Adriatic Sea, the day after his eightieth birthday. There is a certain irony in the fact that the papers had been shipped from Germany. Bernard, the son of Fritz and Louise Gutmann, had fled the Netherlands during the war in his mid-twenties and served in the British army. Distancing himself from the family's past on the continent, he adopted the anglicized surname Goodman and married a descendant of Protestant Highland Scots. The couple baptized their two sons, Nick and Simon, enrolled them in Bible school, and spoke little about the tragic wartime history of the Gutmann family. Bit by bit, Simon recalls, he and his brother began to piece together information from "coded adult conversation that children instinctively pick up on." They learned that their paternal grandparents had "died in the war," and eventually their mother revealed the family's Jewish heritage—a surprise to the boys, who had considered themselves thoroughly Anglican.

Later on, Simon and Nick also learned from relatives that the Gutmanns had been fabulously wealthy and had lost all of their assets during the war.[109] Bernard and his wife eventually divorced, and after living as an aging bachelor in London, he struck up a romance with a German woman named Eva, twenty years his junior. To his sons' surprise, he moved to Tübingen to be with her. They realized only after his death that he had also taken crates of papers with him—the documents Eva sent to Nick's home in Los Angeles.[110]

The brothers began going through Bernard's papers, placing them in stacks on Nick's dining room table. Some were their father's handwritten notes, others were government documents in several different languages—German, French, Dutch, Italian, English, Czech—on official letterhead with stately coats of arms. There were old receipts and bills of sale, expired passports with prewar swastika stamps from Nazi Germany, art exhibition catalogs, and photographic negatives of what appeared to be French Impressionist paintings. The brothers began to piece together the painstaking work their father had carried out after the war to trace the Gutmann family's lost art collection. Bernard had encountered obstacles at every turn but kept the quest secret from his sons.[111] After his death, the brothers and their aunt Lili, Bernard's sister, would revive his mission with far greater success.

Simon, a veteran of the music industry, became an amateur art researcher and initially focused his energy on tracing a painting in one of the photo negatives, a landscape by Degas. In the fall of 1995, he pored over materials housed at UCLA, near his home. One day while wrapping up work at the Arts Library, he was flipping through a book on Degas landscapes by British art historian Richard Kendall when an image suddenly grabbed his attention. "There it was!" he recalled. "As if it jumped off the page, the impact was like a blow to the chest. What had eluded my family for over half a century was staring me in the face: *Landscape with Smokestacks*."[112] The book's publication had coincided with the occasion of a traveling exhibition held the previous year at the Metropolitan Museum of Art in New York and the Houston Museum of Fine Arts, and indicated that the landscape had been loaned by Mr. Daniel Searle, the former chairman of the G. D. Searle pharmaceutical company.[113] After establishing that the painting in question indeed had been owned by Fritz Gutmann, the heirs first unsuccessfully tried to reach an agreement with Searle. When the effort failed, they filed a lawsuit, initially in New York, where Searle had purchased the painting. The case was transferred to Illinois, the defendant's state of residency. Amid extensive television and newspaper coverage in the new era of heightened awareness of

Holocaust-era assets, in August 1998 the two parties reached an unusual settlement. Each side agreed to hold half ownership. Searle donated his half to the Art Institute of Chicago and the Institute paid the Gutmann heirs for their half.[114] While the settlement did not provide restitution nor full compensation, and barely covered their legal fees, the heirs nonetheless considered it a significant victory.[115]

With the assistance of a researcher, Helen Hofhuis, Nick and Simon also pursued works from the Gutmann collection that were still held in custodianship by the Dutch state. Their timing fortuitously coincided with the creation of the Unknown Origins Agency, whose reports included a growing list of works from the Gutmann collection: a Meissen teacup, a couple paintings, several pieces of Chinese porcelain. The heirs enlisted the support of Anne Webber of the Commission for Art Recovery and submitted a formal claim at the end of 1999.[116]

The Ekkart Committee investigated three categories of objects from the Gutmann collection. One was a group of three silver objects purchased by Hofer in 1940 on behalf of Göring. After the war, Bernard and Lili had not claimed them and most likely were unaware of them. However, the committee determined there were "sufficient indications to assume that the sale was involuntary." In the second category were seven paintings sold to Böhler and Haberstock in 1942, to which the heirs had forfeited their rights in July 1954. The third group was the largest, made up of works sold by Gutmann to Böhler and Haberstock in 1941 and 1942, and which Bernard and Lili had declined to repurchase after the war. In addition, the committee had discovered twelve works in the NK collection that it believed were sold by Gutmann to Böhler and Haberstock but were not included in the postwar settlements, nor in Nick and Simon's claim.[117]

Following the Dutch government's restitution guidelines, the committee determined on March 25, 2002, that the Gutmann heirs had presented "new facts" regarding the sale and restitution of the collection. Considering the "special circumstances" in which the sales had taken place, the committee could not assume "that the heirs would be unlawfully enriched by the restitutions if they did not refund the sales proceeds." In addition, the committee found that the actions of the heirs in the early postwar years should not be considered a forfeiture of rights, "since the mere fact that the owners refrained from repurchasing the objects and made a conscious selection does not constitute forfeiture of rights in itself." The fact that sold objects could not be returned without repayment lent "additional poignancy to the case," and the committee found plausible the claimants' argument that such repayment had been prohibitively expensive for the heirs.[118]

In all, the committee recommended the restitution of some 250 works of art and antiques to the Gutmann heirs. Simon was stunned: "We could hardly believe it." The decision was approved by the state secretary shortly afterward, and the Dutch state began the complicated process of gathering all the items from various museums, ministries, and repositories, illustrating the extent to which the NK collection had been scattered among numerous public buildings: tapestries from Maastricht, an Aelbert Cuyp painting from the Dutch embassy in Stockholm, an Etruscan terra-cotta mask from Leiden, Meissen bowls and dishes from a museum in Zwolle, Chantilly vases from the Rijksmuseum, a Louis XV desk from the Dutch embassy in Buenos Aires.[119]

In September 2002, Simon, Nick, and Lili all returned to Bosbeek, the former Gutmann family mansion outside Heemstede, which had been converted into a retirement home for elderly nuns. After the war, the Dutch state had recognized Bernard and Lili as the property's rightful owners, but they relinquished it due to mounting financial and legal burdens. The Catholic Congregation of the Sisters of Providence purchased the mansion in 1950 and converted it into a sanatorium. Fifty-two years later, they allowed the heirs to wander through largely empty rooms.[120] Lili served as tour guide and pointed out the wall where a Gobelin tapestry had hung, another spot where the family had displayed a Louis XV clock and Qing dynasty vases, and "barren walls where there once had been Louis XIV silk damask paneling in between floor-to-ceiling Louis XV mirrors."[121] In the great room, the Dutch state had restored a Jacob de Wit painted ceiling with a gilded frame, "all of which," according to Simon, "contrasted depressingly with the sanatorium's functional furnishings." Glancing back at the mansion as they drove away, the family found some comfort in the fact that the property's exterior and the lawns had been properly maintained, but for Simon "the void inside was still a difficult image to shake."[122]

When the family reached the ICN storage facility, they found on display many of the items that had once graced Bosbeek. The heirs each chose several items they wished to keep and enlisted Christie's to sell some ninety pieces.[123] An initial auction in Amsterdam in May 2003 brought in $983,981, and a month later in London, three highly coveted silver pieces formerly in the custody of the Rijksmuseum sold for more than $3 million.[124] The Rijksmuseum managed to regain possession of one of the pieces through the sale, a silver-gilt ewer by Johannes Lencker. A set of two Petzolt cups went to the Detroit

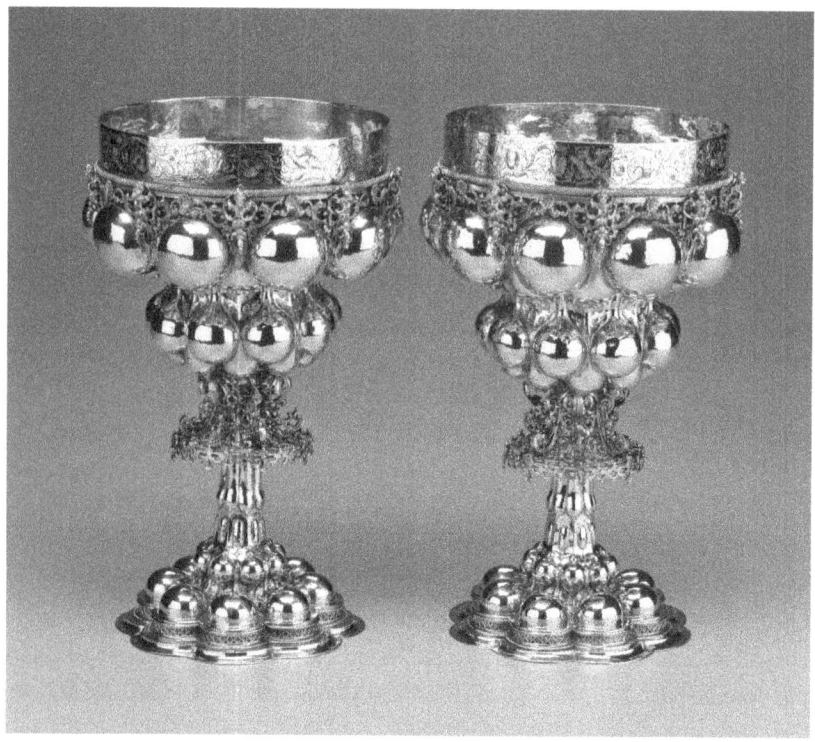

Hans Petoltz, *Double-Cup* (1596), selected by the Dutch state. Restituted to heirs of Fritz Gutmann in 2002. Courtesy of the Detroit Institute of Arts, which purchased the items.

Institute of Arts, and the Art Institute of Chicago purchased a stunning silver-gilt cup, *Horse and Rider* by Hans Ludwig Kienle.[125]

Naturally, the heirs profited from the sales of the valuable objects. According to Simon Goodman, however, the hunt for his family's art was about far more than profit. "All those who had concealed, knowingly or not, the true origins of a work of art obtained by the Nazis between 1933 and 1945," he argued, "were in fact prolonging the Holocaust."[126]

The Goudstikker Collection

By the late 1990s, the Dutch state still held some two hundred pieces from Jacques Goudstikker's former trading stock that had been purchased by

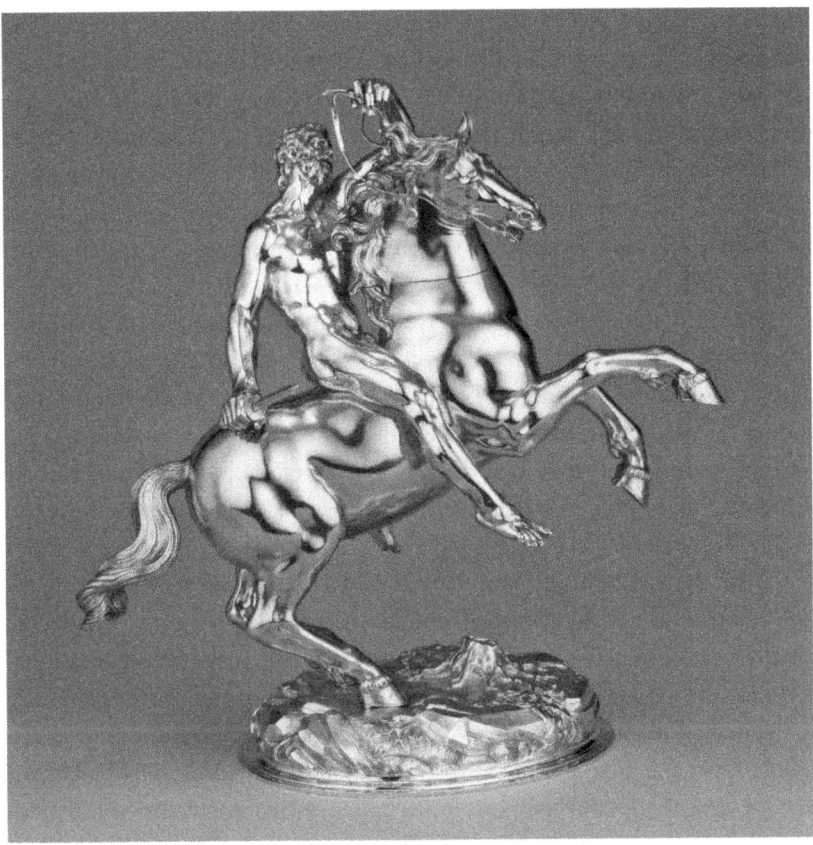

Hans Ludwig Kienle, *Horse and Rider* (1630), selected by the Dutch state and restituted to heirs of Fritz Gutmann in 2002. Courtesy of the Art Institute of Chicago / Art Resource, NY.

Göring. Goudstikker's widow Dési had remained in the United States after the war and married her attorney, August von Saher. She and her son, Eduard, the infant she had held while fleeing the Netherlands with Jacques, both adopted the Von Saher surname. In her negotiations with the postwar Dutch state, Dési faced significant costs to recover works of art and real estate that was sold to the enemy, and she waived restitution rights to the paintings purchased by Göring. They quietly remained in Dutch museums and storage facilities for several decades.[127]

Amid growing public debates about Holocaust-era assets in the mid-1990s, and formal declarations by the Dutch state that it intended to study this troubled history, investigative journalist Pieter den Hollander received a news tip from a senior official in the Dutch finance ministry about the Goudstikker property. "You should take a look at this case," the informant advised, "it stinks to high heaven."[128] Den Hollander pursued the story, and after researching the case in Dutch archives, found that his informant was right. The government was still holding the Goudstikker collection, but had not tracked down an heir. With some additional sleuthing he found Marei von Saher, Eduard's widow, in Greenwich, Connecticut, and shared his findings with her.[129]

Prior to this conversation with Den Hollander, Von Saher had known little about the fate of the art collection. Dési and Eduard had both recently passed away, in 1995 and 1996, respectively, and the family had only obliquely spoken about the art dealership and castles plundered during the war. But with the information provided by Den Hollander, Von Saher knew she needed to pursue restitution of the artworks, to honor her late husband and mother-in-law.[130]

A Dutch court rejected Von Saher's initial claim, submitted in January 1998, on the basis of the statute of limitations provided in the postwar decree E100 on the restoration of property rights. Yet she knew the international tide was turning against this kind of technical defense, and she found an ally in the World Jewish Congress, which urged the Dutch state to appeal the ruling. Over the next few years, with the creation of the Origins Unknown Agency and the Restitution Committee, the environment for Von Saher's claim became much more favorable. By this point, she also was in contact with Nick and Simon Goodman in the wake of their successful claim, and the heirs gave one another advice and moral support. In June 2004 she submitted another claim, which went through a thorough review, including a hearing held on September 12, 2005, featuring testimony of Marei and her daughter, Charlène.[131]

In a landmark decision issued in December 2005, the committee recommended that the state secretary of education allow the restitution of 202 works from Goudstikker's trading stock. The committee determined that Dési had reached a definitive settlement with the Dutch state in 1952, when she had bought back some three hundred other works and declined around twenty that had been purchased by Alois Miedl. A cache of 194 works purchased by Göring, however, were in a separate category, as the heirs had "never waived their ownership rights" to those items. The committee found that the claim previously rejected in 1999 was admissible, owing to the more liberal restitution policy implemented in 2002. The committee determined that twelve pieces purchased by parties other than Miedl and Göring likely had been sold involuntarily and thus it allowed their restitution. Four paintings had "gone missing," which brought the total number of restitutable pieces to 202. In an additional victory for Von Saher, the committee further determined that no repayment for the restituted works of art would be required, as the amount that had been made available to Dési through the wartime sales was "much lower than the amount paid by Miedl and Göring during the war," and she had suffered "significant losses." The committee also recognized that in the 1950s the Dutch state had sold at least sixty-three works from Goudstikker's stock and deposited the proceeds in the national treasury, and that the state "has had the right of usufruct to the works of art for almost 60 years." It further held that no national public interest should have impeded the restitution, as the works had been intended for sale in 1940 and thus could not be considered subject to the protection of Dutch cultural heritage at the time.[132]

Education secretary Maria van der Hoeven disagreed with key aspects of the committee's conclusions and in a letter to the Lower House of parliament on February 6, 2006, explained that she believed the 1999 decision had "conclusively settled the case." Nonetheless, she ultimately recognized that "there are sufficient grounds in this special case to grant restitution in accordance with the Committee's recommendation."[133] The Dutch state had moved beyond strictly legal criteria in examining this restitution case and considered moral justifications as well. Von Saher sold four pictures by Old Masters back to the Dutch state and donated one painting by Bartholomeus van der Helst in gratitude for the work of the Ekkart Committee.[134]

The committee's recommendations from the early 2000s formed the basis of Dutch art restitution policy until July 2012, when a decree incorporated recommendations by then–State Secretary for Education, Culture and Science Halbe Zijlstra. The reform gave the Restitutions Committee more latitude in cases related to works outside the NK collection, allowing consideration of the interests of all parties involved. It also endorsed an advisory council's view that the government's more liberal restitution policy did not "need to be drawn out indefinitely." Zijlstra proposed a shift to the standard of "fairness and justice" (*redelijkheid en billijkheid*) beginning June 30, 2015, two years after the anticipated publication of a study on NK works in Dutch museum collections.[135] This shift created uniformity in the Restitution Committee's assessment of claims, whether involving works held by the state and other entities, but also reversed the benefit of the doubt previously

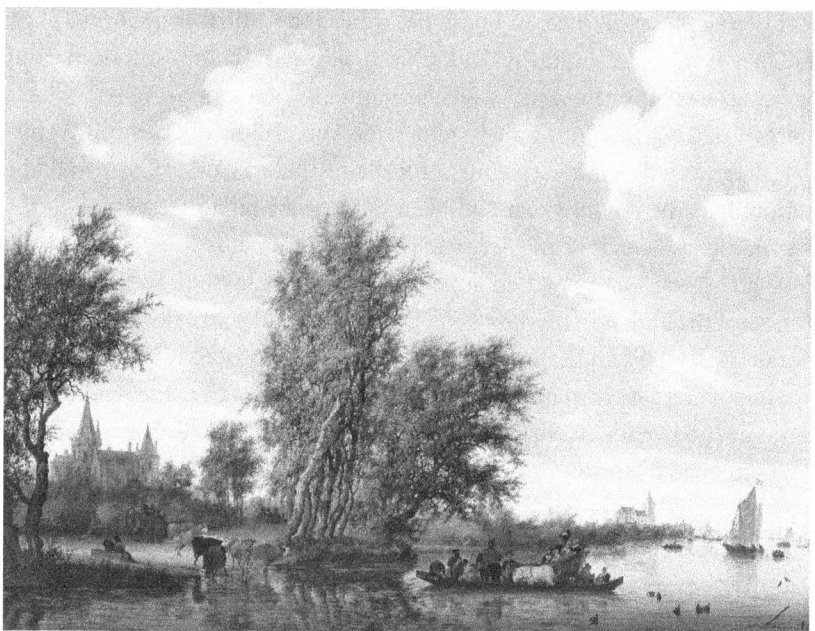

Salomon van Ruysdael, *River Landscape with Ferry* (1649), selected by the Dutch state. Restituted to heirs of Jacques Goudstikker in 2006. Courtesy of the National Gallery of Art in Washington, D.C., which purchased the painting.

given to claimants. The Restitution Committee would now weigh not only the merits of the claim, but also the interest of the current owner—including museums—in holding the object.[136]

Critics of this shift to a "balance of interests" policy argued that it contradicted the Washington Principles and international norms that discount the importance of a work of art to a public collection. In February 2015, attorney Gert-Jan van den Bergh argued in the daily *De Volkskrant* that by considering the length of time a work was held by a museum, the Restitution Committee was allowing a previously rejected statute of limitations argument to be "brought in again by the back door."[137] The following year, the committee reviewed five restitution requests and recommended rejecting restitution in all of them. Committee chair Willibrord Davids appeared to anticipate criticism by stating in an annual report that it would be "irresponsible to conclude that this is the start of a trend which will lead to many applications being rejected."[138] In each of the cases, he argued, claimants had failed to rise to the standard of "very plausible" ownership.[139]

However, the public-relations damage was done. Gideon Taylor, chairman of operations for the World Jewish Congress, told the *New York Times* in May 2017 that the new Dutch approach "is having a chilling effect on claimants."[140] To many in the art world, Dutch museums were poised to benefit at the expense of private claimants.[141] This controversy gave way to yet another set of procedural regulations in April 2021, abandoning the recent "balance of interests" approach. According to this new framework, if the applicant is the plausible owner of an item held by the state and lost it involuntarily, the Restitution Committee advises return of the item "unconditionally." If the item is not held by the state, the Committee also considers whether the current possessor acquired it in good faith.[142] As elsewhere, Dutch Nazi-era art restitution policy is evolving along with the repatriation of colonial items.[143]

Belated Reckoning in Belgium

Belgium was the last of the three countries to create a research commission on the spoliation of Jewish property and postwar restitution. According to Jacques Lust, a contributor to the study commission and a researcher with the Federal Science Policy Office, Belgian authorities learned from the work of commissions in France and the Netherlands, which were progressing far more quickly.[144] Created in July 1997 by the government of Jean-Luc Dehaene, the Belgian Study Commission on Jewish Assets was initially headed by the former governor of the National Bank of Belgium, Baron Jean Godeaux. After commission members expressed concern that Godeaux might be favoring banking interests, he was succeeded by Lucien Buysse, the former grand marshal of the Royal Palace.[145]

The government entity, popularly known as the Buysse Commission, convened civil servants, historians, and other researchers. Historian Rudi Van Doorslaer led a sub-committee of researchers from April 1999. The research group created the Mala Zimetbaum database (MZBD) of around seventy thousand Jews who lived in Belgium during the war, named after a young Jewish girl from Antwerp who was caught trying to escape from Auschwitz and was executed by the Nazis.[146] They documented the spoliation of assets using wartime and postwar archives on an array of assets, including bank accounts, insurance policies, diamonds, works of art, and furniture. The commission's final report was published in July 2001, and in the preface Buysee observed that the document should be "approached and read as a work of remembrance." One should not "divorce the tale of despoliation and redress and the 'material' deficit from its tragic human backdrop," he continued, as the loss of 24,240 Jews from Belgium "cannot ever be quantified in 'moral' terms."[147]

The commission set up a series of meetings in 2000 to learn about the study of Jewish cultural assets in other countries. In March, the Belgian researchers met with Alain Pierret, a member of the French Mattéoli Commission who oversaw the working group on cultural assets, and in June learned about the work of the Dutch Ekkart Committee. The same month, they met with Anne Webber of the Commission for Looted Art in Europe and in October, like members of the Dutch committee, participated in the Vilnius International Forum on Holocaust-Era Looted Cultural Assets. Facing an eight-month deadline, they focused on assessing available archives, building a Jewish Cultural Assets-Belgium (JCA-B) database of looted cultural objects, and investigating whether Belgian institutions were holding spoliated works of art.[148]

The JCA-B database contained information gathered from archives from the Ministry of Public Works and Reconstruction, the DER, and German ERR and furniture operation documents, and was available only to members of the commission due to Belgian privacy laws.[149] It contained 4,196 records on 225 Jewish-owned collections, linked to the broader database on Jews in Belgium through an MZDB number, and grouped the pieces into categories, including paintings, sculpture, furniture, tapestries, archeological artifacts, gold and silverworks, ceramics, and religious objects. The "items" were not strictly works of fine art and included archival collections, musical instruments, and books. Database fields included the artist, work title, medium, dimensions, creation date, site of spoliation, and the release dates and locations for works restituted by the DER.[150]

For the investigation into artworks in Belgian institutions, the commission distributed a survey to 415 cultural institutions, asking about the activities of the given establishment during the war, and whether they held objects that might have Jewish provenance or related archives. Most museums (276) did not respond, but of the 148 respondents, four confirmed they held Jewish-owned items—Autoworld, the Jewish Museum of Belgium, the Royal Museums of Art and History, and the Vleeshuis Museum in Antwerp. Researchers were surprised to see a variety of ambiguous responses about Jewish provenance: "not at first glance," "not as far as we know." The respondents' uncertainty at least clarified a need for more thorough provenance research in Belgian collections. More to the point, none of the responding institutions had previously carried out research on Jewish-owned works of art, prompting researchers to question whether they truly did not hold Jewish items, as most claimed.[151]

The commission sent a second questionnaire to twenty-four cultural institutions, including twelve museums that had received works of art in the custodianship, such as the Royal Museums in Brussels and Antwerp, the Royal Museum for Central Africa in Tervuren, and smaller museums in Liège, Tournai, and Ghent. The questionnaire also went to three government divisions that might have held unclaimed goods or relevant documentation: the Sequestration Office of the state property agency, the committee of recovery of despoiled assets at the Ministry of Economic Affairs, and the Office for War Victims. The survey first asked whether institutions had acquired works of art between the start of the German occupation in 1940 and the last sale of recovered works of art in 1954. It also asked whether Jewish collectors had stored works of art at the museum for safekeeping between 1940 and 1948. Researchers cross referenced names of the collectors with entries in the Mala Zimetbaum database and searched for evidence that the objects had been restituted. Institutions were then asked to detail correspondence with the DER, in an effort to find more information on the 639 recovered objects distributed to Belgian museums. Finally, the commission asked whether each entity received objects between 1940 and 1954 that did not appear in an official inventory. Of the twenty-four institutions, fifteen submitted at least a partial response, a rather meager response rate of 62.5 percent.[152]

In early January 2001, the commission launched site visits based on responses to the second questionnaire and carried out more thorough provenance research on works in the custodianship. The researchers first studied the official inventories of each institution and noted acquisitions during a broadened time frame of 1933 to 1960, covering the beginning of the Nazi era and an extended period of restitution beyond the last sale of recovered artworks. They then studied each acquisition more closely, and in cases of donations and bequests they asked institutions to provide correspondence confirming a voluntary gift. In cases where a collector had stored works at a museum for safekeeping, the researchers requested proof that the items had indeed been restituted. If such evidence was not available, they asked to see the objects themselves. For works purchased by the museum, they asked to see proof of the transaction. If this research raised ownership questions, researchers asked to study the objects more closely to see if seals, stamps, or inscriptions could provide additional clues.[153] While Belgium escaped the high-value restitution lawsuits seen in France and the Netherlands, a phenomenon Jacques Lust called a "tyranny of masterpieces," the government also faced dilemmas due to a lack of documentation on the appropriated items.[154]

For the 639 acquired artworks, researchers attempted to trace the ownership of each piece. They also asked each institution to provide information on works they held by three foreign and Jewish artists who were deported from Belgium: Kopelis Simelovicius, Félix Nussbaum, and Gyorgy Bekefi. The researchers compiled a detailed report for each item with Jewish provenance, whether the owner had been identified, and for those of unknown provenance. Their report excluded works with demonstrated non-Jewish provenance. Of the 639 pieces, the researchers determined that 298 had unidentified Jewish ownership, of which nearly all (292) were distributed to the Royal Museums of Art and History. These items were mostly ceramics, bronzes, gold and silver objects, and Greek, Roman, and Asian antiquities. Other institutions received three horloges, two paintings, and one archive lot of around two hundred documents. An additional seven objects with identified Jewish provenance (one flag with one handle, one lot of 460 Hebrew books, two paintings, one tapestry, and one rug), and twenty-six with possible Jewish provenance (fifteen paintings, two sculptures, six silver pieces, two Torah scrolls, and one badge) brought the total of demonstrated and potentially Jewish-owned assets to 331 cultural items.[155] The researchers admit that these findings likely represented "the tip of the iceberg" given the scope of spoliation during the occupation and the ineffective restitution procedures after the war. Moreover, they addressed only works held by museums and not those sold on the art market that ended up in private and foreign collections. The figures on Jewish-owned items may also be artificially low due to the relatively low response rate of museums to the initial questionnaires.[156] Most of the research on cultural items was not included with the general commission report, given the volume of material. Annex 27 indicates that the extensive material would be published separately, though it has yet to appear.[157]

Recognizing the short period of time granted to researchers for this study, the commission recommended hiring two art historians to continue carrying out provenance research, either through the prime minister's cultural affairs office or the Royal Institute for Artistic Patrimony. These provenance researchers would pursue several goals: identify heirs of objects held by Belgian museums and other institutions, find current owners of recovered works sold by the Belgian state, investigate possible dispersal through the private art market, and search for recovered works that may have ended up in foreign collections, especially in France, the Netherlands, the United States, and eastern Europe. The commission recommended notifying any identified rightful owners and allowing appropriate restorative measures on a case-by-case basis. When researchers could not identify owners of Judaica, sacred objects, or works specifically emanating from the Jewish community in Belgium, the items should be given to Jewish institutions. Other recovered works with no identified owner could be signaled in museum displays with a plaque explaining the history of wartime spoliation.[158]

There is no evidence that the Belgium government hired the researchers. The state did, however, establish a Jewish Community Indemnification Commission to compensate losses not yet paid through the West German BRüG law or previous Belgian measures. In a significant departure from postwar restitution policy, claimants were required to have lived in Belgium between May 10, 1940, and May 8, 1945—not necessarily to have held citizenship—and to have been despoiled of assets due to "anti-Jewish measures or practices of the occupying authorities."[159] Through negotiations among the Belgian State, the National Bank of Belgium, insurance companies, and financial institutions, €110,640,298.30 was paid into a special account at the Belgian National Bank for disposal by the Indemnification Commission. Of this amount, €45,579,587 came from the Belgian state.[160] From September 2002 through the end of 2007, the Indemnification Commission processed 5,620 claims, 58 percent of which originated in Belgium, the next highest percentage coming from the United States and Israel, 14 percent each.[161]

The vast majority of claims sought compensation for lost furniture as a result of the German furniture operation. Indemnification was calculated according to figures established by the German BRüG law of 1957, with a flat-rate figure averaged to compensate a home of four and a half rooms, indexed and rounded up to total €7,000.[162] A total of 1,813 furniture claims were compensated for €12,700,000. The Indemnification Commission also compensated the loss of recovered works sold by the state in response to claims, and researchers determined the merits of each claim based on records of postwar auctions. In all, fifty-seven claims for cultural objects were compensated for €300,000, and researchers were able to determine rightful owners of two pieces, which led to restitution.[163] While the office of the

Indemnification Commission closed at the end of 2007, the prime minister's office intended to manage pending claims. However, it is not clear that systematic provenance research on the appropriated items was carried out, and by 2023, no special restitution commission had been established.

Debates over colonial repatriation, however, may end up prompting further research on Nazi-era items; in March 2019 the Belgian government created a committee charged with researching items of dubious provenance, in response to a flurry of claims to objects and human remains from Congo and New Zealand.[164] In June 2021, a report published by an independent panel of experts urged the state to pursue provenance research on colonial items and facilitate restitution procedures. It referenced the importance of the 1998 Washington Principles, which "set up an important framework, also relevant for dealing with colonial loot, as they require a proactive role of possessors, call for understanding with regard to the problems with evidence, and put forward the importance of just and fair solutions to complicated claims."[165] A few weeks later, the Belgian government approved a plan to create a bilateral agreement with the Democratic Republic of Congo (DRC) to repatriate items stolen or acquired through violence under colonial rule.[166]

The Belgian government did not develop such a systematized approach related to Nazi-era items at the time. According to Jacques Lust, there was less urgency to develop a restitution policy on Nazi-era art, compared to France and the Netherlands, as the state held fewer and less valuable items.[167] One sign of progress: in May 2021, Thomas Dermine, a state secretary who played a key role developing plans for the cultural accord with the DRC, notified the heirs of Gustave and Emma Mayer that the Belgian state would restitute a painting purchased by the government in 1951. The Belgian Study Commission had noted in 2001 that the Corinth painting may have been Jewish-owned, but it took twenty more years for the state to determine that it was indeed stolen from a storage facility at the beginning of the war, after the couple had fled to England. The painting was returned to the Mayer descendants in February 2022.[168] In addition, the Belgian economic ministry created a database of works plundered from Belgium during the war based on DER records, available in Dutch, French and English.[169] Yet without the pursuit and publication of more systematic provenance research, Belgian reckoning with state appropriation of Nazi-era art remains incomplete.

As in France and the Netherlands, the work of investigative journalists keeps the issue in news headlines. Belgian journalist Geert Sels, cultural editor at *De Standaard* and an associate researcher at the Centre d'études de Guerre et Société, has written numerous articles on works plundered in Belgium, and a monograph published in 2022. According to Sels, Belgian museums at the time of his book publication held nine paintings and thirteen other items plundered from private owners by the Nazis and their collaborators. He also emphasizes the fact that works sold from Belgium during the war went to the Netherlands, France and other neighboring countries, thus escaping the recovery effort in former Reich territories.[170]

The legacy of Nazi art plunder thus continues to create legal and ethical dilemmas for art museums, in western Europe and around the globe, amid restitution demands from various constituencies.

Conclusion

A New Age of Museum Ethics

The evening train ride from Zurich to Munich began normally enough. It was early autumn, September 22, 2010, and among the passengers, seventy-seven-year-old Cornelius Gurlitt was returning home. Traveling was difficult for Gurlitt, who struggled with a heart condition, and he preferred the peace, quiet, and predictability of ordinary daily routines, conducted alone in his small apartment in Munich's Schwabing district. He also acutely distrusted authority. When customs officials approached him on the train and asked him routine questions, he became agitated. Suspicious of his odd behavior and evasive answers, the agents escorted him to the train restroom to conduct a search. They found he was carrying €9,000 in cash—not a crime in itself, as the amount was judiciously below the €10,000 cross-border limit for undeclared currency. Lacking evidence of illicit activities, the agents noted his name and address and allowed him to continue the journey. But the incident prompted an investigation by Bavarian authorities, who soon realized they had no record of Gurlitt. He did not report income, pay taxes, use public health insurance, or draw social security benefits. As one journalist later put it, the man was a phantom.[1]

After the unsettling incident on the train, Gurlitt returned to his reclusive daily routine. For a while. About a year and a half later, on February 28, 2012, his peaceful world was shattered when around thirty customs investigators from the Augsburg public prosecutor's office stormed inside his apartment. They found him in a nightshirt, stunned by the intrusion. What began as a tax investigation eventually became a much bigger art crime story that generated headlines around the world: inside the modest flat, the investigators found and seized 121 paintings and 1,285 drawings, watercolors, and prints, many of which were unframed and carefully stored in the drawers of a large art cabinet. The pieces were Gurlitt's "friends," as he called them, the only love of his life, and some had been plundered by the Nazis. He had inherited the artworks from his father, Hildebrand Gurlitt, a dealer tasked with disposing of "degenerate" art on behalf of the Third Reich, and who kept numerous pieces for his own collection. Investigators later found another stash of artworks in Cornelius's home in Salzburg, bringing the total cache to fifteen hundred items.[2]

The Gurlitt story prompted a frenzy in traditional and social media. It was a dramatic tale of hidden treasure, with an intriguing, unsavory character as the protagonist. Initial press reports also sensationally claimed the collection was worth upwards of a billion dollars, given the multimillion dollar value of key works by Matisse, Monet, and Cézanne. The value is now estimated to be far lower, as the collection contains some family heirlooms and numerous works on paper, including serial graphic works; no official valuation has been published.[3] There was also international outrage at the bungled reaction of the German government, which kept silent about the discovery until the story leaked to the magazine *Focus* in early November 2013. Moreover, the news headlines circulated just as the trailer for George Clooney's film *The Monuments Men* was hitting screens of all sizes.[4]

Another key factor in the extensive press coverage of the Gurlitt hoard was a wide consensus by the 2010s, among scholars, journalists, art experts, and a broader public, that states and other entities must reveal holdings of Holocaust-era assets with transparency. Heightening the drama surrounding the collection, Cornelius passed away in May 2014 and bequeathed the artworks to the Kunstmuseum Bern in Switzerland, an apparent final act of defiance against the German government. The museum, which had no prior dealings with Gurlitt, deliberated for several months and accepted the bequest, with the exception of any items determined to have been plundered. Research overseen by the German Lost Art Foundation through 2019 left many questions unanswered. By the time the foundation published its final report in May 2020, only fourteen items had been identified as Nazi plunder, thirteen of which were restituted to rightful owners; the rest of the trove went to Bern. With the conclusion of research in Germany, foundation Director Gilbert Lupfer was confident that nothing more could have been done, but he admitted that for around one thousand items, "there is a large gray zone."[5]

The Gurlitt case illustrates the continued legacy of Nazi looting in the art world, and the importance of transparency and provenance research, whether carried out by governments or private entities. In western Europe, this responsibility above all is borne by states, which benefited from Nazi plunder for decades, and in some cases to this day. These examples of patrimania prolonged the dispossession inflicted by the Nazis and their collaborators, with a disproportionate impact on Jewish art collectors and dealers, in the context of the Final Solution. Despite differences in the extent and nature of Nazi plunder, in postwar restitution agencies and personnel, and in national laws and norms governing the management of cultural property, there was remarkable similarity in the French, Dutch, and Belgian governments' approach to orphaned works of art. These items, once held to be a national interest, are today subject to international scrutiny. The governments of the three countries have an ongoing responsibility to carry out provenance research on items in their care that might have changed hands as a result of Nazi persecution, and to publish findings on searchable websites, in multiple languages.

The renewed attention to Nazi art looting that followed the Gurlitt story came at a time when other aspects of art crime were in the news. Upheaval in the Middle East during the Arab Spring of the early 2010s caused a spike in art trafficking. The Islamic State (IS) shocked the world by publicizing grisly murders and wanton destruction of cultural heritage, such as the ancient site of Palmyra in Syria. It also financed operations through art trafficking, exacerbating the illicit trade of antiquities. One victim of IS was eighty-two-year-old antiquities scholar Khaled al-Asaad, who in the summer of 2015 refused to disclose the location of precious artifacts during a month-long interrogation. The militants beheaded him and hung his mutilated body in the main square of Palmyra.[6]

As concerns over antiquities trafficking deepened, French president Emmanuel Macron amplified debates in Europe over items in museums that had been plundered from former colonies. While speaking to several hundred university students in Burkina Faso in November 2017, he advocated facilitating "the temporary or definitive restitution of African cultural heritage to Africa." The unexpected declaration shocked the art world, French curators and museum directors perhaps most of all. Did he really mean it? There were seventy thousand objects from sub-Saharan Africa in the Quai Branly Museum alone. Rather than backtracking, Macron doubled down on Twitter, declaring that "African heritage cannot remain a prisoner of European museums."[7] Macron had unwittingly stumbled into a noble but thorny proclamation that was exceedingly difficult to uphold, as the deaccession of artworks from national collections required approval from the French parliament.

In a 2018 report commissioned by the French government, Senegalese economist Felwine Sarr and French art historian Bénédicte Savoy advocated the full restitution of numerous colonial objects, drawing sharp rebukes from critics and intensifying debates over colonial heritage that already were circulating elsewhere in Europe.[8] In December 2020, the French National Assembly approved a bill restituting twenty-seven objects to Africa—twenty-six to the Republic of Benin and a sword to Senegal. Apparently aiming to allay fears of excessive restitution, French Culture Minister Roselyne Bachelot explained that the law applied only to those items and would not overturn the inalienability of French national heritage.[9] Over the next few years, debates over colonial collections in France, Belgium, and the Netherlands intensified, prompting governments in all three countries to proclaim a commitment to provenance research and develop procedures for repatriation.[10]

Coinciding with these debates, Dan Hicks, Professor of Contemporary Archeology and Curator at the Pitt Rivers Museum, published *The Brutish Museums*, highly critical of museums around the world with items stolen violently by British forces at the end of the nineteenth century from the Kingdom of Benin, in present-day Nigeria.[11] The book contributed to controversy around the opening of the Humboldt Forum in Berlin, housing the Ethnological Museum and the Museum of Asian Art, amid claims from former German colonies.[12] British museums also faced high-profile claims from India and former African colonies, along with the longstanding conflict between Greece and the British Museum over the Parthenon ("Elgin") Marbles, an emblematic cultural-heritage dispute.[13]

Since the 1990s, various constituencies have challenged the proclaimed right of public and private museums to hold objects acquired through illicit means. Claims to various categories of objects on legal and ethical grounds—Nazi-era art, trafficked antiquities, Native American and Indigenous belongings, colonial collections—have called into question the mission of universal art museums developed in Europe more than two hundred years ago. These encyclopedic public museums have expanded through a kind of cultural *raison d'état*, defending as national heritage works produced and conserved in the country. Across the Atlantic, private museums with cultural power and influence grew in the United States in the nineteenth century, modeled on the great European institutions. Largely built with the wealth of private benefactors, such as J. P. Morgan, Henry Clay Frick, and William Wilson Corcoran, communities running and supporting these museums also developed a sense of heritage and a duty to preserve and display works in the public trust, expanding collections significantly after the Second World War.[14]

In an apparent paradox, globalization, digitization, and ever-expanding forms of social media in the early twenty-first century have reinforced the importance of tangible objects as heritage and sources of identity—local and national, individual and familial, communal and tribal. Advances in digitization and other technologies, by nature unbearably ephemeral and potentially inauthentic, have reinforced the importance of materiality and tangibility, raising the stakes for art restitution. As ever, the act of holding an original work of art signifies control, sovereignty, and power. Today, public attention focuses on the communities and individuals from whom items were plundered.[15]

In the realm of Nazi-era art, activists, claimants, experts, and policymakers will continue to debate the meaning of "fair and just solutions."[16] Proposals for an international body charged with adjudicating cultural property disputes will continue to surface, as they did in the early postwar years.[17] In June 2018, a privately established Court of Arbitration for Art opened in The Hague, addressing issues related to authenticity, contracts, and copyright claims in private proceedings. But Nazi-era cases may be dismissed if claims have not been pursued "with reasonable diligence," making the body a far cry from an international cultural court of justice.[18] With heritage stakes so high and national legal systems protecting current owners, it is highly unlikely that culturally dominant public or private institutions would submit to the authority of such an international body in the near future.

Still, efforts at international cooperation continue. In November 2018, delegates convened in Berlin to assess progress made by the twentieth anniversary of the Washington Principles. The United States, represented once again by Stuart Eizenstat, and Germany issued a joint declaration affirming a commitment to the principles, though Eizenstat gave a qualified assessment. Despite advances in provenance research, notably the use of digital technology to enhance transparency and facilitate restitution, he declared that "the glass is slightly more than half-full, but that is not satisfactory." He placed particular blame on five European countries that, in his view, had failed to implement the principles: Hungary, Poland, Spain, Russia, and Italy. Marc Masurovsky, co-founder of the Holocaust Art Restitution Project (HARP), pushed the point further, challenging Eizenstat by arguing that non-compliance over the previous twenty years had been so widespread that the Washington Principles were simply a failure.[19]

Indeed, the grand international conferences on Holocaust-era assets—in Washington, Vilnius, and Prague—had achieved limited results. The noble declarations remained non-binding agreements among nations with varying legal systems, and they lack any kind of enforcement mechanism. As a result, for instance, Russia has endorsed general statements promoting the restitution of Jewish assets, while continuing to oppose restitution of trophy art seized by the Red Army. According to a 2014 report sponsored by the Claims Conference and the World Jewish Restitution Organization, however, the worst offenders—countries that did not "appear to have made significant progress toward implementing the Washington Principles and the Terezin Declaration"—were Italy and several east European countries, including Poland, Hungary, Bulgaria, Romania, and Ukraine.[20]

While much of the recent criticism from Americans justifiably has targeted these countries, more can and should be done in the United States as well. Prior to widespread concern over Nazi-era art, demands for systematic research in US collections first involved Native American items. The 1990 Native American Graves Protection and Repatriation Act (NAGPRA) requires museums and other entities to study and publicize their holdings of human remains and sacred and funerary items, and allow tribal access to collections for potential repatriation claims.[21] By the late 1990s, when museums also faced growing demands for systematic provenance research on Nazi-era art, professional organizations voluntarily chose to create new codes of ethics. The Association of Art Museum Directors (AAMD) adopted guidelines on best practices in 1998, followed soon afterward by a similar code of ethics issued by the American Association of Museums, renamed the American Alliance of Museums (AAM). With the publication of the PCHA final report in January 2001, the Alliance and AAMD supported the recommendation to create a searchable registry of information provided by museums on works that may have been plundered from Holocaust victims. The PCHA, AAMD, and AAM agreed that museums should strive to identify these assets, make provenance information accessible to the public, and prioritize provenance research "as resources allow."[22]

Many art museums in the United States made progress by carrying out provenance research on their permanent collections as well as loaned and acquired objects, and by creating requisite websites detailing ownership histories. The AAM pursued the goal of creating a searchable online registry and in September 2003, launched the Nazi-Era Provenance Internet Portal, with information provided by museums on works that changed ownership in continental Europe between 1933 and 1945. By the end of 2018, 179 participating museums had listed nearly thirty thousand objects in the portal.[23] Listing these objects in a portal, however, is not the same thing as conducting thorough provenance research and transparently publishing updated findings to the public. The portal quickly became outdated and has not been replaced by a more robust resource. The United States lacks a government mechanism to enforce best practices, as most art museums are private entities. If institutions genuinely aim to facilitate restitution of Nazi-plundered art, as stated in the Washington Principles, they must search for rightful owners through provenance research and the work of genealogists, and not simply wait for heirs to submit claims. Such methods have been used by the Dutch and French governments, as we will see, but remain rare in the United States.[24]

In December 2016, President Obama signed into law the Holocaust Expropriated Art Recovery (HEAR) Act, which aimed to "provide the victims of Holocaust-era persecution and their heirs a fair opportunity to recover works of art confiscated or misappropriated by the Nazis."[25] It addressed a thorny legal issue of varying statutes of limitations across the states by creating a uniform six-year statute of limitations, upon discovery of an artwork's location or the claimant's potential ownership. The act was quickly invoked in court decisions and eliminated one source of technical legal defenses used by museums and dealers.[26]

Since the milestone restitution from the Dutch government in 2006, Goudstikker heir Marei von Saher has pursued other claims to works held by museums and private collectors in the United States, only some of which have been successful. In 2019 she lost a twelve-year legal battle with the Norton Simon Museum in Pasadena, California, over an *Adam and Eve* diptych by Lucas Cranach the Elder, purchased from the Goudstikker stock by Göring and today valued at more than $20 million. After the war the Dutch state had acquired the paintings for the NK collection, and in 1966 it sold them to an exiled Russian aristocrat, George Stroganoff-Sherbatoff, who in turn sold them to the Norton Simon in 1971. The case wound its way through federal district and appellate courts, and the Supreme Court declined twice to review it. The Ninth Circuit Court of Appeals ultimately determined that the Dutch state had acted with proper authority when it sold the paintings, a decision that could not be challenged by US courts, thus confirming the museum's proper title to them.[27] Such protracted and high-profile restitution battles, carried out in the public eye, can take a financial and emotional toll on claimants. Yet Von Saher, who above all seeks acknowledgment of transgressions from the past, believes the struggle is worthwhile. Her message to daunted potential claimants: "You must go forward, for your family."[28]

Today's more engaged and digitally connected public will continue to expect ethical stewardship from art museums and other entities. This expectation of ethical management extends from the ownership and conservation of objects to sources of funding.[29] In this vision, the value of art collections is based not only on appraisals of coveted objects, but also on an institution's commitment to widely accepted codes of ethics. Such an international commitment would further advance early twenty-first-century progress toward greater transparency and belated justice.

Notes

Introduction

1. Simon Goodman, *The Orpheus Clock: The Search for My Family's Art Treasures Stolen by the Nazis* (New York: Scribner, 2015), 132–33.
2. Goodman, *Orpheus Clock*, 76.
3. Goodman, *Orpheus Clock*, 75, 84–89.
4. Goodman, *Orpheus Clock*, 113–28.
5. Goodman, *Orpheus Clock*, 133.
6. Goodman, *Orpheus Clock*, 128–56.
7. Irwin Cotler, "The Holocaust, Thefticide, and Restitution: A Legal Perspective," *Cardozo Law Review* 601 (1998): 602.
8. Commission Consultative des Dommages et des Réparations, *Emprise Allemande sur la Pensée Française*, Monographie P.F. 5: Œuvres d'art ([Paris]: Imprimerie Nationale, 1947), 6.
9. See Dutch postwar exhibition catalog, *Herwonnen Kunstbezit: Tentoonstelling van uit Duitsland Teruggekeerde Nederlandsche Kunstchatten*, Mauritshuis, March–May 1946, preface by J. G. van Gelder, 4. And for Belgium, "Avant-propos," *Chefs-d'Oeuvre Récupérés en Allemagne*, Palais des Beaux-Arts, Brussels, November–December 1948, 7.
10. *The Monuments Men*, directed by George Clooney (Columbia Pictures, 2014); *Woman in Gold*, directed by Simon Curtis (BBC Films, 2015); Robert Edsel with Bret Witter, *The Monuments Men: Allied Heroes, Nazi Thieves, and the Greatest Treasure Hunt in History* (New York: Center Street, 2009).
11. See Herkomst Gezocht (Origins Unknown) pilot study (Netherlands), April 1998, 11, available at https://www.obs-traffic.museum/sites/default/files/ressources/files/origins_unknown_pilot.pdf; Commission d'étude (Belgium), *Les biens des victimes*, 433; Ministère de la culture et de la communication, "Rapport du groupe de travail sur les provenances d'oeuvres récupérées après la seconde guerre mondiale remis à Madame Audrey Azoulay, Ministre de la Culture et de la Communication, March 2017," 14–16, available at https://www.vie-publique.fr/rapport/36809-rapport-du-groupe-de-travail-sur-les-provenances-doeuvres-recuperees-ap.
12. Pim Griffioen and Ron Zeller, "La persécution des Juifs en Belgique et aux Pays-Bas pendant la Seconde Guerre mondiale: une analyse comparative," *Cahiers d'Histoire du Temps Présent/Bijdragen tot de Eigentijdse Geschiedenis*, no. 5 (November 1998/May 1999): 75. Griffioen and Zeller provide the statistic of 320,000 Jews in France on the eve of the Holocaust, less than 1 percent of the total population of around 40 million. See Pim Griffioen and Ron Zeller, "Anti-Jewish Policy and Organization

of Deportations in France and the Netherlands: A Comparative Study," *Holocaust Genocide Studies* 20, no. 3 (December 2006): 437. Total population in 1940 retrieved from Institut national d'études démographiques, ined.fr.

13. I also explore this concept in *Defending National Treasures: French Art and Heritage Under Vichy* (Stanford, CA: Stanford University Press, 2011).

14. See Yvon Lamy, "Patrimoine et culture: l'institutionnalisation," in *Pour une histoire des politiques du patrimoine*, ed. Philippe Poirrier and Loïc Vadelorge (Paris: La Documentation française, 2003), 45–63.

15. Debora Silverman, "Diasporas of Art: History, the Tervuren Royal Museum for Central Africa, and the Politics of Memory in Belgium, 1885–2014," *Journal of Modern History* 87 (September 2015): 617–18.

16. Frits M. van der Meer and Jos C. N. Raadschelders, "In Service of Dutch National Identity: The Discovery, Governance and Management of Historical and Cultural Heritage," in *National Approaches to the Governance of Historical Heritage over Time: A Comparative Report*, ed. Stefan Fisch (Amsterdam: IOS Press, 2008), 136–40.

17. See on the UNESCO website, "Protecting Our Heritage and Fostering Creativity," https://en.unesco.org/themes/protecting-our-heritage-and-fostering-creativity.

18. See, for instance, Willem van Elden, "Juridische Status Gerecupereerd Kunstbezit," December 17, 1945, Nationaal Archief (Netherlands, NAN) 2.08.42/132.

19. See Silverman, "Diasporas of Art." On recent recommendations for cultural repatriation to former colonies, see a report commissioned by the French government: Felwine Sarr and Bénédicte Savoy, "The Restitution of African Cultural Heritage: Toward a New Relational Ethics," November 2018. Original French version available at https://www.vie-publique.fr/rapport/38563-la-restitution-du-patrimoine-culturel-africain. These ideas face wide resistance in the museum world and connect to broader debates on the restitution of antiquities. For perspectives defending the mission of museums, see James Cuno, ed., *Whose Culture? The Promise of Museums and the Debate over Antiquities* (Princeton, NJ: Princeton University Press, 2009).

20. The literature on heritage studies has grown considerably over the past few decades. See David Lowenthal, *The Past Is a Foreign Country* (Cambridge: Cambridge University Press, 1985), and *The Heritage Crusade and the Spoils of History* (Cambridge: Cambridge University Press, 1998); Dominique Poulot, *Une histoire du patrimoine en Occident XVIIIe–XXIe siècle: Du monument aux valeurs* (Paris: Presses Universitaires de France, 2006); Stefan Fisch, ed., *National Approaches to the Governance of Historical Heritage over Time: A Comparative Report* (Amsterdam: IOS Press, 2008).

21. James Rorimer with Gilbert Rabin, *Survival: The Salvage and Protection of Art in War* (New York: Abelard Press, 1950); Thomas Carr Howe, *Salt Mines and Castles: The Discovery and Restitution of European Looted Art* (Indianapolis, IN: The Bobbs-Merrill Company, 1946); Lincoln Kirstein, "Quest of the Golden Lamb," *Town and Country* 100, no. 4276 (September 1945): 114–15, 182–87, 198; Rose Valland, *Le front de l'Art: Défense des collections françaises, 1939–1945*, 2nd ed. (Paris: Réunion des Musées Nationaux, 1997); Walker Hancock, "Experiences of a Monuments Officer," *College Art Journal* 5, no. 4 (May 1946): 271–311; John D. Skilton, *Memoirs*

of a Monuments Officer: Protecting European Artworks (1948; repr., Portland, OR: Inkwater Press, 2008); Walter Farmer, *The Safekeepers: A Memoir of the Arts at the End of World War II* (Berlin: Walter de Gruyter, 2000).
22. Janet Flanner, *Men and Monuments: Profiles of Picasso, Matisse, Braque, and Malraux* (1957; repr., New York: De Capo Press, 1990).
23. Lynn Nicholas, *The Rape of Europa: The Fate of Europe's Treasures in the Third Reich and the Second World War* (New York: Vintage Books, 1995); Hector Feliciano, *The Lost Museum: The Nazi Conspiracy to Steal the World's Greatest Works of Art* (New York: Basic Books, 1997); Michael Kurtz, *America and the Return of Nazi Contraband: The Recovery of Europe's Cultural Treasures* (New York: Cambridge University Press, 2006). Patricia Kennedy Grimsted's extensive bibliography is available at the International Institute of Social History, https://iisg.amsterdam/en/about/staff/patricia-kennedy-grimsted.
24. See Presidential Advisory Commission on Holocaust Assets in the United States, Commission Final Report, "Plunder and Restitution," December 2000, available at http://govinfo.library.unt.edu/pcha/index-1.htm. For France, see Mission d'étude sur la spoliation des Juifs de France, *Rapport Général* (Paris: La Documentation Française, 2000). On art looting in France and the French art custodianship, see Isabelle Le Masne de Chermont and Didier Schulmann, eds., *Le pillage de l'art en France pendant l'Occupation et la situation des 2000 oeuvres d'art confiées aux Musées nationaux* (Paris: La Documentation Française, 2000). The French reports are available at vie-publique.fr, by searching "Mission d'étude sur la spoliation des Juifs de France." For an updated French government report, see David Zivie, Mission sur le traitement des oeuvres et biens culturels ayant fait l'objet de spoliations pendant le Second Guerre mondiale, rapport à Madame Françoise Nyssen, Ministre de la Culture, "'Des Traces Subsistent dans des Registres . . .': Biens culturels spoliées pendant la Second Guerre mondiale: Une ambition pour rechercher, retrouver, restituer et expliquer," February 2018. See also reports by the Dutch Ekkart Committee published annually between 2002 and 2017, at http://www.restitutiecommissie.nl. For Belgium, see Commission d'étude sur le sort des biens des membres de la Communauté juive de Belgique spoliés ou délaissés pendant la guerre 1940–1945. *Les biens des victimes des persécutions anti-Juives en Belgique: Spoliation, Rétablissement des droits, Résultats de la Commission d'étude.* July 2001. The Belgian report is available in French and Dutch, with some sections available in English, at https://www.combuysse.fgov.be/language_selection?destination=index-oldsite.html.
25. On the case of France, an important study from the late 1990s is Claude Lorentz, *La France et les Restitutions Allemandes au lendemain de la Seconde Guerre Mondiale* (Paris: Direction des Archives et de la Documentation, Ministère des Affaires Etrangères, 1998). Among Claire Andrieu's many contributions on Nazi and Vichy plunder is a volume in the Mattéoli Commission report: *La spoliation financière* (Paris: La Documentation Française, 2000). See also Corinne Bouchoux, *"Si les tableaux pouvaient parler . . .": Le traitement politique et médiatique des retours d'oeuvres d'art pillées et spoliées par les Nazis (France 1945–2008)* (Rennes: Presses Universitaires de Rennes, 2013); and Karlsgodt, *Defending National Treasures*.

Jonathan Petropoulos examines the sly maneuvering of Bruno Lohse, a key German dealer in the Nazis' employ, in *Göring's Man in Paris: The Story of a Nazi Art Plunderer and His World* (New Haven, CT: Yale University Press, 2021). On looting and restitution in the Netherlands, see Gerard Aalders, *Nazi Looting: The Plunder of Dutch Jewry during the Second World War*, trans. Arnold Pomerans with Erica Pomerans (Oxford: Berg, 2004), and *Berooid: De beroofde joden en het Nederlandse restitutiebeleid sinds 1945* (Amsterdam: Boom, 2001); Eelke Muller and Helen Schretlen, *Betwist Bezit: De Stichting Nederlands Kunstbezit en de teruggave van roofkunst na 1945* (Zwolle: Waanders Uitgevers, 2002). On the plunder of real estate and household items, see Shannon Fogg, *Stealing Home: Looting, Restitution, and Reconstructing Jewish Lives in France, 1942–1947* (Oxford: Oxford University Press, 2017); Annette Wieviorka and Floriane Azoulay, *Le Pillage des appartements et son indemnisation* (Paris: La Documentation Française, 2000), a volume in the Mattéoli Commission report; and Sarah Gensburger, *Images d'un pillage: Album de la Spoliation des Juifs à Paris, 1940–1944* (Paris: Editions Textuels, 2010). On the theft of books and archives, see Lisa Moses Leff, *The Archive Thief: The Man Who Salvaged French Jewish History in the Wake of the Holocaust* (New York: Oxford University Press, 2015). Important edited volumes include Martin Dean, Constantin Goschler, and Philipp Ther, eds., *Robbery and Restitution: The Conflict over Jewish Property in Europe* (New York: Berghahn Books, 2007): A French translation with updated texts is Constantin Goschler, Philipp Ther, and Claire Andrieu, eds., *Spoliations et restitutions des biens juifs en Europe, XXe siècle*, trans. Odile Demange (Paris: Editions Autrement, 2007). See also Wouter Veraart and Laurens Winkel, eds., *The Post-war Restitution of Property Rights in Europe: Comparative Perspectives* (New York: RVP Press, 2012); Evelien Campfens, ed., *Fair and Just Solutions? Alternatives to Litigation in Nazi-Looted Art Disputes: Status Quo and New Developments* (The Hague: Eleven International Publishing, 2015).

26. See Bianca Gaudenzi and Astrid Swenson, "Looted Art and Restitution in the Twentieth Century—Toward a Global Perspective," *Journal of Contemporary History* 52, no. 3 (2017): 491–518. See also the other contributions in this JCH Special Issue, "The Restitution of Looted Art in the 20th Century." For a critical response to the "transnational turn," see Nancy Green, "Trials of Transnationalism: It's Not as Easy as It Looks," *Journal of Modern History* 89 (December 2017): 874. By the same author, see also *The Limits of Transnationalism* (Chicago: University of Chicago Press, 2019).

27. See J. C. H. Blom, "The Persecution of the Jews in the Netherlands: A Comparative Western European Perspective," *European History Quarterly* 19 (1989): 333–51; Griffioen and Zeller, "La persécution des Juifs en Belgique et aux Pays-Bas," 73–164; Griffioen and Zeller, "Anti-Jewish Policy," 437–73. Deportation statistics vary slightly in these studies. Those cited here are in Jean-Marc Dreyfus, "The Looting of Jewish Property in Occupied Western Europe," in *Robbery and Restitution*, ed. Martin Dean, Constantin Goschler, and Philipp Ther, 54.

28. See, for instance, Martin Dean, "The Seizure of Jewish Property in Europe: Comparative Aspects of Nazi Methods and Local Responses," in *Robbery and Restitution*, ed. Martin Dean, Constantin Goschler, and Philipp Ther, 21–32; Dreyfus,

"Looting of Jewish Property in Occupied Western Europe," 53–67. For a broader comparative analysis of "patriotic memory," see Pieter Lagrou, *The Legacy of Nazi Occupation: Patriotic Memory and National Recovery in Western Europe, 1945–1965* (Cambridge: Cambridge University Press, 2000).

29. Jean-Pierre Bady, "Restitution and Compensation in Four Countries of Western Europe: Belgium, France, Luxemburg and the Netherlands," in *Holocaust Era Assets Conference Proceedings, Prague, 26–30 June 2009*, ed. Jiří Schneider, Jakub Klepal, and Irena Kalhousová (Prague: Forum 2000 Foundation, 2009), 829–30.
30. See Konstantin Akinsha and Grigorii Kozlov, *Beautiful Loot: The Soviet Plunder of Europe's Art Treasures* (New York: Random House, 1995); Konstantin Akinsha, "Stalin's Decrees and Soviet Trophy Brigades: Compensation, Restitution in Kind, or 'Trophies' of War?," *International Journal of Cultural Property* 17, no. 2 (May 2010): 195–216, part of a Special Issue on Russian cultural property law guest edited by Patricia Kennedy Grimsted. See also Sophie Coeuré, "Cultural Looting and Restitution at the Dawn of the Cold War: The French Recovery Missions in Eastern Europe," *Journal of Contemporary History* 52, no. 3 (2017): 588–606.
31. Michael Marrus, *Some Measure of Justice: The Holocaust Era Restitution Campaign of the 1990s* (Madison: University of Wisconsin Press, 2009).

Chapter 1

1. "Report of Professor Jonathan Petropoulos, Clarement McKenna College," expert testimony in dispute between claimant Maria Altmann and the Republic of Austria, July 14, 2005, 2–3, 10, available at http://www.bslaw.com/altmann/Klimt/Petropoulos.pdf.
2. "Report of Professor Jonathan Petropoulos," 6, 16; Melissa Müller, "Adele and Ferdinand Bloch-Bauer," in *Lost Lives, Lost Art: Jewish Collectors, Nazi Art Theft, and the Quest for Justice*, ed. Melissa Müller and Monika Tatzkow (New York: Vendome Press, 2010), 164. Maria Altmann claimed seven paintings by Klimt, but according to Petropoulos, five Klimt paintings appear on the curators' inventory from January 1939. See pp. 12–13 of his report, http://www.bslaw.com/altmann/Klimt/Petropoulos.pdf.
3. "Report of Professor Jonathan Petropoulos," 9; Müller, "Adele and Ferdinand Bloch-Bauer," 164–65.
4. Art collector and founder of the Commission for Art Recovery, Ronald S. Lauder, purchased the golden Adele portrait for a reported $135 million, a record sum at the time. It now hangs in the Neue Galerie in New York, also founded by Lauder. See Müller, "Adele and Ferdinand Bloch-Bauer," 165–71.
5. Jonathan Petropoulos, "German Laws and Directives Bearing on the Appropriation of Cultural Property in the Third Reich," in *Spoils of War*, ed. Elizabeth Simpson, 106–7.
6. Nicholas, *Rape of Europa*, 41–49; Petropoulos, *Art as Politics in the Third Reich*, 90.
7. Petropoulos, *Art as Politics in the Third Reich*, 51–56; Uwe Fleckner, "Marketing the Defamed: On the Contradictory Use of Provenances in the Third Reich," in

Provenance: An Alternate History of Art, ed. Gail Feigenbaum and Inge Reist (Los Angeles: Getty Research Institute, 2012), 140–41.
8. Petropoulos, *Art as Politics in the Third Reich*, 124–26.
9. Jonathan Petropoulos, *The Faustian Bargain: The Art World in Nazi Germany* (New York: Oxford University Press, 2000), 52–55.
10. Petropoulos, *Faustian Bargain*, 52–53.
11. Petropoulos, *Faustian Bargain*, 93.
12. In her memoir, Rose Valland cites a total of 5,350 paintings by Old Masters and ninety-five tapestries. See *Le front de l'art*, 165. Jonathan Petropoulos provides the figure of 8,000 paintings, acknowledging it is a high estimate. See *Faustian Bargain*, 293n205.
13. Nicholas, *Rape of Europa*, 49.
14. See report by Webb on looting and vandalism by Canadian, British, and American soldiers, sent to chief of G-5 Internal Affairs Branch, March 20, 1945, United States National Archives and Records Administration (NARA), RG 331.
15. Report by Bruce Easley to Webb, November 15, 1944, NARA RG 331; Robert Rey, "Violations du Droit International Commises par les Allemands en France dans la Guerre de 1939," *Revue générale de droit international public* 49, no. 2 (1941–45): 43.
16. Report of Combined Services Detailed Interrogation Centre in cooperation with MFAA (United Kingdom), "German Treatment of Works of Art in Occupied Territory," October 16, 1944, NARA RG 260, section on Lille available at https://www.fold3.com/image/269945808.
17. Report by Bernard Foy, curator of the Musée Maritime in Nantes, September 25, 1944, NARA RG 260, https://www.fold3.com/image/114/292890436. A cover letter by Georges Salles, Director of National Museums, dated October 23, 1944, suggests Foy sent the report to M. Auzas, Inspector of Historic Monuments. See NARA RG 260 https://www.fold3.com/image/114/292890438.
18. Bancel LaFarge, "Removal of Works of Art from the Netherlands during the German Occupation," December 29, 1944, NARA RG 331.
19. German poster in AN AJ40/573, folder 12.
20. Valland, *Le front de l'art*, 35–36.
21. Kurtz, *America and the Return of Nazi Contraband*, 31.
22. On Hitler's plan for French museum collections, see Albert Speer, *Inside the Third Reich* (New York: Macmillan, 1970), 214.
23. For a Nazi defense of the confiscation of Jewish-owned artworks, see a report by ERR officer Gerhard Utikal, November 3, 1941, Archives Nationales, France (AN), 3W/122.
24. See Petropoulos, *Art as Politics in the Third Reich*, 15, on the size of Göring's collection, and Chapter 7 on twelve Nazi leaders' collections and acquisition methods.
25. On Lohse's activities, see Petropoulos, *Göring's Man in Paris*.
26. Consolidated Interrogation Report No. 2, The Goering Collection, September 15, 1945, NARA RG 239.
27. Petropoulos, *Art as Politics in the Third Reich*, 127–31.
28. Petropoulos, *Art as Politics in the Third Reich*, 131–33.

29. Petropoulos, *Art as Politics in the Third Reich*, 139-45.
30. Robert O. Paxton and Michel R. Marrus, *Vichy France and the Jews* (Stanford: Stanford University Press, 1981), 6-7.
31. Aalders, *Nazi Looting*, 106-7; Thierry Delplancq, "Des Paroles et des actes: L'administration bruxelloise et le registre des Juifs, 1940-1941," *Cahiers d'histoire du temps présent* 12 (2003): 145.
32. Laurent Joly, *Vichy dans la "Solution Finale": Histoire du commissariat général aux Questions juives (1941-1944)* (Paris: Bernard Grasset, 2006), 81-88.
33. Joly, *Vichy dans la "Solution Finale"*, 229; Julian Jackson, *France: The Dark Years, 1940-1944* (Oxford: Oxford University Press, 2001), 119-20.
34. Petropoulos, *Art as Politics in the Third Reich*, 126.
35. Lust, "Spoils of War Removed from Belgium during World War II," 60; Leistra, "Short History of Art Loss and Art Recovery in the Netherlands," 53, both in *Spoils of War*, ed. Elizabeth Simpson. See also Gensburger, *Images d'un pillage*, 13.
36. Serge Klarsfeld, André Delahaye, Diane Afoumado, et al., *La Spoliation dans les Camps de Province* (Paris: La Documentation Française, 2000), 1-8, 37-50.
37. Nicholas, "World War II and the Displacement of Art and Cultural Property," in *Spoils of War*, ed. Elizabeth Simpson, 41-42; Martin Dean, "The Seizure of Jewish Property in Europe: Comparative Aspects of Nazi Methods and Local Responses," in *Robbery and Restitution*, ed. Martin Dean, Constantin Goschler, and Philipp Ther, 24-29.
38. Géraldine David and Kim Oosterlinck, "War, Inflation, Monetary Reforms and the Art Market," *European Historical Economics Society*, working paper no. 12 (January 2012): 2; Raymonde Moulin, *The French Art Market: A Sociological View*, trans. Arthur Goldhammer (New Brunswick and London: Rutgers University Press, 1987), 21.
39. David and Oosterlinck, "War, Inflation, Monetary Reforms and the Art Market," 2.
40. Cited in David and Oosterlinck, "War, Inflation, Monetary Reforms and the Art Market," 4.
41. Geert Sels, *Kunst voor das Reich: Op zoek naar naziroofkunst uit België* (Tielt: Lannoo, 2022), 9-10. French translation by Pierre Lambert, *Le Trésor de guerre des nazis: Enquête sur le pillage d'art en Belgique* (Brussels: Editions Racine, 2023).
42. John Keegan, *The Second World War* (New York: Penguin, 1989), 65; Michael Lyons, *World War II: A Short History*, fourth edition (Upper Saddle River, NJ: Pearson, 2004), 88; Paul Arblaster, *A History of the Low Countries*, 2nd ed. (Houndmills, NY: Palgrave Macmillan, 2006), 223.
43. Leistra, "A Short History of Art Loss and Recovery in the Netherlands," in *Spoils of War*, ed. Elizabeth Simpson, 53.
44. Petropoulos, *Art as Politics in the Third Reich*, 142; Gerard Aalders, "Le pillage aux Pays-Bas et la Restitution d'après-guerre," in *Spoliations et restitutions des biens juifs en Europe*, ed. Constantin Goschler, Philipp Ther, and Claire Andrieu, 237-38; Dreyfus, "Le pillage des biens juifs dans l'Europe occidentale occupée," in *Spoliations et restitutions des biens juifs en Europe*, ed. Constantin Goschler, Philipp Ther, and Claire Andrieu, 78.
45. Aalders, "Le Pillage aux Pays-Bas," 241.

46. Aalders, "Pillage et (non) restitution des oeuvres d'art aux Pays-Bas (1940–2001)," trans. Claire Darmon, *Revue d'histoire de la Shoah* 186 (January–June 2007): 195; Leistra, "Short History of Art Loss," 54.
47. Leistra, "Short History of Art Loss," 55–56.
48. Aalders, *Nazi Looting*, 6.
49. Aalders, "Le pillage aux Pays-Bas," 237–38.
50. Aalders, *Nazi Looting*, 108–9.
51. Aalders, *Nazi Looting*, 127–30.
52. Aalders, "Pillage et (non) restitution des oeuvres d'art aux Pays-Bas," 200–1.
53. Aalders, "Pillage et (non) restitution des oeuvres d'art aux Pays-Bas," 199.
54. Aalders, *Nazi Looting*, 196.
55. Aalders, *Nazi Looting*, 62–65, 186.
56. Bancel LaFarge, Mission to the Netherlands, to MFAA advisor to SHAEF, December 29, 1944, NARA RG 331.
57. Floris Kunert and Annemarie Marck, "The Dutch Art Market 1930–1945 and Dutch Restitution Policy Regarding Art Dealers," in *Kunst sammeln, Kunst handeln: Beiträge des Internationalen Symposiums in Wien*, ed. Eva Blimlinger and Monika Mayer (Vienna: Böhlau Verlag, 2012), 142.
58. Aalders, *Nazi Looting*, 14.
59. Pieter den Hollander and Melissa Müller, "Jacques Goudstikker," in *Lost Lives, Lost Art*, ed. Melissa Müller and Monika Tatzkow, 221–25.
60. Müller and Tatzkow, *Lost Lives, Lost Art*, 227–28.
61. Advisory Committee on the Assessment of Restitution Applications for Items of Cultural Value and the Second World War, *Annual Report 2005*, 37–40; Müller and Tatzkow, *Lost Lives, Lost Art*, 228.
62. Advisory Committee on the Assessment of Restitution Applications for Items of Cultural Value and the Second World War, *Annual Report 2005*, 33–34.
63. Nicholas, *Rape of Europa*, 111–14.
64. Nicholas, *Rape of Europa*, 110–11.
65. Leistra, "Short History of Art Loss," 54–55; Nicholas, *Rape of Europa*, 110–11. On the contemporary dispute over the drawings, see Patricia Kennedy Grimsted, "Legalizing 'Compensation' and the Spoils of War: The Russian Law on Displaced Cultural Valuables and the Manipulation of Historical Memory," *International Journal of Cultural Property* 17 (2010): 227.
66. Nicholas, *Rape of Europa*, 108–9; Helen Schretlen, "Geschiedenis van de Stichting Nederlands Kunstbezit," in *Betwist Bezit*, ed. Eelke Muller and Helen Schretlen, 54.
67. Aalders, *Nazi Looting*, 70.
68. Leistra, "Short History of Art Loss," 56.
69. Conway, *The Sorrows of Belgium*, 29; Lyons, *World War II*, 88–89.
70. Jean-Michel Veranneman de Watervliet, *Belgium in the Second World War* (Barnsley, South Yorkshire: Pen and Sword, 2014), 94–95; Lust, "The Spoils of War Removed from Belgium," 58.
71. Buchner to Lammers, Reich Chancellery, September 1, 1942, NARA RG 260, https://www.fold3.com/image/114/270141184; Joseph Billiet to Jacques Jaujard,

August 28, 1942, AN 3W/78. Jonathan Petropoulos examines Buchner's service to the Nazis and postwar rehabilitation in *Faustian Bargain*, 16–51.
72. "List of paintings stolen by the Germans at the Musée Royal des Beaux-Arts at Anvers," n.d., RB DER 366.
73. Lust, "Spoils of War Removed from Belgium," 60.
74. Griffioen and Zeller, "La persecution des Juifs en Belgique et aux Pays-Bas pendant la Seconde Guerre Mondiale," 111; Dreyfus, "Looting of Jewish Property," 54.
75. Jacques Lust, "Spoils of War Removed from Belgium," 60–61.
76. Doorslaer, "The Expropriation of Jewish Property and Restitution in Belgium," in *Robbery and Restitution*, in Martin Dean, Constantin Goschler, and Philipp Ther, 156–57.
77. Dreyfus, "Looting of Jewish Property," 55–56; Doorslaer, "Expropriation of Jewish Property," 156–57.
78. Doorslaer, "Expropriation of Jewish Property," 156–57.
79. Commission d'étude (Belgium), *Les biens des victimes*, 142–43.
80. Lust, "Spoils of War Removed from Belgium," 58–59; Jacques Lemaire, *La Franc-Maçonnerie en Belgique: Les loges symboliques* (Paris: Editions Maçonniques de France, 2000), 66–69; Commission d'étude (Belgium), *Les biens des victimes*, 136.
81. Doorslaer, "Expropriation of Jewish Property," 159.
82. Doorslaer, "Expropriation of Jewish Property," 159.
83. Lust, "Spoils of War Removed from Belgium," 60; Commission d'étude (Belgium), *Les biens des victimes*, 135–38.
84. Commission d'étude (Belgium), *Les biens des victimes*, 140.
85. Commission d'étude (Belgium), *Les biens des victimes*, 139. On p. 424, the report indicates that the Commission identified cultural items, broadly defined, from a total of 225 Jewish owners, including items seized by the Möbel-Aktion.
86. German police interrogation of Georg Hoffmann, associate of Andriesse, August 9, 1941, Rijksarchief in België, Brussels (RB), series Dienst voor Economische Recuperatie (DER) 366; Jean Capart statement, November 25, 1941, RB DER 366. For lists of items plundered from the collection, search "Hugo Daniel and Elisabeth Andriesse" and "Elisabeth Andriesse" at https://errproject.org/jeudepaume/.
87. German police interrogation of Georg Hoffmann, associate of Andriesse, August 9, 1941, RB DER 366; Jean Capart to Secretary General of Education, March 9, 1942, RB DER 366; Belgian Secretary General of Education to Military Administration, Section for Culture and Art, April 13, 1942, AEB 366; Lust, "Spoils of War Removed from Belgium," 60.
88. Patricia Kennedy Grimsted, *Reconstructing the Record of Nazi Cultural Plunder: A Guide to the Dispersed Archives of the Einsatzstab Reichsleiter Rosenberg (ERR) and the Postwar Retrieval of ERR Loot*, revised December 2016, BE-7, https://errproject.org/guide/ERR_Belgium_12.2016.pdf.
89. Lust, "Spoils of War Removed from Belgium," 61; Valland, *Le front de l'art*, 80–81. On objects in the Lyndhurst collection registered at the Jeu de Paume, see the database "Cultural Plunder by the Einsatzstab Reichsleiter Rosenberg, https://errproject.org/jeudepaume/. Database sources do not specify the subject in the Hoppner

portrait. On repatriated works, see Commission d'étude (Belgium), *Les biens des victimes*, 237.
90. Commission d'étude (Belgium), *Les biens des victimes*, 145, 424.
91. Commission d'étude (Belgium), *Les biens des victimes*, 9.
92. Lagrou, *The Legacy of Nazi Occupation*, 10.
93. Jackson, *France: The Dark Years*, 355, 371.
94. Jackson, *France: The Dark Years*, 125–26; Robert Paxton, *Vichy France: Old Guard and New Order 1940–1944*, rev. ed. (New York: Columbia University Press, 2001), 6.
95. Marc Olivier Baruch, *Servir l'Etat Français: L'administration en France de 1940 à 1944* (Paris: Fayard, 1997), 65, 68–69.
96. Bertram Gordon, *War Tourism: Second World War France from Defeat and Occupation to the Creation of Heritage* (Ithaca, NY: Cornell University Press, 2018), 67–68; Jackson, *France: The Dark Years*, 142.
97. Jackson, *France: The Dark Years*, 132, 588.
98. Olivier Wieviorka, *Orphans of the Republic: The Nation's Legislators in Vichy France*, trans. George Holoch (Cambridge, MA: Harvard University Press, 2009), 12. According to Wieviorka, 570 deputies "adopted" the measure, as one deputy later changed his vote in favor. See p. 365n2.
99. Keitel to Von Boeckelberg, June 30, 1940; Abetz to military command in Paris, July 1, 1940; Commander in Chief of the Army, Ordinance of July 15, 1940; Ribbentrop to Keitel, August 3, 1940, all reproduced in Jean Cassou, ed., *Le pillage par les Allemands des oeuvres d'art et des bibliothèques* (Paris: Editions du Centre, 1947), 77–83.
100. Telegram from Gerum, German Army Secret Police, to Major Heidschuh, Abwehr, August 30, 1940, AN 3W/357.
101. Valland, *Le front de l'art*, 115–16.
102. Jaujard to Hautecoeur, August 21, 1940, AN AMN R20.6.1.
103. Petropoulos, *Art as Politics in the Third Reich*, 129.
104. "Exposé du Comte F. Wolff-Metternich," in *Le pillage par les Allemands des oeuvres d'art et des bibliothèques*, ed. Jean Cassou (Paris: Editions du Centre, 1947), 165–68.
105. Petropoulos, *Art as Politics in the Third Reich*, 130.
106. Le Masne de Chermont and Schulmann, *Le pillage de l'art en France*, 22–23; Petropoulos, *Art as Politics in the Third Reich*, 131.
107. Carcopino to Darlan, May 29, 1941, AN 3W/121.
108. Michel Rayssac, *L'Exode des musées: Histoire des oeuvres d'art sous l'Occupation* (Paris: Payot, 2007), 272; Carcopino to De Brinon, June 23, 1941, AN 3W/121; Le Masne de Chermont and Schulmann, *Le pillage de l'art en France*, 23.
109. Corinne Bouchoux, *Rose Valland: La Résistance au Musée* (La Crèche: Geste éditions, 2006), 9–20.
110. Jaujard, "Activités dans la Résistance de Mademoiselle Rose Valland, Conservateur des Musées Nationaux," AN AMN R32.1; arrêté establishing Valland's paid position, July 22, 1941, AN AMN O 30-438.
111. Howe, *Salt Mines and Castles*, 24.
112. Valland to Jaujard, February 8, 1944, AN AMN R32.1.

113. Carcopino to de Brinon, June 23, 1941, AN 3W/121; Darlan to de Brinon, June 10, 1941, AN F21/8090, dossier 4.
114. Report from Vallat to Best, August 5, 1941, AN AMN R32.2.
115. Moulin, *The French Art Market*, 17–18.
116. Jacques Jaujard to Louis Hautecoeur, "Ordonnance du 15 juillet concernant les collections particulières," August 21, 1940, AN AMN R20.6.1; "Loi relative à la déchéance de la nationalité à l'égard des Français qui ont quitté la France," *Journal officiel de la République Française*, July 24, 1940, 4569; "Note sur les séquestres," May 18, 1945, AN AMN R32.2.7.
117. "Loi confidant à l'administration de l'enregistrement l'administration et la liquidation des biens mis sous séquestre en conséquence d'une mesure de sûreté générale," *Journal officiel de la République Française*, October 23, 1940, 5389.
118. Salles to Henraux, February 16, 1945, AN AMN R32.3.
119. Le Masne de Chermont and Schulmann, *Le pillage de l'art en France*, 28.
120. Domaines to the education ministry, January 3, 1941, AN AMN R20.4.2.
121. The French government had initially allocated seven million francs (nominal) for acquisitions in 1941 and 1942. See Marie-Claude Genet-Delacroix, "Le budget des Beaux-Arts sous l'Occupation: Un budget de circonstances?," in *La direction du Budget entre doctrines et réalités, 1919–1944*, ed. Comité pour l'histoire économique et financère de la France (Paris: Ministère de l'Economie, des Finances et de l'Industrie, 2001), 436. Portions of the supplementary 66-million-franc acquisition funding were approved incrementally in 1941: first 5 million, then 20 million in October 1941, and 41 million in December 1941, including 6 million for non-sequestered works sold at auction, in December 1941. See Jaujard to Domaines, November 18, 1941, AN AMN R20.4.2; Jaujard to Domaines, January 21, 1942, AN AMN R20.4.2.
122. Budget office to Domaines, March 3, 1942, AN AMN R20.4.2.
123. Karlsgodt, *Defending National Treasures*, 221–26.
124. Huyghe to Jaujard, July 4, 1941, AN F21/4723.
125. Report from René Huyghe to Jacques Jaujard, June 19, 1943, transcribed in a letter from Jaujard to Abel Bonnard, August 10, 1943, AN AMN R32.3.3.
126. René Huyghe to Jacques Jaujard, June 19, 1943, AN AMN R32.3.3.
127. René Huyghe to Jacques Jaujard, August 11, 1943, AN AMN R32.3.3.
128. Three notes from Jaujard to head curator at Versailles and Trianon museums, July 22, 1944, AN AMN R32.2.3.
129. Musées de Versailles et des Trianons (illegible signature) to Jaujard, August 5, 1944, AN AMN R32.2.3.
130. Georges Salles to Jacques May, April 18, 1945, AN AMN R32.3.1.
131. Nicholas, *Rape of Europa*, 153–54.
132. Moulin, *French Art Market*, 21.
133. Jackson, *France: The Dark Years*, 356–57.
134. Michele Cone, *Artists under Vichy: A Case of Prejudice and Persecution* (Princeton: Princeton University Press, 1992), 13–15; Nicholas, *Rape of Europa*, 160.

135. "Special Report on the firm of Wildenstein & Cie, Paris art dealers," NARA RG 260, https://www.fold3.com/image/283745669. Initialed "D. C." for Douglas Cooper. See cross reference in S. L. Faison, Consolidated Interrogation Report No. 4, "Linz: Hitler's Museum and Library," according to which the special report was "issued for British element C.C. by Douglas Cooper, September 1945," https://www.fold3.com/image/283755469. See also Nicholas, *Rape of Europa*, 159.
136. "Special Report on the firm of Wildenstein & Cie, Paris art dealers," NARA RG 260, https://www.fold3.com/image/283745669.
137. Nicholas, *Rape of Europa*, 160.
138. "Special Report on the Firm of Wildenstein & Cie, Paris Art Dealers," NARA RG 260, https://www.fold3.com/image/283745669.
139. See Jonathan Petropoulos, "Art Dealer Networks in the Third Reich and in the Postwar Period," *Journal of Contemporary History* 52, no. 3 (2017): 555–56.
140. Léonce Rosenberg to Commission de Récupération Artistique, February 22, 1945. Recipient specified in cover letter from Jones to Webb, February 28, 1945, NARA RG 331.
141. Report by Central Control Commission for Germany, British Component, Douglas Cooper, Cecil Gould on the Schenker Papers, Part I, including "Index of Paris Art Dealers and Individuals Who Sold Works of Art to German Museums," April 5, 1945, NARA RG 331.
142. Report by Central Control Commission for Germany, British Component, Douglas Cooper, Cecil Gould on the Schenker Papers, Part II, "List of French Art Dealers, Firms, and Individuals Who Sold Works of Art to the Germans during the Occupation," n.d., NARA RG 331.
143. Nicholas, *Rape of Europa*, 157.
144. Petropoulos, *Art as Politics in the Third Reich*, 182.
145. Nicholas, *Rape of Europa*, 157.
146. Laurence Bertrand Dorléac, "Le marché de l'art," in Direction des musées de France, *Pillages et Restitutions: Le Destin des oeuvres d'art sorties de France pendant la Second Guerre Mondiale* (Paris: Adam Biro, 1997), 93.
147. French DGER notice, March 24, 1945, given to MFAA, with cover letter by Jones to Webb, June 5, 1945, NARA RG 331. Dana Thomas, "The Power Behind the Cologne," *New York Times Magazine*, February 24, 2002, https://www.nytimes.com/2002/02/24/magazine/the-power-behind-the-cologne.html.
148. Rorimer journal, November 26, 1944, NGA Rorimer papers.
149. Laurence Bertrand Dorléac, "Le marché de l'art," in *Pillages et Restitutions*, ed. Direction des musées de France, 93.
150. Petropoulos, *Art as Politics in the Third Reich*, 135.
151. Dreyfus, "Looting of Jewish Property," 54; Griffioen and Zeller, "Le persécution des Juifs en Belgique et aux Pays-Bas," 74–75; Maxime Steinberg, *Un pays occupé et ses juifs: Belgique entre France et Pays-Bas* (Gerpinnes: Quorum, 1999), 27. Deportation statistics vary in different sources, though to a relatively small degree. See also Raul Hilberg, *The Destruction of the European Jews*, 3rd ed., vol. 2 (New Haven, CT: Yale University Press, 2003), 599–703.

152. Tony Judt, *Postwar: A History of Europe since 1945* (New York: Penguin Books, 2005), 38.
153. These figures are based on the number of postwar claims, and likely are lower than actual losses. A French commission on war damages and reparations estimated in 1947 that 107,566 objects or assemblages had been lost, based on claims submitted to that point. See Commission Consultative des Dommages et Réparations, *Emprise Allemande sur la pensée francaise*, 12. See also Leistra, "A Short History of Loss and Art Recovery in the Netherlands," 56; Lust, "Spoils of War Removed from Belgium," 62, both in Simpson, *Spoils of War*.

Chapter 2

1. "Laws of War: Laws and Customs of War on Land (Hague II)," July 29, 1899, articles 47 and 56, https://avalon.law.yale.edu/19th_century/hague02.asp. The 1907 Convention continued these provisions.
2. Wayne Sandholtz, *Prohibiting Plunder: How Norms Change* (New York: Oxford University Press, 2007), 102–17.
3. See a list of officers at the Monuments Men and Women Foundation, https://www.monumentsmenandwomenfnd.org/monuments-men-and-women.
4. Roberts Commission meeting minutes, August 25, 1943, NARA RG 239. The United States assigned an embassy staff member as an observer; China and the Soviet Union were not represented. This conference of ministers became the immediate precursor to the United Nations Educational, Scientific, and Cultural Organization (UNESCO).
5. "Protection of Monuments: A Proposal for Consideration during War and Rehabilitation," preliminary draft of petition, December 1942, Archives of American Art (AAA), Constable papers.
6. Nicholas, *Rape of Europa*, 210–11.
7. Roberts Commission meeting minutes, October 8, 1943, NARA RG 239.
8. In *Foreign Relations of the United States Diplomatic Papers (FRUS), 1943*, vol. 1: *General* (Washington, DC: United States Government Printing Office, 1963): Hull to Roosevelt, June 21, 1943, 475–78; Hull to Stone, July 16, 1943; Hull to Roosevelt, August 4, 1943, 479–80.
9. Press release, "The American Commission for the Protection and Salvage of Artistic and Historic Monuments in Europe," August 20, 1943, NARA RG 331. In April 1944, the Commission's official title substituted "War Areas" for "Europe," reflecting its extended responsibilities in Asia.
10. "First List of Possible 50," "First List—Architectural Engineers," both October 15, 1943, in AAA Constable papers; Kurtz, *America and the Return of Nazi Contraband*, 54–55.
11. US Department of State press release, "The American Commission for the Protection and Salvage of Artistic and Historic Monuments in Europe," August 20, 1943, NARA RG 331.

12. Inter-Allied Declaration against Acts of Dispossession committed in Territories under Enemy Occupation and Control, January 5, 1943, in *FRUS 1943*, 443–44. Signatories included the Union of South Africa, the United States, Australia, Belgium, Canada, China, the Czechoslovak Republic, the United Kingdom, Greece, India, Luxembourg, the Netherlands, New Zealand, Norway, Poland, the USSR, and Yugoslavia.
13. Lorentz, *La France et les Restitutions Allemandes*, 10.
14. Lt. Col. Sir Leonard Woolley, *A Record of the Work Done by the Military Authorities for the Protection of the Treasures of Art and History in War Areas* (London: His Majesty's Stationery Office, 1947), 10.
15. Woolley, *Record of the Work Done by the Military Authorities*, 11.
16. Woolley to Dinsmoor, March 2, 1944, AAA Constable papers.
17. Woolley, *Record of the Work Done by the Military Authorities*, 6.
18. Agata Wolska, "The Vaucher Commission as an International Restitution Body—an Abandoned Idea," unpublished paper, March 2017, 3.
19. Memorandum from the American Education Delegation to Shaw, Dickey, and Thompson, April 27, 1944, NARA RG 239; Roberts Commission meeting minutes, July 27, 1944, NARA RG 239.
20. Members included Lord Macmillan (Chair), G. M. Trevelyan, and John Forsdyke representing the British Museum; the Duke of Wellington and Eric Maclagan of the Victoria and Albert Museum; Vincent Massey and Kenneth Clark of the National Gallery; John Clapham and Frederic Kenyon of the British Academy; and J. G. Mann of the Society of Antiquaries.
21. Woolley to Dinsmoor, March 4, 1944, AAA Constable papers.
22. Nicholas, *Rape of Europa*, 222–27.
23. Nicholas, *Rape of Europa*, 237.
24. Eisenhower directive to all commanders, December 29, 1943, NARA RG 331.
25. Nicholas, *Rape of Europa*, 246–47.
26. "For Col. Newton," March 30, 1944, AAA Constable papers.
27. Howe, *Salt Mines and Castles*, 21.
28. Geoffrey Webb to SHAEF Chief of Staff, "Report to June 1944," NARA RG 331.
29. Geoffrey Webb to SHAEF Chief of Staff, "Report to June 1944," NARA RG 331.
30. Walker Hancock with Edward Connery Lathem, *A Sculptor's Fortune* (Gloucester, MA: Cape Ann Historical Association, 1997), 130.
31. Eisenhower to SHAEF Commanders in Chief, May 26, 1944, NARA RG 331.
32. Eisenhower to SHAEF Commanders in Chief, May 26, 1944, NARA RG 331.
33. SHAEF, "France: A General Survey To Be Read in Conjunction with the Handbook for Civil Affairs (France)," March 1944, NARA RG 331.
34. Memorandum from Civil Affairs Division, ComNavEu, to all Naval Civil Affairs Officers, June 3, 1944, NARA RG 331.
35. Lyons, *World War II*, 267.
36. Geoffrey Webb to SHAEF Chief of Staff, "Report to June 1944," NARA RG 331.
37. Claudia Baldoli and Andrew Knapp, *Forgotten Blitzes: France and Italy under Allied Air Attack, 1940–1945* (London: Continuum Books, 2012), 6.
38. Rorimer, *Survival*, 3–5.

39. Journal entry, August 3, 1944, NGA Rorimer papers.
40. Rorimer, *Survival*, 5–6.
41. Rorimer, *Survival*, 37–39.
42. Journal entry, August 18–19, 1944, NGA Rorimer papers.
43. Journal entry, August 18–19, 1944, NGA Rorimer papers.
44. Skilton, *Memoirs of a Monuments Officer*, 19.
45. Skilton, *Memoirs of a Monuments Officer*, 24.
46. Walker Hancock, "Experiences of a Monuments Officer in Germany," *College Art Journal* 5, no. 4 (May 1946): 271.
47. George Stout to Margie Stout, July 14, 1944, AAA Stout papers.
48. See "Ordonnance du 9 août 1944 relative au rétablissement de la légalité républicaine sur le territoire continental," http://www.legifrance.gouv.fr/affichTexte.do?cidTexte=LEGITEXT000006071212.
49. Rorimer letter addressed to "Dear ones," September 25, 1944, NGA Rorimer papers.
50. Valland, *Le front de l'art*, 184–86. A dramatized and entertaining version of these events is depicted in the 1964 film *The Train*, directed by John Frankenheimer.
51. Valland, *Le front de l'art*, 152. Valland mistakenly describes this scene at the "hôtel Continental," actually at Le Meurice.
52. Lyons, *World War II*, 273–79; Ian Buruma, *Year Zero: A History of 1945* (New York: Penguin, 2013), 14–15, 54.
53. Howe, *Salt Mines and Castles*, 25.
54. Rorimer journal, August 26–31, 1944, NGA Rorimer papers.
55. Stout diary, August 29, 1944, AAA Stout papers.
56. Rorimer journal, December 6, 1944, NGA Rorimer papers.
57. Rorimer to "dear ones," September 25, 1944, NGA Rorimer papers.
58. Rorimer journal, September 20, 1944, October 1, 1944, NGA Rorimer papers.
59. Rorimer, *Survival*, 92–94. Rorimer to Lt. Col. R.P. Hamilton, Assistant Chief of Staff, G-5, September 16, 1944, NGA Rorimer papers.
60. Rorimer, *Survival*, 106.
61. LaFarge to Webb, February 4, 1945, NARA RG 331.
62. Webb to Chief of G-5 Internal Affairs Branch, March 20, 1945, NARA RG 331.
63. Stout diary, August 29, 1944, AAA Stout papers.
64. Leslie A. Piña, *Louis Rorimer: A Man of Style* (Kent, OH: Kent State University Press, 1990), 1–5, 123n1.
65. Charles Dellheim, "Framing Nazi Art Loot," in *The Art of Being Jewish in Modern Times*, ed. Barbara Kirshenblatt-Gimblett and Jonathan Karp (Philadelphia: University of Pennsylvania Press, 2008), 324. One letter written on James's behalf as he was seeking a commission with army intelligence describes him as "a Jewish gentleman 37 years of age and married." See Merrill Coseo to Mrs. Marshall, May 1, 1943, AAA Rorimer papers. See also Rorimer, *Survival*.
66. Rorimer, *Survival*, 102.
67. Rorimer journal, September 9, 1944, NGA Rorimer papers.
68. Valland to Salles, October 21, 1944, AN AMN Z15 B 1.
69. Rorimer, *Survival*, 108–9.

70. Rorimer journal, December 18, 1944, NGA Rorimer papers.
71. Rorimer journal, December 22, 1944, and photographs, NGA Rorimer papers; Rorimer, *Survival*, 109–10. For German photographs of the looting of household objects and department store–like displays created for Nazi officials, see Sarah Gensburger, *Images d'un pillage: Album de la Spoliation des Juifs à Paris* (Paris: Editions Textuel, 2010).
72. Rorimer journal, December 18, 1944, NGA Rorimer papers; Valland, *Le front de l'art*, 218–19.
73. Rorimer, *Survival*, 110–11.
74. As recounted by Rorimer, *Survival*, 113.
75. Rorimer, *Survival*, 114; Valland, *Le front de l'art*, 219.
76. Hancock, "Experiences of a Monuments Officer in Germany," 272–73.
77. Hancock, "Experiences of a Monuments Officer in Germany," 273.
78. Hancock, "Experiences of a Monuments Officer in Germany," 271–76.
79. Hancock, "Experiences of a Monuments Officer in Germany," 276.
80. Balfour cited in Greg Bradsher, "The Monuments Men in March 1945: Ronald Balfour and Walker Hancock," United States National Archives, March 31, 2015, text-message.blogs.archives.gov/2015/03/31/the-monuments-men-in-march-1945-ronald-balfour-and-walker-hancock.
81. Woolley cited in Greg Bradsher, "A British Monuments Man Killed in Action: Ronald Balfour," United States National Archives, February 13, 2014, text-message.blogs.archives.gov/2014/02/13/a-british-monuments-man-killed-in-action-ronald-balfour.
82. Finley cited in Greg Bradsher, "Walter J. Huchthausen: A Monuments Man Killed in Action," United States National Archives, December 12, 2013, text-message.blogs.archives.gov/2013/12/12/walter-j-huchthausen-a-monuments-man-killed-in-action.
83. Hancock, "Experiences of a Monuments Officer in Germany," 271.
84. Posey, "Protection of Cultural Materials during Combat," 130–31; Kirstein, "The Quest of the Golden Lamb," 182–83; Nicholas, *Rape of Europa*, 332.
85. Kirstein, "Quest of the Golden Lamb," 183.
86. Posey, "Protection of Cultural Materials during Combat," 130–31; Kirstein, "Quest of the Golden Lamb," 183; Nicholas, *Rape of Europa*, 332.
87. Rorimer, *Survival*, 161.
88. Report by Rorimer to Col. Joseph Canby, June 3, 1945 (Seventeenth Report), NGA Rorimer papers.
89. Rorimer, *Survival*, 163; Skilton, *Memoirs of a Monuments Officer*, 91.
90. Rorimer, *Survival*, 163–64.
91. Rorimer, *Survival*, 164.
92. Rorimer, *Survival*, 182.
93. Journal entries of May 3–4, 1945, NGA Rorimer papers; Rorimer, *Survival*, 164, 181.
94. Rorimer, *Survival*, 183.
95. Rorimer, *Survival*, 185–86.
96. Rorimer, *Survival*, 137–40.
97. Rorimer, *Survival*, 141–47.

98. Nicholas, *Rape of Europa*, 328–29, 331; Hancock, "Experiences of a Monuments Officer," 292.
99. Stout diary, April 2, 1945, AAA; Hancock, "Experiences of a Monuments Officer," 291.
100. Stout diary, April 2, 1945, AAA; Hancock, "Experiences of a Monuments Officer," 292.
101. George Stout oral history, March 21, 1978, AAA; Stout diary, April 12, 1945, AAA Stout papers.
102. Nicholas, *Rape of Europa*, 335.
103. George Stout oral history, March 21, 1978, AAA; Stout diary, April 14 and 15, 1945, AAA.
104. Hancock, "Experiences of a Monuments Officer in Germany," 295–96.
105. Hancock, "Experiences of a Monuments Officer in Germany," 297.
106. Hancock, "Experiences of a Monuments Officer in Germany," 300.
107. Rorimer, *Survival*, 194–97; Nicholas, *Rape of Europa*, 342.
108. Rorimer, *Survival*, 194; Rorimer diary, May 8, 1945, NGA Rorimer papers.
109. Rorimer, *Survival*, 203–4.
110. Rorimer, *Survival*, 198–207. On the exchange negotiations with French national museums and Göring's failure to provide equivalent pieces, see Karlsgodt, *Defending National Treasures*, 246–56.
111. Kirstein, "Quest of the Golden Lamb," 184.
112. Petropoulos, *Art as Politics in the Third Reich*, 254–56.
113. Kirstein, "Quest of the Golden Lamb," 186.
114. Stout diary, May 21, 1945, AAA Stout papers.
115. Stout diary, June 15, 1945, AAA Stout papers.
116. Nicholas, *Rape of Europa*, 371–72.
117. Howe, *Salt Mines and Castles*, 157.
118. Howe, *Salt Mines and Castles*, 157–59.
119. Stout cited in Howe, *Salt Mines and Castles*, 159.
120. Howe, *Salt Mines and Castles*, 159–61.
121. Nicholas, *Rape of Europa*, 373. On MFAA operations in Asia, which prioritized the protection of Japanese heritage over the restitution of works looted by Japan, see Christine Kim, "Colonial Plunder and the Failure of Restitution in Postwar Korea," *Journal of Contemporary History* 52, no. 3 (2017): 607–24.
122. Coeuré, "Cultural Looting and Restitution at the Dawn of the Cold War," 595.
123. Coeuré, "Cultural Looting and Restitution at the Dawn of the Cold War," 595.
124. Michel Florisoone, "La Commission de Récupération Artistique," January 1950, AN AMN O 30-438.
125. Valland, "Récupération d'oeuvres d'art spoliées en France par les Allemands dans le dépôt de Seisseneg [sic], zone Soviétique, Autrichienne," December 15, 1947, AN AMN O 30-438.
126. Coeuré, "Cultural Looting and Restitution at the Dawn of the Cold War," 596.
127. Valland cited in Coeuré, "Cultural Looting and Restitution at the Dawn of the Cold War," 599.

128. Coeuré, "Cultural Looting and Restitution at the Dawn of the Cold War," 600.
129. Valland to Jaujard, November 16, 1950, Ministère de l'Europe et des Affaires Etrangères, Direction des Archives, La Courneuve, France (MEAE), 209SUP/528.
130. Coeuré, "Cultural Looting and Restitution at the Dawn of the Cold War," 605.
131. Anne Rothfeld, "Project ORION: An Administrative History of the Art Looting Investigation Unit (ALIU): An Overlooked Page in Intelligence Gathering," (MA thesis, University of Maryland, 2002), 35–45.
132. Rothfeld, "Project ORION," 66–67, 82.
133. Vaucher Commission meeting minutes, March 2, 1945, AN AMN R.20.2.3.
134. Rothfeld, "Project ORION," 83–84.
135. Howe, *Salt Mines and Castles*, 133–34.
136. Rothfeld, "Project ORION," 85.
137. Rothfeld, "Project ORION," 99. The ALIU reports, in NARA RG 239, are all available on fold3.com. See the final report at https://www.fold3.com/image/232005046. Rousseau later became a curator of European paintings at the Met in New York. According to Petropoulos, rumors circulated that the OSS officer maintained a cozy relationship with Lohse, with the knowledge of then–Met director James Rorimer. See Petropoulos, *Göring's Man in Paris*, 273–74.
138. Greg Bradsher, "A British Art Historian and Collector Monuments Man: Douglas Cooper," February 6, 2014, text-message.blogs.archives.gov/2014/02/06/a-british-art-historian-and-collector-monuments-man-douglas-cooper. Summary of meeting between Cooper and French officials (1er bureau, Guerre économique), September 7, 1945, AN AMN Z 15 B 1.
139. Valland report, "Collection Hitler du Musée de Linz," September 13, 1946, MEAE 209SUP/710.
140. Valland report, "Collection Hitler du Musée de Linz," September 13, 1946, MEAE 209SUP/710.
141. Susan Ronald, *Hitler's Art Thief: Hildebrand Gurlitt, the Nazis, and the Looting of Europe's Treasures* (New York: St. Martin's Press, 2015), 265–77.
142. Ronald, *Hitler's Art Thief*, 293–97; Jeevan Vasagar and Elizabeth Paton, "Art: Lost and Found," *Financial Times*, November 8, 2013, https://www.ft.com/content/b6c4c78e-4860-11e3-a3ef-00144feabdc0; German Lost Art Foundation database, https://www.kulturgutverluste.de/Content/06_ProjektGurlitt/_ORE/Liebermann_ORE_477892.pdf?__blob=publicationFile&v=11.
143. Valland to Captain Harlin, Judge of the Military Tribunal, May 20, 1949, AN AMN O 30-438; statement by Bruno Lohse, May 26, 1949, AN AMN O 30-438.
144. Valland to Florisoone, June 20, 1951, MEAE 209SUP/528; Karlsgodt, *Defending National Treasures*, 218–27.
145. Valland to Florisoone, June 20, 1951, MEAE 209SUP/528.
146. See the Base Rose Valland at pop.culture.gouv.fr and enter "Lohse" in the search feature.
147. Catherine Hickley, "Nazi Art Dealer's Will Disperses Dutch Masters, Expressionists," July 12, 2007, *Bloomberg*, retrieved at https://www.lootedart.com/MKOYSM152431.

For an in-depth investigation of Lohse's dealings in Paris and his continued work as a dealer after the war, see Petropoulos, *Göring's Man in Paris*.
148. Rothfeld, "Project ORION," 108–9.

Chapter 3

1. Meeting minutes, Comité interministériel des restitutions artistiques et culturelles, 7, 8 December 1951, MEAE 209SUP/528.
2. Judt, *Postwar*, 113–14.
3. William I. Hitchcock, *The Struggle for Europe: The Turbulent History of a Divided Continent, 1945 to the Present* (New York: Anchor Books, 2003), 22; Kurtz, *America and the Return of Nazi Contraband*, 60–61.
4. Sandholtz, *Prohibiting Plunder*, 155; Richard Johnson, "Memorandum on the Protection, Restitution, and Reparation of Objets d'Art and Other Cultural Objects," November 17, 1944, in *Foreign Relations of the United States, 1944*, vol. 2: *General: Economic and Social Matters* (Washington, DC: Government Printing Office, 1967), 1052n29.
5. Lorentz, *La France et les Restitutions Allemandes*, 25–27.
6. Lorentz, *La France et les Restitutions Allemandes*, 27–29.
7. Sandholtz, *Prohibiting Plunder*, 157.
8. Richard M. Buxbaum, "A Legal History of International Reparations," *Berkeley Journal of International Law* 23, no. 2 (2005): 323.
9. Memorandum extracted from US State Department, "Report on Reparations, Restitution, and Property Rights—Germany," in FRUS 1944, vol. 2, July 31, 1944, 1037.
10. Roberts Commission, "Memorandum on Principles for the Restitution of Works of Art, Books, Archives, and Other Cultural Property," October 11, 1944, in FRUS 1944, vol. 2, 1043–44.
11. Hein A. M. Klemann and Sergei Kudryashov, *Occupied Economies: An Economic History of Nazi-Occupied Europe, 1939–1945* (London: Berg, 2012), 210.
12. "Restitutions des biens culturels," n.d., NARA RG 331, amg 215. Meeting location is not specified. Cowell of the British Foreign Office summarized Henraux's view of works purchased by the Germans in a note dated April 7, 1945, The National Archives, United Kingdom (UKNA) FO 924/148/2.
13. "Tabeleaux de l'école française se trouvant dans les collections publiques allemandes," n.d., c. 1945, AN AMN Z15 B 1.
14. Kurtz, *America and the Return of Nazi Contraband*, 84–85.
15. Vaucher Commission Report of Progress, September 1, 1944–February 28, 1945, UKNA FO 924/148/1.
16. Macmillan Committee memorandum to Anthony Eden, September 20, 1944, in FRUS 1944, vol. 2, 1047.
17. Memorandum by the United Kingdom Delegation, European Advisory Commission, November 14, 1944, UKNA T209/8.

18. Owen J. Roberts to the Secretary of State, October 30, 1944, in FRUS 1944, vol. 2, 1040–41.
19. Eden to Vincent Massey, Macmillan Committee, October 7, 1944, UKNA T209/8.
20. Law to Macmillan, December 5, 1944, UKNA T209/8.
21. Kurtz, *America and the Return of Nazi Contraband*, 70–71.
22. Judt, *Postwar*, 113–14.
23. Hitchcock, *Struggle for Europe*, 24–25.
24. Hitchcock, *Struggle for Europe*, 24.
25. Judt, *Postwar*, 109.
26. Lorenz, *La France et les Restitutions Allemandes*, 68.
27. Mark Gilbert, *Cold War Europe: The Politics of a Contested Continent* (Lanham: Rowman and Littlefield, 2015), 18.
28. Lorentz, *La France et les Restitutions Allemandes*, 67.
29. Lorentz, *La France et les Restitutions Allemandes*, 67–68.
30. On French domestic political and social dynamics, see Herrick Chapman, *France's Long Reconstruction: In Search of the Modern Republic* (Harvard: Harvard University Press, 2018).
31. "The Quest of [illegible] 'Mystical Lamb,'" *La Libre Belgique*, May 28, 1945, translated excerpt in NARA RG 239, https://www.fold3.com/image/270030439.
32. Hilldring to Sawyer, September 14, 1945, NARA RG 239, https://www.fold3.com/image/270194443; Office of Military Government for Bavaria, Monthly Consolidated Field Report, April 1946, NARA RG 239, https://www.fold3.com/image/270260052; Nicholas, *Rape of Europa*, 408–13.
33. Kurtz, *America and the Return of Nazi Contraband*, 98–99, 136–43; Lorenz, *La France et les Restitutions Allemandes*, 119–24.
34. Ian Locke and Stephen Ward, *Nazi Looted Art: Britain and Post-war Restitution* (London: The Holocaust Educational Trust, 1998), 12–17; Lothar Pretzell, *Das Kunstlager Schloss Celle 1945 bis 1958* (n.p., 1958).
35. Kirrily Freeman, "The Bells, Too, Are Fighting: The Fate of European Church Bells in the Second World War," *Canadian Journal of History* 43, no. 3 (2008): 440.
36. Anne Popham diaries, vol. 1, November 17, 1945, Imperial War Museum (IWM), 87/19/1.
37. Lorentz, *La France et les Restitutions Allemandes*, 119–23; Coeuré, "Cultural Looting and Restitution at the Dawn of the Cold War," 592.
38. Kurtz, *America and the Return of Nazi Contraband*, 71.
39. Hitchcock, *Struggle for Europe*, 29.
40. Kurtz, *America and the Return of Nazi Contraband*, 98–102; Buxbaum, "Legal History of International Reparations," 330–34.
41. Lorenz, *La France et les Restitutions Allemandes*, 74.
42. Memorandum for the Coordinating Committee, Allied Control Authority, "Interim Restitution Deliveries," December 6, 1945, in FRUS 1945, vol. 2, 956–57.
43. "Copy of Text of Agreement of July 8, 1946 with respect to control of cultural property looted by the enemy in counties occupied by it during the war," NARA RG 59.

44. Embassy of the United States, Moscow to Soviet Ministry of Foreign Affairs, January 5, 1948, NARA RG 59.
45. Soviet Ministry of Foreign Affairs to the US Embassy, Moscow, March 4, 1948, NARA RG 59.
46. Judt, *Postwar*, 90–91.
47. Lorentz, *La France et les Restitutions Allemandes*, 95–98; Howard cited in Kurtz, *America and the Return of Nazi Contraband*, 112.
48. Commandement en Chef Français en Allemagne, *Répertoire des biens spoliés en France durant la guerre 1939-1945*, vol. 2: *Tableaux, tapisseries et sculptures* (Berlin: Bureau Central des Restitutions, 1947), 236. Quote on compensation in G. Glasser, "Preface," *Répertoire des biens spoliés*, vii.
49. "Collections publiques allemandes," March 25, 1947, AN AMN Z15 B 2.
50. Note from Mauricheau-Beaupré to Salles, March 25, 1947, AN AMN Z15 B 2.
51. Aubert to Salles, March 22, 1947, AN AMN Z15 B 2.
52. Webb "Restitution Problems: Memorandum to the Macmillan Committee," n.d. (sent to James Mann April 1, 1946), UKNA T209/24.
53. Webb, "Restitution Problems: Memorandum to the Macmillan Committee," n.d. (sent to James Mann April 1, 1946), UKNA T209/24.
54. Kim, "Colonial Plunder and the Failure of Restitution in Postwar Korea," 607–24.
55. Roberts Commission meeting minutes, June 20, 1946, NARA RG 239, https://www.fold3.com/image/115/270224956.
56. Lorentz, *La France et les Restitutions Allemandes*, 98.
57. G. S. Whitham, RDR Division Technical Instruction no. 45, July 23, 1947, RB DER 399. (Whitham's emphasis).
58. "Inter-Allied Declaration against Acts of Dispossession," January 5, 1943, *FRUS 1943*, vol. 1, 443–44.
59. Lucius D. Clay, *Decision in Germany* (New York: Doubleday, 1950), 306–7.
60. Clay, *Decision in Germany*, 309.
61. "U.S. Forces, European Theater, Germany," November 7, 1945, NGA Standen Papers.
62. See excerpt of George Stout's letter to Thomas Howe, January 6, 1946, in Farmer, *Safekeepers*, 70.
63. According to Marion Deshmukh, Fulbright also introduced a bill in 1948 that would have kept the paintings in American custody until the United States formally recognized a German government, which Clay suspected was actually a ruse to expand the National Gallery in Washington. See "Recovering Culture: The Berlin National Gallery and the U.S. Occupation, 1945–1949," *Central European History* 27, no. 4 (Winter 1994): 423–24.
64. Nicholas, *Rape of Europa*, 384–405; Walter Farmer, "The Wiesbaden Manifesto of 7 November 1945," *Jahrbuch Preussischer Kulturbesitz* 33 (1996): 91–119.
65. De Vries to Henraux, November 21, 1946, NAN 2.08.42/318.
66. Memorandum from the United States Political Advisor for Germany, March 8, 1948, NARA RG 59.

67. Military Government, Germany, United States Area of Control, Law no. 59, Restitution of Identifiable Property, November 10, 1947, NARA RG 260, https://www.fold3.com/image/114/303707992.
68. Military Government, Germany, United States Area of Control, Law no. 59, Restitution of Identifiable Property, November 10, 1947, NARA RG 260, https://www.fold3.com/image/114/303707992.
69. "Ordonnance no. 120 relative à des biens ayant fait l'objet d'actes de spoliation," *Journal Officiel du Commandement en Chef Français en Allemagne*, no. 119, November 14, 1947, 1219–22.
70. Constantin Goschler, "Jewish Property and the Politics of Restitution in Germany after 1945," in *Robbery and Restitution*, ed. Martin Dean, Constantin Goschler, and Philipp Ther, 119.
71. Ayaka Takei, "The 'Gemeinde Problem': The Jewish Restitution Successor Organization and the Postwar Jewish Communities in Germany, 1947–1954," *Holocaust and Genocide Studies* 16 (2): 266–67.
72. Takei, "The 'Gemeinde Problem,'" 269–71; Elisabeth Gallas, "Locating the Jewish Future: The Restoration of Looted Cultural Property in Early Postwar Europe," *Naharaim* 9, nos. 1–2 (2015): 35.
73. Leff, *Archive Thief*, 136–40; Michael Kurtz, "Resolving a Dilemma: The Inheritance of Jewish Property," *Cardozo Law Review*, no. 2 (December 1998): 643. On distribution percentages, see Isabelle le Masne de Chermont and Laurence Sigal-Klagsbald, *A qui appartenaient ces tableaux? La politique Française de recherche, de provenance de garde et de restitution des oeuvres d'art pillées durant la Second Guerre Mondiale* (Paris: Editions de la Réunion des Musées Nationaux, 2008), 35.
74. Locke and Ward, *Nazi Looted Art*, 23; Ruth Schreiber, "New Jewish Communities in Germany after World War II and the Successor Organizations in the Western Zones," *Journal of Israeli History* 18, nos. 2–3 (1997), 169.
75. Schreiber, "New Jewish Communities in Germany after World War II," 167–90.
76. Goschler, "Jewish Property and the Politics of Restitution," 121–22.
77. Murray Van Wagoner to Hans Ehard, August 3, 1948, MEAE 209SUP/312.
78. Robert Murphy to the US Secretary of State, October 6, 1948, NARA RG 59.
79. Lorentz, *La France et les Restitutions Allemandes*, 166.
80. Meeting minutes, Commissariat général aux Affaires Allemandes et Autrichiennes, Service des Affaires Intérieures et Culturelles, August 24, 1948, AN AMN Z15 B 2.
81. Armand Bérard, Chargé d'affaires in French Embassy to US Under Secretary of State Robert Lovett, September 18, 1948, NARA RG 59. Informal English translation by the US Department of State.
82. Acting US Secretary of State to the French Embassy, n.d., NARA RG 59. Document date is unclear, though a note in the footer suggests October 12, 1948.
83. Acting US Secretary of State to the French Embassy, n.d., NARA RG 59.
84. Rose Valland, "Rapport sur la fin des restitutions artistiques en zone Américaine et au Central Collecting Point de Munich," March 23, 1949, MEAE 209SUP/312.
85. Robert Murphy to Department of State, March 16, 1948, NARA RG 59.

86. Rose Valland, "Rapport sur la fin des restitutions artistiques en zone Américaine et au Central Collecting Point de Munich," March 23, 1949, MEAE 209SUP/312.
87. "Note," J. L. Bonet-Maury, April 20, 1949, AN AMN O 30-438.
88. Kiefer, "Restitution from Germany," May 18, 1949, with cover note by Brad Patterson, NARA RG 59. The author was likely Alexander F. Kiefer, an economist in the Office of German Economic Affairs. See "Personnel Notes," *Information Bulletin* (June 1951), at http://images.library.wisc.edu/History/EFacs/GerRecon/omg1951June/reference/history.omg1951june.i0020.pdf.
89. Spedding, RDR Detmold to M. E. Bathurst, Office of the Legal Adviser, October 4, 1949, UKNA FO 1057/270.
90. Kiefer, "Restitution from Germany," May 18, 1949, with cover note by Brad Patterson, NARA RG 59.
91. Kiefer, "Restitution from Germany," May 18, 1949, with cover note by Brad Patterson, NARA RG 59; Kurtz, *America and the Return of Nazi Contraband*, 195–96.
92. Kiefer, "Restitution from Germany," May 18, 1949, with cover note by Brad Patterson, NARA RG 59.
93. Kiefer, "Restitution from Germany," May 18, 1949, with cover note by Brad Patterson, NARA RG 59.
94. Ardelia Hall, "Return of Cultural Property," May 18, 1949, NARA RG 59.
95. Ardelia Hall, "Return of Cultural Property," May 18, 1949, NARA RG 59.
96. Ardelia Hall, "The Recovery of Cultural Objects Dispersed during World War II," *Department of State Bulletin* 25 (August 27, 1951): 339.
97. Hitchcock, *Struggle for Europe*, 96.
98. Richard L. Merritt, "Political Perspectives in Germany: The Years of Semisovereignty 1949–1955," *Historical Social Research/Historische Sozialforschung* 13 (January 1980): 17.
99. Rose Valland, "Récupération Artistique en Allemagne, Etat actuel de la question—Projets de reorganization (Mission en zones françaises et américaines du 20 août au 10 septembre 1949)," MEAE 209SUP/528.
100. Rose Valland, "Service Française de remise en place des oeuvres d'art," n.d., MEAE 209SUP/528. This summary was attached to the report in the previous reference and most likely was written in September 1949.
101. Rose Valland, "Compte rendu d'activité," c. 1954, AN AMN O 30-438.
102. Rose Valland, "Récupération Artistique en Allemagne, Etat actuel de la question—Projets de reorganization (Mission en zones françaises et américaines du 20 août au 10 septembre 1949)," MEAE 209SUP/528. Metternich led the German *Kunstschutz* in occupied France from 1940 to 1942. See Karlsgodt, *Defending National Treasures*, 39–41.
103. Rose Valland, "Récupération Artistique en Allemagne, Etat actuel de la question—Projets de reorganization (Mission en zones françaises et américaines du 20 août au 10 septembre 1949)," MEAE 209SUP/528.
104. Rose Valland, "Récupération Artistique en Allemagne, Etat actuel de la question—Projets de reorganization (Mission en zones françaises et américaines du 20 août au 10 septembre 1949)," MEAE 209SUP/528.

105. Lorentz, *La France et les Restitutions Allemandes*, 241n1.
106. S. Lane Faison, Jr., "Transfer of Custody to the Germans," in *The Spoils of War*, ed. Elizabeth Simpson, 140.
107. Jill Lewis, *Workers and Politics in Occupied Austria, 1945–1955* (Manchester: Manchester University Press, 2007), 72.
108. On the American shipment of works from Alt Aussee to the Munich Collecting Point, see Nicholas, *Rape of Europa*, 371–75.
109. French translation of anonymous German summary of meeting between an American officer, "Mr. Wangler," and German cultural officials Hanfstaengle, Röthel and Hoffmann, n.d., MEAE 209SUP/528. The Monuments Men and Women Foundation list of heroes does not contain a Mr. Wangler but does include "William Walker," who served the MFAA in Bavaria. It is possible that Walker met with the German officials and Valland's source misspelled his name. See https://www.monumentsmenandwomenfnd.org/the-heroes.
110. Valland report, "Etat de la question des collecting points et des collections Nazies à la fin du mois de juin," July 10, 1951, MEAE 209SUP/528.
111. S. Lane Faison, Jr., "Transfer of Custody to the Germans," 140.
112. S. Lane Faison, Jr., "Transfer of Custody to the Germans," 140–41.
113. Valland to Neuville, November 8, 1950, MEAE 209SUP/528.
114. Valland to Neuville, May 28, 1951, MEAE 209SUP/528.
115. Valland, "Cession des Oeuvres d'Art des Grandes Collections Nazies à l'Autriche," September 3, 1951, AN AMN O 30-438.
116. Hale statement cited in Ardelia R. Hall, "The Transfer of Residual Works of Art from Munich to Austria," *College Art Journal* 11, no. 3 (Spring 1952): 192.
117. Hall, "The Transfer of Residual Works of Art from Munich to Austria," 193.
118. Valland to Chef du Cabinet de M. le Haut Commissaire de la République Française en Allemagne, February 11, 1952, AN AMN O 30-438.
119. G. H. Pommery to Director of OBIP, March 8, 1952, AN AMN O 30-438.
120. Valland does not specify dates of the transfers to German authorities. See her report, "Distribution des biens des grandes collections nazies avant que le Gouvernement Fédéral n'intervienne dans les restitutions," April 18, 1952, MEAE 209SUP/528.
121. Amphoux note cited in Bouchoux, *"Si les tableaux pouvaient parler...,"* 105.
122. Rose Valland, "Note succincte sur l'activité du Service de Protection des Oeuvres d'Art au cours de l'année 1962," February 16, 1963, AN AMN O 30-438.
123. Valland, *Le front de l'Art*.
124. Hitchcock, *Struggle for Europe*, 147–48.
125. Hitchcock, *Struggle for Europe*, 149.
126. Judt, *Postwar*, 156–57.
127. Judt, *Postwar*, 244–46.
128. Walter Sullivan, "High Court Set Up on Jewish Claims," *New York Times*, October 26, 1953, 7; "New Supreme Restitution Court Starts Functioning in Germany," *Jewish Telegraphic Agency Daily News Bulletin*, January 25, 1956, available at http://pdfs.jta.org/1956/1956-01-25_017.pdf?_ga=2.261928909.1110421645.1571879435-2026163944.1571879435.

129. Le Masne de Chermont and Didier Schulmann, eds., *Le pillage de l'art en France*, 45–46.
130. Goschler, "Jewish Property and the Politics of Restitution," 120–22.

Chapter 4

1. Michel Florisoone, "La Commission de Récupération Artistique," January 1950, AN AMN O 30-438.
2. Ministère de l'éducation nationale, *Les Chefs d'oeuvre des collections françaises retrouvés en Allemagne par la Commission de Récupération Artistique et les Services Alliés*, June–August 1946, preface by Albert Henraux, v.
3. Ministère de l'éducation nationale, *Les Chefs d'oeuvre des collections françaises*.
4. Le Masne de Chermont and Schulmann, eds., *Le pillage de l'art en France*, 37.
5. Le Masne de Chermont and Schulmann, eds., *Le pillage de l'art en France*, 55–56. The exact number of selected items is still unknown, partly due to variations in records on single objects and assemblages. The total of 2,143 items provided by Le Masne de Chermont and Schulmann included works added to the custodianship after the early 1950s, including seventy-three pieces added in the 1990s. See Zivie, "Des traces subsistent dans des registres," 16.
6. See Maud Mandel, *In the Aftermath of Genocide: Armenians and Jews in Twentieth-Century France* (Durham, NC: Duke University Press, 2003), 83; Lisa Moses Leff, "Post-Holocaust Book Restitutions: How One State Agency Helped Revive Republican Franco-Judaism," in *Post-Holocaust France and the Jews, 1945-1955*, ed. Seán Hand and Steven Katz (New York: New York University Press, 2015), 71–84.
7. Florisoone, "La Commission de la Récupération Artistique," January 1950, AN AMN O 30-438.
8. Le Masne de Chermont and Schulmann, eds., *Le pillage de l'art en France*, 34.
9. Arrêté du 24 novembre 1944, "Commission de récupération artistique," *Journal Officiel de la République Française*, January 23, 1945, 315–16.
10. Michel Florisoone, "La Commission de Récupération Artistique," January 1950, AN AMN O 38-348; Bouchoux, *"Si les tableaux pouvaient parler . . ."*, 58; Le Masne de Chermont and Schulmann, eds., *Le pillage de l'art en France*, 34.
11. Michel Florisoone, "La Commission de Récupération Artistique," January 1950, AN AMN O 38-348; minutes of CRA meetings: September 19, 1944, December 14, 1944, December 27, 1944, MEAE 209SUP/296.
12. Bouchoux, *"Si les tableaux pouvaient parler . . ."*, 62.
13. On collaboration, accommodation, and resistance in the fine arts under Vichy, see Karlsgodt, *Defending National Treasures*, 29–39; Laurence Bertrand Dorléac, *L'art de la défaite, 1940-1944* (Paris: Editions du Seuil, 1993), 32–44.
14. Bouchoux, *Rose Valland*, 66–68.
15. Valland details these activities in *Le front de l'art*.
16. Le Masne de Chermont and Schulmann, eds., *Le pillage de l'art en France*, 22, 37–38.

17. Florisoone, "La Commission de Récupération Artistique," January 1950, AN AMN O 30-438; Le Masne de Chermont and Schulmann, eds., *Le pillage de l'art en France*, 35.
18. The *Répertoire* is available at http://www.culture.gouv.fr/documentation/mnr/MnR-rbs.htm.
19. Le Masne de Chermont and Schulmann, eds., *Le pillage de l'art en France*, 35–36.
20. CRA meeting minutes, September 19, 1944, MEAE 209SUP/296; Florisoone, "La Commission de Récupération Artistique," January 1950, AN AMN O 30-438.
21. Florisoone, "La Commission de Récupération Artistique," January 1950, AN AMN O 30-438.
22. Florisoone, "La Commission de Récupération Artistique," January 1950, AN AMN O 30-438.
23. Le Masne de Chermont and Schulmann, eds., *Le pillage de l'art en France*, 35.
24. Minutes from meeting of the Comité interministeriel des restitutions artistiques et culturelles, October 23, 1951, AN AMN O 30-438.
25. "Liquidation frauduleuse de la Succession Jaffé," December 12, 1944, 209SUP/3.
26. Decision of the Tribunal Civil de la Seine, November 7, 1947, 209SUP/3.
27. Minutes from meeting of the Comité interministeriel des restitutions artistiques et culturelles, October 23, 1951, AN AMN O 30-438.
28. Florisoone, "La Commission de Récupération Artistique," January 1950, AN AMN O 30-438. On Aryanization of the Vichy regime and postwar restitution, see Antoine Prost, Rémi Skoutelsky, Sonia Etienne, et al., *Aryanisation économique et restitutions* (Paris: La documentation Française, 2000); Claire Andrieu, "Two Approaches to Compensation in France: Restitution and Reparation," in *Robbery and Restitution*, ed. Martin Dean, Constantin Goschler, and Philipp Ther, 134–54.
29. Florisoone, "La Commission de Récupération Artistique," January 1950, AN AMN O 30-438; Florisoone, "Addendum au Rapport sur la Commission de Récupération Artistique: Tableau numérique des œuvres récupérées et des œuvres restituées," n.d.; addendum cover letter from Henraux to Jaujard, June 7, 1950, AN AMN 2MM6.
30. Florisoone, "La Commission de Récupération Artistique," January 1950, AN AMN O 30-438. On the restitution of household items and pianos, see Mission d'étude sur la spoliation des Juifs de France, *Rapport Général*, 139–48; and Fogg, *Stealing Home*.
31. Le Masne de Chermont and Schulmann, eds., *Le pillage de l'art en France*, 37.
32. Lorentz, *La France et les Restitutions Allemandes*, 266.
33. Lorentz, *La France et les Restitutions Allemandes*, 234–35, 266–67.
34. Henraux to Florisoone, February 5, 1952, AN AMN Z15 B 3; Florisoone to Henraux, February 14, 1952, AN AMN Z15 B.3.
35. CRA meeting minutes, September 27, 1945, AN AMN Z15 B 1; Rayssac, *L'Exode des musées*, 815.
36. Waldemar George, "Les chefs d'oeuvre retrouvés en Allemagne," *La Résistance*, September 19, 1946.
37. Michel Florisoone, "La Commission de Récupération Artistique," January 1950, AN AMN O 30-438.
38. See Karlsgodt, *Defending National Treasures*, 208–27.

39. "Ordonnance du 14 novembre 1944 portant application de l'ordonnance du 12 novembre 1943 sur la nullité des actes de spoliation accomplis par l'ennemi et sous son contrôle," *Journal Officiel de la République Française*, November 15, 1944, 1310.
40. "Ordonnance du 9 août 1944 relative au rétablissement de la légalité républicaine sur le territoire continental," article 3. Available at https://www.legifrance.gouv.fr/affichTexte.do?cidTexte=LEGITEXT000006071212; "Ordonnance du 16 Octobre 1944 relative à la restitution par l'administration des domaines de certains biens mis sous séquestre," *Journal Officiel de la République Française*, October 17, 1944, 964; "Ordonnance du 14 novembre 1944 portant application de l'ordonnance du 12 novembre 1943 sur la nullité des actes de spoliation accomplis par l'ennemi et sous son contrôle," *Journal Officiel de la République Française*, November 15, 1944, 1310.
41. Georges Salles to General Director of Domaines, March 15, 1945, AN AMN R32.2.7; Le Masne de Chermont and Didier Schulmann, eds., *Le pillage de l'art en France*, 29; Secretary of Jacques May to Georges Salles, May 1, 1945, AN AMN R32.2.7.
42. Huyghe to Jaujard, August 18, 1943, AN AMN R32.3.3.
43. Jacques Jaujard to Marcel-Edmond Naegelen, February 20, 1946, AN AMN R32.2.7.
44. Marcel-Edmond Naegelen to the President of the Council of State, February 25, 1946, AN AMN R32.2.7; Jacques Jaujard to Marcel-Edmond Naegelen, April 3, 1946, AN AMN R32.2.7; Maurice de Rothschild retrocession, April 27, 1949, AN AMN R32.2.7.
45. L'Association des Ecrivains Combattants, *L'anthologie des écrivains morts à la guerre, 1939–1945* (Paris: Albin Michel, 1960), 69.
46. Ibid., 68.
47. Ladoué to Jaujard, May 15, 1941, AN AMN R32.3.1; Arrêté, Ministry of National Education, December 31 1942, R32.3.1; Jaujard to Ladoué, July 22, 1944, AN AMN R32.3.1.
48. Restitution order signed by education minister Marcel-Edmond Naegelan, April 4, 1946, AN AMN R32.3.1.
49. Roger Bethout to Georges Salles, July 27, 1953, AN AMN R32.3.1; Court summons, Albert Agnus to Georges Salles, June 16, 1954, AN AMN R32.3.1; Direction des Musées Nationaux, restitution agreement, July 28, 1954, AN AMN R32.3.1.
50. Accountant of the Réunion des Musées Nationaux à M. le Receveur Central des Finances de la Seine, February 9, 1953, AN AMN R32.2.7; "Réponse à la note n°1.115 du 2 août 1951 de la Cour des Comptes," to Director of administration, Ministry of National Education, n.d. but most likely August 1951, AN AMN R32.2.7; Accountant of the Réunion des Musées Nationaux à Mme Henraux, Head of administrative services, Réunion des Musées Nationaux, April 16, 1953, AN AMN R32.2.7.
51. On wartime negotiations over the Schloss collection, see Karlsgodt, *Defending National Treasures*, 218–27.
52. Georges Salles to Mme Prosper-Emile Weil, November 16, 1944, AN AMN R32.3.3; Max Gonfreville to René Huyghe, January 22, 1945, AN AMN R32.3.3.
53. René Huyghe to Georges Salles, January 24, 1945, AN AMN R32.3.3.
54. Georges Salles to the CRA, February 16, 1945, AN AMN R32.3.3.
55. Receipt of paintings signed by Raymond and Henry Schloss, July 26, 1946, AN AMN R32.3.3.

56. Germain Bazin, *Souvenirs de l'exode du Louvre, 1940–1945* (Paris: Somogy, 1992), 97.
57. Michel Raysaac, *L'exode des musées: Histoire des oeuvres d'art sous l'Occupation* (Paris: Payot, 2007), 834–35; minutes from CRA meeting of September 27, 1945, AN AMN Z15 B.1.
58. "Extrait du procès-verbal du Conseil artistique de la Réunion des Musées nationaux," session of December 2, 1948, AN AMN P4. On the Schloss Rembrandt, see Huyghe to Jaujard, August 18, 1943, AN AMN R32.3.3.
59. "Extrait du procès-verbal du Comité des conservateurs des Musées nationaux," session of December 23, 1948, AN AMN P4.
60. Capitant to Minister of Finance, March 27, 1945, AN AMN R32.2.7.
61. "Ordonnance du 21 avril 1945 portant deuxième application de l'ordonnance du 12 novembre 1943 sur la nullité des actes de spoliation accomplis par l'ennemi ou sous son contrôle et edictant la restitution aux victimes de ces actes de ceux de leurs biens qui on fait l'objet des actes de disposition," *Journal officiel de la République française*, April 23, 1945, 2283–85.
62. "Décret n° 47-2105 du 29 octobre 1947 relatif à la restitution des biens spoliés par l'ennemi," *Journal officiel de la République française*, October 31, 1947, 10831–32.
63. "Décret n° 49-1344 du 30 septembre 1949 relatif à la fin des operations de la commission de récupération Artistique," *Journal officiel de la République française*, October 2, 1949, 9815.
64. Henraux to Salles, June 29, 1948, AN AMN Z15 B 2.
65. The art selection committee met on October 27, 1949; November 17, 1949; December 19, 1949; December 21, 1949; October 25, 1950; May 29, 1951; March 28, 1952; and June 17, 1953. List of meeting dates in MEAE 209SUP/528. Membership listed in "Arrêté," October 12, 1949, AN AMN Z15 B 2.
66. Minutes from selection committee meeting, December 21, 1949, AN AMN Z15 B 2.
67. Minutes from selection committee meeting, December 21, 1949, AN AMN Z15 B 2.
68. One example of a looted painting is MNR 410, Joos de Momper, *Paysage Montagneux (avec chapelle)*, stolen from Belgian banker Baron Cassel van Doom in southern France in 1943 and selected for the Louvre. It was restituted to heirs in 2014. See the Base MNR Rose Valland at pop.culture.gouv.fr.
69. Minutes from selection committee meeting, December 21, 1949, AN AMN Z15 B 2. See updated titles and attributions on the Base MNR Rose Valland at pop.culture.gouv.fr.
70. See Florisoone statement in committee meeting of December 21, 1949, AN AMN Z15 B 2. On the Mattéoli Commission findings, see Le Masne de Chermont and Schulmann, eds., *Le pillage de l'art en France*, 65–73.
71. On notions of ordinary versus exclusionary law, see Véronique Parisot, "The Gentili di Giuseppe Case in France," *International Journal of Cultural Property* 10, no. 2 (2001): 268–70.
72. Minutes of selection committee meeting, October 27, 1949, AN AMN R20.3.3.
73. Dorival to Salles, "Oeuvres provenant de la Récupération Artistique et affectées au Musée d'Art Moderne," March 24, 1950, AN AMN R20.3.3.

74. Minutes from selection committee meeting, March 28, 1952, MEAE 209SUP/528; see updated titles and attributions at the MNR catalog on the Base MNR Rose Valland at pop.culture.gouv.fr.
75. Selection committee meeting minutes, December 21, 1949, AN AMN Z15 B 2.
76. The total number of chosen objects varies by source depending on the method used to count "items" such as assemblages with more than one piece. According to David Zivie, the total number of 2,143 cited in the Mattéoli Commission report, held at that time (the year 2000), must be adjusted to account for thirteen pieces given to France by Germany in 1994, sixty objects newly listed on the register in 1999, twenty-eight objects added in folk and Asian art, still held by the French state, plus the first sixty restitutions, for a total number of 2,102 items selected in the early postwar years. (2,143−13−60 + 28 + 60 = 2,102) See Le Masne de Chermont and Schulmann, eds., *Le pillage de l'art en France*, 55–56, 97–100; Zivie, "*Des traces subsistent dans des registres...*," 16n6.
77. See Base MNR Rose Valland at pop.culture.gouv.fr.
78. Florisoone to Salles, November 8, 1951, AN AMN Z15 B 3; Rossignol to Lemaire, May 22, 1953, with list of paintings, RB DER 386; Rossignol to Lemaire, October 9, 1953, RB 6B/68.37813; Service des Ventes Publiques du Palais des Beaux-Arts, "Vente publique: 22.12.1954," December 29, 1954, RB DER 385.
79. Saul Friedländer, *Kurt Gerstein: The Ambiguity of Good*, trans. Charles Fullman (New York: Alfred A Knoft, 1969).
80. "Kurt Gerstein," http://www.ushmm.org/wlc/en/article.php?ModuleId=10005840; Eric Biétry-Rivierre, "La France restitue un Matisse volé par les Nazis," *Le Figaro*, November 24, 2008, http://www.lefigaro.fr/culture/2008/11/24/03004-20081124 ARTFIG00360-la-france-restitue-un-matisse-vole-par-les-nazis-.php.
81. Jean-Baptiste Viaud, "Restitution en grande pompe d'un tableau volé par les Nazis," *L'Express*, November 27, 2008, http://www.lexpress.fr/culture/art-plastique/restitut ion-en-grande-pompe-d-un-tableau-vole-par-les-nazis_713182.html. See the Base MNR Rose Valland at pop.culture.gouv.fr.
82. Biétry-Rivierre, "La France restitue un Matisse volé par les Nazis"; Base MNR Rose Valland at pop.culture.gouv.fr.
83. Valland to Director, Musées de France, May 24, 1957, AN AMN Z15 B 3; Base MNR Rose Valland at pop.culture.gouv.fr.
84. Base MNR Rose Valland at pop.culture.gouv.fr.
85. Valland to Director, Musées de France, May 24, 1957, AN AMN Z15 B 3; Base MNR Rose Valland at pop.culture.gouv.fr.
86. Valland to Director, Musées de France, May 24, 1957, AN AMN Z15 B 3; Base MNR Rose Valland at pop.culture.gouv.fr.
87. Valland to Director, Musées de France, May 24, 1957, AN AMN Z15 B 3.
88. These are the only details about the 1961 agreement on the Base MNR Rose Valland at pop.culture.gouv.fr. Search "OAR 24."
89. "Décret relatif à la fin des opérations de la Commission de récupération artistique," *Journal Officiel de la République Française*, October 2, 1949, 9815.

90. Meeting minutes for Comité interministériel des restitutions artistiques et culturelles, October 23, 1951, AN AMN O 30-438.
91. Florisoone to Salles, March 8, 1955, AN AMN Z15 B 3.
92. Bazin to Salles, December 18, 1956, AN AMN Z15 B 3.
93. Le Masne de Chermont and Schulmann, *Le pillage de l'art en France*, 42.
94. Salles to M. Reichenbach, June 13, 1951, AN AMN Z 15 B 3.
95. Curator of Compiègne museum to Salles, June 13, 1951, AN AMN Z15 B.3; Ministère de Culture et Communication, "Restitution aux ayants droit de M. Richard Neumann et de M. Josef Wiener de sept tableaux spoliés par les Nazis," March 19, 2013, 7; Director of OBIP to Salles, March 27, 1950, AN AMN Z15 B 3; "Formule de décharge," April 20, 1951, AN AMN P15.
96. "Décharge," October 25, 1951, AN AMN P15; Le Masne de Chermont and Schulmann, eds., *Le pillage de l'art en France*, 97–100.
97. See Karlsgodt, *Defending National Treasures*, 95–101.
98. Selection committee meeting minutes, October 27, 1949, AN AMN R20.3.3; the Base MNR Rose Valland indicates the bust is "*d'après*" (modeled on) Houdon, with unknown pre-1940 provenance. See the database at pop.culture.gouv.fr.
99. Bazin to Vergnet-Ruiz, November 17, 1950, AN AMN Z15 B 4.
100. Bazin also mentions talks involving the Corot with the "National Gallery," presumably in London. Bazin to Vergnet-Ruiz, December 8, 1950, AN AMN Z15 B 4; see also the Base MNR Rose Valland at pop.culture.gouv.fr.
101. Karlsgodt, *Defending National Treasures*, 43–45, 267–68; Musée de l'Ordre de la Libération, "Jean Cassou," https://www.ordredelaliberation.fr/fr/compagnons/jean-cassou; Cassou, ed., *Le Pillage par les Allemands*, 9–16.
102. Cassou to Vergnet-Ruiz, October 18, 1950, AN AMN Z15 B 4; Dorival to Vergnet-Ruis, November 22, 1950, AN AMN Z15 B 4.
103. Cassou to Vergnet-Ruiz, October 18, 1950, AN AMN Z15 B 4. The "Gleizes" to which Cassou refers most likely was R 1 P, restituted to the heirs of Alphonse Kann in 1997, and the "Léger" R 2 P, *Woman in Red and Green*, restituted in 2003 to the heirs of Léonce Rosenberg, who had purchased it in 1921 from the sequestered collection of German dealer Daniel-Henry Kahnweiler. See Base MNR Rose Valland at pop.culture.gouv.fr.
104. Bazin to Vergnet-Ruiz, December 8, 1950, AN AMN Z15 B 4.
105. Bazin to Vergnet-Ruiz, May 19, 1951, AN AMN Z15 B 4.
106. Vergnet-Ruiz to Bazin, June 19, 1951, AN AMN Z15 B 4.
107. Bazin to Vergnet-Ruiz, September 18, 1951, AN AMN Z15 B 4. The Guardi, *Le Grand Canal à Venise* (MNR 286), was restituted to heirs of John Jaffé in 2005. The Ingres most likely is *Portrait de "Père Desmarets"* (MNR 156), housed at the Musée des Augustins in Toulouse. See Base MNR Rose Valland at pop.culture.gouv.fr.
108. Mesuret to Duprat, April 20, 1953, AN AMN Z15 B 5.
109. Vergnet-Ruiz to mayor of Cognac, December 11, 1953, AN AMN Z15 B 5; Base MNR Rose Valland at pop.culture.gouv.fr.
110. Andrew Bellisari, "The Art of Decolonization: The Battle for Algeria's French Art, 1962–70," *Journal of Contemporary History* 52, no. 3 (2017): 630–31.

111. Alazard to Salles, January 5, 1950, AN AMN Z15 B 3; minutes of selection committee meeting October 27, 1949, AN AMN R20.3.3.
112. Naegelen to Salles, with "List of works requested by Algerian museums," June 22, 1950, AN AMN Z15 B 3. I have corrected few minor errors in Naegelen's list based on information on the Base MNR Rose Valland, such as the title of the Tiepolo painting and a reference to the painter "Breugel."
113. Florisoone to Vergnet-Ruiz, February 22, 1951, AN AMN Z15 B 4.
114. "Arrêté," December 18, 1952, AN AMN Z15 B 3.
115. The Joos de Momper painting (MNR 418) was transferred to the Louvre in 1961; a different work by the artist was restituted in 2014. The pieces by Maillol were reassigned to the MNAM and housed at the Musée d'Orsay. See Base MNR Rose Valland at pop.culture.gouv.fr. The twenty-nine appropriated pieces were not among some three hundred works that had been evacuated to France, then repatriated to Algeria in 1969, the result of negotiations acknowledging the newly independent country's *patrimoine artistique*. See Bellisari, "The Art of Decolonization," 636.
116. Luisa Vertova, "A New Museum Is Born," *Burlington Magazine* 119, no. 888 (1977): 158–59.
117. See http://www.petit-palais.org/musee/fr/historique-de-la-collection.
118. Vergnet-Ruiz to Florisoone, May 3, 1952, AN AMN Z15 B 4.
119. Correspondance from Vergnet-Ruiz to Bazin and curators of provincial museums, March–April 1954, AN AMN Z15 B 5.
120. André Chastel, "Le Goût des 'Préraphaélites' en France," in *De Giotto à Bellini: Les primitifs italiens dans les musées de France, Mai-Juillet*, ed. Michel Laclotte (Paris: Editions des Musées Nationaux, 1956), xx; untitled Florisoone text, xxvii; Vertova, "A New Museum Is Born."
121. Sources vary on the number of sold objects due to methods of counting "pieces" versus "lots." The Mission Mattéoli report explains, for example, that Ministry of Foreign Affairs archivist Marie Hamon in 1998 provided the figure of 12,463 objects transferred to Domaines, along with an additional 943 sequestered objects. Elsewhere, Hamon refers to 14,263 sold objects, a difference perhaps explained by different counting methods in her sources. See Le Masne de Chermont and Schulmann, eds., *Le Pillage de l'art en France*, 40 n53.
122. Le Masne de Chermont and Schulmann, eds., *Le Pillage de l'art en France*, 40–41; see the Phillips Collection, https://www.phillipscollection.org/collection/browse-the-collection?id=0334.
123. Le Masne de Chermont and Schulmann, eds., *Le Pillage de l'art en France*, 41. No compensation date is provided.
124. "Oeuvres d'art récupérées et remises aux Domaines," hand-written notation at bottom, likely by Rose Valland, "d'après documents transmis par l'OBIP," n.d., AN AMN O 30-438. See historical exchange rate calculator at measuringworth.com.
125. Rose Valland, "Compte rendu d'activité," 1954, AN AMN O 30-438.
126. Quote and price in Bouchoux, *"Si les tableaux pouvaient parler...",* 74.
127. Rose Valland, "Compte rendu d'activité," 1954, AN AMN O 30-438.
128. Châtelain to Valland, April 1, 1965, AN AMN O 30-438.

Chapter 5

1. Exhibition catalog, "Herwonnen Kunstbezit: Tentoonstelling van uit Duitschland teruggekeerde Nederlandsche Kunstschatten," March–May 1946.
2. Exhibition catalog, "Herwonnen Kunstbezit: Keuze-tentoonstelling van uit Duitschland teruggevoerde Nederlandsche Kunstschatten," June 22–September 22, 1946.
3. List of paintings and exhibition catalog, NAN 2.08.42/814. See NK2346, Rembrandt's *Still Life with Peacocks*. (*De Pauwen*) at http://www.herkomstgezocht.nl/nl/nk-collec tie/de-pauwen; and the Rijksmuseum website at https://www.rijksmuseum.nl, or http://hdl.handle.net/10934/RM0001.COLLECT.5220.
4. Leistra, "Short History of Art Loss," 56.
5. "Restitutions and other releases from the Munich Central Collecting Point to October 31, 1949," NARA RG 59. Another report in the record group for the same time period on restitution from Wiesbaden to the Netherlands indicates 13,822 items, including unopened cases, but most likely includes restituted books, as did previous US reports.
6. Helen Schretlen, "Geschiedenis van de Stichting Nederlands Kunstbezit," in *Betwist Bezit*, ed. Eelke Muller and Helen Schretlen, 52.
7. Origins Unknown pilot study, April 1998, section "Custodianship and restitution in the Netherlands," available at the International Council of Museums, International Observatory on Illicit Traffic in Cultural Goods: https://www.obs-traffic.museum/ sites/default/files/ressources/files/origins_unknown_pilot.pdf.
8. Updated information from the Dutch government Cultural Heritage Agency is available in Dutch and English at https://www.cultureelerfgoed.nl/onderwerpen/restituti ebeleid, with a portal on the NK collection at wo2.collectienederland.nl.
9. Andrieu points to the relatively high restitution rate in France, where the Jewish survival rate was around 75 percent. See Andrieu, "Two Approaches to Compensation in France," 140–41. See also Blom, "The Persecution of the Jews in the Netherlands," 333–51; Griffioen and Zeller, "La persécution des Juifs en Belgique et aux Pays-Bas," 73–164; Pim Griffioen and Ron Zeller, "Anti-Jewish Policy and Organization of Deportations in France and the Netherlands," 437–73; Dreyfus, "Looting of Jewish Property," 54.
10. Aalders, "Pillage et (non) restitution des oeuvres d'art aux Pays-Bas," 212.
11. Ekkart Committee, "Recommendations Regarding the Restitution of Works of Art," section "General research findings," April 2001. Formerly available at restitutiecommissie.nl. Due to website updates, not all reports and press releases remain available. The 2001 report can be found on the Internet Archive at https://web. archive.org/web/20160826232346/http://restitutiecommissie.nl/en/2001_private_p roperty.html.
12. Wouter Veraart, "Contrasting Legal Concepts of Restitution in France and the Netherlands," in *The Post-war Restitution of Property Rights in Europe*, ed. Wouter Veraart and Laurens Winkel, 21–22, 24.
13. Le Masne de Chermont and Schulmann, *Le pillage de l'art en France*, 22.
14. Veraart, "Contrasting Legal Concepts of Restitution," 25.

15. Gerard Aalders, "Le pillage aux Pays-Bas et la Restitution d'après-guerre," in *Spoliations et restitutions des biens juifs*, ed. Constantin Goschler, Philipp Ther, and Claire Andrieu, 246–47; Veraart, "Contrasting Legal Concepts of Restitution," 25; Katja Lubina, *Contested Cultural Property: The Return of Nazi Spoliated Art and Human Remains from Public Collections* (Maastrict: Datawyse/Universitaire Pers Maastricht, 2009), 295–96.
16. Veraart, "Contrasting Legal Concepts of Restitution," 25.
17. Aalders, *Nazi Looting*, 89.
18. Judt, *Postwar*, 21.
19. Buruma, *Year Zero*, 14–16, here 14.
20. "Memorandum of the Netherlands Government Containing the Claims of the Netherlands to Reparations from Germany," 1945, reproduced in S. I. P. van Campen, *The Quest for Security: Some Aspects of Netherlands Foreign Policy, 1945–1950* (The Hague: Martinus Nijhoff, 1958), appendix 5, 205.
21. "Memorandum of the Netherlands Government," 211, 217.
22. "Memorandum of the Netherlands Government," 205.
23. Veraart, "Contrasting Legal Concepts of Restitution," 26.
24. Charter cited in Schretlen, "Geschiedenis van de Stichting Nederlands Kunstbezit," 33.
25. Schretlen, "Geschiedenis van de Stichting Nederlands Kunstbezit," 33–34.
26. Origins Unknown pilot report, April 1998, available at https://www.obs-traffic.museum/sites/default/files/ressources/files/origins_unknown_pilot.pdf.
27. See Dictionary of Art Historians, http://arthistorians.info/vriesa, http://arthistorians.info/gelderj.
28. J. Jolles and D. F. Lunsingh Scheurleer, "Overzicht van de werkzaamheden van de Stichting Nederlands Kunstbezit," March 15, 1950, NAN 2.08.42/131.
29. Howe, *Salt Mines and Castles*, 256–57.
30. See the Monuments Men and Women Foundation, "Alphonsus Petrus Antonius Vorenkamp (1898–1953)," monumentsmenandwomenfnd.org/vorenkamp-lt-col-alphonsus-p-a.
31. Howe, *Salt Mines and Castles*, 257.
32. Taylor to education minister Bolkestein, May 19, 1944, NAN 2.08.42/274. See also the Monuments Men and Women Foundation, "Alphonsus Petrus Antonius Vorenkamp (1898–1953)," http://www.monumentsmenfoundation.org/the-heroes/the-monuments-men/vorenkamp-lt-col-alphonsus-p-a.
33. The Monuments Men and Women Foundation, "Alphonsus Petrus Antonius Vorenkamp (1898–1953)," monumentsmenandwomenfnd.org/vorenkamp-lt-col-alphonsus-p-a.; Iris Lauterbach, *The Central Collecting Point in Munich: A New Beginning for the Restitution and Protection of Art*, trans. Fiona Elliott (Los Angeles: Getty Research Institute, 2018), 123.
34. See Monuments Men and Women Foundation, "Hans C. L. Jaffé (1915–1984)," http://www.monumentsmenandwomenfnd.org/jaffe-hans-c.-l.
35. Howe, *Salt Mines and Castles*, 269.
36. SNK meeting minutes, June 18, 1945, NAN 2.08.42/2.
37. SNK meeting minutes, June 18, 1945, NAN 2.08.42/2.
38. SNK meeting minutes, June 18, 1945, NAN 2.08.42/2.

39. Schretlen, "Geschiedenis van de Stichting Nederlands Kunstbezit," 36.
40. "List of Dutch Property from Central Collecting Point, Munich," November 20, 1945, NARA RG 260, fold3.com/image/114/270067732.
41. Howe, *Salt Mines and Castles*, 266–71.
42. See http://www.herkomstgezocht.nl/nl/nk-collectie/de-pauwen.
43. Howe, *Salt Mines and Castles*, 269–70.
44. Leistra, "Short History of Art Loss," 56.
45. Howe, *Salt Mines and Castles*, 257–58.
46. Report by American Consul General Doyle, August 16, 1946, NARA RG 84; Leistra, "Short History of Art Loss," 54.
47. "Total Amount of Works of Fine Art Removed from Holland to Germany during the War, to English Zone Only," April 1, 1947, NAN 2.08.42/303.
48. De Vries to Norris, March 5, 1946, NAN 2.08.42/302.
49. "Total Amount of Works of Fine Art Removed from Holland to Germany during the War, to English Zone Only," April 1, 1947, NAN 2.08.42/303.
50. Anne Olivier Popham diary, vol. 3, November 11, 1946, IWM (her emphasis).
51. Norris to De Vries, February 10, 1947, NAN 2.08.42/302; De Vries to Norris, February 20, 1947, NAN 2.08.42/302. Deirkauf's approach to art recovery also is revealed in an operation carried out in Wevelsburg, where Himmler's chateau was burned and townspeople reportedly stole items, including works of art. Deirkauf was convinced that "we could find her [sic] a lot of the stolen goods, but only by a good organised sudden attack. If we could make an example in some cases, the Wevelsburg people will be very afraid and ready to declare voluntary [sic] what they looted." Translated Deirkauf statement, n.d., NAN 2.08.42/303. He led a raid of some thirty homes and filled two 3-ton trucks with allegedly looted property, favorably reported by the local intelligence section. See statement by D. Jordan in Paderborn, May 7, 1947, NAN 2.08.42/303.
52. Report by US Vice Consul Mary Olmsted, "Return of Art Treasures to the Netherlands," January 13, 1947, NARA RG 84.
53. Origins Unknown pilot study, April 1998, "Custodianship and restitution in the Netherlands," available at https://www.obs-traffic.museum/sites/default/files/ressources/files/origins_unknown_pilot.pdf.
54. Willem van Elden memorandum, "Juridische Status Gerecupereerd Kunstbezit," December 17, 1945, NAN 2.08.42/132.
55. The phrase "generally speaking" (*in algemene zin*) is hand written, a revision of typed and crossed-out "undoubtedly" (*zonder meer*), a modification granting the Dutch state greater latitude. Willem van Elden memorandum, "Juridische Status Gerecupereerd Kunstbezit," December 17, 1945, NAN 2.08.42/132.
56. By "original owner," Van Elden appears to mean not the first owner, but the owner at the time of the first transfer of possession during the German occupation.
57. Willem van Elden memorandum, "Juridische Status Gerecupereerd Kunstbezit," December 17, 1945, NAN 2.08.42/132.
58. Willem van Elden memorandum, "Juridische Status Gerecupereerd Kunstbezit," December 17, 1945, NAN 2.08.42/132.

59. SNK meeting minutes, January 6, 1947, NAN 2.08.42/5.
60. Article 11 of guidelines cited in "Origins Unknown: Report on the Pilot Study," 1998, section "Custodianship and Restitution in the Netherlands," available at https://www.obs-traffic.museum/sites/default/files/ressources/files/origins_unknown_pilot.pdf.
61. Aalders, "Pillage et (non) restitution des oeuvres d'art aux Pays-Bas," 209.
62. Quote by Taper recalling Leonard's description of the Göring interrogation, in "Investigating Art Looting for the MFAA," in *Spoils of War*, ed. Elizabeth Simpson, 138.
63. SNK board of directors meeting minutes, March 8, 1947, NAN 2.08.42/5. The fee appears to be calculated based on the works' value at the time of restitution. See also Schretlen, "Geschiedeis van de Stichting Nederlands Kunstbezit," 37–38.
64. "Origins Unknown: Report on the Pilot Study," 1998, section "Custodianship and Restitution in the Netherlands," available at https://www.obs-traffic.museum/sites/default/files/ressources/files/origins_unknown_pilot.pdf; Vorenkamp's observation relayed by United States Consul General Albert Doyle to the Secretary of State, August 16, 1946, NARA RG 84.
65. Lubina, *Contested Cultural Property*, 297–98.
66. Aalders, "Pillage et (non) restitution des oeuvres d'art aux Pays-Bas," 209–10.
67. SNK meeting minutes, September 23, 1946, NAN 2.08.42/4.
68. SNK meeting minutes, May 13, 1946, NAN 2.08.42/4; "Origins Unknown: Report on the Pilot Study," 1998, section "Voluntary and Forced Sale," available at https://www.obs-traffic.museum/sites/default/files/ressources/files/origins_unknown_pilot.pdf.
69. Edwin Rae to James Goodwin, December 4, 1946, NARA RG 260; https://www.fold3.com/image/269965239/.
70. Helen Schretlen, "De niet-gerestitueerde kunstwerken," in *Betwist Bezit*, ed. Eelke Muller and Helen Schretlen, 245. (The number of sold items in this case is not provided.)
71. Council decision cited in Restitutiecommissie, "Advice Concerning the Application for Restitution of the Gutmann Collection," March 25, 2002, https://www.restitutiecommissie.nl/en/recommendation/the-gutmann-collection-gutmann-i/.
72. Restitutiecommissie, "Advice Concerning the Application for Restitution of the Gutmann Collection," March 25, 2002, https://www.restitutiecommissie.nl/en/recommendation/the-gutmann-collection-gutmann-i/.
73. Pieter den Hollander and Melissa Müller, "Jacques Goudstikker, 1897–1940," in *Lost Lives, Lost Art*, ed. Melissa Müller and Monika Tatzkow, 230.
74. Hollander and Müller, "Jacques Goudstikker, 1897–1940," 230.
75. See Advisory Committee on the Assessment of Restitution Applications for Items of Cultural Value and the Second World War, *Report 2005*, 33–34.
76. Nicholas, *Rape of Europa*, 110–14, 422–23.
77. Curtis to Engelhard, December 1, 1948, NARA RG 84; telegram from Engelhard delivered via Staatsbedrijf der PTT in US State Department files, 1948; hand-written 30/12 most likely indicates receipt on December 30, 1948, NARA RG 84.
78. Provenance information on Chardin, *Soap Bubbles*, at metmuseum.org/art/collection, accession number 49.24.
79. Scheurleer to education minister, April 22, 1952, NAN 2.14.73/951.

80. Leistra, "Short History of Art Loss," 54–55; and Konstantin Akinsha and Grigorii Kozlov, "The Discovery of the Secret Repositories," 162–65, both in *Spoils of War*, ed. Elizabeth Simpson.
81. See the museum web site, https://www.boijmans.nl/over-het-museum.
82. Advisory commission meeting minutes, August 23, 1946, NAN 2.08.42/12.
83. Advisory commission meeting minutes, August 23, 1946, NAN 2.08.42/12.
84. Advisory commission meeting minutes, August 23, 1946, NAN 2.08.42/12.
85. Guidelines established in Commission meeting of August 23, 1946, NAN 2.08.42/12.
86. SNK meeting minutes, September 23, 1946, NAN 2.08.42/4.
87. Heldring speech to museum directors, April 1947 (exact date not provided), NAN 2.08.42/12.
88. Lieftinck to education ministry, November 13, 1948, NAN 2.08.42/546.
89. Heldring speech to museum directors, April 1947 (exact date not provided), NAN 2.08.42/12.
90. H. Schröder, Secretary, to Heldring, February 11, 1947, NAN 2.08.42/12.
91. A. F. Philips to K. G. Boon, May 6, 1947, NAN 2.08.42/12.
92. Eelke Muller, "Visies op de juridische status van teruggevoerde cultuurgoederen," in *Betwist Bezit*, ed. Eelke Muller and Helen Schretlen, 66.
93. Advisory commission meeting minutes, October 14, 1947, NAN 2.08.42/12.
94. Scheurleer to education minister, April 22, 1952, NAN 2.14.73/951.
95. Advisory commission meeting minutes, October 14, 1947, NAN 2.08.42/12.
96. SNK meeting minutes, September 23, 1946, NAN 2.08.42/4.
97. For claims statistics, see "Origins Unknown: Report on the Pilot Study," 1998, available at https://www.obs-traffic.museum/sites/default/files/ressources/files/origins_unknown_pilot.pdf; Aalders, "Le pillage et (non) restitution des oeuvres d'art aux Pays-Bas," 211.
98. These paintings are listed in an extensive catalogue including many works in the NK Collection. See Rijksdienst Beeldende Kunst, *Old Master Paintings: An Illustrated Summary Catalogue* (Zwolle: Waanders Uitgevers, 1992).
99. "Suggesties voor een wetsonwerp op de restitutiegoederen," September 5, 1946, NAN 2.08.42/132.
100. Summary of meeting (Beekhuis, De Vries, Wijsenbeek, Heyning), September 6, 1946, NAN 2.14.73/946.
101. "Suggesties voor een wetsonwerp op de restitutiegoederen," September 5, 1946, NAN 2.08.42/132.
102. "Rapport van de Commissie voor Recuperatiegoederen," n.d., NAN 2.08.42/132. Minutes for the SNK meeting of November 20, 1947, refer to the "forthcoming" commission report. See NAN 2.08.42/5.
103. Heyning, "Positie teruggevoerde Kunstvoorwerpen," January 5, 1948, NAN 2.08.42/132. (his emphasis)
104. Röell to education minister, March 31, 1948, NAN 2.08.42/815.
105. Heyning, "Positie teruggevoerde Kunstvoorwerpen," January 5, 1948, NAN 2.08.42/132.

106. SNK meeting minutes, June 18, 1948, NAN 2.08.42/6.
107. Finance ministry memorandum cited in SNK meeting minutes, September 10, 1948, NAN 2.08.42/6.
108. F. Kuyvenhoven, Rijksdienst voor het Cultureel Erfgoed, "History of the Formation of the Dutch State Collection," n.d., 4–6; formerly available at http://culturalheritageagency.nl/en/a-varied-collection; SNK meeting minutes, September 10, 1948, NAN 2.08.42/6.
109. Lieftinck to the education ministry, November 13, 1948, NAN 2.08.42/546.
110. Muller, "Visies op de juridische status van teruggevoerde cultuurgoedernen," 98; Origins Unknown pilot report, section "Decline of the Netherlands Art Property Foundation," April 1998, available at https://www.obs-traffic.museum/sites/default/files/ressources/files/origins_unknown_pilot.pdf.
111. Schretlen, "De niet-gerestitueerde kunstwerken," 245.
112. Jolles cited in Origins Unknown pilot report, section "Auctions," April 1998, available at https://www.obs-traffic.museum/sites/default/files/ressources/files/origins_unknown_pilot.pdf.
113. Schretlen, "De niet-gerestitueerde kunstwerken," 253–55.
114. Schretlen, "Geschiedenis van de Stichting Nederlands Kunstbezit," 68–76; Nicholas, *Rape of Europa*, 108, 417–18, 426–27.
115. Howe to Coremans, October 12, 1949; Coremans to Howe, October 29, 1949, AAA Howe papers.
116. Schretlen, "Geschiedenis van de Stichting Nederlands Kunstbezit," 76. See photo here of news headline from *De Telegraaf*, May 11, 1951: "De chaos bij Stichting Kunstbezit: Fraudes, Zwarte Kas en Slechte Administratie."
117. SNK meeting minutes, September 10, 1948, NAN 2.08.42/6.
118. Rosebrock, "Kurt Hermann Martin (1899–1975)," in *Hans Haug, homme de musées: une passion à l'oeuvre*, ed. Bernadette Schnitzler and Anne-Doris Meyer (Strasbourg: Editions des Musées de la ville de Strasbourg, 2009), 170.
119. Bernadette Schnitzler, "Hans Haug et l' 'affaire' des tableaux hollandais de Strasbourg," *Cahiers alsaciens d'archéologie, d'art et d'histoire* 51 (2008): 151–52; Bernadette Schnitzler, "Les années de guerre (1939–1945)," in *Hans Haug, homme de musées*, ed. Bernadette Schnitzler and Anne-Doris Meyer, 155–56.
120. Schnitzler, "Hans Haug et l' 'affaire' des tableaux hollandais de Strasbourg," 151.
121. Schnitzler, "Hans Haug et l' 'affaire' des tableaux hollandais de Strasbourg," 153.
122. Haug to Henraux, December 8, 1944, quote with Haug's emphasis in reproduced letter accompanying Schnitzler, "Les années de guerre (1939–1945)," 169.
123. Schnitzler, "Hans Haug et l' 'affaire' des tableaux hollandais de Strasbourg," 155.
124. Schnitzler, "Hans Haug et l' 'affaire' des tableaux hollandais de Strasbourg," 155.
125. Michel Florisoone, "Note sur les achats du Dr. Kurt Martin pour les Musées de Strasbourg et sur le tableau de Pissarro retrouvé en Hollande," September 21, 1951, MEAE 209SUP/528.
126. Michel Florisoone, "Note sur les achats du Dr. Kurt Martin pour les Musées de Strasbourg et sur le tableau de Pissarro retrouvé en Hollande," September 21, 1951, MEAE 209SUP/528.

127. Dutch Ministry of Foreign Affairs to the French Embassy, May 15, 1952, NAN 2.08.42/318.
128. Maurice de Rothschild to Direction générale des Arts et Lettres, May 16, 1952, MEAE 209SUP/528.
129. Schnitzler, "Hans Haug et l' 'affaire' des tableaux hollandais de Strasbourg," 158.
130. French Embassy, The Hague, to the Dutch Ministry of Foreign Affairs, July 1, 1954, NAN 2.08.42/318.
131. Dutch Ministry of Foreign Affairs to the French Embassy in The Hague, October 6, 1954, NAN 2.08.42/318.
132. Jolles and Scheurleer, "Overzicht van de werkzaamheden van de Stichting Nederlands Kunstbezit," March 15, 1950, NAN 2.08.42/131.
133. Jolles and Scheurleer, "Overzicht van de werkzaamheden van de Stichting Nederlands Kunstbezit," March 15, 1950, NAN 2.08.42/131.
134. Origins Unknown pilot report, section "Auctions," April 1998, available at https://www.obs-traffic.museum/sites/default/files/ressources/files/origins_unknown_pilot.pdf.

Chapter 6

1. "Avant-propos," *Chefs-d'oeuvre Récupérés en Allemagne*, Palais des Beaux-Arts, Brussels, November–December 1948, 7.
2. See, for instance, De Vries to Henraux, November 21, 1946, NAN 2.08.42/318; and a Belgian discussion of the need for a government stock of furniture similar to the French Mobilier national, from head curator Lavachery at the Musées royaux d'art et d'histore to the education minister, December 30, 1948, REB 6B 68.378/3.
3. Commission d'étude (Belgium), *Les biens des victimes*, 430–33; on the distribution of items, see annex 26, 237–52.
4. Conway, *Sorrows of Belgium*, 59.
5. Conway, *Sorrows of Belgium*, 58.
6. Conway, *Sorrows of Belgium*, 59.
7. Conway, *Sorrows of Belgium*, 134–36.
8. Lagrou, *Legacy of Nazi Occupation*, 2.
9. Conway, *Sorrows of Belgium*, 43, 62–68.
10. Conway, *Sorrows of Belgium*, 366–73.
11. Dictionary of Art Historians, "Léo Van Puyvelde," http://arthistorians.info/puyveldel. See also Monuments Men Foundation, "Léo van Puyvelde (1882–1965)," https://www.monumentsmenandwomenfnd.org/ van-puyvelde-col-leo.
12. This service was the Direction générale de la protection du patrimoine culturel in the education ministry. See Van Puyvelde to education minister Leo Collard, March 13, 1946, RB 6B/68.378.3.
13. Dictionary of Art Historians, "Léo Van Puyvelde," http://arthistorians.info/puyveldel; Monuments Men Foundation, "Léo van Puyvelde," https://www.monumentsmenfoundation.org/the-heroes/the-monuments-men/puyvelde-leo-van.

14. Nicholas, *The Rape of Europa*, 407.
15. Commission d'étude (Belgium), *Les biens des victimes*, 233.
16. Commission d'étude (Belgium), *Les biens des victimes*, 233–34.
17. Lemaire oversaw numerous conservation projects through the 1970s across Belgium, notably in Bruges, Brussels, and Louvain. See http://arthistorians.info/lemairer.
18. Commission d'étude (Belgium), *Les biens des victimes*, 238.
19. Commission d'étude (Belgium), *Les biens des victimes*, 238.
20. Reul to Count Gobert d'Aspremont Lynden, Belgian minister to Austria, February 5, 1947, RB 6B/68.378/3.
21. Education Minister Herman Vos to Leo Van Puyvelde, January 17, 1947, RB 6B/68.378/3.
22. Doorslaer, "The Expropriation of Jewish Property and Restitution in Belgium," in *Robbery and Restitution*, ed. Martin Dean, Constantin Goschler, and Philipp Ther, 161–62.
23. Doorslaer, "Expropriation of Jewish Property," 161–65.
24. Commission d'étude (Belgium), *Les biens des victimes*, 237.
25. Commission d'étude (Belgium), *Les biens des victimes*, 238;
26. See Freeman, "'The Bells, Too, Are Fighting,'" 417–50; Lust, "Spoils of War Removed from Belgium," 61.
27. Doorslaer, "Expropriation of Jewish Property," 159, 164.
28. Lemaire to Christophe, August 21, 1948, RB 6B/68.37813.
29. The lack of detailed information and imprecise titles and authorship often make it difficult to identify specific paintings. The four listed here most likely were registered in the guardianship as P316, Roelandt Savery, *Chasse au cerf*, assigned to the Royal Museums in Brussels (inventory number 6590, fine-arts-museum.be, collection information only available in French and Dutch); A72, Jan Brueghel, *Paysage*, for the Royal Museums in Brussels (today inventory number 6594, fine-arts-museum.be); A83, Cranach, *Eve*, for the Royal Museum in Antwerp (inventory number 5048, collectie.kmska.be, indicating provenance from Göring's art collection); and A88, Jordaens, *Neptune and Amphitrite*, for the fine arts administration, today at the Rubenshuis in Antwerp (www.rubenshuis.be). See "Liste des tableaux pouvant entrer en ligne de compte pour l'exposition," n.d., and "Note pour Monsieur le Ministre," April 30, 1951, both in RB 6B/68.37813.
30. L. Ninane, "Rapport sur la visite, le 31/8/48, au dépôt d'oeuvres par l'ORE," September 1, 1948, RB 6B/68.37813.
31. Van Mulders, "Directeur délégué" to education minister, September 29, 1948, RB 6B/68.37813.
32. Christophe to Rossignol and Lemaire, October 12, 1948, RB 6B/68.37813.
33. Christophe to Pirlot, November 4, 1948, RB 6B/68.37813.
34. J. Dinjeart, DER director of administration, to education minister, December 4, 1949, RB 6B/68.37813.
35. "Avant-propos," *Chefs-d'oeuvre Récupérés en Allemagne*, Palais des Beaux-Arts, Brussels, November–December 1948, 7.
36. Reul to Dorcq, January 15, 1949, RB DER 386.

37. Reul to Dorcq, January 15, 1949, RB DER 386.
38. Christophe to Huysmans, March 7, 1949, RB 6B/68.37813.
39. Christophe to Huysmans, March 7, 1949, RB 6B/68.37813.
40. Lemaire to Christophe, June 25, 1949, RB DER 387.
41. Rossignol to Domaines collector (*receveur*), November 17, 1949, RB DER 386.
42. Oct. Van Mulders, "Note pour Madame Guerin," August 23, 1949, and list of purchased objects, RB 6B/68.37813.
43. Notice of transfer and list of objects signed by Lemaire, Rossignol, and Pirlot, December 11, 1950, RB 6B/68.37813.
44. "Oeuvres d'art intéressant les Musées Royaux des Beaux-Arts," n.d., RB 6B/68.37813.
45. Notice of transfer and list of artworks signed by Lemaire, Rossignol, and Pirlot, December 11, 1950, RB 6B/68.37813.
46. *Dictionary of Art Historians*, entries for Emile Renders, Friedrich Winkler, http://arthistorians.info/search/node/renders; http://arthistorians.info/winklerf.
47. Franc to Marks calculation at Rodney Edvinsson, ed., historicalstatistics.org; dollar-to-Marks exchange rate calculated at Harold Marcuse, Historical Dollar-to-Marks Currency Conversion page, http://marcuse.faculty.history.ucsb.edu/projects/currency.htm#tables; current dollar value calculated at measuringworth.com.
48. Consolidated Interrogation Report No. 2, The Goering Collection, September 15, 1945, NARA RG 239, fold3.com/image/232001756.
49. Consolidated Interrogation Report No. 2, The Goering Collection, September 15, 1945, NARA RG 239, fold3.com/image/232001798.
50. Consolidated Interrogation Report No. 2, The Goering Collection, September 15, 1945, NARA RG 239, fold3.com/image/232001767.
51. Report by Captain Jan Vlug, Art Looting Investigation Unit, February 1947, RB DER 367.
52. Rossignol to Renders, July 4, 1946, RB DER 391.
53. Rossignol to Coremans, July 5, 1946, RB DER 391.
54. Report "Renders, Emile," n.d., RB DER 393.
55. Attorney Robert van Malderghem to Rossignol, October 26, 1951, RB DER 391.
56. List in RB DER 447, created circa 1994 according to RB finding aid. According to the Web Gallery of Art, the two Memling panels have been "on permanent loan" at the museum since 1952. See wga.hu.
57. "Biens culturels cédés aux musées," c. 1951, RB DER 387; on Lagrand's activities, see Commission d'étude (Belgium), *Les biens des victimes*, 132.
58. Commission for the Protection and Restitution of Cultural Material (London), "A list of art dealers," July 16, 1945, NARA RG 260, fold3.com/image/269883052. A cover page indicates "this list is composed of dealers of enemy nationality (other than Austrian or German); and of "collaborationist" dealers (other than French or Dutch) in the Occupied territories of Europe; and of dealers of neutral nationality who are known to or believed to have traded with the enemy." On the Van Gelder collection, see Lust, "Spoils of War Removed from Belgium," 61.

59. "Biens culturels cédés aux musées," c. 1951, RB DER 387. The description is similar to one listed on Belgian Art Links and Tools (BALaT), held by the Royal Museums of Fine Arts in Brussels: balat.kikirpa.be/object/20026153. However, the latter was acquired in 1895 and has remained in the royal collection ever since, confirmed in email communication with curator Joost Vander Auwera, January 15, 2020. Another list in RB DER 447, created c. 1994, indicates the painting went to the Rubenshuis in Antwerp, but also does not appear on the museum's website. See rubenshuis.be. A similar piece with slightly different dimensions is at the Philadelphia Museum of Art, acquired in 1899. See https://www.philamuseum.org/collections/permanent/104386.html.
60. See DER in provenance at balat.kikirpa.be/object/10137317.
61. "Biens culturels cédés aux musées," c. 1951, RB DER 387.
62. On the Denens piece, see collectie.kmska.be and balat.kikirpa.be/object/91745. On P27, see "Biens culturels cédés aux musées," c. 1951 RB DER 387; and RB DER 447, list of recovered works in public museums, c. 1994. The *Stork* item does not appear on the website of the Royal Museums of Art and History: kmkg-mrah.be.
63. The statement is in the context of the DER resisting demands by the fine arts office to pay fees for storing works of art in the Musées du Cinquantenaire. J. Dinjeart to Dierckx, March 4, 1950, RB DER 386.
64. The Belgian state sold all of the pieces transferred from France, except, it appears, Meunier, *Le Lamineur*. See Service des Ventes Publiques du Palais des Beaux-Arts, "Vente publique: 22.12.1954," December 29, 1954, RB DER 385.
65. Rossignol to Lemaire, May 22, 1953, and list of fourteen paintings, RB DER 386.
66. Rossingol to Lemaire, October 9, 1953, RB 6B/68.37813.
67. Christophe to finance ministry, via Inspection of Finance, September 26, 1953, RB 6B/68.37813.
68. Caris to education minister, October 22, 1953, RB 6B/68.37813.
69. Christophe to education minister, December 11, 1953, RB 6B/68.37813.
70. Service des Ventes Publiques du Palais des Beaux-Arts, "Vente publique: 22.12.1954," December 29, 1954, RB DER 385. Meunier, *Le Lamineur*, does not appear on the auction list, nor on later lists of acquired works. See also "Gerecupereerde Kunstwerken in Belgisch Openbaar (Museum) Bezit," RB DER 447.
71. Curator of Tournai Museum of Fine Arts to Christophe, September 16, 1949, RB 6B/68.37813.
72. Paul Renotte to Huysmans, February 2, 1949, RB 6B/68.37813.
73. L. Somers to Christophe, January 18, 1951, RB 6B/68.37813.
74. Meeting minutes, February 26, 1951, RB 6B/68.37813.
75. Meeting minutes, February 26, 1951, RB 6B/68.37813. The Royal Museums of Fine Arts in Brussels and Antwerp provide websites with information on paintings received from the DER. For Brussels, see the Cultural Goods database at https://cultural-goods-wwii.fine-arts-museum.be/en/artworks, and for Antwerp, see the database at collectie.kmska.be. On the Denens painting, see also Commission d'étude (Belgium), *Les biens des juifs*, annex 26, 246.

76. Meeting minutes, February 26, 1951, RB 6B/68.37813.
77. Christophe to education minister, April 30, 1951, RB 6B/68.37813.
78. Christophe to education minister, September 4, 1951, RB 6B/68.37813. The De Backer picture may be inventory number 76 at the Lier museum; image available at http://balat.kikirpa.be/photo.php?path=X029779&objnr=136757&nr=6.
79. Fierens to Christophe, September 21, 1951, RB 6B/68.37813.
80. See, for instance, "Personal and confidential" note from Rossignol to education minister, n.d., RB 6B/68.37813. The Allies initially aimed to require $20 billion in compensation from Germany, and according to the Paris agreement of January 14, 1946, Belgium would receive 4.5 percent of industrial and other capital equipment, and 2.7 percent of other forms of compensation. See "Reparation from Germany, on the Establishment of Inter-Allied Reparation Agency, and Restitution of Monetary Gold," January 14, 1946, available at https://treaties.un.org/doc/Publication/UNTS/Volume%20555/volume-555-I-8105-English.pdf. On the failure of the IARA distribution mechanism, see Richard Buxbaum, "From Paris to London: The Legal History of European Reparation Claims: 1946–1953," *Berkeley Journal of International Law* 31, no. 2 (2013): 329–34.
81. Commission d'étude (Belgium), *Les biens des victimes*, 250–51.
82. Commission d'étude (Belgium), *Les biens des victimes*, 246, 248.
83. Commission d'étude (Belgium), *Les biens des victimes*, 246.
84. Commission d'étude (Belgium), *Les biens des victimes*, 247.
85. Rossignol to Dorcq, March 2, 1949, RB DER 381.
86. E. Mouteau to Receveur, Domaines, June 20, 1949, RB DER 380.
87. Rossignol to Dorcq, August 5, 1948, RB 380; Dorcq to Rossignol, August 11, 1948; RB 380; Dinjeart to Dierckx, March 4, 1950, RB DER 386.
88. Dinjeart to Dierckx, March 4, 1950, RB DER 386.
89. Dinjeart to Dierckx, March 4, 1950, RB DER 386.
90. A. M. Berryer to Christophe, December 31, 1948, RB 6B/68.37813.
91. H. Lavachery to education minister Huysmans, December 30, 1948, RB 6B/68.37813.
92. Huysmans to finance minister, January 19, 1949, RB 6B/68.37813.
93. Commission d'étude, *Les biens des victimes*, 247.
94. Tiron, "un Bock avec . . . M. X. Amateur d'art, à propos de la vente publique des oeuvres récupérées en Allemagne," *Pourquoi pas?*, n.d., 306, 308, RB DER 381.
95. Commission d'étude (Belgium), *Les biens des victimes*, 242–43. The report does not specify the painters' first names, but they likely were Belgian artists Louis Dubois, Alfred Bastien, and Constant Permeke.
96. See the "Give Them a Face" portrait collection at Kazerne Dossin, http://beeldbank.kazernedossin.eu/.
97. Commission d'étude (Belgium), *Les biens des victimes*, 243–44.
98. "Catalogue des ventes," June 21 and 22, 1951, RB DER 382.
99. Rossignol to Dierckx, November 19, 1952, RB 383; list of objects, "Vente publique du 5 November 1952," RB DER 383.
100. Service des Ventes Publiques, Palais des Beaux-Arts, "Vente publique: 22.12.1954," December 29, 1954, RB DER 385; Commission d'étude, *Les biens des victimes*, 248.

101. Commission d'étude (Belgium), *Les biens des victimes*, 245–46 and annex 26, 237; on Masonic pieces, see Dinjeart to Dierckx, March 4, 1950, RB DER 386. See museum information on the Corinth painting at https://www.fine-arts-museum.be/en/provenance.
102. "Curriculum Vitae du Dr. J.W. von Moltke," n.d., RB DER 399.
103. "Curriculum Vitae du Dr. J.W. von Moltke," n.d., RB DER 399.
104. "Curriculum Vitae du Dr. J.W. von Moltke," n.d., RB DER 399.
105. Statement by Major Vilhelm Evang, "A tous ceux que la chose puisse intéresse," April 12, 1946; statement by bishop of Oslo, "A tous ceux que la chose puisse intéresse," January 10, 1946, RB DER 399. Jacques Mangers's title of bishop appears, along with "former member of the command of the Norwegian resistance," but not his name. It appears to be a joint statement also issued by a "Doctor of Philosophy" formerly in contact with resistance command.
106. Count of Montblanc to Ch. Leeman in education ministry, Antwerp, July 10, 1947, RB DER 398.
107. Ewan Phillips, Assistant Controller MFAA, "Certificate of Character: Dr. Joachim Wolfgang von Moltke," June 7, 1947, RB DER 398.
108. Amand to Rehard, Office of General Koenig, December 31, 1947, RB DER 398.
109. "Rubens appartenant au comte von Moltke," February 12, 1947: RB 398; Lemaire to Henraux, February 28, 1947, RB DER 398; Henraux to Lemaire, March 15, 1947, RB DER 399.
110. L. G. Perry to RDR Detmold, October 27, 1948, RB DER 398.
111. Rossignol to Em. Langui, education ministry, May 15, 1950, RB DER 398.
112. "Note de plaidoirie," March 21, 1953, RB DER 399; Amoetat Akevoth, Dutch Jewish Genealogical Database, dutchjewry.org/genealogy/seijffers/127.htm.
113. Purchase details in letter from L. G. Perry to RDR Detmold, October 27, 1948, RB DER 398.
114. Decision by 5th trial court (*de première instance*), Brussels, April 29, 1954, RB DER 399.
115. Decision by 5th trial court (*de première instance*), Brussels, April 29, 1954, RB DER 399; Statement by Raymond Lemaire, February 24, 1954, RB DER 399.
116. Jean Baiwir, Huissier, "Assignation," n.d., RB DER 399.
117. Van de Moortel, Belgian economic mission in Düsseldorf, to Rossignol, January 15, 1953; Valland to Van de Moortel, February 21, 1953, RB DER 399.
118. Ruling of 5th Chamber of Tribunal *de première instance*, April 29, 1954, RB DER 399.
119. Commission d'étude (Belgium), *Les biens des victimes*, 249.
120. Commission d'étude (Belgium), *Les biens des victimes*, 433.

Chapter 7

1. Goodman, *Orpheus Clock*, 243–46.
2. Interview with Simon Goodman, February 3, 2019.

3. Lyndel V. Prott, "Responding to World War II Art Looting," in *Resolution of Cultural Property Disputes*, The International Bureau of the Permanent Court of Arbitration (The Hague: Kluwer Law International, 2004), 122.
4. Marrus, *Some Measure of Justice*, 38–39.
5. Rose Valland, "Note succincte sur l'activité du Service de Protection des Oeuvres d'Art au cours de l'année 1962," February 16, 1963, AN AMN O 30–438; Ministère de la Culture, dossier de presse "Restitution du tableau 'Triptyque de la Crucifixion' attribué à l'atelier de Joachim Patinir (MNR 386) aux ayants droit d'Hertha et Henry Bromberg," February 12, 2018, 9. Available at http://www.culture.gouv.fr/Presse/Dossiers-de-presse/Restitution-du-tableau-Triptyque-de-la-Crucifixion-attribue-a-l-atelier-de-Joachim-Patinir-MNR-386-aux-ayants-droit-d-Hertha-et-Henry-Bromberg. The dossier de presse indicates the Jonas restitution occurred in 1961, whereas Valland reported it among her activities in 1962. The discrepancy may be a matter of when the restitution decision and actual transfer occurred.
6. Ministère de la Culture, dossier de presse "Restitution du tableau 'Triptyque de la Crucifixion,'" 9.
7. Rijksdienst Beeldende Kunst, *Old Master Paintings*, 409; Commission d'étude (Belgium), *Les biens des victimes* (2001), http://www.combuysse.fgov.be/hoofdframemenufr.html.
8. Jürgen Lillteicher, "West Germany and the Restitution of Jewish Property in Europe," in *Robbery and Restitution*, ed. Martin Dean, Constantin Goschler, and Philipp Ther, 102–3.
9. Marrus, *Some Measure of Justice*, 70–71.
10. Cited in Herf, *Divided Memory: The Nazi Past in the Two Germanys* (Cambridge, MA: Harvard University Press, 1997), 281.
11. Cited in Herf, *Divided Memory*, 282.
12. Marrus, *Some Measure of Justice*, 71; Lillteicher, "West Germany and the Restitution of Jewish Property in Europe," 104.
13. Lillteicher, "West Germany and the Restitution of Jewish Property in Europe," 104.
14. Le Masne de Chermont and Schulmann, *Le pillage de l'art en France*, 46–49.
15. Herf, *Divided Memory*, 288.
16. United Nations Educational, Scientific and Cultural Organization, "Convention for the Protection of Cultural Property in the Event of Armed Conflict with Regulations for the Execution of the Convention 1954," May 14, 1954, available at http://portal.unesco.org/en/ev.php-URL_ID=13637&URL_DO=DO_TOPIC&URL_SECTION=201.html.
17. Kurtz, *America and the Return of Nazi Contraband*, 199. See also the list of signatories, states parties, and declarations and reservations at United Nations Educational, Scientific and Cultural Organization, "Convention for the Protection of Cultural Property in the Event of Armed Conflict with Regulations for the Execution of the Convention 1954," May 14, 1954, available at http://portal.unesco.org/en/ev.php-URL_ID=13637&URL_DO=DO_TOPIC&URL_SECTION=201.html.

18. "Convention on the Means of Prohibiting and Preventing the Illicit Import, Export and Transfer of Ownership of Cultural Property—1970," available at http://www.unesco.org/new/en/culture/themes/illicit-trafficking-of-cultural-property/1970-convention/. See also Ana Filipa Vrdoljak, *International Law, Museums and the Return of Cultural Objects* (Cambridge: Cambridge University Press, 2008), 207–8.
19. "Convention Concerning the Protection of the World Cultural and Natural Heritage," 1972, available at https://whc.unesco.org/en/conventiontext/.
20. Vrdoljak, *International Law, Museums and the Return of Cultural Objects*, 209–11.
21. See the *ICOM Code of Ethics for Museums*, updated in 2004, at icom.museum.
22. Eizenstat, *Imperfect Justice*, 3–5.
23. See Feliciano's description of his sources in the updated French edition of *Le musée disparu: Enquête sur le pillage d'oeuvres d'art en France par les nazis* (Paris: Editions Gallimard, 2008), 12–15.
24. See a list of publications at https://www.cmc.edu/academic/faculty/profile/jonathan-petropoulos.
25. Marrus, *Some Measure of Justice*, 10–19.
26. Marrus, *Some Measure of Justice*, 19–22.
27. Marrus, *Some Measure of Justice*, 22–25. On flaws in the ICHEIC settlement model, see Lawrence Kill and Linda Gerstel, "Holocaust-Era Insurance Claims: Legislative, Judicial and Executive Remedies," in *Holocaust Restitution: Perspectives on the Litigation and Its Legacy*, ed. Michael Bazyler and Roger P. Alford (New York: New York University Press, 2006), 239–49. The estimated face value is cited in the same volume, Sidney Zabludoff, "ICHEIC: Excellent Concept but Inept Implementation," 207.
28. See Eizenstat, *Imperfect Justice*, 5–7.
29. Presidential Advisory Commission on Holocaust Assets in the United States, introduction to final report "Plunder and Restitution," http://govinfo.library.unt.edu/pcha/PlunderRestitution.html/html/Intro_CreationCommission.html.
30. Presidential Advisory Commission on Holocaust Assets in the United States, "Recommendations," http://govinfo.library.unt.edu/pcha/PlunderRestitution.html/html/Recommendations.html.
31. Michael Bazyler, *Holocaust Justice: The Battle for Restitution in America's Courts* (New York: New York University Press, 2003), 305.
32. See Eizenstat's own account of these negotiations in *Imperfect Justice*.
33. "Washington Conference Principles on Nazi-Confiscated Art," December 3, 1998, https://www.state.gov/washington-conference-principles-on-nazi-confiscated-art/.
34. Tabitha Oost, "In an Effort To Do Justice? Restitution Policies and the Washington Principles" (MA thesis, University of Amsterdam, 2011), 121–23.
35. Leistra, "Short History of Art Loss," 56–57; Helen Fawkes, "Netherlands Hails Return of Stolen Art," April 20, 2004, http://news.bbc.co.uk/2/hi/entertainment/3640951.stm.
36. Sandholtz, *Prohibiting Plunder*, 215–23; on Jewish assets held in Russia, see Wesley Fisher and Ruth Weinberger, "Holocaust-Era Looted Art: A Current World-Wide Overview," Conference on Jewish Material Claims against Germany and World Jewish Restitution Organization (September 10, 2014): 38–39.

37. "Vilnius Forum Declaration," October 5, 2000, available at https://www.lootedart.com/MFV7A818610.
38. "Terezin Declaration," June 30, 2009, http://www.eu2009.cz/en/news-and-documents/news/terezin-declaration-26304/.
39. Tabitha Oost, "Restitution Policies on Nazi-Looted Art in the Netherlands and the United Kingdom: A Change from a Legal to a Moral Paradigm?" *International Journal of Cultural Property* 25 (2018): 172–74.
40. Ministère de la Culture, dossier de presse "Restitution du tableau 'Triptyque de la Crucifixion'," February 12, 2018, 8–9, http://www.culture.gouv.fr/Presse/Dossiers-de-presse/Restitution-du-tableau-Triptyque-de-la-Crucifixion-attribue-a-l-atelier-de-Joachim-Patinir-MNR-386-aux-ayants-droit-d-Hertha-et-Henry-Bromberg.
41. Lorentz, *La France et les Restitutions Allemandes*, 296–97. Mitterrand at the time referred to the painting title *Route de Louveciennes*, but it appears to be MNR 1001, *Neige au soleil couchant*, held at the Musée d'Orsay. See François Mitterrand, "Allocution de M. François Mitterrand, Président de la République, sur la restitution à la France d'une collection de tableaux, notamment du peintre Claude Monet, l'amitié et la coopération franco-allemandes, Mulhouse le 30 mai 1994," available at https://www.vie-publique.fr/discours/130508-allocution-de-m-francois-mitterrand-president-de-la-republique-sur-l; and the MNR catalog at the Site Rose Valland, http://pop.culture.gouv.fr.
42. Mitterrand, "Allocution de M. François Mitterrand," https://www.vie-publique.fr/discours/130508-allocution-de-m-francois-mitterrand-president-de-la-republique-sur-l.
43. French titles of the restituted paintings are available at Ministère de la Culture, dossier de presse "Restitution du tableau 'Triptyque de la Crucifixion'," 9.
44. See Direction des Musées de France, *Pillages et Restitutions*.
45. Louis Amigues, "Restitutions et récupération artistique depuis 1950," in Direction des Musées de France, *Pillages et Restitutions*, 125–28, 161–62.
46. Philippe Dagen and Hector Feliciano, "Les musées détiennent près de deux mille oeuvres volées par les nazis pendant l'Occupation," *Le Monde*, January 28, 1997: 6.
47. Alain Juppé to Jean Mattéoli, February 5, 1997, in Mission d'étude sur la spoliation des Juifs de France, *Rapport Général*, 9–10.
48. CIVS September 2019 report available at http://www.civs.gouv.fr/images/pdf/lacivs/Chiffres-cles_SEPTEMBRE_2019_FR.pdf.
49. Mission d'étude sur la spoliation des Juifs de France, *Rapport Général*, 79.
50. See Le Masne de Chermont and Schulmann, eds., *Le pillage de l'art en France*, 28–29. I address the French sequestration and selection of works from the Schloss collection in *Defending National Treasures*, 208–27.
51. Le Masne de Chermont and Schulmann, eds., *Le pillage de l'art en France*, 65–74.
52. Christiane Gentili di Giuseppe et al. v. Musée du Louvre, Court of Appeal of Paris, June 2, 1999 (English), available in the ArThemis database, Art-Law Centre, University of Geneva, https://plone.unige.ch/art-adr/cases-affaires/five-italian-paintings-2013-gentili-di-giuseppe-heirs-v-musee-du-louvre-and-france/christiane-gentili-di-giuseppe-et-al-v-musee-du-louvre-court-of-appeal-of-paris-june-2-1999-english/view.

53. Christiane Gentili di Giuseppe et al. v. Musée du Louvre; Corinne Hershkovitch, *La restitution des oeuvres d'art: Solutions et impasses* (Paris: Editions Hazan, 2011), 54; Parisot, "The Gentili di Giuseppe Case in France," 264–65.
54. "Loi relative à la déchéance de la nationalité à l'égard des Français qui ont quitté la France," July 23, 1940, *Journal Officiel de la République Française*, July 24, 1940, 4569; Christiane Gentili di Giuseppe et al. v. Musée du Louvre.
55. Christiane Gentili di Giuseppe et al. v. Musée du Louvre.
56. Hershkovitch, *La restitution des oeuvres d'art*, 55.
57. Christiane Gentili di Giuseppe et al. v. Musée du Louvre; Rose Valland (initialed "RV"), "Visite à Maître Moulin," January 18, 1956, MEAE 69; Parisot, "The Gentili di Giuseppe Case in France," 265; Hershkovitch, *La restitution des oeuvres d'art*, 54.
58. Parisot, "The Gentili di Giuseppe Case in France," 265.
59. Parisot, "The Gentili di Giuseppe Case in France," 265.
60. "Liste des tableaux reconnus au Musée du Louvre," n.d., MEAE 209SUP/49.
61. Notice from the Service des Restitutions artistiques et Culturelles, OBIP, "Objet: Spoliation Gentili di Giuseppe Salem," June 5, 1951, MEAE 209SUP/49.
62. Adriana, Raphaël Salem to Poullin, Service de la Récupération, June 21, 1950, MEAE 209SUP/40.
63. Kraemer-Bach to Berthoin, November 30, 1955, MEAE 209SUP/69.
64. Jacques Bordeneuve to Marcelle Kraemer-Bach, February 15, 1956, MEAE 209SUP/69.
65. Valland to Seyrig, December 19, 1961, MEAE 209SUP/69.
66. Valland to Seyrig, January 12, 1962, MEAE 209SUP/69.
67. Christiane Gentili di Giuseppe et al. v. Musée du Louvre.
68. Christiane Gentili di Giuseppe et al. v. Musée du Louvre.
69. Parisot, "The Gentili di Giuseppe Case in France," 271.
70. Walter Robinson, "MFA Exhibition Acknowledges Background, Theft of Monet Work," *Boston Globe*, December 5, 1998, B1.
71. Audrey Gillian, "Monet Painting Looted by Nazis Withdrawn from Exhibition," *The Guardian*, December 31, 1998, 4.
72. HA-Dienst Telegraph Service, "Hamburg: Paintings 'acquired' by Ribbentrop found," October 30, 1945, NARA RG 239, https://www.fold3.com/image/271388196.
73. Commandement en Chef Français en Allemagne, *Répertoire des biens spoliés en France durant la guerre*, vol. 2. English translation of preface by G. Glasser on works of exceptional cultural value, p. vii; the Monet water lily painting owned by Paul Rosenberg listed on p. 236.
74. Compte-rendu de la quatrième reunion de la Commission de Choix des Oeuvres d'art, December 21, 1949, AN AMN Z15 B 2.
75. See Bazyler, *Holocaust Justice*, 225.
76. See catalogue of the Site Rose Valland, http://pop.culture.gouv.fr.
77. Catherine Trautmann, "Déclaration de Mme Catherine Trautmann, ministre de la culture et de la communication, sur la restitution du tableau de Claude Monet 'Nymphéas' à la famille de Paul Rosenberg spoliée par les nazis durant la seconde guerre mondiale, Paris le 29 avril 1999," https://www.vie-publique.fr/discours/188994-declaration-de-mme-catherine-trautmann-ministre-de-la-culture-et-de-la.

78. Interview with Marianne Rosenberg, October 18, 2019.
79. Bazyler, *Holocaust Justice*, 225.
80. See Corinne Bouchoux, "Oeuvres culturelles spoliées ou au passé flou et musées publics: bilan et perspectives," January 2013, http://www.senat.fr/fileadmin/Fichiers/amdcom/cult/6P_C_Bouchoux_oeuvres_spoliees_.pdf; Ministère de la Culture, dossier de presse "Restitution du tableau 'Triptyque de la Crucifixion,'" February 12, 2018, 26–27. Available at http://www.culture.gouv.fr/Presse/Dossiers-de-presse/Restitution-du-tableau-Triptyque-de-la-Crucifixion-attribue-a-l-atelier-de-Joachim-Patinir-MNR-386-aux-ayants-droit-d-Hertha-et-Henry-Bromberg.
81. Zivie, "Des traces subsistent dans les registres." See also Antoine Froidefond, "Report Lashes France's 'Lack of Ambition' to Return Looted Jewish Art," *The Times of Israel*, April 3, 2018, https://www.timesofisrael.com/report-lashes-frances-lack-of-ambition-to-return-looted-jewish-art/; Agence France-Presse, "Françoise Nyssen met en place une nouvelle mission de restitution des biens juifs spoliés," *Le figaro*, July 26, 2018, http://www.lefigaro.fr/culture/2018/07/26/03004-20180726ARTFIG00264-francoise-nyssen-met-en-place-une-nouvelle-mission-de-restitution-des-biens-juifs-spolies.php?redirect_premium.
82. David Zivie, "The Search for and Return of Looted Cultural Property: A New Turn," presentation for the Association of Art Museum Directors advanced provenance research training workshop, Washington, DC, November 19, 2019.
83. "France to Return 15 Artworks Stolen from Jews during WWII," February 15, 2022, https://www.france24.com/en/europe/20220215-france-to-return-15-artworks-stolen-from-jews-during-wwii; "French Parliament Authorises 'Historic' Return of Art by Klimt and Chagall to Jewish Families," February 21, 2022, https://www.euronews.com/culture/2022/02/16/french-parliament-authorises-historic-return-of-art-by-klimt-and-chagall-to-jewish-familie.
84. With Agence France-Presse, "L'Assemblée nationale décide de faciliter la restitution des oeuvres spoliées par les nazis," *Le Figaro*, June 29, 2023, https://www.lefigaro.fr/flash-actu/l-assemblee-nationale-decide-de-faciliter-la-restitution-des-oeuvres-spoliees-par-les-nazis-20230629.
85. Philippe Dagen, "Dix oeuvres du Louvre sont issues de la collection d'Armand Dorville, spolié sous Vichy," January 22, 2020, https://www.lemonde.fr/culture/article/2020/01/22/dix-uvres-du-louvre-sont-issues-de-la-collection-d-armand-dorville-spolie-sous-vichy_6026791_3246.html; Vincent Noce, "French Museums Face Fresh Legal Action over Refusal to Restitute Works to Jewish Families," July 15, 2021, https://www.theartnewspaper.com/2021/07/15/french-museums-face-fresh-legal-action-over-refusal-to-restitute-works-to-jewish-families.
86. Origins Unknown pilot study, April 1998, "Reason for the Project," https://www.obs-traffic.museum/sites/default/files/ressources/files/origins_unknown_pilot.pdf.
87. Origins Unknown pilot study, April 1998, "Reason for the Project," https://www.obs-traffic.museum/sites/default/files/ressources/files/origins_unknown_pilot.pdf.
88. Eelke Muller, *Rapport museale verwervingen 1940–1948* (Amsterdam: Nederlandse Museumvereniging, 1999), 5.
89. Muller, *Rapport museale verwervingen 1940–1948*.

90. Origins Unknown pilot study, April 1998, "Organization and Implementation of the Research," "Results of the Pilot Research Project," https://www.obs-traffic.museum/sites/default/files/ressources/files/origins_unknown_pilot.pdf.
91. Origins Unknown pilot study, April 1998, "Results of the Pilot Research Project," "Conclusions," https://www.obs-traffic.museum/sites/default/files/ressources/files/origins_unknown_pilot.pdf.
92. Ekkart Committee, "Recommendations Regarding the Restitution of Works of Art," April 2001. Formerly available at restitutiecommissie.nl. Due to website updates, not all reports and press releases remain available. The 2001 report can be found on the Internet Archive at https://web.archive.org/web/20160826232346/ http://restitutiecommissie.nl/en/2001_private_property.html. For later annual reports, see Advisory Committee on the Assessment of Restitution Applications for Items of Cultural Value and the Second World War, Report 2003 at https://www.obs-traffic.museum/sites/default/files/ressources/files/Restitution_Committee_Report_2003.pdf, and Report 2004 at https://www.obs-traffic.museum/sites/default/files/ressources/files/Restitution_Committee_Report_2004.pdf.
93. Ekkart Committee, "Recommendations Regarding the Restitution of Works of Art," section "General research findings," April 2001, available at Internet Archive, https://web.archive.org/web/20160826232346/http://restitutiecommissie.nl/en/2001_private_property.html.
94. Ekkart Committee, "Recommendations Regarding the Restitution of Works of Art," section "Basic principles," April 2001 (their emphasis), available at Internet Archive, https://web.archive.org/web/20160826232346/http://restitutiecommissie.nl/en/2001_private_property.html.
95. Ekkart Committee, "Recommendations Regarding the Restitution of Works of Art," section "Forced sale," April 2001, available at Internet Archive, https://web.archive.org/web/20160826232145/http://restitutiecommissie.nl/en/4_forced_sale.html.
96. Ekkart Committee, "Recommendations Regarding the Restitution of Works of Art," section "Repayment of sales proceeds," April 2001, available at Internet Archive, https://web.archive.org/web/20160826221949/http://restitutiecommissie.nl/en/5_repayment_of_sales_proceeds.html.
97. Ekkart Committee, "Recommendations Regarding the Restitution of Works of Art," section "Repurchasing," April 2001, available at Internet Archive, https://web.archive.org/web/20160826201857/http://restitutiecommissie.nl/en/7_period_allowed_for_repurchasing.html.
98. Ekkart Committee, "Recommendations Regarding the Restitution of Works of Art," section "Proof of title," April 2001, available at Internet Archive, https://web.archive.org/web/20160826223018/http://restitutiecommissie.nl/en/6_proof_of_title.html.
99. Ekkart Committee, "Recommendations Regarding the Restitution of Works of Art," section "Proof of title," April 2001, available at Internet Archive, https://web.archive.org/web/20160826223018/http://restitutiecommissie.nl/en/6_proof_of_title.html.
100. Annemarie Marck and Eelke Muller, "National Panels Advising on Nazi-Looted Art in Austria, France, the United Kingdom, the Netherlands and Germany," in *Fair and Just Solutions?*, ed. Campfens, 75.

101. "Decree Advisory Committee on the Assessment of Restitution Applications for Items of Cultural Value and the Second World War," Article 2, point 5, November 16, 2001. Full text available in *Fair and Just Solutions?*, ed. Campfens, Appendix 11, 289–92. See also "The Restitutions Committee," www.restitutiecommissie.nl/en and "Regulations binding expert opinion procedure," issued in 2011 and updated in 2014, available at Internet Archive, http://web.archive.org/web/20210923085604/https://www.restitutiecommissie.nl/en/regulations_binding_expert_opinion_procedure.html. The Committee issued new regulations in January 2019, available at Internet Archive, http://web.archive.org/web/20211114031802/https://www.restitutiecommissie.nl/en/system/files/Regulations2019.pdf.
102. Restitutiecommissie, "2003: Art dealerships," "Introduction," available at Internet Archive, https://web.archive.org/web/20160826220110/http://www.restitutiecommissie.nl/en/1_introduction.html.
103. Restitutiecommissie, "2003: Art dealerships," section "Theft and Confiscation," available at Internet Archive, https://web.archive.org/web/20160826210154/http://restitutiecommissie.nl/en/4_theft_and_confiscation.html.
104. Restitutiecommissie, "2003: Art dealerships," section "Involuntary Sale," available at Internet Archive, https://web.archive.org/web/20160826211329/http://restitutiecommissie.nl/en/6_involuntary_sale.html.
105. Restitutiecommissie, "2004: Final Recommendations," section "Duration of Liberalized Policy," available at Internet Archive, https://web.archive.org/web/20160826214234/http://restitutiecommissie.nl/en/duration_of_the_term_of_the_current_liberalized_restitution_policy.html; Brief van de Staatssecretaris van Onderwijs, Cultuur en Wetenschap, H. Zijlstra, aan de Voorzitter van de Tweede Kamer der Staten-Generaal, June 22, 2012, https://zoek.officielebekendmakingen.nl/kst-25839-41.html.
106. Restitutiecommissie, "2004: Final recommendations," section "Unjustly recuperated art," available at Internet Archive, https://web.archive.org/web/20160827031628/http://restitutiecommissie.nl/en/artworks_that_were_possibly_unjustly_recuperated_to_the_netherlands_after_the_war.html.
107. Restitutiecommissie, "2004: Final Recommendations," section "Unreturnable stolen art," http://www.restitutiecommissie.nl/en/unreturnable_stolen_works_of_art.html; available at Internet Archive, https://web.archive.org/web/20160826205938/http://restitutiecommissie.nl/en/unreturnable_stolen_works_of_art.html; section "Allocation of repayments," http://www.restitutiecommissie.nl/en/the_allocation_of_any_possible_repayments_for_the_restitution_of_works_of_art.html, available at Internet Archive, https://web.archive.org/web/20160826211317/http://restitutiecommissie.nl/en/the_allocation_of_any_possible_repayments_for_the_restitution_of_works_of_art.html.
108. Restitutiecommissie, "2004: Final Recommendations," section "Preserving research results," http://www.restitutiecommissie.nl/en/preserving_the_results_of_the_research_carried_out.html, available at Internet Archive, https://web.archive.org/web/20160826205938/http://restitutiecommissie.nl/en/unreturnable_stolen_works_of_art.html.
109. Goodman, *Orpheus Clock*, 7–8.
110. Goodman, *Orpheus Clock*, 3, 13–14.

111. Goodman, *Orpheus Clock*, 4–5.
112. Goodman, *Orpheus Clock*, 201–3.
113. Feliciano, *Lost Museum*, 193.
114. Nicholas O'Donnell, *A Tragic Fate: Law and Ethics in the Battle over Nazi-Looted Art* (Chicago: American Bar Association, 2017), 100–1.
115. Goodman, *Orpheus Clock*, 219.
116. Goodman, *Orpheus Clock*, 238.
117. "The Gutmann Collection (Gutmann I)," March 25, 2002, http://www.restitutiecommissie.nl/en/recommendations/recommendation_12.html#anchor-4.
118. "The Gutmann Collection (Gutmann I)," March 25, 2002, http://www.restitutiecommissie.nl/en/recommendations/recommendation_12.html#anchor-4.
119. Goodman, *Orpheus Clock*, 241.
120. Goodman, *Orpheus Clock*, 189.
121. Goodman, *Orpheus Clock*, 242–43.
122. Goodman, *Orpheus Clock*, 243.
123. Goodman, *Orpheus Clock*, 243–48.
124. "Christie's International Announces Worldwide Sales of $947 million," September 16, 2003, *Antiques and the Arts Weekly*, https://www.antiquesandthearts.com/christies-international-announces-worldwide-sales-of-947-million/.
125. Goodman, *Orpheus Clock*, 249–53.
126. Goodman, *Orpheus Clock*, 321.
127. Pieter den Hollander and Melissa Müller, "Jacques Goudstikker," in *Lost Lives, Lost Art*, ed. Melissa Müller and Monika Tatzkow, 230.
128. Cited in Hollander and Müller, "Jacques Goudstikker," 218.
129. Hollander and Müller, "Jacques Goudstikker," 217.
130. Interview with Marei von Saher, October 2, 2019.
131. Restitutiecommissie, recommendation "Goudstikker," December 19, 2005, https://www.restitutiecommissie.nl/en/recommendation/goudstikker/. On communications with the Goodman brothers, interview with Marei von Saher, October 2, 2019.
132. Restitutiecommissie, recommendation "Goudstikker," December 19, 2005, https://www.restitutiecommissie.nl/en/recommendation/goudstikker/.
133. Restitutiecommissie, recommendation "Goudstikker," December 19, 2005, https://www.restitutiecommissie.nl/en/recommendation/goudstikker/.
134. Hollander and Müller, "Jacques Goudstikker," 231.
135. Brief van de Staatssecretaris van Onderwijs, Cultuur en Wetenschap, H. Zijlstra, aan de Voorzitter van de Tweede Kamer der Staten-Generaal, June 22, 2012, https://zoek.officielebekendmakingen.nl/kst-25839-41.html.
136. Brief van de Staatssecretaris van Onderwijs, Cultuur en Wetenschap, H. Zijlstra, aan de Voorzitter van de Tweede Kamer der Staten-Generaal, June 22, 2012, https://zoek.officielebekendmakingen.nl/kst-25839-41.html.
137. Gert-Jan van den Bergh, "New Rules for Returning Art Stolen by the Nazis Are Not Always Fair," March 5, 2015, https://www.dutchnews.nl/features/2015/03/new-rules-for-returning-art-stolen-by-nazis-are-not-always-fair/. Also published in Dutch, February 25, 2015, "Geef alle roofkunst terug aan nazaten," https://www.volkskrant.nl/columns-opinie/geef-alle-roofkunst-terug-aan-nazaten~b5e00ae0/.

138. Willibrord Davids, foreword to Restitutiecommissie, *Report 2016*, 5.
139. See "Recommendations issued in 2016," in Restitutiecommissie, *Report 2016*, 23–44.
140. Nina Siegal, "Are the Dutch Lagging in Efforts to Return Art Looted by the Nazis?," *The New York Times*, May 12, 2017, https://www.nytimes.com/2017/05/12/arts/design/are-the-dutch-lagging-in-efforts-to-return-art-looted-by-the-nazis.html.
141. Oost, "Restitution Policies on Nazi-Looted Art in the Netherlands and the United Kingdom," 153.
142. "New Decree Establishing the Restitutions Committee and Restitutions Committee Regulations," April 21, 2021, https://www.restitutiecommissie.nl/en/news/new-decree-rc/.
143. See Government of the Netherlands press release, "Colonial collections to be returned to Indonesia and Sri Lanka," July 6, 2023, https://www.government.nl/latest/news/2023/07/06/colonial-collections-to-be-returned-to-indonesia-and-sri-lanka.
144. Lust, "Provenance and World War II: Art, Research, and Illusion," in *Holocaust Era Assets*, ed. Jiří Schneider, Jakub Klepal, and Irena Kalhousová, 1050.
145. Doorslaer, "The Expropriation of Jewish Property and Restitution in Belgium," 155.
146. Commission d'étude (Belgium), *Les biens des victimes*, 26, 32n9.
147. Lucien Buysse preface, Commission d'étude (Belgium), *Les biens des victimes*, 8–9.
148. Commission d'étude (Belgium), *Les biens des victimes*, 423–24.
149. Commission d'étude (Belgium), *Les biens des victimes*, 424–25.
150. Commission d'étude (Belgium), *Les biens des victimes*, 424.
151. Commission d'étude (Belgium), *Les biens des victimes*, 426.
152. Commission d'étude (Belgium), *Les biens des victimes*, 429–30.
153. Commission d'étude (Belgium), *Les biens des victimes*, 431.
154. Lust, "Provenance and World War II," 1049.
155. Commission d'étude (Belgium), *Les biens des victimes*, 433.
156. Commission d'étude (Belgium), *Les biens des victimes*, 434.
157. Commission d'étude (Belgium), *Les biens des victimes*, annexe 27, "Rapports de la 2e enquête au sein des institutions culturelles," 253.
158. Commission d'étude (Belgium), *Les biens des victimes*, 454–56.
159. The Commission for the indemnification for the Belgian Jewish community's assets, which were plundered, surrendered, or abandoned during the war 1940–45, *Final Report*, February 4, 2008, 10.
160. Commission for indemnification, *Final Report*, 9.
161. Commission for indemnification, *Final Report*, 17.
162. Commission for indemnification, *Final Report*, 31.
163. Commission for indemnification, *Final Report*, 74. On the restitution of the two items, for which no further details are provided, see Oost, "In an Effort To Do Justice?," 84.
164. Fisher and Weinberger, "Holocaust-Era Looted Art," 14–15. On the research committee, see Karen Chernick, "'We're Coming Late to the Matter Here': Belgian Museums Continue to Struggle With a Flurry of Restitution Claims," artnet.com, December 13, 2019, https://news.artnet.com/art-world/belgium-art-restitution-1731726.

165. Restitution Belgium, "Ethical Principles for the Management and Restitution of Colonial Collections in Belgium," June 2021, https://restitutionbelgium.be/en/report.
166. Catherine Hickley, "'There has been a generational shift': Belgian government to collaborate with Democratic Republic of Congo to return colonial-era Loot," June 22, 2021, https://www.theartnewspaper.com/2021/06/22/there-has-been-a-generational-shift-belgian-government-to-collaborate-with-democratic-republic-of-congo-to-return-colonial-era-loot.
167. Lust interview cited in Oost, "In an Effort To Do Justice?," 82n146.
168. Jennifer Rankin, "'Justice Can Triumph': Painting Looted by Nazis Returned to Owners after 80 Years," February 10, 2022, https://www.theguardian.com/artanddesign/2022/feb/10/justice-can-triumph-painting-looted-by-nazis-returned-to-owners-after-80-years.
169. See lootedart.belgium.be/en/database-unrecovered-works-art-looted-during-second-world-war-belgium.
170. Sels, *Kunst voor Das Reich*; French translation *Le Trésor de guerre des nazis* published in 2023. See also "Nazi-looted artwork still hangs in Belgian museums," *The Brussels Times*, November 30, 2022, https://www.brusselstimes.com/329468/nazi-looted-artwork-still-hangs-in-belgian-museums.

Conclusion

1. Özlem Gezer, "Interview with a Phantom: Cornelius Gurlitt Shares His Secrets," *Spiegel Online*, November 17, 2013, https://www.spiegel.de/international/germany/spiegel-interview-with-cornelius-gurlitt-about-munich-art-find-a-933953.html.
2. Gezer, "Interview with a Phantom"; Ronald, *Hitler's Art Thief*, 314–17.
3. See Deutsches Zentrum Kulturgutverluste, "Provenienzrecherche Gurlitt," https://www.kulturgutverluste.de/Webs/DE/ProjektGurlitt/Provenienzrecherche-Gurlitt/Index.html;jsessionid=CEEEFA042CA47A12C4392568AF2F6573.m1
4. See the official trailer on IMDb, https://www.imdb.com/title/tt2177771/.
5. See Deutsches Zentrum Kulturgutverluste, "Provenienzrecherche Gurlitt," https://www.kulturgutverluste.de/Webs/DE/ProjektGurlitt/Provenienzrecherche-Gurlitt/Index.html;jsessionid=CEEEFA042CA47A12C4392568AF2F6573.m1; Nadine Wojcik, "Gurlitt Trove: Research on Nazi-Looted Art Ends," May 28, 2020.
6. Kareem Shaheen and Ian Black, "Beheaded Syrian Scholar Refused to Lead Isis to Hidden Palmyra Antiquities," *The Guardian*, August 19, 2015, https://www.theguardian.com/world/2015/aug/18/isis-beheads-archaeologist-syria.
7. Tweet by Emmanuel Macron, November 28, 2017, https://twitter.com/EmmanuelMacron/status/935488489663156226.
8. Felwine Sarr and Bénédicte Savoy, "The Restitution of African Cultural Heritage: Toward a New Relational Ethics," trans. Drew S. Burk, November 2018.
9. See "Restitution de 26 oeuvres à la République du Bénin," https://www.quaibranly.fr/fr/collections/vie-des-collections/actualites/restitution-de-26-oeuvres-a-la-republique-du-benin/; Gareth Harris, "Looted African Works that France Has

304   NOTES TO PAGES 245–247

Promised to Return to Benin Will Be Shown in Paris Museum for One Last Time," September 15, 2021, https://www.theartnewspaper.com/2021/09/15/looted-african-works-that-france-has-promised-to-return-to-benin-will-be-shown-in-paris-museum-for-one-last-time.

10. In 2023, the French Minister of Culture proposed to parliament three laws that would facilitate restitution of colonial items, human remains and Nazi-era art. The law related to Nazi-era art passed both houses of parliament unanimously in May and June 2023. See "Trois lois-cadres sur les restitutions seront soumises au vote du Parlement en 2023," *Le Monde,* January 16, 2023, https://www.lemonde.fr/culture/article/2023/01/16/trois-lois-cadres-sur-les-restitutions-seront-soumises-au-vote-du-parlement-en-2023_6158013_3246.html; With Agence France-Presse, "L'Assemblée nationale décide de faciliter la restitution des oeuvres spoliées par les nazis," *Le Figaro,* June 29, 2023, https://www.lefigaro.fr/flash-actu/l-assemblee-nationale-decide-de-faciliter-la-restitution-des-oeuvres-spoliees-par-les-nazis-20230629. See also Government of the Netherlands press release, "Colonial collections to be returned to Indonesia and Sri Lanka," July 6, 2023, https://www.government.nl/latest/news/2023/07/06/colonial-collections-to-be-returned-to-indonesia-and-sri-lanka; Restitution Belgium, "Ethical Principles for the Management and Restitution of Colonial Collections in Belgium," June 2021, https://restitutionbelgium.be/en/report.

11. Dan Hicks, *The Brutish Museums: The Benin Bronzes, Colonial Violence and Cultural Restitution* (London: Pluto Press, 2020).

12. See Humboldt Forum, https://www.humboldtforum.org.

13. See, for instance, Jo Angouri, Marina Paraskevaidi, and Ruth Wodak, "Discourses of Cultural Heritage in Times of Crisis: The Case of the Parthenon Marbles," *Journal of Sociolinguistics* 21, no. 2 (April 2017): 208–37.

14. See Nancy Einreinhofer, *The American Art Museum: Elitism and Democracy* (London: Leicester University Press, 1997).

15. See Gaudenzi and Swenson, "Looted Art and Restitution in the Twentieth Century," 517.

16. See contributions to Campfens, *Fair and Just Solutions?*

17. See, for instance, Judge Arthur Tompkins, "A Permanent International Art Crime Tribunal?," *Art Crime* (2016): 327–36, https://doi.org/10.1007/978-1-137-40757-3_24.

18. See the Court of Arbitration for Art, https://www.cafa.world/cafa/.

19. Eizenstat cited in David d'Arcy, "Washington Principles—'A Glass More than Half-Full,' The Anniversary Berlin Conference," *IFAR Journal* 19, no. 3 (2018): 24; William Cohan, "Five Countries Slow to Address Nazi-Looted Art, U.S. Expert Says," *New York Times,* November 26, 2018, https://www.nytimes.com/2018/11/26/arts/design/five-countries-slow-to-address-nazi-looted-art-us-expert-says.html.

20. Wesley Fisher and Ruth Weinberger, "Holocaust-Era Looted Art: A Current World-Wide Overview," Conference on Jewish Material Claims against Germany and World Jewish Restitution Organization, September 10, 2014, 5.

21. Laetitia La Follette, "Looted Antiquities, Art Museums and Restitution in the United States since 1970," *Journal of Contemporary History* 52, no. 3 (2017): 675–77.

22. American Alliance of Museums, "Unlawful Appropriation of Objects during the Nazi Era," https://www.aam-us.org/programs/ethics-standards-and-professional-practices/unlawful-appropriation-of-objects-during-the-nazi-era/. See also Nancy H. Yeide, Konstantin Akinsha, and Amy L. Walsh, *The AAM Guide to Provenance Research* (Washington, DC: American Association of Museums, 2001).
23. See the Nazi-Era Provenance Internet Portal at www.nepip.org. The information is outdated and not recommended for provenance research. An updated AAMD statement of principles related to Nazi-era art from May 2007 is available at https://aamd.org/sites/default/files/document/Nazi-looted%20art_clean_06_2007.pdf. An AAM statement, "Unlawful Appropriation of Objects during the Nazi Era," is available at https://www.aam-us.org/programs/ethics-standards-and-professional-practices/unlawful-appropriation-of-objects-during-the-nazi-era.
24. The Museum of Fine Arts, Boston, after facing controversy in the late 1990s for displaying Nazi-looted art and acquiring stolen antiquities, has in recent years taken a more proactive approach to provenance research. In 2010, the museum created an endowed Curator of Provenance position and in several cases has initiated settlement agreements with rightful owners discovered through research. See Geoff Edgers, "A Detective's Work at the MFA," *Boston Globe*, December 11, 2011, https://www.bostonglobe.com/arts/2011/12/11/detective-work-mfa/6iaei4YOQOj83s9u3YfDXO/story.html; Museum of Fine Arts, Boston, "Provenance Research," https://www.mfa.org/collections/provenance.
25. The full text of the HEAR Act is available at https://www.gpo.gov/fdsys/pkg/BILLS-114hr6130enr/pdf/BILLS-114hr6130enr.pdf.
26. See, for instance, the decision by the New York State Supreme Court, appellate division, on July 9, 2019, in *Reif v. Nagy*. The lawsuit was filed by heirs of Fritz Grünbaum over two Egon Schiele drawings held by dealer Richard Nagy: https://www.courthousenews.com/wp-content/uploads/2019/07/Reif-v-Nagy.pdf. On museums' use of legal technicalities, see Jennifer Kreder, "The New Battleground of Museum Ethics and Holocaust-Era Claims: Technicalities Trumping Justice or Responsible Stewardship for the Public Trust?," *Oregon Law Review* 88, no. 37 (2009): 37–47.
27. Court decisions and other information on the Norton Simon case can be found through the US Supreme Court docket system, case no. 18–1057, at supremecourt.gov/docket.
28. Interview with Marei von Saher, October 2, 2019.
29. See, for instance, protests against opioid money at the Guggenheim Museum: Liam Stack, "Guggenheim Museum Says It Won't Accept Gifts From Sackler Family," *New York Times*, March 22, 2019, https://www.nytimes.com/2019/03/22/arts/guggenheim-sackler-family-donations.html. On broader museum ethics, see Elaine A. King and Gail Levin, eds., *Ethics and the Visual Arts* (New York: Allworth Press, 2006); Janet Marstine, Alexander Bauer, and Chelsea Haines, eds., *New Directions in Museum Ethics* (London: Routledge, 2013); Jane Milosch and Nick Pearce, eds., *Collecting and Provenance: A Multidisciplinary Approach* (Lanham, MD: Rowman & Littlefield, 2019).

Selected Bibliography

Archives

Archives Nationales, France
   3W, Haute Cour de Justice
   AMN, Archives des Musées Nationaux
   AJ/40, Archives Allemandes
   F21, Beaux-Arts
Archives of American Art, Smithsonian Institution, Washington, DC
   W. G. Constable papers
   Walker Hancock oral history
   Thomas Carr Howe papers
   James Rorimer papers
   George Leslie Stout oral history
   George Leslie Stout papers
Imperial War Museum, London
   87/19/1, Private papers of Miss A. O. Popham
Ministère de l'Europe et des Affaires Etrangères, La Courneuve, France
   209SUP, Récupération artistique
Nationaal Archief, The Hague, Netherlands
   2.08.42, Stichting Nederlands Kunstbezit
   2.14.73
National Archives of the United Kingdom
   T 209
   F.O. 371
   F.O. 924
   F.O. 1047
   F.O. 1057
National Gallery of Art Archives (NGA), Washington, DC
   James Rorimer papers
   Edith Standen papers
Rijksarchief in België, Brussels (RB)
   6B/68.37813, Ministry of Instruction
   DER, Dienst voor Economische Recuperatie
United States National Archives and Records Administration (NARA), College Park, Maryland
   RG 59, The State Department
   RG 84, The State Department
   RG 239, The Roberts Commission
   RG 260, Office of Military Government, United States (OMGUS)
   RG 331, Monuments, Fine Arts and Archives

Newspapers and Periodicals

Antiques and the Arts Weekly
The Art Newspaper
Bloomberg
Boston Globe
The Brussels Times
Burlington Magazine
College Art Journal
Deutsche Welle
Le Figaro
Financial Times
The Guardian
Jewish Telegraphic Agency
Journal Officiel de la République Française
Le Monde
The New York Times
The Outlook
Résistance
Der Spiegel
The Times of Israel
De Waarheid

Memoirs and Other First-Hand Accounts

Breker, Arno. *Paris, Hitler et Moi*. Paris: Presses de la Cité, 1970.
Clay, Lucius D. *Decision in Germany*. New York: Doubleday, 1950.
Farmer, Walter I. *The Safekeepers: A Memoir of the Arts at the End of World War II*. Berlin: Walter de Gruyter, 2000.
Farmer, Walter. "The Wiesbaden Manifesto of 7 November 1945." *Jahrbuch Preussischer Kulturbesitz* 33 (1996): 91–119.
Goodman, Simon. *The Orpheus Clock: The Search for My Family's Art Treasures Stolen by the Nazis*. New York: Scribner, 2015.
Hall, Ardelia. "The Recovery of Cultural Objects Dispersed during World War II." *Department of State Bulletin* 25 (August 27, 1951): 337–44.
Hall, Ardelia R. "The Transfer of Residual Works of Art from Munich to Austria." *College Art Journal* 11, no. 3 (Spring 1952): 192–94.
Hancock, Walker. "Experiences of a Monuments Officer in Germany." *College Art Journal* 5, no. 4 (May 1946): 271–311.
Hancock, Walker, with Edward Connery Lathem. *A Sculptor's Fortunes*. Gloucester, MA: Cape Ann Historical Association, 1997.
Howe, Thomas C., Jr. *Salt Mines and Castles: The Discovery and Restitution of Looted European Art*. Indianapolis, IN: Bobbs-Merrill, 1946.
Kirstein, Lincoln. "The Quest of the Golden Lamb." *Town and Country* 100, no. 4276 (September 1945): 114–15, 182–87, 198.
Posey, Robert K. "Protection of Cultural Materials during Combat." *College Art Journal* 5, no. 2 (January 1946): 127–31.

Rorimer, James, with Gilbert Rabin. *Survival: The Salvage and Protection of Art in War*. New York: Abelard Press, 1950.
Salles, Georges. *Au Louvre: Scènes de la vie du musée*. Paris: Editions Domat, 1950.
Skilton, John D., Jr. *Memoirs of a Monuments Officer: Protecting European Artworks*. 1948. Reprint, Portland, OR: Inkwater Press, 2008.
Speer, Albert. *Inside the Third Reich*. New York: Macmillan, 1970.
Valland, Rose. *Le front de l'art: Défense des collections françaises, 1939–1945*. 1961. Reprint, with a foreword by the publisher. Paris: Réunion des Musées Nationaux, 1997.
Woolley, Lt.-Col. Sir Leonard. *A Record of the Work Done by the Military Authorities for the Protection of the Treasures of Art and History in War Areas*. London: His Majesty's Stationery Office, 1947.

Other Primary Sources

Advisory Committee on the Assessment of Restitution Applications for Items of Cultural Value and the Second World War. *Annual Report*. The Hague, 2005.
Association des écrivains combattants. *Anthologie des écrivains morts à la guerre, 1939–1945*. Paris: Albin Michel, 1960.
"Atlantic Charter." August 14, 1941. http://avalon.law.yale.edu/wwii/atlantic.asp.
Bouchoux, Corinne. "Oeuvres culturelles spoliées ou au passé flou et musées publics: bilan et perspectives." Report of the French Senate. January 2013, senat.fr/fileadmin/Fichiers/amdcom/cult/6P_C_Bouchoux_oeuvres_spoliees_.pdf.
Cassou, Jean, ed. *Le pillage par les Allemands des oeuvres d'art et des bibliothèques*. Paris: Editions du Centre, 1947.
Chefs-d'Oeuvre Récupérés en Allemagne. Palais des Beaux-Arts, Brussels, November–December 1948.
Christiane Gentili di Giuseppe et al. v. Musée du Louvre, Court of Appeal of Paris, June 2, 1999 (English). Available in the ArThemis database, Art-Law Centre, University of Geneva, plone.unige.ch/art-adr.
Commandement en Chef Français en Allemagne. *Répertoire des biens spoliés en France durant la guerre 1939–1945*. Vol. 2 of *Tableaux, tapisseries et sculptures*. Berlin: Bureau Central des Restitutions, 1947.
Commission Consultative des Dommages et des Réparations, *Emprise Allemande sur la Pensée Française*. Monographie P.F. 5: Œuvres d'art. [Paris]: Imprimerie Nationale, 1947.
Commission d'étude sur le sort des biens des membres de la Communauté juive de Belgique spoliés ou délaissés pendant la guerre 1940–1945 (Buysse Commission). *Les biens des victimes des persécutions anti-Juives en Belgique: Spoliation, Rétablissement des droits, Résultats de la Commission d'étude*. July 2001.
The Commission for the indemnification for the Belgian Jewish community's assets, which were plundered, surrendered, or abandoned during the war 1940–1945. *Final report*. February 4, 2008. https://www.combuysse.fgov.be/sites/default/files/eindrapport_commissie_schadeloosstelling_2_en_2.pdf.
"Declaration of the United Nations." January 1, 1942. http://avalon.law.yale.edu/20th_century/decade03.asp.
La Documentation Française. *Spoliations et Restitutions des biens culturels publics et privés (objets d'art ou précieux)*. No. 1109, April 1949.

Fisher, Wesley, and Ruth Weinberger. "Holocaust-Era Looted Art: A Current World-Wide Overview." Conference on Jewish Material Claims against Germany and World Jewish Restitution Organization, September 10, 2014.

Foreign Relations of the United States. *The Conference of Berlin (Potsdam Conference), 1945*. 2 vols. Washington, DC: United States Government Printing Office, 1960.

Foreign Relations of the United States. *Diplomatic Papers, 1943*. Vol. 1, *General*. Washington, DC: United States Government Printing Office, 1963.

Herkomst Gezocht (Origins Unknown, Netherlands). Pilot study, April 1998. https://www.obs-traffic.museum/sites/default/files/ressources/files/origins_unknown_pilot.pdf.

"Herwonnen Kunstbezit: Keuze-tentoonstelling van uit Duitschland teruggevoerde Nederlandsche Kunstschatten." Centraal Museum Utrecht, June 22–September 22, 1946.

"Herwonnen Kunstbezit: Tentoonstelling van uit Duitschland tereggekeerde Nederlandsche Kunstschatten." March–May 1946.

Laclotte, Michel, ed. *De Giotto à Bellini: Les primitifs italiens dans les musées de France, Mai-Juillet*. Paris: Editions des Musées nationaux, 1956.

"Laws of War: Laws and Customs of War on Land (Hague II)." July 29, 1899.

"Memorandum of the Netherlands Government Containing the Claims of the Netherlands to Reparations from Germany." 1945. Reproduced in S. I. P. van Campen, *The Quest for Security: Some Aspects of Netherlands Foreign Policy, 1945–1950*. The Hague: Martinus Nijhoff, 1958, Appendix 5, 205–18.

Ministère de la culture et de la communication (France). "Rapport du groupe de travail sur les provenances d'oeuvres récupérées après la Seconde Guerre mondiale remis à Madame Audrey Azoulay, Ministre de la Culture et de la Communication, March 2017." https://www.ladocumentationfrancaise.fr/rapports-publics/174000602-rapport-du-groupe-de-travail-sur-les-provenances-d-oeuvres-recuperees-apres-la.

Ministère de la Culture et de la Communication. "Restitution aux ayants droit de M. Richard Neumann et de M. Josef Wiener de sept tableaux spoliés par les Nazis." March 19, 2013.

Ministère de l'Education Nationale. "Les Chefs-d'Oeuvre des Collections Françaises retrouvées en Allemagne par la Commission de Récupération Artistique et les Services Alliés." June–August 1946.

Mission d'étude sur la spoliation des Juifs de France. *Rapport Général*. Paris: La Documentation Française, 2000.

Mitterrand, François. "Allocution de M. François Mitterrand, Président de la République, sur la restitution à la France d'une collection de tableaux, notamment du peintre Claude Monet, l'amitié et la coopération franco-allemandes, Mulhouse le 30 mai 1994." https://translanth.hypotheses.org/ueber/mitterand [sic].

Muller, Eelke. *Rapport museale verwervingen 1940–1948*. Amsterdam: Nederlandse Museumvereniging, 1999.

"Ordonnance du 9 août 1944 relative au rétablissement de la légalité républicaine sur le territoire continental." legifrance.gouv.fr/affichTexte.do?cidTexte=LEGITEXT000006071212.

Presidential Advisory Commission on Holocaust Assets in the United States. Commission Final Report. "Plunder and Restitution." December 2000. http://govinfo.library.unt.edu/pcha/index-1.htm.

Restitutiecommissie, the Netherlands. Annual reports at restitutiecommissie.nl.

Restitution Belgium, "Ethical Principles for the Management and Restitution of Colonial Collections in Belgium," June 2021. https://restitutionbelgium.be/en/report.

Sarr, Felwine, and Bénédicte Savoy. "Rapport sur la restitution du patrimoine cultural africain – Vers une nouvelle éthique relationnelle, November 29, 2018. https://www.vie-publique.fr/rapport/38563-la-restitution-du-patrimoine-culturel-africain.

"St. James Agreement." June 12, 1941. http://avalon.law.yale.edu/imt/imtjames.asp.

Terezin Declaration. June 30, 2009. https://www.state.gov/prague-holocaust-era-assets-conference-terezin-declaration/.

Trautmann, Catherine. Déclaration de Mme Catherine Trautmann, ministre de la culture et de la communication, sur la restitution du tableau de Claude Monet "Nymphéas" à la famille de Paul Rosenberg spoliée par les nazis durant la seconde guerre mondiale, Paris. April 29, 1999. https://www.vie-publique.fr/discours/188994-declaration-de-mme-catherine-trautmann-ministre-de-la-culture-et-de-la.

Vilnius Forum Declaration. October 5, 2000. https://www.lootedartcommission.com/vilnius-forum.

Washington Conference Principles on Nazi-Confiscated Art. December 3, 1998. state.gov/washington-conference-principles-on-nazi-confiscated-art/.

Zivie, David. Mission sur le traitement des oeuvres et biens culturels ayant fait l'objet de spoliations pendant le Second Guerre mondiale. Rapport à Madame Françoise Nyssen, Ministre de la Culture. *"Des Traces Subsistent dans des Registres . . ." Biens culturels spoliées pendant la Second Guerre mondiale: Une ambition pour rechercher, retrouver, restituer et expliquer.* February 2018.

Zivie, David. "The Search for and Return of Looted Cultural Property: A New Turn." Presentation for the Association of Art Museum Directors Advanced Provenance Research Training Workshop. November 19, 2019. Washington, DC.

Interviews and Conversations

Thierry Bachou
Evelien Campfens
Simon Goodman
Corinne Hershkovitch
Marc Masurovsky
Marianne Rosenberg
Marei von Saher
Perry Schrier
Filip Strubbe
Wouter Veraart
David Zivie

Websites

Agence France-Presse: afp.com
ArThemis database, Art-Law Centre, University of Geneva: plone.unige.ch/art-adr
The Art Newspaper: theartnewspaper.com
artnet: artnet.com

Barron's: barrons.com
British Broadcasting Corporation: bbc.com
Burris, Schoenberg & Walden, LLP: bslaw.com
The Avalon Project: Documents in Law, History and Diplomacy: avalon.law.yale.edu
Commission pour l'indemnisation des victimes de spoliations intervenues du fait des législations antisémites en vigueur pendant l'Occupation (France): civs.gouv.fr
The Court for Arbitration of Art: cafa.world/cafa/
Courthouse News Service: courthousenews.com
Cultural Plunder by the Einsatzstab Reichsleiter Rosenberg: errproject.org/jeudepaume
The Database on the Unrecovered Works of Art Looted during the Second World War in Belgium: lootedart.belgium.be/en/database-unrecovered-works-art-looted-during-second-world-war-belgium
Dictionary of Art Historians: arthistorians.info
Dutch Jewish Genealogical Database: dutchjewry.org
Euronews.com
France24.com
German Lost Art Foundation: kulturgutverluste.de
Government of the Netherlands: government.nl
Herkomst Gezocht (Origins Unknown, Netherlands): herkomstgezocht.nl. Updated information available at Rijksdienst voor het Cultureel Erfgoed (see below).
Historicalstatistics.org: Portal for Historical Statistics, ed. Rodney Edvinsson: historicalstatistics.org
Historical Dollar-to-Marks Currency Conversion page, ed. Harold Marcuse: marcuse.faculty.history.ucsb.edu/projects/currency.htm#tables
Humboldt Forum: humboldtforum.org
Institut national d'études démographiques: ined.fr
International Council of Museums: icom.museum
International Institute of Social History: iisg.amsterdam/en
Kazerne Dossin: kazernedossin.eu
Legifrance: legifrance.gouv.fr
MeasuringWorth: measuringworth.com
Metropolitan Museum of Art: metmuseum.org
Ministry of Culture, France: culture.gouv.fr
Ministry of Culture, France. Base Rose Valland (MNR-Jeu de Paume): pop.culture.gouv.fr
Monuments Men and Women Foundation: monumentsmenandwomenfnd.org
Musée de l'Ordre de la Libération: ordredelaliberation.fr
Musée du Petit Palais, Avignon: petit-palais.org
Musées Royaux des Beaux-arts de Belgique: fine-arts-museum.be
Musées Royaux d'Art et d'Histoire: kmkg-mrah.be
Museum Boijmans Van Beuningen: boijmans.nl
Philadelphia Museum of Art: philamuseum.org
The Phillips Collection: phillipscollection.org
République Française, Vie Publique: vie-publique.fr
Restitutie Commissie (Netherlands): restitutiecommissie.nl
Restitution Belgium: restitutionbelgium.be
Rijksdienst voor het Cultureel Erfgoed (Cultural Heritage Agency, Netherlands): cultureelerfgoed.nl; portal on items in Nederlands Kunstbezit collectie (NK Collection): wo2.collectienederland.nl

Rijksmuseum, Amsterdam: rijksmuseum.nl
Supreme Court of the United States: supremecourt.gov
Twitter: twitter.com
United Nations Treaty Collection: treaties.un.org
United States Department of State: state.gov
United States Holocaust Memorial and Museum: ushmm.org
United States National Archives and Records Administration Text Message blog: https://text-message.blogs.archives.gov
Web Gallery of Art: wga.hu

Films

George Clooney, director. *The Monuments Men*. Columbia Pictures, 2014.
John Frankenheimer, director. *The Train*. United Artists, 1964.
Simon Curtis, director. *Woman in Gold*. BBC Films, 2015.

Books, Articles, Government Studies

Aalders, Gerard. *Berooid: De beroofde joden en het Nederlandse restitutiebeleid sinds 1945*. Amsterdam: Boom, 2001.
Aalders, Gerard. *Nazi Looting: The Plunder of Dutch Jewry during the Second World War*. Translated by Arnold Pomerans with Erica Pomerans. Oxford: Berg, 2004.
Aalders, Gerard. "Pillage et (non) restitution des oeuvres d'art aux Pays-Bas (1940–2001)." Translated by Claire Darmon. *Revue d'histoire de la Shoah* 186 (January–June 2007): 195–216.
Akinsha, Konstantin, and Grigorii Kozlov. *Beautiful Loot: The Soviet Plunder of Europe's Art Treasures*. New York: Random House, 1995.
Akinsha, Konstantin. "Stalin's Decrees and Soviet Trophy Brigades: Compensation, Restitution in Kind, or 'Trophies' of War?" *International Journal of Cultural Property* 17 (2010): 195–216.
Andrieu, Claire. *La spoliation financière*. Paris: La Documentation Française, 2000.
Angouri, Jo, Marina Paraskevaidi, and Ruth Wodak. "Discourses of Cultural Heritage in Times of Crisis: The Case of the Parthenon Marbles." *Journal of Sociolinguistics* 21, no. 2 (April 2017): 208–37.
Arblaster, Paul. *A History of the Low Countries*. 2nd ed. Houndmills, NY: Palgrave Macmillan, 2006.
L'Association des Ecrivains Combattants, *L'anthologie des écrivains morts à la guerre, 1939–1945*. Paris: Albin Michel, 1960.
Baldoli, Claudia, and Andrew Knapp. *Forgotten Blitzes: France and Italy under Allied Air Attack, 1940–1945*. London: Continuum, 2012.
Baruch, Marc Olivier. *Servir l'Etat Français: L'administration en France de 1940 à 1944*. Paris: Fayard, 1997.
Bazyler, Michael. *Holocaust Justice: The Battle for Restitution in America's Courts*. New York: New York University Press, 2003.
Bazyler, Michael, and Roger P. Alford, eds. *Holocaust Restitution: Perspectives on the Litigation and Its Legacy*. New York: New York University Press, 2006.

Bellisari, Andrew. "The Art of Decolonization: The Battle for Algeria's French Art, 1962–70." *Journal of Contemporary History* 52, no. 3 (2017): 625–45.

Bertrand Dorléac, Laurence. *L'art de la défaite, 1940–1944*. Paris: Seuil, 1993.

Blom, J. C. H. "The Persecution of the Jews in the Netherlands: A Comparative Western European Perspective." *European History Quarterly* 19 (1989): 333–51.

Bouchoux, Corinne. *Rose Valland: La Résistance au Musée*. La Crèche: Geste éditions, 2006.

Bouchoux, Corinne. *"Si les tableaux pouvaient parler . . .": Le traitement politique et médiatique des retours d'œuvres d'art pillées et spoliées par les nazis (France 1945–2008)*. Rennes: Presses Universitaires de Rennes, 2011.

Bradsher, Greg. "A British Art Historian and Collector Monuments Man: Douglas Cooper." US National Archives, February 6, 2014. text-message.blogs.archives.gov/2014/02/06/a-british-art-historian-and-collector-monuments-man-douglas-cooper.

Bradsher, Greg. "A British Monuments Man Killed in Action: Ronald Balfour." US National Archives, February 13, 2014. text-message.blogs.archives.gov/2014/02/13/a-british-monuments-man-killed-in-action-ronald-balfour.

Bradsher, Greg. "The Monuments Men in March 1945: Ronald Balfour and Walker Hancock." US National Archives, March 31, 2015. text-message.blogs.archives.gov/2015/03/31/the-monuments-men-in-march-1945-ronald-balfour-and-walker-hancock.

Bradsher, Greg. "Walter J. Huchthausen: A Monuments Man Killed in Action." US National Archives, December 12, 2013. text-message.blogs.archives.gov/2013/12/12/walter-j-huchthausen-a-monuments-man-killed-in-action.

Buruma, Ian. "The Argument that Saved Paris." *NYRblog*, October 14, 2014. nybooks.com/blogs/nyrblog/2014/oct/15/argument-saved-paris/.

Buruma, Ian. *Year Zero: A History of 1945*. New York: Penguin, 2013.

Buxbaum, Richard. "From Paris to London: The Legal History of European Reparation Claims: 1946–1953." *Berkeley Journal of International Law* 31, no. 2 (2013): 323–47.

Buxbaum, Richard. "A Legal History of International Reparations." *Berkeley Journal of International Law* 23, no. 2 (2005): 314–46.

Campbell, Elizabeth. "Claiming National Heritage: State Appropriation of Nazi Art Plunder in Postwar Western Europe." *Journal of Contemporary History* 55, no. 4 (October 2020): 793–822.

Campfens, Evelien, ed. *Fair and Just Solutions? Alternatives to Litigation in Nazi-Looted Art Disputes: Status Quo and New Developments*. The Hague: Eleven International Publishing, 2015.

Chapman, Herrick. *France's Long Reconstruction: In Search of the Modern Republic*. Harvard: Harvard University Press, 2018.

Coeuré, Sophie. "Cultural Looting and Restitution at the Dawn of the Cold War: The French Recovery Missions in Eastern Europe." *Journal of Contemporary History* 52, no. 3 (2017): 588–606.

Cone, Michèle. *Artists under Vichy: A Case of Prejudice and Persecution*. Princeton, NJ: Princeton University Press, 1992.

Conway, Martin. *The Sorrows of Belgium: Liberation and Political Reconstruction, 1944–1947*. Oxford: Oxford University Press, 2012.

Cotler, Irwin. "The Holocaust, Thefticide, and Restitution: A Legal Perspective." *Cardozo Law Review* 601 (1998): 602.

D'Arcy, David. "Washington Principles—'A Glass More than Half-Full,' The Anniversary Berlin Conference." *IFAR Journal* 19, no. 3 (2018): 22–26.

David, Géraldine, and Kim Oosterlinck. "War, Inflation, Monetary Reforms and the Art Market." *European Historical Economics Society*, working paper no. 12 (January 2012): 1–32.

Dean, Martin, Constantin Goschler, and Philipp Ther, eds. *Robbery and Restitution: The Conflict over Jewish Property in Europe*. New York: Berghahn Books, 2007.

Deshmukh, Marion. "Recovering Culture: The Berlin National Gallery and the U.S. Occupation, 1945–1949." *Central European History* 27, no. 4 (Winter 1994): 411–39.

Dellheim, Charles. "Framing Nazi Art Loot." In *The Art of Being Jewish in Modern Times*, edited by Barbara Kirshenblatt-Gimblett and Jonathan Karp, 319–34. Philadelphia: University of Pennsylvania Press, 2008.

Delplancq, Thierry. "Des Paroles et des actes: L'administration bruxelloise et le registre des Juifs, 1940–1941." *Cahiers d'histoire du temps présent* 12 (2003): 141–79.

Direction des musées de France. *Pillages et Restitutions: Le Destin des oeuvres d'art sorties de France pendant la Second Guerre Mondiale*. Paris: Adam Biro, 1997.

Edsel, Robert. *The Monuments Men: Allied Heroes, Nazi Thieves, and the Greatest Treasure Hunt in History*. New York: Center Street, 2009.

Einreinhofer, Nancy. *The American Art Museum: Elitism and Democracy*. London: Leicester University Press, 1997.

Eizenstat, Stuart. *Imperfect Justice: Looted Assets, Slave Labor, and the Unfinished Business of World War II*. New York: Public Affairs, 2003.

Feigenbaum, Gail, and Inge Reist, eds. *Provenance: An Alternate History of Art*. Los Angeles: Getty Research Institute, 2012.

Feliciano, Hector. *The Lost Museum: The Nazi Conspiracy to Steal the World's Greatest Works of Art*. New York: Basic Books, 1997.

Fisch, Stefan, ed. *National Approaches to the Governance of Historical Heritage over Time: A Comparative Report*. Amsterdam: IOS Press, 2008.

Flanner, Janet. *Men and Monuments: Profiles of Picasso, Matisse, Braque, and Malraux*. 1957. Reprint, New York: Da Capo Press, 1990.

Fogg, Shannon. *Stealing Home: Looting, Restitution, and Reconstructing Jewish Lives in France, 1942–1947*. Oxford: Oxford University Press, 2017.

Freeman, Kirrily. "The Bells, Too, Are Fighting: The Fate of European Church Bells in the Second World War." *Canadian Journal of History* 43, no. 3 (2008): 417–50.

Friedländer, Saul. *Kurt Gerstein: The Ambiguity of Good*. Translated by Charles Fullman. New York: Alfred A Knopf, 1969.

Frijhoff, Willem, and Marijke Spies. *Dutch Culture in a European Perspective: 1950, Prosperity and Welfare*. New York: Palgrave Macmillan, 2004.

Gallas, Elisabeth. "Locating the Jewish Future: The Restoration of Looted Cultural Property in Early Postwar Europe." *Naharaim* 9, nos. 1–2 (2015): 25–47.

Gaudenzi, Bianca, and Astrid Swenson. "Looted Art and Restitution in the Twentieth Century—Toward a Global Perspective." *Journal of Contemporary History* 52, no. 3 (2017): 491–518.

Genet Delacroix, Marie Claude. "Le budget des Beaux-Arts sous l'Occupation: Un budget de circonstances?" In *Comité pour l'histoire économique et financère de la France, La direction du Budget entre doctrines et réalités, 1919–1944*, 413–38. Paris: Ministère de l'Economie, des Finances et de l'Industrie, 2001.

Gensburger, Sarah. *Images d'un pillage: Album de la Spoliation des Juifs à Paris*. Paris: Editions Textuel, 2010.

Gilbert, Mark. *Cold War Europe: The Politics of a Contested Continent*. Lanham: Rowman and Littlefield, 2015.
Gordon, Bertram. "Warfare and Tourism: Paris in World War II." *Annals of Tourism Research* 25, no. 3 (1998): 616–38.
Gordon, Bertram. *War Tourism: Second World War France from Defeat and Occupation to the Creation of Heritage*. Ithaca, NY: Cornell University Press, 2018.
Goschler, Constantin, Philipp Ther, and Claire Andrieu, eds. *Spoliations et restitutions des biens juifs en Europe, XXe siècle*. Paris: Editions Autrement, 2007.
Green, Nancy. *The Limits of Transnationalism*. Chicago: University of Chicago Press, 2019.
Green, Nancy. "Trials of Transnationalism: It's Not as Easy as It Looks." *The Journal of Modern History* 89 (December 2017): 851–74.
Griffioen, Pim, and Ron Zeller. "Anti-Jewish Policy and Organization of Deportations in France and the Netherlands: A Comparative Study." *Holocaust Genocide Studies* 20, no. 3 (December 2006): 437–73.
Griffioen, Pim, and Ron Zeller. "La persécution des Juifs en Belgique et aux Pays-Bas pendant la Seconde Guerre mondiale: une analyse comparative." *Cahiers d'Histoire du Temps Présent/Bijdragen tot de Eigentijdse Geschiedenis* 5 (November 1998/May 1999): 73–164.
Grimsted, Patricia Kennedy. "Legalizing 'Compensation' and the Spoils of War: The Russian Law on Displaced Cultural Valuables and the Manipulation of Historical Memory." *International Journal of Cultural Property* 17 (2010): 217–55.
Grimsted, Patricia Kennedy. *Reconstructing the Record of Nazi Cultural Plunder: A Guide to the Dispersed Archives of the Einsatzstab Reichsleiter Rosenberg (ERR) and the Postwar Retrieval of ERR Loot*. Amsterdam: International Institute of Social History, 2011.
Hand, Seán, and Steven Katz, eds. *Post-Holocaust France and the Jews, 1945–1955*. New York: New York University Press, 2015.
Herf, Jeffrey. *Divided Memory: The Nazi Past in the Two Germanys*. Cambridge, MA: Harvard University Press, 1997.
Hershkovitch, Corinne. *La restitution des oeuvres d'art: Solutions et impasses*. Paris: Editions Hazan, 2011.
Hicks, Dan. *The Brutish Museums: The Benin Bronzes, Colonial Violence and Cultural Restitution*. London: Pluto Press, 2020.
Hilberg, Raul. *The Destruction of the European Jews*. 3 vols. 3rd ed. New Haven, CT: Yale University Press, 2003.
Hitchcock, William. *The Struggle for Europe: The Turbulent History of a Divided Continent, 1945 to the Present*. New York: Anchor Books, 2003.
Jackson, Julian. *France: The Dark Years, 1940–1944*. Oxford: Oxford University Press, 2001.
Joly, Laurent. *Vichy dans la "Solution Finale": Histoire du commissariat général aux Questions juives (1941–1944)*. Paris: Bernard Grasset, 2006.
Judt, Tony. *Postwar: A History of Europe since 1945*. New York: Penguin, 2005.
Karlsgodt, Elizabeth Campbell. *Defending National Treasures: French Art and Heritage under Vichy*. Stanford, CA: Stanford University Press, 2011.
Keegan, John. *The Second World War*. New York: Penguin Books, 1989.
Kim, Christine. "Colonial Plunder and the Failure of Restitution in Postwar Korea." *Journal of Contemporary History* 52, no. 3 (2017): 607–24.
King, Elaine A., and Gail Levin, eds. *Ethics and the Visual Arts*. New York: Allworth Press, 2006.

Kirshenblatt-Gimblett, Barbara, and Jonathan Karp, eds. *The Art of Being Jewish in Modern Times*. Philadelphia: University of Pennsylvania Press, 2008.

Klarsfeld, Serge, André Delahaye, Diane Afoumado, et al. *La Spoliation dans les Camps de Province*. Paris: La Documentation Française, 2000.

Klemann, Hein A. M., and Sergei Kudryashov, *Occupied Economies: An Economic History of Nazi-Occupied Europe, 1939-1945*. London: Berg, 2012.

Knapp, Andrew. *Les Français sous les bombes alliées 1940-1945*. Paris: Editions Tallandier, 2014.

Kreder, Jennifer. "The New Battleground of Museum Ethics and Holocaust-Era Claims: Technicalities Trumping Justice or Responsible Stewardship for the Public Trust?" *Oregon Law Review* 88, no. 37 (2009): 37-93.

Kunert, Floris, and Annemarie Marck. "The Dutch Art Market 1930-1945 and Dutch Restitution Policy Regarding Art Dealers." In *Kunst sammeln, Kunst handeln: Beiträge des Internationalen Symposiums in Wien*, edited by Eva Blimlinger and Monika Mayer, 133-53. Vienna: Böhlau Verlag, 2012.

Kurtz, Michael. *America and the Return of Nazi Contraband: The Recovery of Europe's Cultural Treasures*. New York: Cambridge University Press, 2006.

Kurtz, Michael. "Resolving a Dilemma: The Inheritance of Jewish Property." *Cardozo Law Review* 20, no. 2 (December 1998): 625-55.

Kuyvenhoven, F. "History of the Formation of the Dutch State Collection." N.d. Formerly available at culturalheritageagency.nl.

Laclotte, Michel, ed. *De Giotto à Bellini: Les primitifs italiens dans les musées de France, Mai-Juillet*. Paris: Editions des Musées Nationaux, 1956.

La Follette, Laetitia. "Looted Antiquities, Art Museums and Restitution in the United States since 1970," *Journal of Contemporary History* 52, no. 3 (2017): 669-87.

Lagrou, Pieter. *The Legacy of Nazi Occupation: Patriotic Memory and National Recovery in Western Europe, 1945-1965*. Cambridge: Cambridge University Press, 2000.

Lauterbach, Iris. *The Central Collecting Point in Munich: A New Beginning for the Restitution and Protection of Art*. Translated by Fiona Elliott. Los Angeles: Getty Research Institute, 2018.

Le Masne de Chermont, Isabelle, and Didier Schulmann, eds. *Le pillage de l'art en France pendant l'Occupation et la situation des 2000 oeuvres d'art confiées aux Musées nationaux*. Paris: La Documentation Française, 2000.

Le Masne de Chermont, Isabelle, and Laurence Sigal-Klagsbald. *A qui appartenaient ces tableaux? La politique Française de recherche, de provenance de garde et de restitution des oeuvres d'art pillées durant la Second Guerre Mondiale*. Paris: Editions de la Réunion des Musées Nationaux, 2008.

Leff, Lisa. *The Archive Thief: The Man Who Salvaged French Jewish History in the Wake of the Holocaust*. New York: Oxford University Press, 2015.

Lemaire, Jacques. *La Franc-Maçonnerie en Belgique: Les loges symboliques*. Paris: Editions Maçonniques de France, 2000.

Lewis, Jill. *Workers and Politics in Occupied Austria, 1945-1955*. Manchester: Manchester University Press, 2007.

Locke, Ian, and Stephen Ward. *Nazi Looted Art: Britain and Post-war Restitution*. London: The Holocaust Educational Trust, 1998.

Lorentz, Claude. *La France et les Restitutions Allemandes au Lendemain de la Seconde Guerre Mondiale*. Paris: Direction des Archives et de la Documentation, Ministère des Affaires Etrangères, 1998.

Lowenthal, David. *The Heritage Crusade and the Spoils of History*. Cambridge: Cambridge: University Press, 1998.
Lowenthal, David. *The Past Is a Foreign Country*. Cambridge: Cambridge University Press, 1985.
Lubina, Katja. *Contested Cultural Property: The Return of Nazi Spoliated Art and Human Remains from Public Collections*. Maastrict: Datawyse/Universitaire Pers Maastricht, 2009.
Lustig, Jason. "Who Are to Be the Successors of European Jewry? The Restitution of German Jewish Communal and Cultural Property." *Journal of Contemporary History* 52, no. 3 (2017): 519–45.
Lyons, Michael. *The Second World War: A Short History*. 4th ed. Upper Saddle River, NJ: Pearson, 2004.
Mandel, Maud. *In the Aftermath of Genocide: Armenians and Jews in Twentieth-Century France*. Durham, NC: Duke University Press, 2003.
Marrus, Michael. *Some Measure of Justice: The Holocaust Era Restitution Campaign of the 1990s*. Madison: University of Wisconsin Press, 2009.
Marstine, Janet, Alexander Bauer, and Chelsea Haines, eds. *New Directions in Museum Ethics*. London: Routledge, 2013.
Merritt, Richard L. "Political Perspectives in Germany: The Years of Semisovereignty 1949–1955." *Historical Social Research/Historische Sozialforschung* 13 (January 1980): 16–25.
Milosch, Jane, and Nick Pearce, eds. *Collecting and Provenance: A Multidisciplinary Approach*. Lanham, MD: Rowman & Littlefield, 2019.
Ministère de la Culture et de la Communication, Direction des Musées de France. *Pillages et restitutions: Le destin des oeuvres d'art sorties de France pendant la Seconde guerre mondiale*. Paris: Editions Adam Biro, 1997.
Moulin, Raymonde. *The French Art Market: A Sociological View*. Translated by Arthur Goldhammer. New Brunswick, NJ: Rutgers University Press, 1987.
Muller, Eelke, and Helen Schretlen, *Betwist Bezit: De Stichting Nederlands Kunstbezit en de teruggave van roofkunst na 1945*. Zwolle: Waanders Uitgevers, 2002.
Müller, Melissa, and Monika Tatzkow. *Lost Lives, Lost Art: Jewish Collectors, Nazi Art Theft, and the Quest for Justice*. New York: Vendome Press, 2010.
Nicholas, Lynn. *The Rape of Europa: The Fate of Europe's Treasures in the Third Reich and the Second World War*. New York: Vintage, 1995.
O'Donnell, Nicholas. *A Tragic Fate: Law and Ethics in the Battle over Nazi-Looted Art*. Chicago: American Bar Association, 2017.
Oliver, Bette. *From Royal to National: the Louvre Museum and the Bibliothèque Nationale*. Lanham, MD: Lexington Books, 2007.
Oost, Tabitha. "In an Effort To Do Justice? Restitution Policies and the Washington Principles." MA thesis, University of Amsterdam, 2011.
Oost, Tabitha. "Restitution Policies on Nazi-Looted Art in the Netherlands and the United Kingdom: A Change from a Legal to a Moral Paradigm?" *International Journal of Cultural Property* 25 (2018): 139–78.
Parisot, Véronique. "The Gentili di Giuseppe Case in France." *International Journal of Cultural Property* 10, no. 2 (2001): 264–75.
Paxton, Robert O. *Vichy France: Old Guard and New Order 1940–1944*. 2nd ed. New York: Columbia University Press, 2001.

Paxton, Robert O., and Michel R. Marrus. *Vichy France and the Jews*. Stanford, CA: Stanford University Press, 1981.
Petropoulos, Jonathan. *Art as Politics in the Third Reich*. Chapel Hill: University of North Carolina Press, 1996.
Petropoulos, Jonathan. "Art Dealer Networks in the Third Reich and in the Postwar Period." *Journal of Contemporary History* 52, no. 3 (2017): 546–65.
Petropoulos, Jonathan. *The Faustian Bargain: The Art World in Nazi Germany*. New York: Oxford University Press, 2000.
Petropoulos, Jonathan. *Göring's Man in Paris: The Story of a Nazi Art Plunderer and His World*. New Haven, CT: Yale University Press, 2021.
Petropoulos, Jonathan. "Report of Professor Jonathan Petropoulos, Claremont McKenna College." July 14, 2005, http://www.bslaw.com/altmann/Klimt/Petropoulos.pdf.
Poirrier, Philippe, and Loïc Vadelorge, eds. *Pour une histoire des politiques du patrimoine*. Paris: La Documentation Française, 2003.
Poulot, Dominique. *Une histoire du patrimoine en Occident XVIIIe–XXIe siècle: Du monument aux valeurs*. Paris: Presses Universitaires de France, 2006.
Pretzell, Lothar. *Das Kunstlager Schloss Celle 1945 bis 1958*. N.p., 1958.
Prost, Antoine, Rémi Skoutelsky, Sonia Etienne, et al. *Aryanisation économique et restitutions*. Paris: La documentation Française, 2000.
Prott, Lyndel V. "Responding to World War II Art Looting." In *Resolution of Cultural Property Disputes*, edited by the International Bureau of the Permanent Court of Arbitration, 113–37. The Hague: Kluwer Law International, 2004.
Raysaac, Michel. *L'Exode des musées: Histoire des oeuvres d'art sous l'Occupation*. Paris: Payot, 2007.
Piña, Leslie A. *Louis Rorimer: A Man of Style*. Kent, OH: Kent State University Press, 1990.
Rey, Robert. "Violations du Droit International Commises par les Allemands en France dans la Guerre de 1939." *Revue générale de droit international public* 49, no. 2 (1941–45): 1–127.
Rijksdienst Beeldende Kunst. *Old Master Paintings: An Illustrated Summary Catalogue* Zwolle: Waanders Uitgevers, 1992.
Ronald, Susan. *Hitler's Art Thief: Hildebrand Gurlitt, the Nazis, and the Looting of Europe's Treasures*. New York: St. Martin's, 2015.
Rothfeld, Anne. "Project ORION: An Administrative History of the Art Looting Investigation Unit (ALIU): An Overlooked Page in Intelligence Gathering." MA thesis, University of Maryland, 2002.
Sandholtz, Wayne. *Prohibiting Plunder: How Norms Change*. New York: Oxford University Press, 2007.
Schneider, Jiří, Jakub Klepal, and Irena Kalhousová, eds. *Holocaust Era Assets Conference Proceedings, Prague, 26–30 June 2009*. Prague: Forum 2000 Foundation, 2009.
Schnitzler, Bernadette. "Hans Haug et l' 'affaire' des tableaux hollandais de Strasbourg." *Cahiers alsaciens d'archéologie, d'art et d'histoire* 51 (2008): 151–60.
Schnitzler, Bernadette, and Anne-Doris Meyer, eds. *Hans Haug, homme de musées: une passion à l'oeuvre*. Strasbourg: Editions des Musées de la ville de Strasbourg, 2009.
Schreiber, Ruth. "New Jewish Communities in Germany after World War II and the Successor Organizations in the Western Zones." *Journal of Israeli History* 18, nos. 2–3 (1997): 167–90.

Sels, Geert. *Kunst voor das Reich: Op zoek naar naziroofkunst uit België*. Tielt: Lannoo, 2022. French translation by Pierre Lambert, *Le Trésor de guerre des nazis: Enquête sur le pillage d'art en Belgique*. Brussels: Editions Racine, 2023.

Silverman, Debora. "Diasporas of Art: History, the Tervuren Royal Museum for Central Africa, and the Politics of Memory in Belgium, 1885–2014." *Journal of Modern History* 87 (September 2015): 615–67.

Simpson, Elizabeth, ed. *Spoils of War: World War II and Its Aftermath: The Loss, Reappearance, and Recovery of Cultural Property*. New York: Bard Graduate Center for Studies in the Decorative Arts, 1997.

Takei, Ayaka. "The 'Gemeinde Problem': The Jewish Restitution Successor Organization and the Postwar Jewish Communities in Germany, 1947–1954." *Holocaust and Genocide Studies* 16, no. 2 (2002): 266–88.

Tompkins, Arthur. "A Permanent International Art Crime Tribunal?" *Art Crime* (2016): 327–36. https://doi.org/10.1007/978-1-137-40757-3_24.

Van Campen, S. I. P. *The Quest for Security: Some Aspects of Netherlands Foreign Policy, 1945–1950*. The Hague: Martinus Nijhoff, 1958.

Van Kalck, Michèle, ed. *Les Musées royaux des Beaux-Arts de Belgique: Deux siècles d'histoire*. Brussels: Editions Racine, 2003.

Vrdoljak, Ana Filipa. *International Law, Museums and the Return of Cultural Objects*. Cambridge: Cambridge University Press, 2008.

Veranneman de Watervliet, Jean-Michel. *Belgium in the Second World War*. Barnsley, South Yorkshire: Pen and Sword, 2014.

Veraart, Wouter, and Laurens Winkel, eds. *The Post-war Restitution of Property Rights in Europe: Comparative Perspectives*. New York: RVP Press, 2012.

Wieviorka, Annette, and Floriane Azoulay. *Le Pillage des appartements et son indemnisation*. Paris: La Documentation Française, 2000.

Wieviorka, Olivier. *Orphans of the Republic: The Nation's Legislators in Vichy France*. Translated by George Holoch. Cambridge, MA: Harvard University Press, 2009.

Wolska, Agata. "The Vaucher Commission as an International Restitution Body—An Abandoned Idea." Unpublished paper, March 2017.

Yeide, Nancy H., Konstantin Akinsha, and Amy L. Walsh. *The AAM Guide to Provenance Research*. Washington, DC: American Association of Museums, 2001.

Index

For the benefit of digital users, indexed terms that span two pages (e.g., 52–53) may, on occasion, appear on only one of those pages.

Tables and figures are indicated by *t* and *f* following the paragraph number.

Aalders, Gerard, 22, 148
AAM (American Alliance of Museums), 247–48
AAMD (Association of Art Museum Directors), 247–48
Abetz, Otto, 34
ACC (Allied Control Council), 88, 91–92, 93–94, 95, 96–97, 98
Acheson, Dean, 113–14
ACLS (American Council of Learned Societies), 48, 51–52
Adele Bloch-Bauer I, 12f
Adenauer, Konrad, 113–14, 202, 206
Adom, Magen David, 134
agents of Nazi art plunder, 13–20
Alazard, Jean, 140–41
Albert I (King), 27
Alexander, Harold, 53
Alexander the Great and Campaspe in the Studio of Apelles, 131f
ALIU (Art Looting Investigation Unit), US, 17, 82–85
Alliance Israélite, 29
Allied-caused damage, in France, 61–63, 67
Allied Control Council (ACC), 88, 91–92, 93–94, 95, 96–97, 98
Allied High Commission, 108
Allied Military Government (AMGOT), 51–52
Allied occupation, end of, 113–15
Alt Aussee salt mine art recovery, 78–80, 86f, 93
Altmann, Maria, 12–13, 255n.2
American Alliance of Museums (AAM), 247–48

American Commission for the Protection and Salvage of Artistic and Historic Monuments in Europe (Roberts Commission), 48–49, 52–53, 89, 90–91, 98
American Council of Learned Societies (ACLS), 48, 51–52
American Defense Harvard Group, 48, 51–52
AMGOT (Allied Military Government), 51–52
Andriesse, Elisabeth, 182
Andriesse, Hugo, 30, 182
Angerer, Josef, 135
anti-modernism, antisemitism and, 13–14
antisemitism
  anti-modernism and, 13–14
  art dealers and, 19–20
  France repealing laws of, 125
  French laws and, 18
  in US, 63
Arab Spring, 244
Army Museum, Les Invalides, 15–16
Arnstein, Hermann, 142–43
Art as Politics in the Third Reich (Petropoulos), 208
art dealers
  antisemitism and, 19–20
  Ekkart Committee recommendations for, 225
  in France, 42, 45
  Nazi's employing, 2–3, 20, 23
  in the Netherlands, 172, 173, 174–75
  transaction confidentiality of, 205
Art Institute of Chicago, 227–28

Art Looting Investigation Unit (ALIU), US, 17, 82–85
art market
　antisemitism in, 19–20
　confidentiality in, 205
　in France, 41–42, 44–45
　missing objects lists and global, 96, 119–20
　war profiteers and, 20
art plunder. *See* Nazi art plunder
art trafficking, IS and, 244
al-Asaad, Khaled, 244
Association of Art Museum Directors (AAMD), 247–48
Attlee, Clement, 91
Aubert, Marcel, 97
Auschwitz concentration camp, 4
Austria
　cultural restitution and, 110–13
　Nazi art plunder in, 11–13
　occupation zones of, 110
Auwera, Joost Vander, 291n.59
Azoulay, Audrey, 220–21

BALaT (Belgian Art Links and Tools), 291n.59
Balfour, Ronald, 54, 67–68
Basaiti, Marco, 137
Baudouin, Franz, 181
Bayeux tapestry, 60
Bazin, Germain, 40, 127–28, 136–37, 138–40
Beckmann, Max, 84–85
Behr, Kurt von, 17–18, 35–36, 37, 59–60
Bekefi, Gyorgy, 238
Belgian artistic heritage, 7. *See also* Office for Economic Restitution
　exhibitions promoting, 177–78
　museums enriched by, 185–91
　museum-worthy object distribution and, 191–93
　political stability progress and, 1944–1951, 178–79
　recovered art exhibitions by DER for, 183–85
　recovered art for, 179–83
Belgian Art Links and Tools (BALaT), 291n.59

Belgian Study Commission on Jewish Assets, 235–41
Belgium. *See also* Office for Economic Restitution
　BTG in, 28–29, 182
　cultural heritage in, 7
　cultural restitution challenges in, 87
　deficit payments and, 89–90
　Freemason assets in, 29
　French MFAA distrust of, 201
　incomplete reckoning in, 235–41
　JCA-B database of, 236
　Jewish Community Indemnification Commission of, 239–40
　Jewish deportations from, 45–46
　Jewish misappropriated assets in, 5–6
　Jewishness defined in, 18
　Jewish refugees in, 28
　liberation of, 60
　Möbel Aktion in, 29–30
　Moltke case and, 199–203
　MZBD in, 235–37
　Nazi art plunder in, 27–31
　Nazi invasion of, 27
　ownerless art auctioned by, 193–99, 194*t*
　political stability progress in, 1944–1951, 178–79
　replacement art for cultural restitution and, 90
　sequestered collections of, 193–94
　value of artworks lost from, 30, 31
Belinfante, W. J., 168–69
Bérard, Armand, 104
Berchtesgaden art recovery, 76–78
Bergh, Gert-Jan van den, 234
Bernterode art recovery, 75–76
Berryer, A. M., 195–96
Berthoin, Jean, 217
Bertrand Dorléac, Laurence, 45
Beuningen, Daniël George van, 25–26, 176
Blinder, Samuel, 103*f*
Bloch-Bauer, Adele, 11, 12*f*
Bloch-Bauer, Ferdinand, 11–13
Blumberg, Marina, 134
Boijmans Museum, Rotterdam, 21
Bois, Elie-Joseph, 125–26
Bonet-Maury, J. L., 106–7
Bonn accords, 114

INDEX 323

Bonnard, Abel, 118
Borchers, Walter, 135
Bormann, Martin, 26, 77–78
Bornheim, M., 134
Bornheim, Walter, 44–45
Bouchoux, Corinne, 220–21
Bouts, Dieric, 27–28
Bradley, Omar Nelson, 77f
Brauchitsch, Walther von, 35
Braun, Eva, 44–45
Brown, John Nicholas, 93
Bruce, David, 82–83
Brueghel, Jan, 289n.29
Brueghel, Pieter, 85
BRüG (Federal Restitution Law), 206–7, 239–40
Brussels Trustee Corporation *(Brüsseler Treuhandgesellschaft)* (BTG), 28–29, 182
Bruyn, Edmond de, 184
Buchner, Ernst, 27–28
Bührle, Emil, 171
Bundesamt für äussere Restitutionen (Federal Office for External Restitutions), 114
Bunjes, Hermann, 68–69
Buxheim monastery art recovery, 70–71
Buysse, Lucien, 31, 235–36
Buysse Commission, 235–41

Cachin, Françoise, 213, 218
Cailleux, Paul, 44
Caïn, Julien, 117–18
Cairns, Huntington, 48–49, 98
Campana, Giampietro, 141–42
Capart, Jean, 30
Capitant, René, 128–29
Carcopino, Jérôme, 37–38, 61, 118
Caris, J. L., 189–91
Carré, Louis, 42
Cassou, Jean, 138–39
Central Collecting Point (CCP), 93–94, 94f
Cézanne, Paul, 41–42
Chagall, Marc, 220–21
Chamson, André, 95
Chardin, Jean Siméon, 162–63, 163f
Charles (Prince), 178–79
Chase, George, 48

Chasse au cerf, 289n.29
Châtelain, Jean, 144–45
Choltitz, Dietrich von, 60
Christ before Pilat, 189–91
Christophe, Lucien, 183, 184–85, 189–93, 195–96
Christophe, Robert, 125–26
church bells, DER recovering, 182–83
Churchill, Winston, 91–92
CIVS (Commission pour l'indemnisation des victimes de spoliations), 214, 221
Claims Conference (Conference on Jewish Material Claims against Germany), 114–15, 206
Clay, Lucius, 56, 93–94, 96–97, 99–100
Clinton, Bill, 209
Clooney, George, 220–21, 243
Code of Ethics for Museums, ICOM, 207–8
College Art Journal, 112
Commission for Art Recovery (CRA), France, 100–1
  claims process of, 119–21
  dissolution of, 129
  first meetings members of, 117–18
  on forced sales, 120–21
  Jaujard heading, 118
  location of works repatriated to, 121t
  mission of, 117
  recovery rate of, 123
  restitution of private collections and, 117–24, 122t
  restitution of sequestered collections and, 124–28
  SNK dispute with, 172–75
  specialists working for, 120
Commission pour l'indemnisation des victimes de spoliations (Commission for the Compensation for Victims of Spoliation) (CIVS), 214, 221
compensation. *See also* cultural restitution
  in Belgium, 239–40
  BRüG and, 206–7, 239–40
  ICHEIC and, 208–9
  through 1980s, 205–8
  1990s awakening on, 208–12
  reparations and, 206
  Terezin Declaration on, 211–12
  Washington Principles and, 210–12, 246

Conference on Jewish Material
  Claims against Germany (Claims
  Conference), 114–15, 206
Consolidated Interrogation Report, 83–84
Conway, Martin, 178
Cooper, Douglas, 84, 123
Coordinating Committee of the ACC
  (CORC), 95, 96–97
Coremans, Paul, 171, 187–88
Corot, Jean-Baptiste-Camille, 138, 144f
Cotler, Irwin, 4
Council for the Restoration of Rights
  (Raad voor het Rechtsherstel), 149,
  157, 168–69
Court of Arbitration for Art, 246
CRA. See Commission for Art Recovery
Cranach the Elder, 130, 140, 289n.29
cultural heritage. See Belgian artistic
  heritage; Dutch cultural heritage;
  French cultural patrimony
cultural restitution. See also Musées
  Nationaux Récupération pieces;
  recovered art
  from August 1945-December 1947,
    93–101
  Austria and, 110–13
  in British zone, 94–95, 107
  challenges of, 87
  deficit payments and, 89–90
  defining, 92
  end of Allied occupation and, 113–15
  France and the Netherlands dispute
    over, 172–75
  from France to Senegal, 244–45
  in French zone, 95, 107–8
  under FRG, 1949–1952, 109–13
  toward German sovereignty and,
    1947–1949, 101–9
  of Goudstikker collection, 230–35, 234f
  of Gutmann collection, 226–30, 230f, 231f
  ICOM and, 108–9, 207–8
  Inter-Allied Declaration and, 88
  international discussions over, 90–92,
    95–99
  Linz museum project and, 105–6
  mistakes in, 132–35
  in the Netherlands, 148, 149–56
  through 1980s, 205–8

1990s awakening on, 208–12
ownerless art challenge and, 102
private buyers issues with, 97–98
of private collections, 117–24
Répertoire des biens spoliés for, 97,
  119–20
replacement art for, 90, 99
Russia on, 210–11
of sequestered collections, 124–28
SNK exhibitions leading to claims of,
  167
SNK guidelines for, 153–54, 158, 224
in Soviet zone, 95, 107
SROA and, 109–10
Terezin Declaration on, 211–12
UNESCO and, 108–9, 207–8
US Military Law 59 on, 101–2
US transferring responsibilities to
  Germany, 102–6
in US zone, 93–94
wartime diplomacy from 1943–1945
  on, 88–92
Washington Principles and, 210–12, 246
"Wiesbaden Manifesto" and, 99
Curaçao, 166–67
Currency Control Commando
  (Devisenschutzkommando), 19
Curtis, Glion, 162–63
Cyrenaica, 49–51

Dagen, Philippe, 213
D'Amato, Alfonse, 209
Darlan, François, 37–38
Davids, Willibrord, 234
David-Weill, David, 36, 70–72, 119, 124
dealers. See art dealers
deficit payments, cultural restitution and,
  89–90
de Gaulle, Charles, 59, 91
Degenerate Art Exhibition, 1937, 13–14
"degenerate" paintings, 36f
Dehaene, Jean-Luc, 235
Deirkauf, C. J. N., 155–56, 284n.51
Dellheim, Charles, 265n.65
Democratic Republic of Congo (DRC),
  239–40
Denens, Jan, 190f
Dequoy, Roger, 42–44

DER. *See* Office for Economic Restitution
Dermine, Thomas, 240
Deshmukh, Marion, 271n.63
Devisenschutzkommando (Currency Control Commando), 19
Dienst Economische Recuperatie. See Office for Economic Restitution
Dienst voor Rijks Verspreide Kunstvoorwerpen (State Art Collections Service), 170
Dietrich, Maria Almas, 44–45
Dinsmoor, William, 48
Directorate of Reparations, Deliveries and Restitutions (RDR), ACC, 93–94, 98
Doom, Baron Cassel van, 278n.68
Dorléac, Laurence Bertrand, 213
Dorville, Armand, 221
Double-Cup, 229–30, 230*f*
DRC (Democratic Republic of Congo), 239–40
Druène, Bernard, 81–82
Duchartre, Pierre-Louis, 95, 118
Dupont, Jacques, 95
Dutch Art Property Foundation. *See Stichting Nederlands Kunstbezit*
Dutch cultural heritage, 7. *See also Stichting Nederlands Kunstbezit*
   artworks found and lost and, 156–63
   French cultural patrimony dispute with, 172–75
   museums enriched by, 163–68
   ownership debates and, 168–71
   "Recovered Art Property" shows and, 146–47
   repatriation of assets and, 149–56
   State Art Collections Service and, 170

E133 (Enemy Property Decree), 149–50, 151, 168–69
EAC (European Advisory Commission), 88
East Asia, MFAA in, 98, 267n.121
economic Aryanization, Jewish assets and, 28–29, 42
Eden, Anthony, 88, 90–91
Edsel, Robert, 4–5
Eggens, Jannes, 149
Ehard, Hans, 102–4
Eigruber, August, 78–79

Einsatzstab Reichsleiter Rosenberg (ERR), 17–18, 21–22, 29–30, 35–36, 182
Eisenhower, Dwight, 51–53, 54–55, 77*f*
Eizenstat, Stuart, 209–10, 246
Ekkart committee, Netherlands, 222–26, 228
Elden, Willem van, 156–58
Elslander, Jean-François, 20
Enemy Property Decree (E133), 149–50, 151, 168–69
Engelhard, Charles, 162–63
ERR *(Einsatzstab Reichsleiter Rosenberg)*, 17–18, 21–22, 29–30, 35–36, 182
Errera, Alfred, 195, 196–97, 198
Errera, Jacques, 29
ethics. *See* museum ethics
European Advisory Commission (EAC), 88
European Coal and Steel Community, 113–14
European Defense Community, 114
European Steel and Coal Community, 7–8
Evang, Vilhelm, 199–200
Eve, 289n.29
Ewer in the shape of a triton and a nereid, 161*f*
Eyck, Hubert van, 186

Fabiani, Martin, 45
Faison, S. Lane, 82–84, 85, 110, 111
Federal Office for External Restitutions *(Bundesamt für äussere Restitutionen)*, 114
Federal Republic of Germany (FRG), 109–13. *See also* Germany
Federal Restitution Law (BRüG), 206–7, 239–40
Federation of Zionists, 29
Feliciano, Hector, 208, 213
Fiduciary Administration for Cultural Assets *(Treuhandverwaltung von Kulturgut)* (TVK), 114
Fierens, Paul, 184
Final Solution, Jewish assets seizure and, 4, 6, 19, 243–44
Finlay, William, 82–83
Finley, David, 48–49, 68
Fischböck, Hans, 21

Fischer, Theodor, 84
Flanner, Janet, 8
Flechtheim, Alfred, 84–85
Florisoone, Michel, 117, 118, 121–23, 136, 173–74
Flute Player, 27–28
Fontebasso, Salvator Francesco, 140
forced sales
 CRA on, 120–21
 Gentili di Giuseppe collection and, 215–18
 of Goudstikker collection, 23–25, 232–33
 Renders and, 186–88
 for "safekeeping measures," 2–3
 SNK on, 158–59, 160, 224
forgery, Göring duped by, 158
Four-Year Plan, 19
"Framing Nazi Art Loot" (Dellheim), 265n.65
France. *See also* Commission for Art Recovery; French cultural patrimony; Musées Nationaux Récupération pieces
 acquisitions budget of, 261n.121
 Allied-caused damage in, 61–63, 67
 antisemitic laws repealed by, 125
 antisemitism in laws of, 18
 art dealers in, 42, 45
 art market in, 41–42, 44–45
 Belgian MFAA distrust of, 201
 CIVS of, 214, 221
 cultural heritage in, 6–7
 cultural restitution challenges in, 87
 cultural restitution in zone of, 95, 107–8
 deficit payments and, 89–90
 German reconciliation with, 92, 97, 101–2
 Jewish asset seizure in transit camps in, 19
 Jewish deportations from, 45–46
 Jewish misappropriated assets in, 5–6
 Jewishness defined in, 18
 Jewish population in, 251–52n.12
 JTC and, 102
 liberation of, 59–60
 liquidated items by, 122*t*
 location of works repatriated to, 121*t*
 MFAA handbook on, 55
 Möbel Aktion in, 35
 Nazi art plunder in, 31–45
 Nazi art plunder report of, 214
 Nazi invasion in, 31–34, 32*f*
 the Netherlands' restitution dispute with, 172–75
 other items held by, 122*t*
 ownerless art of, 116–17
 ownerless art seized by ERR in, 35–36
 recovered art of, 116–17, 275n.5
 Répertoire des biens spoliés of, 97, 119–20
 replacement art for cultural restitution and, 90
 restitution of private collections in, 117–24, 122*t*
 restitution of sequestered collections in, 124–28
 sales of less worthy objects in, 142–45
 SCAP in, 42
 Senegal and cultural restitution from, 244–45
 sequestered collections approach of, 38–41, 125
 on US transfer of cultural restitution responsibilities to Germany, 104–5
 war damages according to, 263n.153
Frankenheimer, John, 265n.50
Freemason assets, 41
 in Belgium, 29
 in the Netherlands, 21–22
French cultural patrimony, 6–7, 116–17, 275n.5, *See also* Musées Nationaux Récupération pieces
 CRA mission on, 117
 Dutch cultural heritage dispute with, 172–75
 museum collection enrichment and, 137–42
 objects held in interest of, 130–32
 ownerless art and, 128–37
FRG (Federal Republic of Germany), 109–13. *See also* Germany
Friedländer, Max, 186
Friedländer, Saul, 132–34
Friedmann, David, 84–85
The Fruit Seller, 193*f*

Führer, Erich, 11
Fulbright, William, 99–100, 271n.63
Fuld, Harry, 132–34
Furniture Operation (Möbel Aktion), 19, 29–30, 35

Gangnat, Philippe, 81–82
Garden at Pontoise, 173–75
Gaudenzi, Bianca, 9
Gelder, Jan Gerrit van, 151–52, 164–65, 166
Gelder, Michel van, 188–89
genocide
  Jewish assets seizure and Final Solution, 4, 6, 19
  Nazi art plunder and, 45–46
Gentili di Giuseppe, Adriana, 215–18
Gentili di Giuseppe, Federico, 131f, 215–16
Gentili di Giuseppe, Marcello, 215–16, 217, 218
Gentili di Giuseppe collection, 215–18
Genzano, 142–43, 144f
George, Waldemar, 124
George VI (King), 180
Germain, Thomas, 143–44
German Lost Art Foundation, 243
German National Gallery, 99–100
Germany. *See also* Nazi art plunder; Nazis
  BRüG and compensation from, 206–7, 239–40
  deficit payments and, 89–90
  end of Allied occupation and, 113–15
  Federal Office for External Restitutions of, 114
  Federal Republic of, 1949–1952, 109–13
  French reconciliation with, 92, 97, 101–2
  Israel and reparations paid by, 206
  Kunstschutz and, 16, 30, 35, 199–200
  Nazi art plunder protection efforts of, 15–16
  postwar planning for control of, 88–89
  private buyers and cultural restitution issues in, 97–98
  replacement art for cultural restitution and, 90
  SNK receiving shipments from, 154–55
  toward sovereignty of, 1947–1949, 101–9

TVK of, 114
US cultural restitution responsibilities transferred to, 102–6
Gerstein, Kurt, 132–34
Ghent altarpiece, 27–28, 79, 93
Giraud, Julien, 216
Godding, Emile, 27–28
Godeaux, Baron Jean, 235
Goebbels, Joseph, 13–14, 17
Gonfreville, Max, 127
Goodman, Bernard, 226–27
Goodman, Lili, 204, 227, 229
Goodman, Nick, 204, 226–30
Goodman, Simon, 204, 226–30
Göpel, Erhard, 23
Göring, Hermann, 40, 76–78, 86, 134, 135, 173–74, 232–33
  collection of, 17, 23–24
  ERR and, 17–18
  forgery duping, 158
  Four-Year Plan and, 19
  Goudstikker, J.'s, assets sold to, 24–25
  Renders' claim of forced sales to, 186–88
Gossaert, Jan, 134
Gottschalk, Max, 29
Goudstikker, Dési, 23–25, 160–62, 230–33
Goudstikker, Eduard (Eduard von Saher), 23–24, 161–62, 230–32
Goudstikker, Jacques, 23–25, 160–61, 230–31
Goudstikker collection
  forced sale of, 23–25, 232–33
  recovery of, 154, 160–62
  restitution of, 230–35, 234f
Goya, Francisco, 120–21
Great Britain
  cultural preservation efforts launched by, 49–51
  cultural restitution in zone of, 94–95, 107
  EAC and, 88
  JTC and, 102
  SNK receiving shipments from zone of, 155–56
Griffioen, Pim, 251–52n.12
Guardi, Francesco, 120–21
Gunzburg, Niko, 29
Gurlitt, Cornelius, 242–44

Gurlitt, Hildebrand, 45, 84–85, 137–38
Gutmann, Fritz and Louise, 1–4, 3f, 160, 161f, 226–27
Gutmann collection
　Nazi plunder of, 1–4, 2f
　restitution of, 226–30, 230f, 231f

Haagen, Jan Karel van der, 163–64, 166
Haberstock, Karl, 14, 42–44, 84, 128, 228
Hague Conventions of 1899 and 1907, 47
Hale, Oron, 112
Hall, Ardelia, 108–9, 112
Hals, Franz, 137, 154
Hamel, Pierre, 192–93
Hammond, Mason, 51–52
Hamon, Marie, 281n.121
Hancock, Walker, 57, 67
　Bernterode art recovery and, 75–76
　Siegen copper mine art recovery and, 72–74
Hannema, Dirk, 25–26
HARP (Holocaust Art Restitution Project), 246
Hathaway, Calvin, 54, 76–77
Haug, Hans, 172–74
Hautecoeur, Louis, 118
Head of a Woman, 200–1
HEAR (Holocaust Expropriated Art Recovery) Act, 248
Heilbronn salt mine art recovery, 72
heirless Jewish assets. *See* ownerless art
Heldring, E., 163–64, 165–66
Hendrik (Prince), 21–22
Henraux, Albert, 64, 100–1, 104, 116, 118, 123–24, 129–30, 172–73
HERGO (Office for Reparation Payments and Restitution of Property), 147–48, 170, 175–76
Herwonnen Kunstbezit ("Recovered Art Property") shows, 146–47
Hess, Emil, 40
Heyning, C., 169
Himmler, Heinrich, 17, 284n.51
Hitchcock, William, 113–14
Hitler, Adolf, 13–14
　Dietrich selling to, 44–45
　Linz museum project hopes of, 78–79
Hoeven, Maria vann der, 233

Hofer, Walter Andreas, 17
Hofhuis, Helen, 228
Hollander, Pieter den, 231–32
Holocaust Art Restitution Project (HARP), 246
Holocaust Era Assets Conference, Prague, 211–12
Holocaust Expropriated Art Recovery (HEAR) Act, 248
Hooge Veluwe museum, Otterloo, 15–16
Hoppner, John, 30–31
Hornbeck, Stanley, 154
Horse and Rider, 229–30, 231f
Houdon, Jean-Antoine, 137–38
Howard, Richard, 96–97
Howe, Thomas Carr, 8, 37, 53–54, 80, 83–84, 110, 154, 171
Huchthausen, Walter, 68
Hull, Cordell, 48, 88
Hunger Winter, in the Netherlands, 60, 150
Huntzinger, Charles, 31–32
Husky Operation, 51–52
Huyghe, René, 40–41, 118, 125, 127–28, 221
Huysmans, Camille, 185, 196–97

IARA (Inter-Allied Restitution Agency), 95
ICHEIC (International Commission on Holocaust-Era Insurance Claims), 208–9
ICN (Institute for Cultural Heritage), the Netherlands, 204, 222–23
ICOM (International Council of Museums), 108–9, 207–8
Institute for Cultural Heritage (ICN), the Netherlands, 204, 222–23
Inter-Allied Commission for the Protection and Restitution of Cultural Materials (Vaucher Commission), 51, 82–83
Inter-Allied Committee for Study of the Armistice, 88–89
Inter-Allied Declaration, 1943, 88, 98, 193–94, 264n.12
Inter-Allied Restitution Agency (IARA), 95
International Commission on Holocaust-Era Insurance Claims (ICHEIC), 208–9

INDEX   329

International Council of Museums (ICOM), 108–9, 207–8
Islamic State (IS), 244
Israel, reparations and, 206
Italy, 49–51

Jaffé, Alphons, 23
Jaffé, Anna, 120–21
Jaffé, Hans, 153, 172–73
Jaffé, John, 120–21
Japanese seizure of cultural objects from Korea, 98
Jaujard, Jacques, 61, 104, 129–30
   CRA and, 118
   Jewish asset vulnerability and, 34–35
   sequestered art purchases and, 38–40, 41, 125
   Valland and, 36–37, 59–60
   Wolff Metternich and, 35–36
JCA-B (Jewish Cultural Assets-Belgium) database, 236
JCR (Jewish Cultural Reconstruction), 102
Jeannel, A. M., 104
Jeu de Paume museum, 35–37, 36f
Jewish art historians, Linz museum project working with, 23
Jewish assets. *See also* cultural restitution; Nazi art plunder; private collections; recovered art
   in Austria, 11–13
   Belgian Study Commission on, 235–41
   DER and foreign, 182
   economic Aryanization of, 28–29, 42
   Ekkart committee on plunder of, 222–26, 228
   Final Solution and seizure of, 4, 6, 19, 243–44
   French transit camps and seizure of, 19
   Jaujard and vulnerability of, 34–35
   misappropriation of, 5–6
   MZBD and, 235–37
   repercussions for loss of, 46
Jewish Community Indemnification Commission, Belgium, 239–40
Jewish Cultural Assets-Belgium (JCA-B) database, 236
Jewish Cultural Reconstruction (JCR), 102
Jewish deportations, 45–46

Jewish Historical Museum, Amsterdam, 21–22
Jewishness, defining, 18, 22
Jewish refugees, in Belgium, 28
Jewish resettlement, in Israel, 206
Jewish Restitution Successor Organization (JRSO), 102, 114–15
Jewish Trust Corporation (JTC), 102
Jolles, Jolle, 147–48, 170, 175–76
Jonas, Edouard, 44
Jonas, Paul, 205
Jordaens, Jacob, 188–89, 193f, 289n.29
JRSO (Jewish Restitution Successor Organization), 102, 114–15
JTC (Jewish Trust Corporation), 102
Judt, Tony, 46
Juppé, Alain, 214

Kahnweiler, Daniel-Henry, 42
Kaiser Friedrich Museum, 99–100
Kaltenbrunner, Ernst, 78–79
Katz, Nathan, 26, 171
Katz, W., 195
Keitel, Wilhelm, 34
Kendall, Richard, 227–28
Kesselring, Albert, 53
Kienle, Hans Ludwig, 229–30, 231f
Kirstein, Lincoln, 68–69, 78–79
Klein, Martha, 71
Klein, Otto, 71
Klimt, Gustav, 11, 12f, 220–21, 255n.2
Koenigs, Franz, 5–6, 25–26, 222–23
Kohl, Helmut, 212
Korea, Japanese seizure of cultural objects from, 98
Kraemer-Bach, Marcelle, 217
Kuhn, Charles, 61
Kümmel, Otto, 14
Künsberg, Eberhard Freiherr von, 34–35
Kunstschutz, 16, 30, 35, 199–200

LaFarge, Bancel, 23, 54, 56, 93–94, 154
Landscape, the Pink Wall, 132–34
Landscape with Smokestacks, 227–28
Langui, E., 184
Lanz, Otto, 5–6, 26, 222–23
The Last Supper, 27–28
Lathouwer, Auguste de, 27–28

Lauder, Ronald S., 255n.4
Lavachery, H., 195, 196–97
Laval, Pierre, 33–34, 40
Lavalleye, Jacques, 186
Law, Richard, 90–91
Lebrun, Albert, 31–32
Léger, Fernand, 133f
Leiris, Louise, 42
Lemaire, Raymond, 181–82, 183–84, 189
Lencker, Johannes, 161f
Leonard, H. Steward, 158
Leopold II (King), 7, 178–79
Leopold III (King), 27
Levin, Itamar, 208–9
Libya, 49–51
Liebermann, Max, 84–85
Linz museum project
  acquisition costs for, 14–15
  cultural restitution and, 105–6
  Dietrich purchasing for, 44–45
  Hitler's hopes for, 78–79
  Jewish art historians working for, 23
  Liro and, 22
  Lugt's collection seized for, 26–27
  Mannheimer's estate acquired for, 25
  plans for, 13
  Posse leading efforts for, 14–15
  private collections seized for, 16–17
  storage for, 27–28
The Lion Tamer, 84–85
Lippmann, Rosenthal & Co. bank (Liro), 22
Lisser-Rosencrantz Bank of Amsterdam, 25–26
Lohse, Bruno, 17, 37, 64, 85
looting. *See* Nazi looting
The Lost Museum (Le Musée Disparu) (Feliciano), 208
Louvre, 35–36, 40–41, 61
  MNR enriching collections of, 137–42
  private collection donations to, 124
  provincial museum exchanges with, 139–41
Lugt, Frits, 26–27
Lust, Jacques, 235, 237–38, 240
Luxemburg, 9–10
Lyndhurst, Eric-Emil, 30–31, 182

MacLeish, Archibald, 48–49

Macmillan, Hugh Patton, 51
Macron, Emmanuel, 244
Madonna and Child, 27–28
Maillol, Aristide, 138–39, 141, 281n.115
Mala Zimetbaum database (MZBD), 235–37
Les Malheurs de la France (Bois), 125–26
Manet, Edouard, 81f
Mangers, Jacques, 199–200, 293n.105
Mannheimer, Fritz, 25, 162–63, 163f, 222–23
Mannheimer, Jane, 162–63
market. *See* art market
Marrus, Michael, 10
Martin, Gisela, 134
Martin, Kurt, 172–75
Masne de Chermont, Isabelle Le, 214–15, 275n.5
Masurovsky, Marc, 246
Matisse, Henri, 132–34
Mattéoli Commission, 123, 130–31, 137, 142–43, 214–15, 220–21, 279n.76
Mauricheau-Beaupré, Charles, 41, 97
Maxse, F. H. J., 51–52
May, Jacques, 125
Mayer, Emma, 240
Mayer, Gustave, 240
Mayer, Raoul, 120
McCloy, John, 109–10
Meegeren, Han van, 158
Men and Monuments, 8
Mendelsohn Bank, Amsterdam, 25
The Merchant's Quay at Rouen, 138
Merkers mine art recovery, 74–75, 77f, 81f
Mesuret, Robert, 140
Metsys, Quentin, 134
Meynier, Charles, 140
MFAA. *See* Monuments, Fine Arts, and Archives
Michelangelo, 27–28, 86f
Miedl, Alois, 24–25, 232–33
  Renders' claim of forced sales to, 186–88
Military Law 59, US, 101–2
missing objects lists, global art market and, 96, 119–20
Mitterand, François, 212
MNAM (Musée national d'art moderne), 126, 137–39

MNR. *See* Musées Nationaux Récupération
Möbel Aktion (Furniture Operation), 19, 29–30, 35
Molotov, Vyacheslav, 88
Moltke, Joachim von, 199–203
Momper, Joos de, 141, 281n.115
Monet, Claude, 218–21
Monnet, Jean, 92, 113–14
Monte Cassino bombing, 53, 55
Mont Saint Michel, 56–57, 58f
Monuments, Fine Arts, and Archives (MFAA), 8, 10. *See also* cultural restitution; recovered art
  authority of, 54, 57
  Belgian and French distrust within, 201
  Bunjes interrogated by, 68–69
  casualties of officers in, 67–68
  Central Collecting Point and, 93–94
  creation of, 47–49
  early stages of, 51–54
  in East Asia, 98, 267n.121
  France handbook of, 55
  lost preservation battles of, 67–68
  mistakes made by, 132–35
  Nazi art plunder investigated by, 82–86
  the Netherlands receiving objects from, 147–48
  officers of, 54
  recovered art by, 68–82
  responsibilities of, 47
  Rorimer leading Seine section of, 61
  transnational success of, 177–78
  transportation for, 56
  "Wiesbaden Manifesto" and, 99
The Monuments Men, 4–5, 220–21, 243
Monuments Men and Women Foundation, 274n.109
Moore, Lamont, 80
Morgenthau, Henry, 48
Moulin, M., 216
Mühlmann, Kajetan, 22–23, 26–27
Muller, Eelke, 222
Murphy, James, 82–83
Murphy, Robert, 105
Le Musée Disparu (The Lost Museum) (Feliciano), 208
Musée Maritime des Salorges, Nantes, 15–16

Musée national d'art moderne (MNAM), 126
Musée National de l'Orangerie, 116
Musées Nationaux Récupération (National Museums Recovery, MNR)
  category of, 132
  Gentili di Giuseppe collection and, 215–18
  influential books on, 208
  mistakes made with, 132–35, 213
  museum collections enriched with, 137–42
  in provincial museum exchanges, 139–41
  rhetoric compared to reality of, 212–15
  Rosenberg collection and, 218–21
  statute of limitations on, 144–45
  unclear legal status of, 136–37
Musées Royaux des Beaux-Arts, Brussels, 30
museum ethics
  AAM, AAMD on, 247–48
  current claims questioning, 245, 249
  ICOM's Code of Ethics for Museums, 207–8
  responsibilities of, 10, 241
  value of, 249
Museum of Fine Arts, Boston, 218, 305n.24
MZBD (Mala Zimetbaum database), 235–37

Naegelen, Marcel-Edmond, 140–41
NAGPRA (Native American Graves Protection and Repatriation Act), 247
National Museums Recovery pieces. *See* Musées Nationaux Récupération pieces
Native American Graves Protection and Repatriation Act (NAGPRA), 247
NATO (North Atlantic Treaty Organization), 7–8, 109, 114
Nazi art plunder. *See also* cultural restitution; Jewish assets
  agents of, 13–20
  ALIU interrogations on, 82–85
  in Austria, 11–13
  in Belgium, 27–31

332   INDEX

Nazi art plunder (*cont.*)
  Consolidated Interrogation Report on, 83–84
  Ekkart committee on, 222–26, 228
  in France, 31–45
  French report on, 214
  genocide and, 45–46
  German efforts to protect against, 15–16
  impact of, 4
  influential books on, 208
  investigations into, 208–10
  legacy of, 243–44
  methods of, 4, 11, 13
  MFAA investigating, 82–86
  MZBD and, 235–37
  in the Netherlands, 20–27
  Nuremberg Trials on, 86
  in popular culture, 4–5
  re-contextualizing, 9
  Rorimer on, 63–64
  scholarly literature on, 8–9
  Wolff Metternich protesting, 16
Nazi-Era Provenance Internet Portal, 247–48
Nazis. *See also* Germany
  art dealers employed by, 2–3, 20, 23
  Belgium invaded by, 27
  France invaded by, 31–34, 32*f*
  Gutmann home invaded by, 1, 2–4
  laws refashioned by, 2–3
  the Netherlands invaded by, 20–21
Nederlands Kunstbezit-collectie (Netherlands Art Property Collection, NK), 6
  creation of, 176
  Ekkart Committee on claims to works in, 225–26
  Origins Unknown Agency and, 223
Neptune and Amphitrite, 289n.29
the Netherlands. *See also* Dutch cultural heritage; *Stichting Nederlands Kunstbezit*
  art dealers in, 172, 173, 174–75
  art losses from, 147–48
  Council for the Restoration of Rights in, 149, 157, 168–69
  cultural heritage in, 7
  cultural restitution challenges in, 87
  cultural restitution in, 148, 149–56
  deficit payments and, 89–90
  Ekkart committee of, 222–26, 228
  Enemy Property Decree in, 149–50, 151, 168–69
  Freemason assets in, 21–22
  French restitution dispute with, 172–75
  HERGO of, 147–48, 170, 175–76
  Hunger Winter in, 60, 150
  ICN of, 204, 222–23
  Jewish deportations from, 45–46
  Jewish misappropriated assets in, 5–6
  Jewishness defined in, 18, 22
  liberation of, 60
  looted and purchased property defined by, 150–51
  MFAA objects released to, 147–48
  museums enriched by works recovered by, 163–68
  Nazi art plunder in, 20–27
  Nazi invasion of, 20–21
  Origins Unknown Agency of, 223, 228, 232
  reconstruction challenges in, 150–51
  Restitution Committee of, 225, 232, 233–35
  State Art Collections Service of, 170
  value of artworks lost from, 27
Neuschwanstein Castle art recovery, 71–72, 73*f*, 76*f*
Nicholas, Lynn, 208, 213
Nicolas, Etienne, 128
Night Watch, 154
NK. *See Nederlands Kunstbezit-collectie*
Norris, Christopher, 155
North Atlantic Treaty Organization (NATO), 7–8, 109, 114
Northcote, James, 30–31
Norway, 199–200
Nuremberg Trials, 86
Nussbaum, Félix, 238
Nymphéas, 218–21

Obama, Barack, 248
OBIP (Office for Personal Property and Interests), 112, 120
Occupied Western Europe, 15*f*
Office for Economic Restitution *(Dienst Economische Recuperatie)* (DER)
  administrators of, 181–82
  church bells recovered by, 182–83

creation of, 180–81
dissolution of, 202–3
foreign Jewish assets and, 182
liquidation of less worthy objects by, 193–99
museums enriched by, 185–91
museum-worthy objects distributed by, 191–93
ownerless art and, 185
priorities of, 181
recovered art by, 179–83
recovered art exhibitions by, 183–85
Renders' claim of forced sales and, 186–88
responsibilities of, 180–81
Office for Personal Property and Interests (OBIP), 112, 120
Office for Reparation Payments and Restitution of Property (HERGO), 147–48, 170, 175–76
Office of Strategic Services (OSS), US, 43–44
Oost, Tabitha, 235
Operation Overlord, 54, 55–56
ORE. *See* Office for Economic Restitution
Origins Unknown Agency, the Netherlands, 223, 228, 232
OSS (Office of Strategic Services), US, 43–44
ownerless art
 Belgium auctioning, 193–99, 194*t*
 causes of, 5
 cultural restitution challenge with, 102
 DER and, 185
 ERR seizing French, 35–36
 of France, 116–17
 French cultural patrimony and, 128–37
 national opportunities provided by, 7–8
 SNK and, 158–60, 165–66

"Paintings looted from Holland" tour, 146–47
Palais des Beaux-Arts (PBA) auctions, 194–95, 194*t*
Palmyra, Syria, 244
patrimania, definition of, 6
Patton, George, 77*f*
Paysage, 289n.29
PBA (Palais des Beaux-Arts) auctions, 194–95, 194*t*

PCHA (Presidential Commission on Holocaust Assets), US, 8–9, 209–10, 247
The Peahens, 146–47, 154
Perkins, J. B. Ward, 50–51
Pernot, M. J., 136
Perry, Lionel, 201
Pétain, Philippe, 31–32, 33–34, 40
Le Petit-Parisien, 125–26
Petoltz, Hans, 229–30, 230*f*
Petropoulos, Jonathan, 14, 208, 268n.137
Philipps, Ewan, 200
Philips, Anton Frederik, 166
Picasso, Pablo, 45
Pierlot, Hubert, 178–79
Pierret, Alain, 236
Pissarro, Camille, 173–75
Plas, L. O. van der, 168–69
Plaut, James, 82–84, 86
Pleven, René, 114
Polack, Emmanuelle, 221
Pommery, G. H., 112
Popham, Anne Olivier, 155–56
Portrait of an Old Woman, 137
Posey, Robert, 68–69, 78–79
Posse, Hans, 14–15, 25–26
Pourquoi Pas?, 197–98
Prague Holocaust Era Assets Conference, 211–12
Presidential Commission on Holocaust Assets (PCHA), US, 8–9, 209–10, 247
private buyers, cultural restitution issues with, 97–98
private collections. *See also specific collections*
 donations from, 124
 France and restitution of, 117–24, 122*t*
 Linz museum project and seizure of, 16–17
provincial museum exchanges, MNR and, 139–41
Puyvelde, Leo Van, 93, 179–82

Quadripartite Procedure for Restitution, 81–82

Raad voor het Rechtsherstel (Council for the Restoration of Rights), 149, 157, 168–69
Raoul Wallenberg Centre for Human Rights, 4
The Rape of Europa (Nicholas), 208

Rauter, Hanns Albin, 21
RDR (Directorate of Reparations, Deliveries and Restitutions), ACC, 93–94, 98
recovered art. *See also* cultural restitution
  from Alt Aussee salt mine, 78–80, 86*f*, 93
  from Berchtesgaden, 76–78
  from Bernterode, 75–76
  from Buxheim monastery, 70–71
  by DER, 179–83
  DER exhibitions of, 183–85
  of France, 116–17, 275n.5
  from Heilbronn salt mine, 72
  from Merkers mine, 74–75, 77*f*, 81*f*
  by MFAA, 68–82
  from Neuschwanstein Castle, 71–72, 73*f*, 76*f*
  protective measures for, 80
  from Siegen copper mine, 72–74
  SNK categories of, 157
  from Soviet zone, 80–82
"Recovered Art Property" *(Herwonnen Kunstbezit)* shows, 146–47
Rembrandt, 40–41, 120–21, 146–47, 154
Renders, Emile, 186–88
Renoir, Pierre-Auguste, 40
Renotte, Paul, 191
reparations, for Israel, 206
Reparations and Restitutions, US, 104
Répertoire des biens spoliés, 97, 119–20
replacement art for cultural restitution, 90, 99
restitution. *See* cultural restitution
Restitution Committee (Restitutiecommissie), the Netherlands, 225, 232, 233–35
"The Return of the Old Masters" exhibition, 154
Return of the Prodigal Son, 198–99
Reynaud, Paul, 31–32
Ribbentrop, Joachim von, 17, 218–19
Rigaud, Jean, 95
Rijksmuseum, Amsterdam, 7, 159–60, 165–66, 167
River Landscape with Ferry, 234*f*
Roberts, Own, 48–49
Roberts Commission, 48–49, 52–53, 89, 90–91, 98
Rodrigo, Evert, 204
Röell, D. C., 151–52, 162–63

Rombouts, Théodore, 198–99
Roosevelt, Franklin Delano, 91–92
Rorimer, James, 8, 266n.71
  Berchtesgaden art recovery and, 76–78
  Buxheim monastery art recovery and, 70–71
  Central Collecting Point and, 93–94
  destruction documented by, 55–56
  on French liberation, 59
  Heilbronn salt mine art recovery and, 72
  Jewish heritage of, 63
  lopsided sales investigated by, 45
  at Louvre, 61
  MFAA Seine section lead by, 61
  Mont Saint Michel concerns of, 56–57
  on Nazi art plunder, 63–64
  Neuschwanstein Castle art recovery and, 71–72, 73*f*, 76*f*
  spy accusations against, 57
  Valland working with, 64–66, 73*f*
  Versailles museum and, 62
Rosenberg, Alfred, 17–18, 86
Rosenberg, Léonce, 44
Rosenberg, Marianne, 220
Rosenberg, Paul, 39*f*, 42, 43*f*, 119, 120, 124, 133*f*, 137, 218–21
Rosenberg collection, 218–21
Ross, Marvin, 54
Rossignol, A., 187–88, 189
Rothschild, Alexandrine de, 119, 120
Rothschild, Edmond de, 119
Rothschild, Edouard de, 118–19
Rothschild, Maurice de, 119, 124, 173–74
Rothschild family collections, 35, 37–38, 41, 70–72, 119, 125
Rousseau, Henri, 45, 268n.137
Rousseau, Theodore, 82–84
Royal Museum of Arts, Antwerp, 191–92
Royal Museums of Art and History, Brussels, 177–78, 191–92
Rubens, Peter Paul, 137, 200–2
Rundstedt, Gerd von, 27
Russia, on cultural restitution, 210–11
Ruysdael, Salomon van, 234*f*

Sachs, Paul, 48–49
"safekeeping measures," forced sales for, 2–3
Saher, August von, 230–31

INDEX 335

Saher, Eduard von (Eduard Goudstikker), 23–24, 161–62, 230–32
Saher, Marei von, 231–32, 248
Salem, Raphaël, 215–17
sales of less worthy objects, in France, 142–45
Salles, Georges, 97, 118, 124, 125, 127–28, 129–30, 136–37
Sarr, Felwine, 244–45
Savery, Roelant, 85, 289n.29
Savoy, Bénédicte, 244–45
SCAP (Service de Contrôle des administrateurs provisoires), 42
Schenker International Transport, 84
Scheurleer, D. F. Lunsingh, 166–67
Schiedlausky, Günther, 83–84
Schloss, Adolphe, 40–41, 85, 127–28
Schloss, Henry, 137
Schloss, Lucie, 40–41
Schmitz, M., 134
Schoeller, André, 44
Schooten, Floris Gerritsz van, 147*f*
Schotel, Pieter Jan, 27–28
Schulmann, Didier, 214–15, 275n.5
Schuman, Robert, 113–14
Searle, Daniel, 227–28
Seligmann family collection, 113, 119
Senegal, French cultural restitution to, 244–45
sequestered collections
 of Belgium, 193–94
 French approach to, 38–41, 125
 restitution of, 124–28
Service de Contrôle des administrateurs provisoires (SCAP), 42
Service for the Protection of Artworks (SPOA), 113, 205
Service for the Return of Works of Art (SROA), 109–10
Seyffers, Léon, 195, 201
Seyrig, Henri, 217
Seyss-Inquart, Arthur, 21
SHAEF (Supreme Headquarters Allied Expeditionary Force), 53–54, 55, 61
Sheeps and Hens, 27–28
Sidorov, Evgenii, 210–11
Siegen copper mine art recovery, 72–74
Simelovicius, Kopelis, 238
Simonin, Victor, 198–99
Sizer, Theodore, 54
Skilton, John, 57, 69–70
SNK. *See Stichting Nederlands Kunstbezit*
Snyders, Frans, 188–89
Soap Bubbles, 162–63, 163*f*
Soviet Union
 cultural restitution challenges in, 87
 cultural restitution in zone of, 95, 107
 EAC and, 88
 recovered art from, 80–82
Speyer, Herbert, 29
SPOA (Service for the Protection of Artworks), 113, 205
SROA (Service for the Return of Works of Art), 109–10
Stalin, Joseph, 80
Standen, Edith, 106*f*
State Art Collections Service *(Dienst voor Rijks Verspreide Kunstvoorwerpen)*, 170
statute of limitations, on MNR pieces, 144–45
Stedelijk Museum, Amsterdam, 166
Steltzer, Helmut, 199–200
Steltzer, Theodore, 199–200
Stephany, Erich, 67
Stern family collection, 119
Sternheim, D. A., 24–25
Stichting Nederlands Kunstbezit (Dutch Art Property Foundation, SNK), 148
 administrative costs and fees of, 151–52
 archives of, 222–23
 artworks found and lost and, 156–63
 board of directors and administrators of, 151–53
 British zone shipments to, 155–56
 CRA dispute with, 172–75
 dissolution of, 175–76
 economic issues of, 169–71
 on forced sales, 158–59, 160, 224
 German shipments received by, 154–55
 legal issues of, 156–58, 168–69
 mismanagement by, 171–72
 museums enriched by works recovered by, 163–68
 ownerless art and, 158–60, 165–66
 ownership debates in, 168–71
 recovered art categories of, 157
 responsibilities of, 151
 restitution claims from exhibitions of, 167

Stichting Nederlands Kunstbezit (Dutch Art Property Foundation, SNK) (*cont.*)
  restitution guidelines of, 153–54, 158, 224
  Vries arrest and, 162–63, 171–72
Stone, Harlan, 48
Stout, George Leslie, 48, 54, 56, 57–59, 61
  Alt Aussee salt mine art recovery and, 79–80, 86*f*
  Bernterode art recovery and, 75–76
  Merkers mine art recovery and, 74–75
  Siegen copper mine art recovery and, 72–74
Stroganoff-Sherbatoff, George, 248
Supreme Headquarters Allied Expeditionary Force (SHAEF), 53–54, 55, 61
Suriname, 166–67
Swenson, Ingrid, 9
Syria, 244

Taper, Bernard, 158
Taussig, Alice von, 198
Taylor, Francis Henry, 48, 82–83, 152–53
Taylor, Gideon, 235
Terezin Declaration, 211–12
"thefticide," 4
Theresienstadt concentration camp, 4
Tiepolo, Giovanni Battista, 131*f*
Tieschowitz, Bernhard von, 16
Todt, Fritz, 205
Torah scrolls, recovered, 102, 103*f*
The Train, 265n.50
transit camps, French, 19
transportation, for MFAA, 56
Trautmann, Catherine, 219–20
Treaty of Paris, 113–14
Treaty of Versailles, 15–16, 27–28, 47
Treuhandverwaltung von Kulturgut (Fiduciary Administration for Cultural Assets) (TVK), 114
Truman, Harry, 80, 91–92
TVK *(Treuhandverwaltung von Kulturgut)*, 114
Two Riders on the Beach, 84–85

United Nations Educational, Scientific and Cultural Organization (UNESCO), 7–8, 108–9, 207–8

United States (US). *See also* Monuments, Fine Arts, and Archives
  AAM, AAMD and, 247–48
  antisemitism in, 63
  Art Looting Investigation Unit of, 17, 82–84
  cultural preservation efforts launched by, 47–49
  cultural restitution in zone of, 93–94
  cultural restitution responsibilities transferred to Germany, 102–6
  EAC and, 88
  HEAR Act of, 248
  Military Law 59 of, 101–2
  NAGPRA of, 247
  National Gallery, 99–100, 100*f*
  OSS, 43–44
  "Paintings looted from Holland" tour in, 146–47
  PCHA and, 8–9, 209–10, 247
  Reparations and Restitutions of, 104
  Roberts Commission of, 48–49, 52–53, 89, 90–91, 98
unrecovered art. *See* ownerless art; recovered art
Utrillo, Maurice, 138–39

Valadon, Suzanne, 138–39, 217
Valland, Rose, 59–60, 104, 106*f*, 118, 123
  on Austria and cultural restitution, 110–13
  French zone cultural restitution and, 95
  Jaujard and, 36–37, 59–60
  on Moltke case, 202
  Nazi art plunder interrogations by, 84–85
  Rorimer working with, 64–66, 73*f*
  Soviet zone recovered art assistance of, 80–82
  SPOA and, 113, 205
  SROA and, 109–10
  on statute of limitations on MNR pieces, 144–45
  on US transfer of cultural restitution responsibilities to Germany, 104, 105–6
Van-Abbe Museum, Eindoven, 166
Vanitas, 190*f*
Van Mulders, O., 184, 185–86

Vaucher, Paul, 51
Vaucher Commission (Inter-Allied Commission for the Protection and Restitution of Cultural Materials), 51, 82–83
VE (Victory in Europe) Day, 60
Veit Stoss altarpiece, 93
Veken, Joseph van der, 186
Veraart, Wouter, 148
Verboeckhoven, Eugène Joseph, 27–28
Vergnet-Ruiz, Jean, 138–42
Versailles museum, 41, 62, 125
Viau, Georges, 41–42
Victory in Europe (VE) Day, 60
Village Street under Snow, 138–39
Vilnius International Forum on Holocaust-Era Looted Cultural Assets, 211–12
Virgin Adoring the Child, 135
Virgin and Child, 191
Virgin with Child and Saint John, 137
Virgin with Grapes, 134
Vlug, Jan, 83–84, 187
Voigtländer, Otto, 134
Vorenkamp, Phonse, 146–47, 152–55, 171–72
Vos, Herman (Belgian education minister), 181
Voss, Hermann (German museum director), 14–15, 84
Vries, Ary Bob de, 100–1
    arrest of, 162–63, 171–72
    British zone frustrations of, 155–56
    as controversial administrator, 151–52
    on ownerless art, 159

Wagoner, Murray van, 102–4
Wallraf Richards museum, 200–1
war profiteers, art market and, 20
wartime diplomacy, 1943–1945, 88–92
Washington Principles, 210–12, 246
Wassermann, Robert von, 198
Wavell, Archibald, 49–50
Webb, Geoffrey, 53–54, 62–63, 97–98, 155–56
Webber, Anne, 228, 236
Weil, André, 42
Weiller, Paul-Louis, 41, 62, 205
Wertheimer, Pierre, 45
Western Europe, Occupied, 15*f*
Weyden, Rogier van der, 191, 192–93
What the English Did in Cyrenaica pamphlet, 50–51
Wheeler, Mortimer, 50–51
"Wiesbaden Manifesto," 99
Wilde, Edy de, 166
Wildenstein, Georges, 42–44, 119
Wildenstein collection, 34–35, 36
Wilhelmina (Queen), 20–22
William I (King), 7
Winkelman, H. G., 20–21
Winkler, Friedrich, 186
Wintergarden, 81*f*
Wittelsbach collection, 71–72
Wolff Metternich, Franz Graf, 16, 35–36, 109–10
Woman in Gold, 4–5
Woman in Red and Green, 133*f*
Woolley, Leonard, 49–51, 52–53, 67–68
World Jewish Congress, 232
Woudstra, J., 168–69

Zeller, Ron, 251–52n.12
Zijlstra, Halbe, 233–34
Zimetbaum, Mala, 237
Zivie, David, 220–21, 279n.76
Zoller, A., 77–78

www.ingramcontent.com/pod-product-compliance
Lightning Source LLC
Chambersburg PA
CBHW052318150825
31165CB00004B/193